Media in War and Armed Conflict

This book focuses on the social process of conflict news production and the emergence of public discourse on war and armed conflict. Its contributions combine qualitative and quantitative approaches through interview studies and computer-assisted content analysis and apply a unique, comparative and holistic approach over time, across different cycles of six conflicts in three regions of the world and across different types of domestic, international and transnational media. In so doing, it explores the roles of public communication through traditional media, social media, strategic communication and public relations in informing and involving national and international actors in conflict prevention, resolution and peacekeeping. It provides a key point of reference for creative, innovative and state-of-the-art empirical research on media and armed conflict.

Romy Fröhlich is Professor at the Institute of Communication Studies and Media Research at Ludwig-Maximilians-Universität (LMU) München, Germany.

Routledge Research in Communication Studies

Populist Political Communication in Europe
Edited by Toril Aalberg, Frank Esser, Carsten Reinemann,
Jesper Strömbäck, and Claes H. de Vreese

Setting Agendas in Cultural Markets
Organizations, Creators, Experiences
Philemon Bantimaroudis

Communication, Advocacy, and Work/Family Balance
Jenny Dixon

Integrative Framing Analysis
Framing Health through Words and Visuals
Viorela Dan

The Discourse of Special Populations
Critical Intercultural Communication Pedagogy and Practice
Edited by Ahmet Atay and Diana Trebing

Interrogating the Communicative Power of Whiteness
Edited by Dawn Marie D. McIntosh, Dreama G. Moon, and
Thomas K. Nakayama

Media in War and Armed Conflict
The Dynamics of Conflict News Production and Dissemination
Edited by Romy Fröhlich

For more information about this series, please visit: https://www.routledge.com

Media in War and Armed Conflict

The Dynamics of Conflict News Production and Dissemination

Edited by
Romy Fröhlich

NEW YORK AND LONDON

First published 2018
by Routledge
52 Vanderbilt Avenue, New York, NY 10017, USA

and by Routledge
2 Park Square, Milton Park, Abingdon, Oxon OX14 4RN

First issued in paperback 2020

Routledge is an imprint of the Taylor & Francis Group, an informa business

© 2019 Taylor & Francis

Library of Congress Cataloging-in-Publication Data
CIP data has been applied for.

ISBN 13: 978-0-367-58361-3 (pbk)
ISBN 13: 978-1-138-05162-1 (hbk)

Typeset in Sabon
by codeMantra

Contents

List of Figures and Tables   ix
Foreword   xiii
SCOTT ALTHAUS

PART I
Comparative, Diachronic and Holistic: Conceptualizing
Theoretical Paths for the Analysis of Conflict News
Coverage and Public Discourse on Armed Conflicts   1

    Introduction: Media's Role in the Creation of Knowledge
    and Images of Wars: More Relevant and More
    Complicated Than Ever   3
    ROMY FRÖHLICH

  1 Dissecting Media Roles in Conflict: A Transactionist
    Process Model of Conflict News Production,
    Dissemination and Influence   23
    CHRISTIAN BADEN AND CHRISTOPH O. MEYER

PART II
The Dynamics of Public Discourse(s) on Wars
and Armed Conflicts: Media Content, Strategic
Communication and Conflict-Related Cognition   49

  2 Not So Bad News? Investigating Journalism's
    Contribution to What Is Bad, and Good, in News on
    Violent Conflict   51
    CHRISTIAN BADEN AND KEREN TENENBOIM-WEINBLATT

3 The Dynamics of Strategic Communication Over Time:
   Patterns of Persuasive Communication and Its Relevance
   for the Construction of Discourse on War and Conflict   76
   ROMY FRÖHLICH AND MARC JUNGBLUT

4 The Dynamics of Parliamentary Debates on War and
   Conflict: Assessing the Impact and Role of the Media
   on the Political Agenda   111
   ROSA BERGANZA, BEATRIZ HERRERO-JIMÉNEZ
   AND ADOLFO CARRATALÁ

5 #iProtest: The Case of the *Colourful Revolution*
   in Macedonia   136
   DIMITRA DIMITRAKOPOULOU AND SERGIOS LENIS

PART III
The Dynamics of Conflict News Production
as a Social Process: Key Actors' (Changing)
Roles and Their Interrelations   167

6 Journalism of War and Conflict: Generic and
   Conflict-Related Influences on News Production   169
   THOMAS HANITZSCH AND ABIT HOXHA

7 The Enduring Value of Reliable Facts: Why NGOs
   Have Become More Influential in Conflict Discourse   191
   ERIC SANGAR AND CHRISTOPH O. MEYER

8 Political Leaders, Media and Violent Conflict
   in the Digital Age   218
   GADI WOLFSFELD AND LINOR TSIFRONI

9 A Game of Frames in Conflict Transformation:
   Mapping the Media-Active Publics' Nexus of
   Competing Conflict Frames   243
   IGOR MICEVSKI AND SNEZANA TRPEVSKA

10 Balancing Plausible Lies and False Truths:
   Perception and Evaluation of the Local and
   Global News Coverage of Conflicts in the DRC   271
   MARIE-SOLEIL FRÈRE AND ANKE FIEDLER

PART IV
Recapitulation, Consolidation, Implication 285

11 The Integration of Findings: Consequences of Empirical
Results for the Advancement of Theory Building 287
ROMY FRÖHLICH

12 Practical Implications and Suggestions for the Applied
Fields of Journalism, Media Assistance, NGOs and Politics 310
ROMY FRÖHLICH

Afterword 335
PHILIP SEIB

List of Contributors 339
Index 345

List of Figures and Tables

Figures

Figure 1.1 Transactionist process model of media roles 29
Figure 1.2 Three levels of media influence 39
Figure 2.1 Significant associates of 'Holocaust', 'Nazism'
and 'Hitler' in Palestinian news during escalation 62
Figure 2.2 In-group- (bold) and out-group (thin) evaluations
in opposing parties' domestic coverage 63
Figure 2.3 Violence orientation in the domestic (bold) and
foreign (thin) coverage of six conflicts 65
Figure 2.4 Frame similarity between Israeli and Palestinian
media and *Al Jazeera* 67
Figure 3.1 Analysis structure for strategic narratives 86
Figure 3.2 Analysis structure for agendas for action 87
Figure 3.3 Number of texts with references to escalative
narratives across time by conflict 91
Figure 3.4 Number of texts with references to agendas for
action across time by conflict 95
Figure 3.5 Number of texts with references to de-escalative
measures, escalative narratives and conflict
casualties across time per conflict 101
Figure 4.1 Presence of traditional media and social
media in the European parliamentary debates
concerning the Syrian conflict 122
Figure 5.1 Flow chart of the steps of the study 145
Figure 5.2 Time series of total tweets between April 12,
2016 and July 27, 2016 146
Figure 5.3 Timeline of used languages 148
Figure 5.4 Most active users (tweeted most during the
studied timeline) 148
Figure 5.5 Network of mentions (@) between users 151
Figure 5.6 Strongly connected users (@) 151

Figure 5.7   Hashtags community detection   154
Figure 5.8   Topic modelling   156
Figure 5.9   Infographic posted on Twitter on April 25, 2016
             (@Mkcolorful)   158
Figure 5.10 Screenshot of digital collection of a total of 41
             graphic materials for #ColourfulRevolution   159
Figure 5.11 Infographic posted on Twitter on April 20,
             2016 (@Protestiram)   159
Figure 6.1   Influences on news production   175
Figure 7.1   NGO occurrences across the six INFOCORE
             Conflict Contexts (Relative Frequencies)   201
Figure 7.2   Forecast of NGO presence based on observed
             relative frequencies from 2010 to 2014   201
Figure 7.3   Absolute frequencies of NGO references and
             proportional share of references to local NGOs   203
Figure 7.4   Relative frequencies of NGO references and
             monthly conflict casualties   203
Figure 7.5   Absolute frequencies of NGO references and
             proportional share of references to local NGOs   206
Figure 7.6   Total number of sampled articles and relative
             frequency of NGO references   207
Figure 9.1   A map of competing conflict frames and framing
             interactions of media active publics in Macedonia   266
Figure 9.2   A map of competing conflict frames and framing
             interactions of media active publics in Kosovo   267
Figure 11.1 INFOCORE's actors and roles in the conflict news
             production process   288
Figure 11.2 INFOCORE's comparative dimensions: contextual
             factors shaping the roles of media   288

Tables

Table 2.1   Sample of domestic conflict news coverage   70
Table 2.2   Sample of foreign conflict news coverage   72
Table 3.1   Sample   85
Table 3.2   Share of texts of all communicators/actors with
            references to strategic narratives per conflict
            (multiple answers set)   89
Table 3.3   Share of texts with references to conflict measures
            per conflict (multiple answers set)   94
Table 3.4   Partial correlations between conflict narratives
            and measures (per actor, per month, controlled
            for the number of texts ($n_{Burundi}$ = 52;
            n_{DRC} = 157; n_{Israel} = 162; n_{Syria} = 175;
            n_{Kosovo} = 139; $n_{Macedonia}$ = 88, n_{total} = 773)   98

Table A   Concepts used for the escalative "Ethnocentrism/
             Patriotism/Religious Superiority" narrative   104
Table B   Concepts used for the escalative "Responsibility
             to Protect" narrative (R2P)   105
Table C   Concepts used for the escalative
             "(Self-)Defence" narrative   105
Table D   Concepts used for de-escalative
             "Moral Values" narrative   105
Table E   Concepts used for the de-escalative
             "Economic Necessity" narrative   105
Table F   Concepts used for the de-escalative "Last Resort/
             No Other Way than Peace" narrative   106
Table G   Concepts used for "Escalative" conflict measures   106
Table H   Concepts used for "De-Escalative" conflict measures 106
Table I   Concepts used for "Non-Violent Escalative"
             conflict measures   106
Table 4.1   Distributions of the parliamentary minutes
             concerning CW crisis and analysed in-depth
             (frequencies)   120
Table 4.2   Descriptive measures for the indicators of social
             media, media and public opinion presence   121
Table 4.3   Averages and standard deviations of the
             indicators for the presence of traditional
             media, social media and public opinion
             in parliamentary debates   122
Table 4.4   Averages and standard deviations of the
             summation of the media presence with respect
             to nationality in parliamentary debates   123
Table 5.1   Media activities on a daily basis   142
Table 5.2   Interaction with media on a weekly basis   142
Table 5.3   List of most mentioned users (@)   149
Table 5.4   Users classified by degree centrality   152
Table 5.5   Users classified by page rank   153
Table 6.1   Generic influences on news production   172
Table 6.2   Media sample distribution per conflict and country   177
Table 7.1   Number of identified NGOs and sampled articles   200
Table 9.1   Representation of the functioning of the four
             types of conflict framing interactions   260

Foreword

Conflict is inherently communicative. As the scale of conflict rises from individuals to groups to states, conflict also becomes increasingly mediated. Yet far less is known about the role of media in violent, large-scale conflict than most people suspect.

It is unusual to study mediated conflict processes outside North America and Western Europe. It is rarer still to study more than one conflict at a time, across more than one language, or to examine the flow of information about a conflict in both domestic and international public spheres. It is almost unheard of to study how conflicts unfold across the full cycle of information production, transmission and reception, or to trace how the full range of actors in a conflict – governments, citizens, journalists, NGOs and combatants – attempt to shape the public discourse that is being produced about a conflict as it evolves over time. The (In)Forming Conflict Prevention, Response and Resolution (INFOCORE) project does all of these, and more.

This book is a landmark contribution to our understanding of how media coverage affects violent conflict, and is shaped in turn by conflict actors. It advances the empirical and theoretical boundaries of conflict scholarship while also providing practical insights for understanding how media coverage can help or hinder the peaceful resolution of armed struggles. Its appearance could hardly be more timely.

A topic so vast required a large team of researchers representing diverse approaches, methods and bodies of expertise. The INFOCORE effort organized 33 scholars into 10 working teams to conduct research in six countries across eight languages over a span of three years. The result of this unprecedented effort is a deeper understanding of how decentralized channels of communication are influenced by multiple actors competing across diverse centres of gravity to jointly construct public information flows about conflict processes. The book's rich insights describe how entire systems of conflict communication operate in the early years of the 21st century, with an eye toward informing points of vulnerability within these systems that can be exploited by internal actors to escalate conflict for maximum advantage, and that can also be leveraged by outsiders to increase the odds of peaceful resolution.

There are no easy answers here. Instead, the pages that follow unfold a rich multi-perspective story of how media operate in armed conflicts, a story based on hundreds of in-depth interviews with parties to (or embedded observers of) armed conflict, scores of focus groups from within conflict countries, and thousands of survey respondents. This story is also enriched by the latest data science technologies that allowed the research team to conduct large-scale analysis of conflict discourse across media channels, languages, countries and deliberative spaces. Together, these nuanced reports and quantitative findings are structured in ways that invite the reader to draw generalizable insights across particular conflicts and about particular actor types.

I had the distinct pleasure of serving in an advisory role for the INFOCORE project over the last several years, and it is from this perspective that I offer this observation about a project designed to provide original insights for scholars that are also actionable for practitioners. From its inception, INFOCORE was an ambitious and perhaps audacious scholarly effort. This book demonstrates without question that its formative ambition has been realized.

Scott Althaus
University of Illinois at Urbana-Champaign
April 2018

Part I

Comparative, Diachronic and Holistic

Conceptualizing Theoretical Paths for the Analysis of Conflict News Coverage and Public Discourse on Armed Conflicts

Introduction

Media's Role in the Creation of Knowledge and Images of Wars: More Relevant and More Complicated Than Ever

Romy Fröhlich

According to the Uppsala Conflict Data Program (UCDP), in 2016 there were 49 state-based armed conflicts across the world – 47 of these were intrastate conflicts, and of these, 38% (18) were internationalized (external states contributed troops to one or both sides in the conflict). In the category of non-state conflicts, for 2016 UCDP counted 60 conflicts (organized violence)[1] – the majority of these (33) were in Africa, followed by 17 in the Middle East and eight in South America (all of those in South America were in Mexico) (Allansson, Melander, & Themnér, 2017, pp. 576, 578).[2] However, we hear almost nothing about the vast majority of these armed conflicts because the media report on very few of them.

In war and violent conflict, media are an important source of information; they provide (or fail to provide) early warnings, intelligence and succinct analysis. How conflict is covered in the news is important because it is consequential for citizens and policymakers – both inside and outside conflict areas (e.g. mobilization, polarization, reconciliation). When deciding which conflicts they will report on and which not, journalists use unique criteria highly specific to their profession (cf. for example, O'Neill & Harcup, 2009). These criteria are not always in agreement with those that typical recipients or political decision makers would use to make their selection. The question of whether mass media make relevant selection decisions when reporting on armed conflicts could therefore be discussed controversially by the audience depending on their specific expectations. This also applies to selection decisions that affect specific individual events within an armed conflict, the respective storylines and narratives chosen by journalists, the voice-overs chosen, etc.

What is more, conflict reporting is continually accused of having, in large part, an escalation-oriented and pro-conflict perspective. In individual case studies, attempts have even been made to prove that there is a link between escalation-oriented war and conflict reporting on the one hand and military escalation on the other (cf. for instance,

Hoijer, Nohrstedt, & Ottosen, 2002). As Christian Baden and Keren Tenenboim-Weinblatt show in this volume (Chapter 2), these kinds of accusations are not only made by particularly critical scientists but also are a relatively dominant and widespread position even in mainstream research on journalism and conflict. Compounding the problem, conflict reporters today are challenged by two very serious developments that I will briefly describe in the following.

Changing (Conflict) Conditions of War Reporting

First, there is the fact that the nature, form and course of wars have changed all over the world. For example, today the circle of actors who are capable of conducting war has expended immensely, which has brought about quasi-privatized wars (e.g. warlords). The circle of these actors has expanded in part because war has become cheap today – one reason for this is that instead of professional soldiers, child soldiers or suicide bombers are being used. Wars have also become cheaper and their nature has changed because acts of war are no longer directed exclusively at the opponents' professional armies but instead at the highly vulnerable civilian population. Adding to this is the trend toward completely privatizing military functions and tasks (cf. Singer, 2008). In such a scenario, one cannot count on the combatants quickly running out of economic resources, and armed conflicts and war can continue on for nearly any length of time. Or: The number of interstate wars has decreased, and the number of (mandated and non-mandated) military interventions has increased. With such developments, the once (more or less) clear differentiation between civil war and interstate wars disappears. These changes in the nature, form and course of wars also have consequences for the terms used to talk about them: If the term "war" was previously reserved for the (symmetric) confrontation of state armies, today it is also applied to include, for example, (asymmetric) terrorist acts against the civilian population and the fight against this terrorism.[3] Scholars of international law and peace researchers rarely use the term "war" anymore and prefer to speak of "armed conflict".

The second serious development that confronts today's war reporting is the fact that the media landscape and process of public opinion-forming has changed greatly. Keywords here are 'digitalization', 'Internet', 'social media' or 'real-time world' (cf. Matheson & Allan, 2009; Seib, 2002). Outside of the online media world, as well, significant changes can be observed. The former information monopolies have been dissolved. The near monopoly of Western media in global news no longer exists as such; *Al-Jazeera* et al. therefore pose the greatest challenges for the previously dominant power of the Western media to define world news (Seib, 2005). In addition, wars are increasingly withdrawing from direct observation by media. Limor and Nossek (2006) characterized this relationship between media and military as a "deactivation model". This changes the role of war reporting, which is less and less able to report on war activities as an eye witness because the activities are largely hidden from its view. In the course of this development, classic media formats are increasingly losing their gatekeeper monopoly in the selection and production of news. And that is also a global trend. In addition, today institutions and organizations beyond classic media are also increasingly involved in the production of the publicly disseminated pictures of wars and armed conflicts – especially non-governmental organizations (NGOs), communicators from the area of political decision-making, the military and even terror organizations. They now all have communication staff and departments, hire communication strategy consultants from public relations (PR) companies and/or produce their own online and print media in which they simulate (sometimes very sophisticated) professional journalism. Hoskins and O'Loughlin (2010, 2015) refer to those developments when characterizing current interrelations between technologies, media ecology and mediatization, on the one hand, and perceptions and actual practices of warfare, on the other, as concepts of "diffused war" and "arrested war".

With the background of changes and challenges described, the question of the media's role in the creation of our knowledge and our images of wars and armed conflicts is more relevant than ever – and the answers are more difficult. The fact that media coverage not only shapes but is also shaped by public discourse (politics and parliamentary debates, civil society, strategic communicators, etc.) on armed conflict does not make things any less complicated. We are therefore dealing with a highly complex, reciprocal scenario that is very difficult to research using previously existing approaches, theories and methods. The research field is already complex enough without the current changes described above because different media and different public and expert discourses play different roles (constructive vs. destructive) in different (phases/cycles of) conflicts in different regions of the world in different circumstances that are determined by different context-specific factors, and because, vice versa, different communicators participating in public discourses can shape media coverage as well as general and specialized discourses on war and armed conflicts in different ways. It can therefore be assumed that the influence various actors and communicators can have on the production and forming of media reporting on wars and armed conflict and which is reflected in general and specialized (public) discourses is manifested in very different ways.

This is where the research reported on in this book picks up. The individual contributions are entirely based on the international, collaborative research project *INFOCORE*[4] – *(In)Forming Conflict Prevention, Response and Resolution: The Role of Media in Violent Conflict.*

INFOCORE

The literature, which up until now has been widely fragmented, describes a series of various roles and functions that media can take on in connection with the emergence, development and course of armed conflicts. In contrast to the research projects, which are mostly only able to look at scenarios specific to individual conflicts, contexts or media, these roles and functions often overlap to a large extent in the actual daily praxis of war journalism – not least because of the conditions briefly described above. INFOCORE's various individual sub-studies therefore had the objective of overcoming usual limitations, namely by: linking influences of various aspects in their process perspective on news production/dissemination; varying contextual factors in their comparative strategy to detect relevant influences of different media types, for different audience types, and in different conflicts; taking a genuinely dynamic perspective on ongoing conflict cycles to trace developments within conflicts and across conflicts (media/conflict dynamics); pursuing a combined emphasis on the roles of media inside (domestic) and outside the conflict areas and their role of informing and involving national and international actors. In doing so, the project applied a comparative and holistic approach that included the following aspects of investigation – although the different chapters of this volume will not in all cases report on all of these aspects[5]:

a The analysis of the workings of *different media's conflict news production and coverage* (professional Western, non-Western, international and domestic news media;[6] social media; semi-public expert media (e.g. NGO media); organizational PR media) in *eight languages*[7] across *six different armed conflict cases* in *three regions* of the world:

Region 1: The Middle East
  The **Israeli–Palestinian conflict** (including the military operations "Molten Lead" and "Pillar of Defense" and the preceding/subsequent latent conflict phases) and the **Syrian Civil War.**

Region 2: The West Balkans
  The **Kosovo conflict** (focusing on the peace-building process after the war in 1998–1999, including Kosovo's declaration of independence and ensuing tensions with Serbia and their possible impacts on the region) and the **interethnic conflict in Macedonia** (including recent outbreaks of violence between Albanian and Macedonian groups).

Region 3: The Great Lakes in Africa
 Conflict in the Democratic Republic of Congo (DRC) (specifically: the ongoing violence in Eastern DRC, including the recent rise of the rebel group M23) and the **conflict in Burundi** (including the electoral success of rebel groups in 2010 and daily violence).

INFOCORE focused on violent conflicts between collective actors. Following Wallensteen (2002), we firstly assume that conflicts consist of "three components: incompatibility, action and actors"; and we secondly understand conflict "as a social situation in which a minimum of two actors (parties) strive to acquire at the same moment in time an available set of scarce resources" (pp. 17–18).[8] Our understanding of *violent* conflict rests upon Coser's (1956) definition of conflict as "a struggle in which the main aims of opponents are to neutralize, injure, or eliminate rivals" (p. 8).[9] Furthermore, all our selected (violent) conflicts either meet the AKUF definition of war[10] at some point in time, or they constitute violent conflicts that have the potential to develop into full-fledged war: A violent mass conflict that is settled by at least two armed forces (official/regular troops, no paramilitary units or police forces) at gunpoint, in the course of which the respective violence must be more than just sporadic, spontaneous or isolated (Gantzel & Schwinghammer, 2000; Kende, 1971).[11] All of our six conflicts are the subject of political conflict prevention, management or resolution, and they involve dispersed actor groups and audiences that imply the relevance of mass media communication. However, they differ with regard to several characteristics known or theorized to influence the process wherein media have the potential to themselves influence the development of conflicts and political conflict prevention, management and resolution (Ruigrok, van Attefeldt, & Takens, 2009). These characteristics include the following:

- various modes of conflict party organization (**interstate conflicts, anti-regime conflicts, intrastate conflicts**) between formally organised or loose groupings;
- the nature of the conflict (ethnic/religious, autonomy/status-based, resource-based);
- the **degree of international involvement** (military, economic, cultural/ideational, diplomatic, legal such as possible prosecutions by the International Criminal Court; Brown, 2002; Livingston, 1997).

Among those differences that pertain specifically to the role of media, we need to consider

- the **relative communicative power of warring parties** (balanced, selective, uneven; Hickey, 2002);

- **characteristics of the media system** (media-state-relations, journalistic and political communication culture, fragmentation and polarization, social media penetration; Hallin & Mancini, 2004);
- the **geopolitical embedding** of the conflict (e.g. cultural/economic proximity; Sheafer & Gabay, 2009);
- political and legal threats to media reporting, and the amount of physical violence.

INFOCORE's comparative and holistic approach includes further aspects of investigation:

b   The analysis of *social interactions* that underlie the processes of conflict news production and public discourse formation, with a focus on *interactions among four key actor types*: professional journalists, political and strategic actors/authorities/entities, experts/NGOs and lay publics/citizens.

c   The analysis of the role and impact of *persuasive strategic communication, PR and the propaganda* of relevant players, functioning as sources of news and public discourse as well as providing their own 'news'.

d   The analytical consideration of the *temporal dynamics* of *conflict, news* and *public discourse* (polarization, escalation, conflict resolution as *long*-term processes), resulting in a *period of investigation from 2006 to 2014* (depending on the respective conflict).

e   The analytical consideration of *context-specific factors* (e.g. the global/domestic communication environment, routine power relations between journalists and sources, professional norms/routines of the key actors, characteristics of political systems, conflict situations/phases).

On the basis of this INFOCORE-specific approach and along a story line from 'these are the sources' to 'these are the media contents' to 'this is how it comes into being and how it affects audiences', this book goes beyond merely analysing and describing media conflict content. It provides insights into selected aspects of the social process of conflict news production and the emergence of public discourse on war and armed conflict. The contributions explain if and why particular content patterns (e.g. (de-)escalative) arise under certain circumstances, who can influence the media (e.g. politicians, military, NGOs, PR practitioners, etc.) in which way and under which circumstances, what are the roles and functions the media perform as information providers/brokers, for whom they do it (e.g. NGOs, parliamentary debates, the general public) and in which situations (phase of conflict).

The research presented here combines qualitative and quantitative approaches through interview studies and computer-assisted (big data) content analysis,[12] explaining if and why particular patterns of content arise under certain circumstances, why the media/journalists and strategic communicators (e.g. politicians, NGOs) communicate in specific ways, who has a voice in public discourse under what circumstances, what roles/functions media and strategic communicators have as information providers/brokers, for whom and in which situations. By applying a unique comparative and holistic approach over time, across different cycles of six conflicts in three regions of the world, and across different types of domestic, international and transnational media, this book explores the roles of public communication through media, social and expert media, and PR for informing and involving national and international actors in conflict prevention, resolution and peacekeeping. The authors build their contributions on the analysis of results which are extracted from:

- a big-data computer-assisted algorithmic text analysis (content analysis toolkit *JAmCAT*)[13] of approximately one million news articles (more than 60 newspapers, including news agencies from 11 countries), TV manuscripts from seven transnational broadcasters, 200,000 texts from various strategic communicators/ PR institutions, more than 13,000 minutes of parliamentary debates, and thousands of relevant social media posts from different communicators;
- several hundreds of in-depth interviews with journalists from across the world, in-depth expert interviews with relevant international politicians and representatives of NGOs, around 50 qualitative focus group discussions (ca. 300 participants) with lay publics/citizens in the three conflict regions;
- surveys with media audiences in selected conflicts (Macedonia, Syria, Israel–Palestine) – around 3,000 respondents.

The Contributions

The innovative approach of INFOCORE described above generates findings that enable a view of the roles and functions of media in violent conflict that encompasses many conflicts, contexts and media. Before the individual contributions in Parts I–III of this volume give impressive evidence related to specific questions, Scott Althaus provides a foreword. As a former member of INFOCORE's External Experts Advisory Board, he has supported the project from the very beginning with his top-class expertise and enthusiasm. I greatly appreciate his willingness to also contribute to this volume. With his foreword, he skilfully paves the way for Christian Baden and Christoph Meyer's fundamental contribution in **Part I** (Chapter 1). The two authors start us off by elaborating on the major theoretical conceptualization of our collaborative research. Here, the authors develop and introduce the transactionist process model of conflict news production, dissemination and influence, which forms the basis of our comparative and holistic research idea. The chapter first provides a systematic discussion of various concepts of media roles in war. Baden and Meyer then conceptualize these roles as the implications of characteristic patterns in news contents for the beliefs, attitudes and behaviours of specific actors and groups in conflict. The authors thereby assume that media roles can typically be varied, that they overlap and that, depending on the specific process situation, sometimes one role dominates, while at other times another role dominates (for instance, the role of journalists/media as senders and receivers of information). The goal of the authors is to offer a conceptual analysis grid which can be used to research and better understand two things: firstly, the interactive and transactional character of the production and dissemination of conflict news coverage of different types of media, and, secondly, the mechanism that can be used to explain how this news then influences various actors and groups whose beliefs, attitudes and actions are capable of influencing the course of war and armed conflicts. Baden and Meyer suggest a three-level model of conflict news' medial influence. For the media content, the model differentiates among 'evidential claims' (specific informative assertions about the conflict and its context), 'interpretative frames' (which render information meaningful while structuring and shaping audiences' knowledge and evaluative attitudes) and 'agendas for action' (advocating specific courses of action in response to perceived conflict). These three different types of media content are then presented to diverse types of publics (lay publics, experts, decision makers, etc.). In addition, they differentiate among short-term and long-term cumulative effects that can lead to changes in knowledge, attitudes and/or behaviour. The model allows us to more precisely analyse specific transactions of information and commentary between journalists and various other communicators while accounting for prevalent structural constraints. It also allows us to study the dynamics of competitive social interactions between diverse media and non-media actors within the news production and dissemination process. And in addition, we can use it to investigate how both informational transactions and social interactions are continuously structured by, and contribute to the structuration of, the underlying power balances, institutions and established routines, the configuration of audiences, media, and conflict actors, as well as the embedded conflict situation.

The emphasis of **Part II** is on the comparison of the dynamics and on patterns of content and information diffusion over time and across conflicts and contexts. The four chapters included here are based on complex content-analytical studies, which explore (1) the content of professional news media and (2) persuasive content in strategic communication material, (3) the reception of conflict news and its (re) construction in parliamentary debates and, finally, (4) conflict-related discourses in social media. This part of the book starts with a contribution by Christian Baden and Keren Tenenboim-Weinblatt (Chapter 2), which provides a thoroughly contextualized, weighted assessment of journalists' contribution to covering conflict. The authors recognize that there is a great deal of evidence that war and conflict reporting is subject to many different, undesirable influences and restrictions, making this reporting seem somewhat less than perfect. However, they also show why the criticism of war and conflict reporting collected by the research – criticism which in part was very harsh – is too hasty and the arguments used are insufficient. Previous research on this topic is criticized in particular because it is based largely on the analysis of only a few, mostly opinion-leading, Western outlets. However, a much more fundamental concern lies in the co-creation between journalists and the sources that get a chance to speak in the news – that is, those that were selected for exactly this purpose by the journalists. Previous studies have occasionally acknowledged this but rarely systematically accounted for. With a view to the subsequent Chapter 3 on strategic communication, Baden and Tenenboim-Weinblatt therefore also make a clear demand: "In order to understand the specific contribution that journalists make to conflict news, we need to systematically compare the produced news to available inputs presented by relevant sources, and to salient developments in the conflict itself." Their third point of criticism of relevant research that critically analyses war reporting is the observation that the vast majority of this research ignores the question of precisely which normative standards are used to evaluate war and conflict reporting. With this background, Baden and Tenenboim-Weinblatt's comparative content analysis across different conflicts, media and events reveals which factors are causal for systematic changes in the respective journalistic practice and could therefore explain the seeming "failure" and errors of war reporting in times of escalative events. The findings of these complex content analyses show that it is worth putting effort into a highly differentiated look at journalistic conflict coverage because much more meaningful findings are generated.

In Chapter 3, Romy Fröhlich and Marc Jungblut present and discuss results from their content analysis of strategic communication material in times of violent and armed conflicts. The study looks into 'strategic narratives' that are produced by various communicators and actors from the areas of both political actors and NGOs in armed conflicts and wars in their strategic communication and are disseminated through their PR material. The research interest is inspired by the question of how different actors use their importance and influence in specific situational and historical contexts to influence the thinking and behaviour of other actors and which role strategic narratives play in this (cf. Miskimmon, O'Loughlin, & Roselle, 2013, pp. 16, 183). The findings show which strategic actors work communicatively at which times in a specific conflict with which strategic narratives and thus with which type of persuasive tactic. A particular focus is thereby placed on the variation of strategic narratives (for instance, escalative and de-escalative narratives) in relation to contextual factors and variances in the conflict. In their approach, the authors differentiate between strategic narratives, on the one hand, that are used to describe, interpret and characterize conflicts, and conflict measures, on the other hand, that represent suggestions or demands in response to the question of how to react to a conflict, how it can/could be resolved, etc. The findings of this content analysis reveal that the theoretical differentiation between 'measures' and 'narratives' makes sense when analysing persuasive conflict communication of strategic communicators in times of war and armed conflict. The picture obtained with this differentiated approach generates detailed findings and enables more complex interpretations.

Parliament is a key institution of contemporary democracies. Its collective political actors so far have considered issues in international affairs to be the exclusive domain of the executive. However, the 20th century changed the classic division of tasks: With the birth of international or multilateral cooperation and the emergence of regional integration processes, some authors now talk about "the parliamentarisation of international affairs" (cf. Beetham, 2006, pp. 172–175; Stavridis & Jančić, 2017). And precisely due to this background, today more than ever before, it makes sense to take a closer scientific look at parliamentary debates on war and armed conflicts. Rosa Berganza, Beatriz Herrero-Jiménez and Adolfo Carratalá have done this in INFO-CORE and report in Chapter 4 on selected findings on the dynamics of parliamentary debates about the Syrian crisis between 2011 and 2015. They investigate possible patterns of parliamentary discourses and the reception and citation of conflict news by members of selected parliaments. With their research, they map the roles that media content, both directly and indirectly cited, played in parliamentary debates on the Syrian conflict. The authors thus fill in a gap that had thus far not been examined scientifically. A large amount of data was used by the study, as the team looked into the relevant debates in Great Britain, France, Germany and the EU Parliament in Brussels based on parliamentary minutes. Berganza, Herrero-Jiménez and Carratalá also transfer the question of the role and function of content conveyed by the media in parliamentary debates to social media, comparing the relevant findings with those of traditional mass media. They examine the extent to which parliamentarians referred to the often-cited 'public opinion' in addition to traditional and social media in their speeches and in which argumentative situations they did this and how. This approach is thus far unique. For some it might come as a surprise, but the findings show that the parliamentarians – at least in the case of the Syrian crisis – often refer to 'public opinion' in their speeches, saying that this 'public opinion' supposedly thinks a certain way or demands a certain action. References to public opinion are more frequent than references to traditional or social media content. It is also interesting that in a direct comparison between traditional and social media, the importance of social media content for parliamentary debates continually increased in the course of the Syrian crisis: While traditional mass media were still more important than social media in the early stages of the conflict, this lead disappears throughout the conflict until June 2015. The authors offer interesting explanations for this effect and additional intriguing details of the findings.

In the last chapter of the content-analytical part of the book (Chapter 5), authored by Dimitra Dimitrakopoulou and Sergios Lenis, social media are in the focus. The sub-project is oriented on the role of social networks and alternative information providers in conflictual collective allotments. As a case for their analysis, the authors choose the so-called *Colourful Revolution,* a social movement that was formed during the ongoing political crisis in Macedonia in 2015. Rightly, Dimitrakopoulou and Lenis point out that research into the role of social media in social movements and violent conflicts has previously been limited largely to regions in the Middle East (e.g. Syria, Egypt, Israel). Other crisis regions such as the Western Balkans have, in contrast, been mostly neglected by research. And yet, the *Colourful Revolution* is an almost ideal-typical example for the formation and spreading of a social protest in which a large number of active, engaged citizens participated and which was covered and negotiated to a great extent online through social media networks. With their content analysis of around 89,700 tweets, Dimitrakopoulou and Lenis show why and how social media contribute to the influence and power of social movements such as the *Colourful Revolution* in social conflict situations.

The study of influences on conflict news is essential to our understanding of the way media cover conflicts and journalists interact with sources in both the absence of conflict and during conflict. Thus, **Part III** of the book is dedicated to the INFOCORE's qualitative interview studies and surveys that elaborate on influences on and conditions of conflict news production, dissemination and reception. The body of work reflected here explores the key actors' particular de facto roles in the news production process, the interactions between these actors and their impacts on lay publics' perspectives on mediated conflict information and their contestation. In Chapter 6, Thomas Hanitzsch and Abit

Hoxha cover the results from the analysis of influences on the journal-istic news production process and the interplay of journalistic routines and journalists' interactions with sources. The authors suggest that the existing research on this problem does not sufficiently acknowledge the practical limits of time, talent and energy nor the determining condi-tions of conflict reporting like the various external constraints imposed on the individual reporter(s). Thus they differentiate between generic and conflict-related influences. Furthermore, they expose the relations of influences in the conflict news production process in three stages: *ide-ation* (sources, choices and implicit influences), *narration* (angle, con-struction of the central narrative and framing) and *presentation* (of the story; selection of information, links and cues). In doing so, Hanitzsch and Hoxha also look at the sources and interactions of journalists with influences in the form of political, professional, institutional, safety-mil-itary and audience feedback factors. Using retrospective reconstructive interviews, they explore the genesis of a news account through the journalist's recollections of specific choices and considerations during the process of news production. With 215 qualitative interviews in the various native languages of conflict journalists who routinely cover armed conflicts on the ground and through the exploration of 314 re-constructed articles, this study goes far beyond classical methodologi-cal approaches. Another unique aspect of this study is that it looks at news coverage from six different conflicts: the war in Syria, the Israeli–Palestinian conflict and the ethnic violence in the Great Lakes regions (Burundi and DRC) as well as in the Western Balkans (Kosovo and Macedonia). With their creative approach, Hanitzsch and Hoxha make an important contribution to both the theoretical understanding of con-flict news production and the empirical mapping of its contextualities.

Next is Chapter 7, on findings regarding the influential roles of NGOs as media-like actors and sources for journalists and political decision makers. Eric Sangar and Christoph Meyer have conducted a study of the evolving role of NGOs in mediated conflict discourses that com-bines quantitative and qualitative methodologies and data analysis. The authors present convincing evidence of the overall growing presence of NGOs' media discourses but also of important disparities among dif-ferent NGO activity profiles, conflict contexts and types of discursive influence. For instance, they find that local NGOs overall fill gaps in conflict coverage when conflict correspondents cannot (for financial or security reasons, etc.) cover conflicts directly from the ground. Sangar and Meyer develop and introduce their 'supply-and-demand model' to explain why NGOs have become more attractive sources of news pro-duction. On the basis of their results, they warn that journalists relying exclusively on NGO reports may therefore promote public perceptions shaped by compassion and anger, which can, for example, result in increased pressure on political decision makers to exclude 'evil perpetrators' from any diplomatic processes. Hard-pressed journalists sometimes trust some of the major advocacy superpowers' NGOs too much, using their content directly and without taking alternative sources and perspectives sufficiently into account. This can lead to them failing to appreciate when NGOs statements are moving beyond their specialized expertise, for instance, when making policy recommendations. Since NGOs necessarily have a different focus on conflict dynamics, and without the use of additional sources, their framing may not be sufficient to develop holistic perceptions of a conflict that enable diplomatic negotiation rather than public condemnation. Not all journalists are sufficiently aware of and transparent about how the NGOs funding may be influencing their conflict coverage. The authors' plea is clear: Media organizations need to step up their support for quality journalism and carefully consider in what ways collaboration with NGOs can help to advance rather than undermine public trust in journalism (and vice versa!).

It is a truism that the relationship between political leaders/decision makers and journalists and media gains a very specific importance during times of violence and armed conflict. Gadi Wolfsfeld and Lino Tsifroni argue in Chapter 8 that this relationship is changing in the age of digital communication. While their original INFOCORE study dealt with a wide range of issues, here they focus specifically on the question of how political leaders mired in decisions and discourses about war and/or peace have been dealing with the media since the dawn of the digital age. More specifically, they ask how political leaders attempt to use the Internet and especially social media in order to achieve their political goals. Their exploratory study is one of the very few that analyses the ways in which social media have both provided opportunities and posed threats for political leaders involved in conflict. For this study as well, a distinctive characteristic is that it approaches the topic from a cross-cultural perspective. That makes it fairly unique. It is based on 55 one-hour in-depth interviews, conducted in person in 2015 in the local language of the respective government officials and members of the opposition stemming from four entities involved in armed conflict: Israel, Palestine, Kosovo and Macedonia. The professional breadth of interviewees is impressive: Some were elected to their positions, some were officials involved in diplomacy, while others were leaders of political organizations. On the basis of their results, Wolfsfeld and Tsifroni provide an initial list of the most important changes that emerged from their interviews. And they can reveal interesting cross-cultural differences between countries in conflict: Where it is difficult for oppositional actors to gain access to the mainstream media, these political actors are much more dependent on social media.

Part III concludes with two chapters that both investigate media's audiences and lay publics in conflict escalation or de-escalation: In the first one (Chapter 9), Igor Micevski and Snezana Trpevska deal with lay publics' interpretations of conflict news content and strategic communication content on wars and armed conflicts. For this purpose, the two researchers develop and apply the specific concept of *media active publics* – defined as members of recent protest movements in the societies under investigation that are active on social media. The study identifies the repertoires of conflict frames used by media active publics in the post-conflict societies of Kosovo and Macedonia and then investigates the interaction(s) of competing conflict frames. The aim is to better understand the roles and functions of those frames by deconstructing their potential for conflict transformation, which reaches from the creation of future frictions and the support of relapses into violence (for instance, ethno-nationalist conflict frames) to the potential of conflict frames to transfigure violent conflict into non-violent (or at least less violent) conflict outcomes (for instance, counter-hegemonic conflict frames). The authors provide interesting explanations for the dominance and/or absence of (particular) frames within media active publics' discourses in the two cases of moderately violent post-conflict episodes in Kosovo and Macedonia. And they provide interesting insights for politicians and strategic actors in the field of conflict resolution – for instance, how to make use of the nexus of *competing* conflict frames in conflict transformation processes. At the same time, they criticize the usual practice of insisting on public circulation of ideas of interethnic understanding and harmony in order to counteract future ethnic conflict escalations – a strategy that often fails.

In Chapter 10, Marie-Soleil Frère and Anke Fiedler present the findings of a field research implemented in Goma (Eastern Congo). Based on eight focus groups, the chapter raises a question about the way audiences use local and international media in a context of continuing unsecurity. The study demonstrates that audience members in Goma, whatever their social background and level of education, show a wide degree of critical media literacy: Participants to the focus groups have a very clear idea of political or institutional affiliations of media outlets, public and private media financing, corruption or restrictions to press freedom and to information. Obviously, they use a range of criteria in order to assess the credibility of the source of information they get access to, in a context where getting reliable information may be an issue of life or death. Even though they claim to have a limited trust in media content, especially when the crisis intensifies, the audience members keep listening to local and international radios, in search of coincidence between media narratives and the information they get from other channels (word of mouth, social media, interpersonal communication). Audience members appreciate more positively the media outlets that show a certain degree of internal pluralism and demonstrate their independence from the public authorities. But they are also aware of the precarious working conditions and constraints under which Congolese journalists practice their job. Frère and Fiedler show that, even though they do not trust them totally, or do not trust them at all, audience members in Goma continue to listen to the radio stations available, in order to reduce uncertainty, which is highly anxiety provoking and stressful. Media consumption in a context of conflict is a part of a strategy to reduce uncertainty, and gives a sense of predictability and control over a much unstable present and future (even though reducing uncertainty does not lead to reaching certainty).

Finally, **Part IV** of the book provides two concluding chapters that aim to function as integrative contributions – integrating the results from the content analyses (Chapters 2–5) and the interview studies (Chapters 6–10). The aim is twofold: first, to demonstrate internal connections, similarities and relationships of results among the content-analytical studies on the one hand and among the interview studies on the other (what we call '*intra*-connectivity'); and second, to demonstrate connections, similarities and relationships between the content-analytical results and the results from the interview studies (what we call '*inter*-connectivity'). In doing so, we highlight the significance and implications of our research and offer readers an overview and focused synthesis of the separate findings as well as specific guidance about what was accomplished. In the synopsis, our different results question, for instance, the popular assumption and claim that political source frames are introduced directly into the news. However, political actors who are directly involved on the ground have higher impacts on news coverage than political actors outside the conflict zones. Or: Concerning the usage of and references to sources, foreign coverage seems to be more balanced than domestic coverage. And while domestic coverage during all stages of the conflict(s) is much steadier, foreign media focus their attention on the escalation and move on to something else quickly. Our research also shows that in contexts with elevated intensity of violence, NGOs appear as highly influential actors on the journalistic production process.

With the background of this integrative wish and on the basis of the collective project experience in INFOCORE, Chapter 11 discusses what consequences our individual findings could have for the further development of theory building. This is done with consideration to the constraints and limitations of the overall international collaborative multi-method study, its complexity, its comparative approach across time, different conflicts, media and languages of analysis and the big-data approach of its content-analytical studies.

On the basis of the project's findings, Chapter 12 elaborates on (practical) implications and suggestions concerning our selected fields of practice: journalism, media assistance, NGOs and politics. In doing so, we aim to contribute to the improvement of professional journalism in war and conflict coverage, its consolidation and stabilization as well as to the improvement of journalistic education and continuing education in this field. We also hope that our suggestions here might contribute to the improvement and further development of media assistance programs and engagement. Here, we provide references for the improvement of NGOs' (fair, transparent and effective) strategic communication in the field of conflict prevention and resolution as well as peacekeeping, and for a profound awareness of the advantages and risks of increasingly blurred boundaries between media and political actors. Concerning the latter, our results and suggestions are also meant to contribute to effective de-escalative strategic communication in politics in the field of war and armed conflicts. For these purposes, Chapter 12 provides and discusses knowledge of how media and policy actors can cooperate to build policy capabilities for understanding ongoing conflicts and formulating/implementing suitable policies. And for these purposes, the contribution develops evidence-based strategies for communicating toward/via media in a manner suitable for assisting mediation and dialogue, reaching out to conflict parties and combating escalative content.

An afterword is provided by Philp Seib, internationally acknowledged by scientists and media as an expert on public diplomacy and international relations as well as for his research on global terrorism and new media. Like Scott Althaus, he served as a member of INFOCORE's advisory board and has accompanied our project since it took its first steps. I am very thankful for his closing view on this volume.

We hope that this book does justice to the goals that it must fulfil according to the EU-funded research project upon which it is based: On the one hand, showing the scientific community how sophisticated basic research can generate application-oriented findings, and on the other hand, showing practitioners in the fields we examined that the usefulness and effectiveness of communication consulting is always greatest when this consulting can refer to scientific findings. Beyond that, it is also our objective to use this book to show students why and for what purpose one can study communication research, media studies, public relations, or political science and international relations.

Acknowledgements

The editor would like to thank all members of the project for their contribution to this book with special thanks to Christian Baden and Marc Jungblut for their valuable comments on this introduction. Moreover, all the contributors would like to express their gratitude to the hundreds of interviewees who have given generously of their time to speak to our researchers. Without their contribution this book would not have been possible. Furthermore, we would like to give special thanks to the members of the Advisory Board and the practitioners and scholars who provided us with advice and feedback at numerous workshops in Brussels as well as the three conflict regions.

Funding

The author(s) disclosed receipt of the following financial support for the research: The research project reported in this book was funded by the EU's FP7 programme under the Grant Agreement No 613308 for the INFOCORE project (www.infocore.eu).

Notes

1 The respective datasets are found at http://ucdp.uu.se/downloads/
2 Depending on which definition is used for "war", other numbers also exist – e.g. the Conflict Barometer 2017: 385 conflicts worldwide (222 violent and 163 non-violent conflicts); 36 wars (20 full-scale wars and 16 limited wars) (Heidelberg Institute for International Conflict Research, 2018, p. 14).
3 For instance, the military campaign "War on Terror" (WoT), called into being by the US government as a response to the terrorist attacks in the US on September 11, 2001.
4 Funded by the EU's Seventh Framework Programme for Research, Technological Development and Demonstration under Grant Agreement No. 613308, 1 Jan. 2014–31 Dec. 2016.
5 For further results/publications beyond this volume, please consult www.infocore.eu
6 Domestic coverage of a conflict: opinion-leading media from within each conflict area; variation in left–right alignment; pro-government/independent/anti-government stance; ethnic/language group affiliation; broadsheet/tabloid style and dominant funding; specific media outlets affiliated with particular relevant groups (e.g. Hamas-affiliated papers in the Israeli–Palestinian conflict; a UN radio station in the DRC). Foreign coverage of the same conflict: range of foreign opinion-leading newspapers (the UK, France, Germany; one leading left-leaning and one right-leaning broadsheet paper, one influential news magazine or tabloid where relevant), transnational broadcasters (leading outlets from the UK, France, Germany, Euronews (English), the Qatari broadcaster Al Jazeera (Arabic), the US news network CNN), the New York Times; the news agencies AP,

AFP and Xinhua. In order to be included in the sample, the media had to possess textual archives of past news coverage.

7 Albanian, Arabic, English, French, German, Hebrew, Macedonian and Serbian/Croatian.

8 Besides measurable/tangible realities (money, territory, access to diverse forms of power, etc.), this includes socially constructed intangibles (collective values/norms, psychological needs like recognition or apology, etc.) (cf. Meyer, Baden, & Frère, 2018, p. 4, or Baden & Meyer in this volume).

9 Depending on their respective research question, some contributions in this volume offer more specific/detailed definitions of (violent) conflict. Their general understanding of conflict, however, rests on the definition presented here. See also Frère and Wilen (2015).

10 "Arbeitsgemeinschaft Kriegsursachenforschung [Working Group Research on Causation of War]" (AKUF) at the University of Hamburg; www.wiso. uni-hamburg.de/fachbereich-sowi/professuren/jakobeit/forschung/akuf/kriegs-definition.html For an English version of the definition see Kiza (2006, p. 75).

11 "Violence", accordingly, is, "the exercise of physical force so as to inflict injury on or cause damage to persons and property" (Mackenzie, 1975, p. 39). War thus involves, "purposive and lethal violence among two or more social groups pursuing conflicting political goals that results in fatalities, with at least one belligerent group organized under the command of authoritative leadership" (Cioffi-Revilla, 1996, p. 8).

12 The construction of the code book, INFOCORE's dictionary, is described in Baden and Stalpouskaya (2015): From a detailed, qualitative analysis of relevant texts, the INFOCORE researchers generated a long list of the so-called 'concepts' (more than 3,700, ranging from actors, places and events to activities, objects, relations and qualities) "that are important for defining the meaning of conflict in various contexts and cultures (...)". As a result, the team obtained "a large number of concept definitions including a list of ways used to express these in the various languages and discourses – the dictionary – and a refined theoretical understanding of the subtleties in the use of these concepts in discourse" (p. 2).

13 http://jamcat.mscc.huji.ac.il/accounts/login/?next=/

References

Allansson, M., Melander, E., & Themnér, L. (2017). Organized violence, 1989–2016. *Journal of Peace Research, 54*, 574–587.

Baden, C., & Stalpouskaya, K. (2015). *Common methodological framework: Content Analysis. A mixed-methods strategy for comparatively, diachronically analyzing conflict discourse.* INFOCORE Working Paper 2015/10. Available online at www.infocore.eu/wp-content/uploads/2016/02/Methodological-Paper-MWG-CA_final.pdf

Beetham, D. (2006). *Parliament and democracy in the twenty-first century: A guide to good practice.* Geneva, Switzerland: Inter-Parliamentary Union. Available online at http://archive.ipu.org/PDF/publications/democracy_en.pdf

Brown, R. (2002). Information operations, public diplomacy and spin: The United States & the politics of perception management. *Journal of Information Warfare, 1*(3), 40–50.

Cioffi-Revilla, C. (1996). Origins and evolution of war and politics. *International Studies Quarterly, 40*, 1–22.

Coser, L. (1956). *The functions of social conflict.* New York, NY: Free Press.

Frère, M.-S., & Wilen, N. (2015). *INFOCORE definitions: "Violent conflict".* Bruxelles, Belgium: ULB. Available online at www.infocore.eu/wp-content/uploads/2016/02/def_violent-conflict.pdf

Gantzel, K. J., & Schwinghammer, T. (2000). *Warfare since the Second World War.* New Brunswick, NJ: Transaction.

Hallin, D. C., & Mancini, P. (2004). *Comparing media systems: Three models of media and politics.* New York, NY: Cambridge University Press.

Heidelberg Institute for International Conflict Research. (2018). *Conflict barometer 2017.* Heidelberg, Germany: HIIK at the University of Heidelberg. Available online at https://hiik.de/conflict-barometer/current-version/?lang=en

Hickey, N. (2002). Access denied. *Columbia Journalism Review, January/February*, 26–31.

Hoijer, B., Nohrstedt, S. A., & Ottosen, R. (2002). The Kosovo war in the media analysis of a global discursive order. *Conflict & Communication Online, 1*(2). Available online at www.cco.regener-online.de

Hoskins, A., & O'Loughlin, B. (2010). *War and media. The emergence of diffused war.* Cambridge, UK: Polity.

Hoskins, A., & O'Loughlin, B. (2015). Arrested war: After diffused war. *Global Policy Blog, 14*. January. Available online at www.globalpolicyjournal.com/blog/14/01/2015/arrested-war-after-diffused-war

Kende, I. (1971). Twenty-five years of local wars. *Journal of Peace Research, 15*, 227–239.

Kiza, E. (2006). Victimization in wars – a framework for further inquiry. In U. Ewald, & K. Turković (Eds.), *Large-scale victimization as a potential source of terrorist activities. Importance of regaining security in postconflict societies* (pp. 73–88) [NATO Security Through Science Series]. Amsterdam, Netherlands: IOS Press.

Limor, Y., & Nossek, H. (2006). The military and the media in the twenty-first century: Towards a new model of relations. *Israel Affairs, 12*, 484–510.

Livingston, S. (1997). *Clarifying the CNN effect: An examination of media effects according to type of military intervention.* Research paper R-18, Cambridge, MA: The Joan Shorenstein Barone Center on the Press, Politics and Public Policy at Harvard University. Available online at http://genocidewatch.info/images/1997ClarifyingtheCNNEffect-Livingston.pdf

Mackenzie, W. J. M. (1975). *Power, violence, decision.* Hannondsworth, UK: Penguin.

Matheson, D., & Allan, S. (2009). *Digital war reporting.* Cambridge, UK: Polity.

Meyer, C. O., Baden, C., & Frère, M.-S. (2018). Navigating the complexities of media roles in conflict: The INFOCORE approach. *Media, War & Conflict, 11*, 3–21.

Miskimmon, A., O'Loughlin, B., & Roselle, L. (Eds). (2013). *Strategic narratives. Communication power and the new world order.* New York, NY, London, UK: Routledge.

O'Neill, D., & Harcup, T. (2009). News values and selectivity. In K. Wahl-Jorgensen, & T. Hanitzsch (Eds.), *The handbook of journalism studies* (pp. 161–174). New York, NY: Routledge.

Ruigrok, N., van Atteveldt, W., & Takens, J. (2009). *Shifting frames in a deadlocked conflict?* Paper presented at the annual meeting of the ISA's 50th Annual Convention on "Exploring the Past, Anticipating the Future", New York, NY: USA.

Seib, P. (2002). *The global journalist: News and conscience in a world of conflict.* Lanham, MD: Rowman & Littlerfield.

Seib, P. (2005). Hegemonic no more: Western media, the rise of Al-Jazeera, and the influence of diverse voices. *International Studies Review, 7,* 601–615.

Sheafer, T., & Gabay, I. (2009). Mediated public diplomacy: A strategic contest over international agenda building and frame building. *Political Communication, 26,* 447–467.

Singer, P. W. (2008). *Corporate warriors: The rise of the privatized military industry.* Ithaca, NY: Cornell University Press.

Stavridis, S., & Jančić, G. (2017). Introduction: The rise of parliamentary diplomacy in international politics. In S. Stavridis, & G. Jančić (Eds.), *Parliamentary diplomacy in European and global governance* (pp. 1–15). Leiden, Netherlands: Brill Nijhoff.

Wallensteen, P. (2002). *Understanding conflict resolution: War, peace and the global system.* London, UK: Sage.

1 Dissecting Media Roles in Conflict

A Transactionist Process Model of Conflict News Production, Dissemination and Influence

Christian Baden and Christoph O. Meyer

As long as there is violent conflict, people have wondered about the role of communication in fanning, shaping and also redressing hostilities. From the deeply media-penetrated West, over the TV-saturated East and to more radio-reliant African societies, the role of media in violent conflict has long assumed a central space in the scholarship of media, communication, political science and increasingly also international relations.[1] However, while there is widespread agreement that media potentially, powerfully influence the evolution and trajectory of violent conflict, it remains heavily contested wherein their primary influence lies. Scholars continue to argue whether media take on specific roles due to innate media logics, economic interest or political influence and, indeed, whether it makes sense to talk about "the media" or even "cumulative media effects", given the progressing heterogeneity of media and media-like actors, their coverage and uses among media audiences. Any review of the widely fragmented literature yields a wealth of proposed media roles, from potential contributions to early warning and intelligence (e.g. Otto & Meyer, 2012), over their involvement in inter-group communication and mediation (e.g. Wolfsfeld, 2004), to widespread worries about incitement and propaganda (e.g. Nohrstedt, Kaitatzi-Whitlock, Ottosen, & Riegert, 2000). Yet many of the proposed media roles overlap in practice and are described in highly conflict-, media- and context-specific terms. What is more, most roles have been formulated against a separate background of theoretical and normative assumptions, which complicates the integration of accumulated knowledge as well as the identification of factors conducive to each role.

In this chapter, we aim to bring some order to the variety of media roles by conceptualizing them as outcomes of two recursive transactional processes: On the one hand, conflict actors, media and other non-media players interact in the creation and transformation of conflict-related news into particular patterns of conflict news coverage (*news production*). On the other hand, the resulting news contents are selectively amplified towards different audiences and influence their beliefs, attitudes and behaviour in characteristic ways (*news dissemination*). Depending on the specific constellation of interactions between media, sources, audiences, authorities and others, the underlying transactions foreground different selections and kinds of information and interpretations, which are represented in the news and shape the perceptions of participants in the conflict. At the same time, both the transactions and interactions are continuously structured by, and contribute to, the structuration of underlying power balances, institutions and practices, as well as other conflict-related factors. In order to account for different media roles manifested in a wide variety of contexts, our model seeks to capture and account for those different ways in which media representations of conflict may influence the perceptions and possibly actions of media audiences.

We understand conflict in a broad sense as a "severe disagreement between at least two sides, where their demands cannot be met by the same resources at the same time"; resources are here not just measurable, tangible realities such as money, territory or access to other forms of power but can also involve socially constructed intangibles such as collective values, norms or psychological needs of actors for recognition or apology from other actors (Wallensteen, 2007, pp. 14–18). Conflict does not arise directly from objective competition over scarce resources but requires that specific issues be perceived as vital but incompatible with the demands, actions or presence of conflicting parties. Conflict may remain latent with few or no attempts to resolve the underlying issue, or turn manifest, involving a broad spectrum of actions ranging from peaceful protest and political dispute, over violent riots and terrorism, to full-blown war. We expect that each conflict provides different opportunities and vulnerabilities for media influence depending on key factors such as the nature of the incompatibility among the most relevant domestic conflict parties and their variable strategies, the conflict's intensity and phase, and the degree of involvement of foreign state actors. Accordingly, there is no single recipe for conflict prevention, peace building and reconciliation, wherein specific kinds of media behaviour are desirable, nor do we assume that all conflicts can or should be prevented. Rather, we aim to understand what different influences media may exert in conflict, and what conditions give rise to different media roles (see also Meyer, Baden, & Frère, 2018).

In our view, media predominantly influence conflict by shaping the conflict perceptions of involved actors or groups, such as political and military elites, radical groups or broad lay populations: First, conflict news advances specific *evidential claims* – reported statements about the real world which are endowed with some epistemic status – that inform audiences' beliefs about present, past or future realities in the conflict. Second, to render such evidential claims meaningful, news stories embed available information into a selective context of background information, common myths and shared values. By constructing such *interpretive frames*, media contribute to structuring audiences' knowledge and understanding of conflict-related issues and influence their evaluative attitudes towards these. Third, the news often conveys explicit or implicit *agendas for action* – directive statements that indicate what could or should be done about a present situation. Such agendas for action hold the potential to motivate, orient and coordinate the individual, political and collective behaviour of media audiences with regard to the conflict, possibly altering the further course of events. In consequence, different media roles arise from specific qualities of the news, and these qualities influence the beliefs, attitudes and behaviour of different actors and groups in consequential ways: For instance, early warning about conflict implies the provision of accurate, timely and relevant evidential claims about the future to challenge prevailing beliefs and facilitate preventive action by policymakers; conflict mediation requires a multidirectional exchange of evidential claims and interpretive frames among conflicting elites or groups, which enables mutual understanding and a reduction of hostile attitudes; and incitement implies the advocacy of escalation-oriented agendas for action that motivate hateful behaviour among susceptible, radical groups or general populations, mostly within conflict areas, but sometimes also abroad.

Our approach is intended to integrate existing knowledge about very different roles of the media, which have been documented in both domestic and international responses to diverse conflict scenarios and situations. It is generally applicable to any kind of media (commercial, public service, state-controlled, organizational or alternative) and can be easily extended to include also non-news communications. Nevertheless, we focus here on publicly disseminated, professionally produced news media – mostly journalistic news, but also the media-like publications produced by different kinds of NGOs and political and other institutional actors (see also Sangar & Meyer, this issue).[2] Such media, which can be distributed via print, broadcast or various digital or social media technologies, are contrasted against (mostly social media based) lay communications (see Dimitrakopoulou & Boukala, this volume), as well as non-public information channels (e.g. intelligence briefings), which may also be influential, but are not in focus here. Moreover, we focus on conflicts that (a) have turned violent at least at some point during their existence; (b) have developed over a period of multiple years, including phases of escalation and de-escalation; and (c) combine domestic conflict with some form of international involvement. While our emphasis on ongoing, violent conflict ensures their sufficient visibility in both domestic and foreign news media, enabling cross-sectional and diachronic comparisons, our focus on professional media is intended to heighten the theoretical generalizability of relevant media practices: Unlike the contributions of media-active laypeople (see Micevski & Trpevska, this volume), both the *production* of professional news contents (interactions with sources and stakeholders, transformation practices, etc.) and their *dissemination* towards specific audiences are structured by institution-alized norms and routines that react to external incentives and pressures, input and demands in a somewhat regular fashion (see Baden & Tenenboim-Weinblatt, this volume). Accordingly, it is possible to connect specific forms of media coverage and resulting roles to those contexts from which these arise: Both through an appraisal of the heavily case-focused, thick accounts of media roles found in the literature, and through systematic empirical comparison within the INFOCORE project, we can investigate what contextual factors induce media to generate what kinds of contents and influence their audience in which ways, thus assuming different roles in a conflict.

Towards a Transactionist Process Model

In violent conflict, media do not perform one out of several possible static roles; rather, their specific impacts can be multiple, variable, and emerging from the confluence of different media practices in the production and dissemination of conflict-related news. Both the production of conflict-related news and its ability to influence the perceptions of different groups and actors in conflict can be conceptualized as a dynamic, interactive and multidimensional process of contestation over available information, prevalent interpretations and appropriate avenues for future actions through means of communication. During news production, strategic communicators, authorities and other actors interact with journalists and other media content producers to gain visibility in the public debate and shape its content in ways that serve their interests vis-à-vis relevant audiences. Various kinds of media content producers, in turn, interact with and rely on diverse sources and other stakeholders to obtain newsworthy information and transform it into news that is valued by intended audiences and/or those who employ, pay or protect the journalists or the content provider. Given the complex economic, political and other dependencies of journalistic and media-like organizations (e.g. NGOs), what is considered newsworthy and valuable is not just a function of professional norms, production routines or commercial objectives, but also a function of the conflict itself and the power relations within which media organizations operate. During news dissemination, then, media interact with their audiences, amplifying contents to update and influence recipients' conflict perceptions, while audiences interact with media in an effort to obtain valuable information, meaning and direction. As the news is interpreted against a body of prior knowledge and beliefs, media trust and other available information, its reception among audiences depends not only on the contents amplified by the media but also on the conflict itself and the information ecology wherein audiences are situated. Throughout both interactive processes of news production and dissemination, evidential claims, interpretive frames and agendas for action are negotiated competitively among a plurality of actors both inside and outside the media. In a recursive, dynamic process, different actors influence the representation of conflict in the news, which in turn influences the perceptions – and possibly, actions – of the same actors involved in the conflict.

Following Simon Cottle's (2006) schematic distinction of theoretical paradigms in the study of mediatized conflict, our model can therefore be broadly located within the media contest model best exemplified by the work of Wolfsfeld (1997, 2004). It rests upon the assumption that different actors compete for access to the media and public debate, aiming to shape dominant media representations of conflict in pursuit of their objectives. Media roles are not holistic, stable and analytically distinct, but respond to the dynamic competition of actors endowed with greater or lesser power as well as to specific conflict situations and settings. While the contested, interactive process of news production shapes how conflict is covered in the media, what media roles result from this coverage depends on the contested, interactive process of news dissemination and reception among relevant audiences – notably, decision makers, radical groups and lay publics, to the extent that these are capable of influencing the development of the conflict through their actions. In this model, evidential claims capture the important role of information about key events and facts shaping audiences' perceptions of the conflict; interpretive frames reflect the role of sociocultural and ideological environments, and agendas for action delineate the behavioural and political choices available to audiences in order to respond to the evolving conflict situation. The model leaves room for understanding the influence of different types of (news, social, organizational/NGO) media, regardless of where they are based, of various kinds of actors (including active audiences joining the competition via digital media) and of diverse conflict scenarios and situations shaping their interactions.

Due to the dynamism of the competitive process, media roles are typically multiple, overlapping and shifting in prominence. Moreover, communication is both ongoing and circular, as both media and extramedia actors appear as both senders and receivers of information in a recursive transaction process (Barnlund, 1970). Focusing on the primary distinction between media as complex actors engaged in the representation of conflict, and those actors and groups involved in the conflict and (possibly) represented in the media, we can organize our model into both an upward process, wherein mediated representations of conflict are produced, and a downward process, wherein these representations influence those actors involved in the conflict. As is schematically summarized in Figure 1.1, evidential claims, interpretive frames and agendas for action are (1) created through a process of both cooperative and conflictual interaction between media actors and actors involved in the conflict itself. Subsequently, they are (2) transformed according to the editorial and technical requirements of different media, given genre and channel, to become (3) represented as specific media contents. These contents are then (4) amplified towards different audiences, gaining different reach and visibility, and thus result in these audiences being exposed to, and making use of, more or less consonant representations of the conflict. These representations, finally, have the capacity to (5) influence audiences' knowledge, attitudes and behaviours towards other actors within a conflict setting and thus (6) shape the sociopolitical and ultimately physical reality of the conflict, its escalation or de-escalation. Importantly, the entire process is constantly reiterated over time between various constellations of actors and media, updating prior news and incrementally adding to audiences' understanding of the conflict. In consequence, each interaction is shaped both by the legacy of prior interactions and, to some extent, actors' anticipation of further, future interactions.

Mediated representations of conflict are both constructed and received against an awareness of past evidential claims, frames and agendas, as well as the prior beliefs, attitudes and behaviours of involved actors. How exactly these various interactions and constructions shape both the representation and social reality of conflict depends on a wide range of contextual factors – such as the freedom and diversity of the media, the intensity and scenario of the conflict, and the specific configuration of conflict actors, media and audiences – that enable, incentivize or constrain different actors and endow them with specific cultural-semantic, political, economic, legal and other resources relevant to their respective contributions. In the following section, we will sketch the main distinctions relevant for understanding each consecutive step and discuss their contribution to shaping different media roles.

The Creation of Conflict News

Compared to the extant scholarship focusing on the contents and influences of conflict news, less research has illuminated the production of these media contents. While news is generally produced by journalists and other media actors, it does not originate within the media. Rather, media cover events, actions and statements that are, to a large extent, created by actors outside the media – most notably, political and military elites, experts, NGOs and business organizations. As Wolfsfeld (2004) has observed, actors' control over events generally translates into these actors also having the power to influence the news – be it by creating newsworthy events, issuing statements that gain media coverage or by regulating media actors' access to sources, sites, and other relevant information. However, the power of any one actor to shape the news is limited by a complex process of social interactions.

First, even powerful executives are only one of many sources competing for media attention. Executives' ability to control many conflict-related

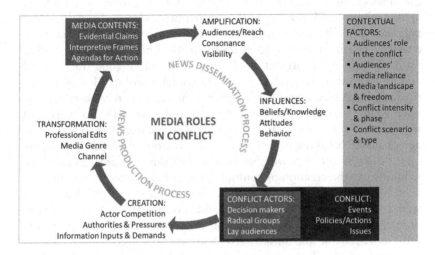

Figure 1.1 Transactionist process model of media roles.

events, act as sources and also regulate media's access to information and other sources puts them at an advantage. However, considerable determination is needed to fully dominate the process of news creation (e.g. far-reaching censorship as in China, systematic intimidation as in Turkey or elaborate media management activities such as those during the US military's Operation Desert Storm; see also Bennett & Paletz, 1994; Hanitzsch & Hoxha, this volume). Unified elites may be able to coerce domestic media into cooperation, but their leverage is weaker towards foreign media, and crumbles where elites are divided, unwilling or unable to sanction media or lose control over conflict events. Competing against the communication power of executives, there exists an increasingly professionalized, diversified network of alternative information sources, including opposition groups, NGOs, experts and business sources as well as a wide variety of non-professional sources (Kampf & Liebes, 2013). Each rival source brings its characteristic set of resources and constraints, which enables it to interact with media and respond to external pressures in different ways. For instance, many NGOs – especially major international ones – work with contacts in inaccessible conflict zones, enabling them to gather information independent of official control. Others possess expertise to provide analysis on specific conflict issues or sustain professional media relations offices to spread awareness and advocacy. International NGOs may be reasonably resilient against pressure from specific conflict parties and sometimes – as do some domestic NGOs – enjoy credibility as impartial brokers, while others are enmeshed within the ongoing conflict (see also Sangar & Meyer, this volume). Also, laypeople increasingly participate in the news creation process, using digital media to provide live footage, upload photos and videos or offer eyewitness accounts and local expertise, especially concerning conflict scenes where journalists lack access (e.g. Hermida, Lewis, & Zamith, 2014). Wherever possible, media normally privilege contributions from sources with a good track record and an interest in preserving a cooperative relationship. However, particularly large media and news agencies increasingly rely on experts in open-source intelligence to harvest, verify and analyse the huge array of user-generated content in an effort to be first and exclusive in the coverage of major breaking events. Which sources prevail depends not only on the distribution of power, but also on the value of source-specific contributions to the creation of conflict news. For instance, foreign media's need for balancing conflict leaders' claims might elevate think tanks or well-known NGOs to key sources; sudden occurrences of violence temporarily increase media's reliance on non-professional sources on site until more reliable and authoritative sources catch up.

Second, media also compete with one another over access to sources and information. Aiming to discover news that is more attractive and valuable to their audiences than that offered by other outlets, media may invest considerable resources to go beyond widely available contents (e.g. press releases, news agency material, online material) and seek out additional information and viewpoints. For this purpose, different media pursue different editorial policies, journalistic styles and strategies and curate strategically developed sourcing networks. In media published by political institutions or NGOs, organizational missions and objectives, as well as the supply of in-house expertise and resources, shape what kinds of contributions will be included in the news. At the same time, both journalists' and other media actors' contributions to news creation follows a distinct media logic that constrains sources' ability to simply 'push' contents into the news. Instead, media actors recruit and privilege sources capable of providing interesting content for their audiences, be it due to traditional news values (relevance, negativity, etc.), its entertaining or evocative qualities, or other properties that increase the attractiveness of created news. Other logics – e.g. censorship, mandated input from conflict parties or owners, media organizations' political allegiances or dependencies, economic considerations – may interfere with this innate logic of media production but can rarely fully supplant it: Lacking media competition and freedom, political restrictions, commercial and language barriers, especially within conflict, sometimes enables media to survive even though they fail to address audiences' need for trusted information. However, such interference threatens to diminish the relevance and trustworthiness of the media to their audiences and reduce their influence on public perceptions.

In consequence, the initial stage of news creation can be understood as a structured interactive process that involves a wide range of media actors, sources and authorities, but is fully controlled by none of these. For the analysis of media roles as depicted in Figure 1.1, the stage of news creation thus foregrounds the question how specific conflict scenarios, situational factors and established media–source relationships shape what kinds of information and commentary are entered into the coverage of conflict.

The Transformation of Conflict News

Following the solicitation and selection of sources' newsworthy input during news creation, the gathered information and commentary needs to be transformed into publishable news. Unlike news creation, this transformation stage is largely controlled by actors in the media: Journalists evaluate sources' content against professional standards and then re-narrate it as news, often departing significantly from the meanings intended by original sources (Tenenboim-Weinblatt & Baden, 2018; for the perspective of political actors as sources, see Wolfsfeld, this volume). NGOs subordinate the further treatment and presentation of available information to their organizational missions, analysing, recontextualizing and trimming input to support specific conclusions or advocacy. Even institutional communication services, which are closely responsible to the policies of their embedding institutions, repurpose quotes and data to spin news-like bulletins that obey a distinct media logic (Seib, 2009). To render their news relevant and attractive to their prospective audiences, all kinds of communicators need to substantively transform the available contents (see also Baden & Tenenboim-Weinblatt, this volume).

The transformation of sources' input into news can thus be conceptualized as a set of professional interventions intended to craft narratives that reflect the stated and non-stated mission of the media organization, and conform to certain requirements regarding their content, form and presentation. From the standpoint of independent, professional journalism, the primary mission (ideally) consists in alerting news audiences to important new events in a conflict and enabling them to understand the underlying issues. Accordingly, journalists need to evaluate sources' input for their credibility and societal relevance and explain their implications for the life worlds of their readers, viewers or listeners. Where journalists are less free, their practices are colonized by considerations such as their allegiance within the conflict or political mission or the interests of the powerful actors financing, protecting or potentially sanctioning their news organization. Journalistic transformation practices are typically structured by professional news values and evaluation criteria, which (for instance) privilege statements by powerful actors or prioritize violent and threatening events over broader social or economic issues, diplomatic talks and political negotiations (Galtung &

Ruge, 1965). Professional routines guide journalists' efforts at checking the facticity and public relevance of news or procuring additional, balancing perspectives – at least to the extent that their situation permits (Frère, 2017). Different news media may have different emphases – e.g. on political choices, economic consequences or the emotional involvement raised by tabloid-style media. Journalists may assume different professional roles (e.g. dispassionate observer, critical watchdog, educator, or political advocate; Hanitzsch et al., 2010), each time foregrounding different aspects of available input, and craft different kinds of news.

Moreover, while all media organizations have to pay attention to the audiences they seek to reach, there is huge variability as to the intentions. Especially in countries affected by conflicts, media content producers also, sometimes even predominantly, adhere to the written and unwritten editorial guidelines of their organizations or the powers that stand behind them, which may pursue distinct agendas and may sanction propagandistic means to achieve their objectives. For those news-like publications issued by NGOs and political institutions, organizational missions are likely to be more narrowly defined – e.g. to further awareness of specific conflict-related issues or raise support for particular political agendas or conflict actors. Absent a common professional ethos, transformations are less structured by shared criteria and routines but rely heavily on organizational practices – e.g. specific quality management procedures established by 'thinking' NGOs (Evans, 2011). Others impose narrow topical constraints, collect input from normally unheard sources or produce news-like contents on specific topics of interest – in conflict, notably, documenting human rights violations and other actors' conflict propaganda. Advocacy groups may apply strong ideological filters to select, curate or generate contents that support specific political viewpoints or agendas ranging from humanitarian causes to inciting collective violence. For an analysis of the transformation of conflict-related news, we can therefore examine those specific missions and role conceptions pursued by different media organizations and study how these are reflected in the selections and interventions applied to available source input. Similarly, we need to investigate how the specific news narratives created refer to those social and cultural beliefs held among news audiences, mobilizing established stereotypes and myths or appealing to collective interests and identities in the conflict.

At the same time, the transformation of conflict-related news also requires several reconfigurations that concern its narrative and rhetorical structure and presentation. Most fundamentally, media actors normally need to integrate diverse source input into unified, coherent news stories. This transformation typically involves shifting the narrative perspective from the subjective claims of sources towards a more authoritative voice – which may present a more distanced, neutral assessment where media are sufficiently free or merely endow specific partisan viewpoints with the authority of the news (Baden & Tenenboim-Weinblatt, 2016). Different media impose different kinds of constraints upon the volume, form and content that can be mediated. From specific narrative styles practised by particular media organizations to the requirements and affordances of different media beats and genres and the technological configuration of different media channels, media actors need to adapt their presentation of news to match the relevant format. Within journalism, common formats range from quickly updating news tickers and brief reports to more opinion-oriented features and commentary and interpretive, magazine-style and long-form journalism. Each format is distinguished not only by its requirements concerning sourcing and evidence, balance and authority, but also by its support for different rhetorical styles and narrative perspectives, or by the use of visualization, sound or video footage, or interactive components. The same is true also for the publications of NGOs and other media-like actors, whose conventions and practices for presenting the news have largely developed in close resemblance to established journalistic formats. Some outlets – e.g. those run by think tanks, but also by some political organizations – allow selected sources to provide conflict assessments and analyses relatively free from editing, primarily adding illustration and some positioning information. Others resemble journalistic news bulletins, or serve as link collections to refer to additional background material. Each media format and dissemination channel implies specific affordances for constructing different (e.g. more or less emotional, authoritative, multi-perspectival, detached) news narratives.

With regard to its contribution to shaping media roles, an analysis of news transformation needs to consider not only the specific edits that media actors effect in their narration of available information, but also their adaptations of the news to specific beats and genres, formats and channels. As is depicted in the second stage of Figure 1.1, we can understand the transformation of conflict-related news as a process by which media actors reconfigure both the contents and presentation of sources' collected input to match the substantive and formal requirements for being published as news. At the same time, also the transformation of news proceeds in a reflexive manner that evaluates novel claims, frames and agendas in relation to those ideas presented in prior news, familiar and relevant to anticipated audiences. Within the constraints of respective outlets' missions and formats, the transformation of conflict-related news thus contributes to a gradual evolution of contents in the news.

The Contents of Conflict News

Through the interrelated processes of news creation and news transformation, authors both outside and inside the media contribute to the production of specific representations of conflict in the news. Throughout the unending literature on conflict news coverage, researchers have documented a large variety of patterns in the contents of conflict news that contribute to specific media roles: For instance, media have been accused of conveying untruths and subduing doubt about presented factual claims; they have been found to construct biased, ethnocentric interpretations that position a valiant in-group against vile enemies; or they have been suspected of excusing or inciting violence and only rarely considering peaceful conflict management as a viable option (see, for instance, Kampf & Liebes, 2013; Robinson, Goddard, Parry, Murray, & Taylor, 2010; Wolfsfeld, 2004). Despite the astounding variety of media contents discussed in relation to their various roles in conflict, the contributions that media make to representing violent conflict can be organized into only three main levels of contents – evidential claims, interpretive frames and agendas for action – which are characterized by a short set of key qualities.

First, media convey a broad range of *evidential claims* about the believed present, past or future reality of conflict, ranging from detailed intelligence (e.g. that a certain kind of chemical agent was used in an attack) to broad assessments (e.g. that a besieged city is expected to fall within days; see Meyer, 2016, for an elaborate definition). Evidential claims can be explicitly qualified (e.g. as contested or likely true), warranted or challenged (e.g. by presenting evidence or sources), or they can be presented as authoritative truth claims, suggesting different certitude about the proposed facts (see also Baeriswyl, 1989; DeAndrea, 2014). Given the preliminary and often contested nature of factual knowledge in conflict, however, it is often not so easy to evaluate the accuracy of presented evidential claims. While there are occasionally evidential claims that are demonstrably false, in many situations, the relevant desiderate is rather that presented claims should be duly qualified. By acknowledging possible corroboration or challenging evidence, and discussing sources' respective competence and trustworthiness in providing dependable information, media can greatly advance audiences' ability to accurately gauge the certitude of presented claims. Moreover, we can try to distinguish possibly accurate but misleading evidential claims from those that support valid conclusions. To the extent that presented evidential claims are duly qualified and relevant, decision makers can found their policies on sound intelligence, civilians can devise actions to avoid possible harm, and all audiences gain the ability to check offered interpretations against what they know to be true. By contrast, where media coverage lacks important information, omits appropriate qualifications of certainty and doubt or conveys inaccurate or misleading claims, an audience's grasp of a conflict is likely to be skewed. In particular, the widely debated practice of 'fake news', which may be sponsored strategically as propaganda by conflict actors or emerge from online rumours or commercial clickbaiting, routinely combines the distortive presentation of accurate but non-indicative facts with false, unwarranted claims to suggest a misleading interpretation.

Second, media interpret available information employing a more or less diverse selection of *interpretive frames*, ranging from incendiary, ethnocentric narratives (e.g. suggesting hostile conspiracies by outside powers) to balanced and reasoned accounts of present disputes. On the one hand, frames explain events and issues by attributing causes, motives and responsibility, define their significance and project their expected future implications. On the other hand, frames evaluate information against the backdrop of specific values or objectives and endow the news with moral and affective charging (e.g. suggesting guilt, justifying aims and raising anxiety or hope; see Entman, 1993). Interpretive frames can be evaluated primarily based on their ability to account for the available information (Neuman, Just, & Crigler, 1992). While there are occasionally frames that are clearly unwarranted by the present evidence, any situation can be valuably interpreted based on a multitude of frames. Accordingly, a second criterion for evaluating the media framing of conflict concerns the provision of multiple, diverse frames that interpret the news from different perspectives and normative backgrounds (Baden & Springer, 2017). However, frame contestation occurs not just due to legitimate differences in the interpretation of the available evidence according to journalists' expertise, but also because of successful frame building by conflict actors advancing their strategic objectives. In covering conflict, the media are typically drawing on a small number of frames that can on occasion converge to form dominant narratives of a conflict that subdue contestation and further examination (Porto, 2007; e.g. framing the Rwandan conflict as a genocide or the US intervention in Afghanistan as part of the War on Terror). Inversely, conflict actors and their sponsored media outlets may also contest emerging media consensus in an effort to maintain ambiguity and thus prevent public opinion or political actors from swinging behind specific positions (e.g. blaming the Assad regime for the use of chemical weapons). Accordingly, not only the diversity of presented frames, but also their specific qualities – notably, their plausibility and coherence, their reliance on crude stereotypes and their propagandistic claim to exclusive truth – must be taken into account.

Third, media often convey explicit or implicit *agendas for action*, which propose possible avenues for collective or individual action and present possible justifications for specific kinds of behaviour (Stalpouskaya & Baden, 2015; for an elaborate definition, see also Baden & Tenenboim-Weinblatt, 2015). For instance, media may endorse or reject specific policies, or highlight opportunities for individuals to act – be it to avert or avoid unwelcome developments (e.g. circumnavigate dangerous places or disguise their religious affiliation in public; protest policies believed to be harmful or warn others), or to attain valued objectives (e.g. campaign, donate or volunteer to support militias, activist groups or paramedics; engage in sabotage or violent action). To evaluate the media's provision of agendas for action, a first criterion concerns the presentation of relevant choices. Just as any conflict situation allows different interpretations, there are generally multiple courses of action that can be derived. Where media fail to present viable choices and alternatives, they unduly restrict the range of political choices. Likewise, agendas for action need to be based upon viable frames, whose analysis points at important problems and causes underlying the conflict (see Benford & Snow, 2000, for an analogous argument in the context of social movements). Where there is no particular reason to expect specific desired outcomes of a proposed course of action, the presented agenda deserves critique. Agendas for action can, in addition, be qualified by various normatively based criteria. For instance, one might evaluate the conformity of proposed agendas with human rights and dignity or assess their demands upon the concessions made by different groups. Likewise, we can evaluate their advocacy of punitive or violent measures or gauge their fairness or acceptability also to other sides in the conflict.

Agendas for action, interpretive frames and evidential claims build upon one another, shaping and constraining the coverage of conflict. On the one hand, what courses of action are plausible depends on the interpretive framing of the situation, which in turn responds to what is known about it. Presented evidential claims thus constrain the range of warranted frames, which in turn legitimize or delegitimize different proposed agendas for action. On the other hand, media attention to and presentation of evidential claims react to available interpretations of the situation, which may in turn be shaped by available or preferred courses of action. Strategic actors may construct frames instrumentally to justify specific agendas, and what claims appear plausible and relevant depends also on how a situation is framed. Taken together, the characteristic selection and presentation of evidential claims, interpretive frames and agendas for action captures most of those contents of conflict news held responsible for particular media roles. As mediated representations of conflict, they are constructed through an interactive transaction process involving both media and non-media actors, as depicted in the lower left half of Figure 1.1. Through their public dissemination in the news, these representations then potentially shape the perceptions of various actors and actor groups involved in the conflict.

The Amplification of Conflict News

For conflict news to exert any influence, it must be publicly amplified. Most immediately, this concerns which audiences are exposed to certain news contents, both via media outlets specifically addressing them and due to audiences' discretional reliance on particular media. Conflict news coverage plays fundamentally different roles when amplified primarily towards audiences within or outside the conflict. To foreign audiences, media coverage is often the only or primary source of information about the conflict. Audiences are likely to base large parts of their perceptions of a conflict upon mediated information. By contrast, domestic audiences often have many ways of receiving information about the conflict – including first-hand experiences, word of mouth, contact with actors involved in the conflict (e.g. soldiers, activists) or exposure to certain effects of the conflict (e.g. resource scarcity, destruction, security measures). In addition, due to the much higher priority of conflict coverage in domestic media, domestic audiences tend to receive conflict news through multiple media channels, which is not necessarily true for foreign audiences. Domestic audiences can vary greatly in their levels of media literacy, education, language proficiency and access to media channels, thus influencing what kind of media content they can access, how they interpret it and whom they trust. Most media cater primarily to either domestic or foreign audiences, with transnational media (and, in some rare cases, media addressing audiences on both sides of the conflict) located somewhere in between.

A critical distinction concerns whether media primarily address *decision-making elites* or wide *lay publics*. Decision makers are much less likely to rely on specific media as their sole or primary source of information. Rather, media constitute only one (not necessarily preferred) source that is likely to be cross-referenced with other sources, such as intelligence briefings or diplomatic channels. By contrast, lay publics mostly rely on media for comprehending conflict. Even where domestic publics have access to additional, non-mediated information, conflict news is critical for putting anecdotal experiences and information into perspective. Highbrow-quality media and analysis-oriented NGO publications are geared more towards addressing (especially foreign) decision-making elites (US President Trump's primary reliance on Fox News appears to be exceptional). Tabloids and other popular media cater to wide audiences, but may also be consulted by domestic leaders aiming to gauge public beliefs and sentiments.

Within each targeted audience, the potential impact of conflict news depends on its visibility and consonance. Where single media outlets reach large shares of a population, their specific way of representing conflict has the potential to powerfully coordinate popular perceptions – consider, for instance, the dominant role of CNN for broadcasting news from the Gulf War to a US audience (Robinson, 2002). However, where different media reach different parts of a population, or where audiences rely on a diverse diet of media, no single outlet's representation of the conflict can dominate prevalent perceptions. Instead, the emphasis then lies on the extent to which different media agree in their way of presenting conflict, exposing audiences to similar news despite their diversified media uses. Arguably, consonance among media is more critical for influencing popular conflict perceptions, whereas decision makers' access to extra-media sources should reduce their reliance on the news. Nevertheless, also media with limited reach have the potential to shape the perceptions of specific audience groups. For instance, radical media may not be consumed much outside ideological communities, but it can powerfully shape the views of those reached. With regard to the analysis of media roles in violent conflict (Figure 1.1), we can distinguish four major scenarios of conflict news amplification that enable media to influence violent conflict: First, multiple media may converge to amplify relatively consonant contents to large shares of a population either inside or outside conflict, building consensus. Second, selected quality media may provide decision-making elites with specific analysis and intelligence on a conflict, augmenting their sources. Third, selected popular media may inform (primarily domestic) decision-making elites about the likely perceptions prevalent among the population. Finally, selected radical outlets may shape the conflict perceptions of small extremist communities.

The Influences of Conflict News

As purveyors of information and commentary, media primarily exercise influence by shaping the perceptions of the audiences that consume and use them. However, evidential claims, interpretive frames and agendas for action each influence audiences' perceptions in characteristic, distinct ways, which are illustrated in Figure 1.2. One can furthermore distinguish between elite or lay audiences, between audiences that are directly (notably, domestic) or at best indirectly affected by the conflict (most foreign audiences) and between media influences that manifest themselves in the short, medium or long term.

Evidential claims presented in the media inform people's *evidential beliefs* about conflict, particularly about the interpretation of key formative events in the conflict and who caused them. Just as evidential claims, evidential beliefs are assumptions about the real world that are endowed with some epistemic status. They shape what people believe they know about conflict, its underlying issues, events and likely developments, and determine the degree of confidence they have in these beliefs. For instance, British media coverage convinced many Britons that Syrian President Assad had used chemical weapons in the civil war, while Russian media cast doubt on the reported incident and inspired confidence in Assad's innocence. Many audiences learn about (claimed) facts about conflict primarily from the media, taking over evidential claims as beliefs relatively easily. Over time and with frequent repetition in the media, evidential claims are credited with growing certainty, morphing increasingly into firmly held evidential beliefs that shape interpretations of subsequent events or choices in a conflict. For instance, as long as many Israelis firmly believe that Arabs wish to eradicate their country from the map, they are unlikely to agree to any measures that

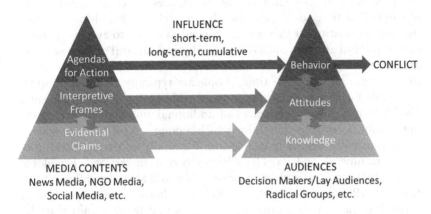

Figure 1.2 Three levels of media influence.

require a leap of trust and increase their vulnerability. At the same time, the degree of cognitive openness to new evidential claims will be lower in situations where conflict-related news touches on collective identities and memories of domestic in- and out-groups or raises foreign audiences' perceptions of postcolonial ties, shared histories or relations with relevant diaspora or migrant groups. Audiences that identify with specific conflict parties, especially within conflict areas but also abroad, are likely to try and insulate themselves from dissonant evidential claims that could challenge their pre-existing beliefs about their own community's role in a conflict as well as the intention of others. Where polarization is high, audiences can resort to psychological belief system defences to repudiate evidential claims seen as hostile fabrications and propaganda (Baden & Stalpouskaya, 2015; Nyhan & Reifler, 2010); for instance, many allegations about human rights violations by the Israeli military are confidently dismissed among Israeli audiences. Evidential claims made in the media are particularly influential in situations of crisis and high uncertainty following major events, when even senior officials and top decision makers sometimes turn to the media, rather than their in-house intelligence, for up-to-date information as we know from interviews.

Interpretive frames influence people's perceptions in two interrelated ways. On the one hand, frames organize available knowledge and render it meaningful, suggesting specific causes, logics and consequences relevant for understanding the significance of evidential claims and beliefs. For instance, British media interpreted the use of chemical weapons in Syria as the act of a desperate, immoral dictator, while Russian media framed the event as staged setup intended to discredit the presidency. On the other hand, frames present relevant normative standards for evaluating specific information, enabling audiences to form *evaluative attitudes* towards the events and actors, issues and choices in a conflict. For example, Assad's actions, or those of North Korean leader Kim Jong Un, raise different evaluations if they are interpreted as efforts to avert what happened in Libya and Iraq and ensure the physical survival of their families and supporting groups, rather than the acts of unyielding despots clinging to power. At the same time, people are typically aware of multiple frames that can be used to interpret and evaluate conflict-related events. Media frames inform audiences of additional suitable interpretations but do not necessarily determine which among several familiar frames a recipient will consider most relevant. Especially in heterogeneous media environments, audiences have been shown to discretionarily endorse frames that resonate with their prior values and attitudes. However, as Gamson (1992) has shown, people primarily choose among those frames offered to them in the media, which means that frames omitted in the news remain unavailable to them. Accordingly, at least where high consonance in news framing narrowly restricts the range of offered frames, media should be able to exercise a strong influence upon people's understandings and attitudes.

Agendas for action, finally, inform audiences about possible courses of behaviour. Together with the motivational force sustained by evaluative attitudes, they thus hold the potential to direct and coordinate the behavioural intentions, and possibly, the actual *behaviour* of media audiences. For instance, mediated agendas may suggest taking shelter or otherwise avoiding an impending threat; they may incite hateful groups and individuals to engage in violent action; or they may suggest that specific policies are suitable to achieve common objectives. Whether agendas for action successfully orient individual or collective action, of course, depends on a large number of intervening factors. Only if individuals are convinced of the appropriateness of specific courses of action (compared to other choices), are capable of carrying them out and are sufficiently motivated is there reason to expect direct behavioural impacts. Unless these criteria are met, suggested policies are bound to lack sufficient backing, attempted behaviours may be stalled by a lack of resources or other obstacles and behavioural intentions may never manifest themselves. Where agendas for action shape conflict elites' decision-making or incite radical groups or entire populations to use violence, they hold the potential to directly influence the course of conflict. However, such situations are quite demanding on the specific nature of consonant agendas and their widespread reception and adoption.

Similarly to the hierarchy of evidential claims, interpretive frames and beliefs, the psychological states affected by conflict news are also interdependent. People are capable of forming their own frames to make sense of acquired evidential beliefs and drawing their own conclusions about appropriate attitudes and behavioural responses. Especially where people hold strong assumptions about the conflict, they have shown themselves capable of imputing evidential beliefs without the help of media or even in direct contradiction to mediated claims. Likewise, actors determined to follow certain courses of action are typically capable of constructing frames that legitimize their behavioural choice, all the way to inventing the evidential beliefs needed to sustain these. In consequence, the influence of conflict news upon conflict-related behaviour can take a variety of paths, most of which require a confluence of mediated claims, frames and agendas with the prior beliefs, attitudes and behavioural dispositions of the individual. Media forcefully inform (especially lay) audiences' evidential beliefs, but the conclusions drawn from this knowledge may still follow from idiosyncratic or culturally engraved interpretations unaided by the media. Media may suggest specific frames for making sense of, and evaluating, conflict-related events, but audiences are not compelled by these suggestions. Mediated agendas offer specific behavioural directions, but even if these are adopted – which is by no means inevitable – many factors may interfere before actual behaviour follows. While some evidential claims, frames and agendas may result in relatively immediate responses among audiences (e.g. protests or political condemnations following reports of extremist violence), in many cases, media contents shape audiences' beliefs, attitudes and behaviours cumulatively over time (e.g. growing inter-group distrust or hatred, or slowly building political support for conflict intervention).

Depending on the specific audiences targeted, several different paths of media influence can therefore be expected. Political decision makers are commonly thought to possess reasonably well-formed prior attitudes and policy preferences, a well-developed ability to systematically process and appraise available information and access to a wide range of additional information sources. Mediated agendas and frames are expected to meet with considerable resistance unless these can convince even when under scrutiny or align with preferences already held by the recipient. Accordingly, most studies investigating media influences upon elites have invoked *rationalist paradigms* and considered media contributions mostly through a lens of providing certified evidence and informed analysis. News may convey early warning before established intelligence channels can corroborate, or it may provide on-the-ground assessments distinct from available official or diplomatic channels (e.g. Otto & Meyer, 2012). By contrast, foreign lay publics are commonly deemed to possess limited prior information, attitudes and behavioural preferences. Laypeople are less likely to engage in effortful analysis to form their own frames and preferences, rendering them susceptible to mediated frames and agendas. Accordingly, scholars studying media effects on laypeople typically highlight the role of conflict *frames and narratives*, evocative visuals and *emotional appeals* and downplay the importance of evidence and rational appraisal. Especially when the coverage of different media is consonant, advocates specific interpretations of foreign conflict persistently over extended periods of time and suggests solutions that tap into underlying identity constructions and worldviews, it can more easily shift public attitudes in support of advocated policies (Peter, 2004). In crisis situations where uncertainty is high and psychologically intolerable, the quickest interpretation can make a considerable and lasting impact and may prove difficult to shift even when the facts underlying this initial frame later turn out to be erroneous. Audiences that are directly affected by the conflict tend to follow the news much more closely and often possess relevant information unavailable to remote publics; however, they may also be more susceptible to fearmongering, lack access to alternative viewpoints or live in denial about present risks. They are also more likely to choose media whose content confirms rather than challenges their view of themselves and the intentions of opposing conflict parties. However, domestic audiences are more likely than foreign audiences to respond to agendas for action presented in their media, as their stakes are higher, as is their ability to influence the situation, be it via political activities addressing relevant conflict actors, through personal behaviour such as hiding or fleeing or through their becoming involved in violent action. Also among extremist groups, recipients' willingness to act upon resonant agendas should be increased; however, as such groups possess strong, preformed attitudes, media frames are unlikely to change how individuals interpret conflict and are mostly restricted to reinforcing pre-existing conceptions.

Finally, media may influence conflict developments not only *directly* – by influencing audiences' beliefs, attitudes and behavioural preferences concerning a conflict – but also *indirectly,* by enabling strategic observers to gauge the likely interpretations and reactions of other groups and actors. Conflict leaders may follow the framing of foreign media in order to estimate the likelihood of third publics supporting sanctions or military intervention; foreign decision makers may monitor violent agendas amplified inside conflict areas to anticipate further escalation. Strategic actors may even anticipate media coverage and take it into account in their policies – for instance, the presence of foreign media capable of raising global outrage may deter militaries from engaging in atrocities; and the expected media framing of specific stances as valiant or weak may motivate political leaders to adjust their conflict-related policies (e.g. Wolfsfeld, 2004). While such indirect effects are hardly an intended influence of the media, they nevertheless contribute to influencing the beliefs, attitudes and behaviours of strategic actors in conflict and thus give rise to possible media roles.

The Roles of Media in Conflict

From the creation and transformation of conflict news contents to their amplification and influence upon different audiences, the specific nature of those media considered, the conflict scenario and various other factors can come into play to modulate media influence on conflicts. For instance, armed conflicts with conflict parties that kidnap, torture and kill journalists limit journalists' ability to safely interact with many sources; in addition, the sanctions imposed by local conflict actors and partisan audiences predispose journalists to provide rather biased coverage. Neutral parties such as regional or foreign media as well as certain NGOs might be in a better position to collect valuable information and analysis if they can still safely operate within the country or if they have access to a network of local sources. Complex security threats hold the potential to constrain the amplification activities of local print media, while online outlets' and broadcasters' ability to reach across conflict lines is less affected. By contrast, in classic interstate conflict, domestic elites may powerfully constrain the freedom of domestic (and to some extent also foreign) media to gather and amplify news. Also, leaders can rely on administrative channels and exercise considerable control over conflict events. Among foreign decision makers, established diplomatic channels and intelligence are usually capable of conveying sufficient information and analysis at least for relatively salient conflicts and outside of high-pressure crisis situations, reducing the role of domestic media as purveyors of policy-relevant intelligence. However, evocative frames and agendas for action in the foreign news might still play a role for pressurizing executives towards taking action, particularly where elites are weak or divided. In low-intensity, identity-based conflict, media are often incentivized, pressured or directly used to transform and amplify news tailored to support ethnocentric perspectives, as we have seen in the case of Macedonia. To the extent that conflicting identities also structure news dissemination and consumption, opposing groups get primarily exposed to contrasting narratives, possibly fuelling polarization and escalation.

At the same time, the expectable impact of conflict news depends also on audiences' respective power to intervene in the course of conflict-related events. The more specific conflict actions are controlled by powerful elites – e.g. military operations, negotiations with limited public involvement – the more likely the media's roles depend on those media actually consumed by these elites. Inversely, the more the considered change in conflict developments depends on voluntary collective action and popular support – e.g. in identity-based conflicts or civil war – the more possible media roles revolve around the consonant coverage found across a variety of news pieces and outlets. For instance, hostile ethnocentrism in Rwandan media arguably facilitated the genocide, just as coverage replete with anti-Semitic stereotypes contributed to the many pogroms in the early 20th century. A hybrid case concerns the radicalization of non-elite individuals or *extremist groups*, which does not require widespread media consensus but depends on a consistent build-up of specific patterns in selected media's news; for instance, online platforms carrying incendiary contents have been linked to recruiting Islamist terrorists in Western countries (Weimann, 2015). Terrorism, hate crimes and other small-scale forms of violence – and with these, extremist media advocating such behaviour – matter mostly within inter-group conflict situations, where widespread fear and hostility fuel retaliatory violence or reactive security policies. In practice, of course, many conflict situations cannot be reduced to just one kind of scenario. While executive elites may decide on some conflict actions without considering public support (e.g. Israeli airstrikes against Gaza, European marine forces' participation in the Operation Atalanta anti-piracy mission in Somalia), major escalations or de-escalations in conflict, longer-term conflict policies, and most actions that tangibly involve or affect domestic populations typically require some kind of popular mobilization and consensus (e.g. activating reservists for ground operations in Gaza; Russian and Ukrainian public backing for military action in Eastern Ukraine). Inversely, widespread public hostility may incentivize political elites to pursue 'hawkish' policies even if that was not originally their intention, and the potential damage, political costs and sometimes popular fallout caused by violent extremist groups often set powerful constraints for political conflict management (consider, for instance, the ability of radical minorities among both Palestinians and Israelis to prevent either side's leaders from making noteworthy concessions; Wolfsfeld, 2004). Theorizing media roles in conflict will always need to combine insights about which factors matter generally for shaping specific media roles with an understanding and analysis of the case-specific features of each conflict case. It forces us to combine area studies, country and conflict knowledge with insights from political communication, cognitive psychology and journalism studies.

Conclusion

As has been amply documented in the extant scholarship on media and conflict, media may play very different roles in violent conflict. However, with its heavy focus on thick, case-oriented accounts of media roles actualized in specific moments (typically, of major escalation), the existing literature has had little to say on what kinds of factors and contexts lead media to assume specific kinds of roles in a conflict. By contrast, our transactionist process model enables a nuanced, comparative investigation of a wide range of influences that media have on different audiences. Our account looks from the perspective of audiences at the different media roles and the contestation among various media and non-media actors shaping these. Media affect the perceptions of lay audiences as well as decision makers, albeit in different ways. To determine what relevant roles media play in a given conflict, an analysis needs to start from determining which audiences matter most, and in which ways, to the trajectory of a given conflict. It needs to consider which media different groups consume and trust, and what kinds of news contents are capable of engendering specific changes in these audiences' beliefs, attitudes, and behaviours in the short term or through sustained, cumulative influences (e.g. consonant, ethnocentric framing; timely, well-backed evidential claims; radicalized, incendiary agendas). Based on an examination of relevant contents in the news, it needs to investigate how those transformations applied by the media, as well as their interactions with political and military actors, NGOs, lay audiences and others, contributed to shaping the specific representation of conflict.

At each stage of the recursive process, we can analyse (1) the specific *transactions* that shape how information and commentary are exchanged and adapted through the interplay of actors' input and prevalent structural constraints (e.g. derived from the media's distinctive logic, the affordances of the specific news production and dissemination process, and the embedding conflict situation); we can study (2) the dynamics of competitive social *interactions* between diverse media and non-media actors attempting to co-shape or control each stage of the news production and dissemination process; and we can investigate (3) how both informational transactions and social interactions are continuously structured by and contribute to the *structuration* of the underlying power balances, institutions and established routines, the configuration of audiences, media and conflict actors, as well as the embedding conflict situation. Underneath the rapidly unfolding stream of specific interactions and transactions, the structuration of persistent interaction and transaction patterns evolves mostly slowly, unless major disruptions (e.g. government closures of key outlets; major leaks) suddenly reconfigure the situation. Our model connects the specific representations of conflict and resulting roles of media to a wide range of contextual factors, most notably, (a) culturally embedded conflict perceptions and belief systems; (b) audiences' media reliance and trust; (c) the configuration, diversity and freedom of relevant media; (d) the constellation of conflict actors, including regional and international powers; and (e) the course and intensity of conflict. This focus on context-sensitive interactions and transactions underlying the creation and transformation, amplification and influences of conflict-related media contents upon the conflict-related perceptions and behaviour allows a flexible, nuanced, yet theoretically grounded examination of different media roles in conflict. In the remaining chapters of the present volume, the authors involved in the INFOCORE team will unfold their respective contributions to this concerted effort, which aims to illuminate several key practices, patterns, conditions and connections and thus add to an increasingly nuanced understanding of those specific factors and processes involved in shaping relevant media roles.

Notes

1 For influential contributions to the ongoing debate, see, for instance, Allan & Zelizer, 2004; Bennett & Paletz, 1994; Carruthers, 2000; Cottle, 2006; Eskjær, Hjarvard, & Mortensen, 2015; Hoskins & O'Loughlin, 2010; Robinson, Goddard, Parry, Murray, & Taylor, 2010 and Wolfsfeld, 1997.
2 This includes professional contents distributed on social and digital media (e.g. webpages and Facebook feeds of professional news organizations or other institutions), as well as all other distribution channels; however, it excludes user-generated contents published by laypeople, political leaders, or even journalists writing in a private faculty, where the interactive production–transformation–amplification–influence process laid out below does not apply.

References

Allan, S., & Zelizer, B. (2004). *Reporting war. Journalism in wartime*. London, UK: Routledge.

Baden, C., & Springer, N. (2017). Conceptualizing viewpoint diversity in news discourse. *Journalism, 18*, 176–194.

Baden, C., & Stalpouskaya, K. (2015). *Maintaining frame coherence between uncertain information and changing agendas: The evolving framing of the Syrian chemical attacks in the US, British, and Russian news*. Paper presented at the 65th ICA annual conference, San Juan, Puerto Rico.

Baden, C., & Tenenboim-Weinblatt, K. (2015). *INFOCORE definitions: "Agenda for Action"*. Jerusalem, Israel: The Hebrew University of Jerusalem. Online available at www.infocore.eu/results/definitions/

Baden, C., & Tenenboim-Weinblatt, K. (2016). Viewpoint, testimony, action: How journalists reposition source frames within news frames. *Journalism Studies, 19*, 143–161.

Baeriswyl, O. (1989). *Gewissheitsgrade in Zeitungstexten. Eine Analyse gewissheitsreduzierender Elemente informativer Texte der Schweizer Zeitungen "Neue Zürcher Zeitung", "Tages-Anzeiger" und "Blick"* [Degree of certainty in news texts. An analysis of certainty reducing elements of informative texts in the Swiss dailies "Neue Zürcher Zeitung", "Tages-Anzeiger" and "Blick"]. Freiburg, Switzerland: Universitäts-Verlag.

Barnlund, D. C. (1970). A transactional model of communication. In J. Akin, A. Goldberg, G. Myers, & J. Stewart (Eds.), *Language behavior: A book of readings in communication* (pp. 43–61). The Hague, The Netherlands: Mouton.

Benford, R. D., & Snow, D. A. (2000). Framing processes and social movements: An overview and assessment. *Annual Review of Sociology, 26*, 611–639.

Bennett, W. L., & Paletz, D. L. (1994). *Taken by storm. The media, public opinion, and U.S. foreign policy in the Gulf War*. Chicago, IL: University of Chicago Press.

Carruthers, S. L. (2000). *The media at war: Communication and conflict in the twentieth century*. Basingstoke, UK: Palgrave Macmillan.

Cottle, S. (2006). *Mediatized conflict: Understanding media and conflicts in the contemporary world*. Maidenhead, UK: McGraw-Hill.

DeAndrea, D. C. (2014). Advancing warranting theory. *Communication Theory, 24*, 186–204.

Entman, R. M. (1993). Framing: Toward clarification of a fractured paradigm. *Journal of Communication, 43*, 51–58.

Eskjær, M. F., Hjarvard, S., & Mortensen, M. (2015). *The dynamics of mediatized conflicts. Global crises and the media.* New York, NY: Peter Lang.

Evans, G. (2011). *Preventing violent conflict: What have we learned?* USIP second annual conference on preventing violent conflict. Online available at www.gevans.org/speeches/speech438.html

Frère, M.-S. (2017). "I wish I could be the journalist I was, but I currently cannot": Experiencing the impossibility of journalism in Burundi. *Media, War & Conflict, 10*, 3–24.

Galtung, J., & Ruge, M. H. (1965). The structure of foreign news. The presentation of the Congo, Cuba and Cyprus crisis in four Norwegian newspapers. *Journal of Peace Research, 2*, 64–91.

Gamson, W. A. (1992). *Talking politics.* Cambridge, UK: Cambridge University Press.

Hanitzsch, T., Hanusch, F., Mellado, C., Anikina, M., Berganza, R., Cangoz, I. et al. (2010). Mapping journalism cultures across nations. *Journalism Studies, 12*, 273–293.

Hermida, A., Lewis, S. C., & Zamith, R. (2014). Sourcing the Arab spring: A case study of Andy Carvin's sources on Twitter during the Tunisian and Egyptian revolutions. *Journal of Computer-Mediated Communication, 19*, 479–499.

Hoskins, A., & O'Loughlin, B. (2010). *War and media: The emergence of diffused war.* Cambridge, UK: Polity.

Kampf, Z., & Liebes, T. (2013). *Transforming media coverage of violent conflicts: The new face of war.* Basingstoke, UK: Palgrave Macmillan.

Meyer, C. O. (2016). *INFOCORE definitions: "Evidential claims and beliefs".* London, UK: King's College London. Online available at www.infocore.eu/results/definitions/

Meyer, C. O., Baden, C., & Frère, M.-S. (2018). Navigating the complexities of media roles in conflict: The INFOCORE approach. *Media, War & Conflict, 11*, 3–21.

Neuman, W. R., Just, M. R., & Crigler, A. N. (1992). *Common knowledge: News and the construction of political meaning.* Chicago, IL: University of Chicago Press.

Nohrstedt, S. A., Kaitatzi-Whitlock, S., Ottosen, R., & Riegert, K. (2000). From the Persian Gulf to Kosovo: War journalism and propaganda. *European Journal of Communication, 15*, 383–404.

Nyhan, B., & Reifler, J. (2010). When corrections fail: The persistence of political misperceptions. *Political Behavior, 32*, 303–330.

Otto, F., & Meyer, C. O. (2012). Missing the story? Changes in foreign news reporting and their implications for conflict prevention, *Media, War & Conflict, 5*, 205–221.

Peter, J. (2004). Our long 'return to the concept of powerful mass media': A cross-national comparative investigation of the effects of consonant media coverage. *International Journal of Public Opinion Research, 16*, 144–168.

Porto, M. P. (2007). Frame diversity and citizen competence: Toward a critical approach to news quality. *Critical Studies in Media Communication, 24*, 303–321.

Robinson, P. (2002). *The CNN effect: The myth of news, foreign policy and intervention.* London, UK: Routledge.

Robinson, P., Goddard, P., Parry, K., Murray, C., & Taylor, P. M. (2010). *Pockets of resistance: British news media, war and theory in the 2003 invasion of Iraq.* Manchester, UK: Manchester University Press.

Seib, P. M. (2009). Public diplomacy and journalism: Parallels, ethical issues, and practical concerns. *American Behavioral Scientist, 52,* 772–786.

Stalpouskaya, K., & Baden, C. (2015). *To do or not to do: The role of agendas for action in analyzing news coverage of violent conflict.* In ACL-IJCNLP Annual Meeting 2015. Beijing, China. Online available at www.aclweb.org/anthology/W15-4504

Tenenboim-Weinblatt, K., & Baden, C. (2018). Journalistic transformation: How source texts are turned into news stories. *Journalism, 19,* 481–499

Wallensteen, P. (2007). *Understanding conflict resolution: War, peace and the global system.* London, UK: Sage.

Weimann, G. (2015). *Terrorism in cyberspace: The next generation.* New York, NY: Columbia University Press.

Wolfsfeld, G. (1997). *Media and political conflict: News from the Middle East.* Cambridge, UK: Cambridge University Press.

Wolfsfeld, G. (2004). *Media and the path to peace.* Cambridge, UK: Cambridge University Press.

Part II

The Dynamics of Public Discourse(s) on Wars and Armed Conflicts

Media Content, Strategic Communication and Conflict-Related Cognition

2 Not So Bad News? Investigating Journalism's Contribution to What Is Bad, and Good, in News on Violent Conflict

Christian Baden and Keren Tenenboim-Weinblatt

Across all disciplines concerned with the study of conflict, most scholars are united in their criticism of conflict news. Extant scholarship has documented an impressive variety of dysfunctions and failures in conflict journalism, extending from a disproportional focus on violence to aggravated ethnocentric biases and a susceptibility to false rumours, manipulation and propaganda. The coverage of conflict escalation and major conflict events, which constitutes the focus of most existing research, has especially been accused of distorting the facts, promoting double standards and inciting to hostility and violence. In consequence, many have doubted journalism's ability to cover violent conflict in a balanced or even constructive fashion. The verdicts range from proclaiming a recurrent failure of the news media in the face of violent conflict, to the dire conclusion that journalism might be fundamentally flawed: When it comes to war and violence, in this view, the way in which journalists provide coverage tends to make a bad situation worse.

In this chapter, we take issue with this perspective, which dominates not only the critical scholarship, but also much mainstream research on journalism and conflict.[1] While we acknowledge the mounting evidence of biases and failures in conflict news coverage, in our view, the conclusion drawn from this is premature in at least three important ways. First, the overwhelming majority of condemning evidence derives from examinations of rather few, mostly opinion-leading, Western outlets covering selected, exalted moments in conflict. By contrast, we know rather little about how the same conflicts were covered at other, less heated times and in other media elsewhere. Do the findings of ethnocentric, incendiary coverage transfer also to those moments and media that were not selected for study? In order to know whether the critiqued patterns in conflict news exist persistently or only temporarily, across a wide range of media or only in certain kinds of outlets, a systematic, comparative and diachronic assessment is required.

Second, while journalists are of course key actors in the production of news, their coverage is in a fundamental sense co-created by those sources and conflict-related events represented in the news. From examining an outlet's news coverage alone, it is impossible to say whether rising antagonism reflects rising tensions in the reality of conflict, hostile communications pushed forward by belligerent elites, or is indeed an outcome of journalistic practices. If we wish to evaluate the performance of journalism, we need to study how journalism *makes a difference* in how the conflict is presented in the news media: How do journalists select, present, transform and contextualize available information, and what deficiencies in conflict coverage can thus plausibly be attributed to journalistic practice? In order to understand the specific contribution that journalists make to conflict news, we need to systematically compare the produced news to available input presented by relevant sources and to salient developments in the conflict itself.

Third, while there is widespread agreement that certain patterns of coverage deserve critique, it is much less clear by what normative standards the journalistic performance is being judged. From the far-reaching postulates of peace journalism, which occasionally conflict with journalistic conceptions of what constitutes news, to the mostly formal standards of professional journalistic ethics, very different verdicts can be formulated. It is neither our intention nor within our capabilities to resolve the many contradictions in the ongoing normative debate. However, we believe that any appraisal of journalistic performance is incomplete unless also its possible positive contributions are taken into account. Furthermore, we need to distinguish between dysfunctions incurred in the pursuit of competing, but legitimate journalistic aims, and the abandonment of professional ethics. In order to gain some traction for distinguishing and evaluating journalistic conflict coverage, we need to consider how those ways in which journalists process conflict-related news relate to their specific, valuable or problematic roles in covering conflict.

In the following, we aim to provide a more contextualized, weighted assessment of journalists' contribution to covering conflict. Our argument is based both on a critical appraisal of the existing scholarship, and the systematic examination of journalistic conflict coverage in a comparative, empirical fashion. Departing from an analysis of journalistic transformations applied to available source materials, we begin by arguing that journalists alter the content of conflict news coverage in meaningful ways. While some interventions – notably, those involved in the domestication of news (Clausen, 2004) – are indeed prone to producing or reinforcing ethnocentric bias, from a standpoint of professional journalism, none can be described as dysfunctional *per se*. In fact, some transformations also serve to contain or counter incendiary tendencies innate to the communications of important sources, or the conflict situation itself. In a second step, we investigate journalistic conflict coverage in a comparative perspective, aiming to uncover what factors appear to drive systematic changes in journalistic practices, and might therefore explain a recurrent failure of the media during escalation. This analysis suggests that journalists possess several very different routines for covering major crises, which are triggered by specific kinds of situations in the conflict. Only very few responses to violent escalation hold consistently across different conflicts, media and events, suggesting that the evaluation of journalistic practices requires considerable additional nuance. In a third step, finally, we examine the proposition that journalism might be generally biased toward aggravating conflict. Focusing on those patterns in journalistic coverage that persist throughout both escalation and comparatively calm phases, we find a remarkable amount of consistency in the way in which media cover the same events, even on opposing sides in a conflict. We therefore argue that the polarized, ethnocentric presentation of conflict news needs to put into perspective against a powerful undercurrent of professional news work that is relatively unaffected by conflict-related or political biases.

In sum, our analysis supports a much more differentiated, ambivalent appraisal of journalistic conflict coverage. Despite a marked tendency to play up violence and privilege ethnocentric views, we argue, there are also many valuable transformations suitable to mitigate the distortions and incitement of other conflict actors, and improve the quality of available information.

Data and Approach

In order to address these questions, we investigated the coverage generated by journalists covering six ongoing conflicts, employing a combination of qualitative and quantitative, comparative as well as diachronic approaches. We collected news produced by opinion-leading news outlets within Macedonia and Kosovo, Burundi and the Democratic Republic of the Congo (DRC), Syria, Israel and the Palestinian Territories, as well as the coverage of the same conflicts in German, French, British and selected transnational media. Within each conflict area, we additionally selected specific outlets representing important conflict parties (e.g. two Hamas-affiliated newspapers in the Israeli–Palestinian conflict and a UN-funded radio station in the DRC). From each outlet, we collected all coverage related to the conflict over a period of multiple years (2006–2016 for the Israeli–Palestinian conflict, 2010–2016 for Macedonia, Kosovo and Burundi, 2011–2016 for Syria and the DRC, or as far back as archives would allow; see Tables 2.1 and 2.2 for the domestic and foreign coverage, respectively).[2]

To analyse the coverage provided by these outlets, we relied on three complementary approaches. Using a large, fine-grained dictionary capable of recognizing more than 3,700 relevant concepts mentioned in eight languages, we automatically recognized the topical contents of each article as well as the patterns with which different concepts were put into relation. This strategy enabled a systematic comparative analysis of specific contents raised in the news, identifying (for instance) various forms of references to violence or negotiation, uncertainty or ethnocentric perspective, as well as the evaluative tendency of coverage.[3] For a more holistic analysis, we identified slowly evolving latent structures organizing the use of these concepts in the coverage of different media, using Evolutionary Factor Analysis (Motta & Baden, 2013). This analysis reveals to what extent the coverage of different media, or of the same media at different times, is structured by the same patterns of issue attention and association, or provides structurally different representations of conflict events. These two quantitative strategies were complemented by the qualitative, in-depth investigation of selected moments and media within specific conflicts, which provided a nuanced contextualization of the provided news: By comparing specific news texts to the portfolio of source materials used for creating the news, the coverage of the same events in different media, and the same outlets' coverage of related events, we were able to illuminate the specific selections and interventions achieved by journalists and separate their contributions from other factors shaping the news.

For the further contextualization of our analyses, we drew upon existing data collections of conflict-related casualties.[4] Based on detailed timelines for each conflict, we distinguished phases of relative calm and pacification from those phases characterized by different kinds of escalation, or sustained high levels of violence. Through the combination of micro- and macroscopic, cross-sectional and diachronic as well as quantitative and qualitative analyses, we were able to separate common and persistent patterns from media-specific and temporary deviations in the coverage and distinguish the influences of shared sources and reported events from the distinctive contribution of journalistic news production.

Delineating the Journalistic Contribution

Journalists' authorship and control of the news is both far-reaching and severely limited. In one sense, journalists, editors and other media workers (e.g. news agency writers, fixers) each exercise considerable control over the news. Their contact networks, information diets and research activities are responsible for large parts of the information that reaches the attention of the media; their selections and agendas shape what issues and events receive coverage; and it is ultimately their words that convey the news and endow it with different meaning. Nevertheless, attributing authorship solely to journalists severely "overemphasize[s] the determining agency of media professionals" (Boesman, d'Haenens, & van Gorp, 2016, p. 233). Sources and strategic communicators exercise profound influence over available information, they provide specific interpretation, and otherwise create input for journalists to use in their coverage (Althaus, Edy, Entman, & Phalen, 1996; Bennett, Lawrence, & Livingstone, 2006; see also Fröhlich & Jungblut, this volume). Authorities and political actors, as well as security forces and (para-) militaries in the case of conflict, constrain journalists' ability to produce coverage in many ways (e.g. by regulating access to sources and locations, imposing sanctions and censorship upon media). In a fundamental sense, finally, news is also driven by the succession of real world events – which range from the statements and actions of sources to occurrences largely or entirely beyond discretionary control (e.g. terror attacks, accidents, disasters). Yet, inversely crediting the contents of conflict news essentially to the media management of powerful sources and conflict actors severely understates journalists' substantial contribution to covering conflict-related events. Given the many interactive ways in which journalists, sources and events co-shape the news, attempting to determine who, if anyone, 'leads the dance' (and thus holds responsibility for specific news contents) adds little to our understanding of conflict journalism.

Instead, we suggest looking at news as the outcome of a journalistic-controlled process that *transforms* available information – which originates from sources or direct observations outside journalistic production – into newsworthy, meaningful accounts. In our view, journalists can and should be held accountable for the ways in which they select, transform and present the information available to them but not for the quality of this information itself. For instance, a TV station might broadcast footage of soldiers abusing civilians, followed by sound bites from a rally protesting the event. In such a case, our question is not whether such coverage sparks outrage (maybe it should!), possibly fanning escalation; rather, we must ask whether the abuse and demonstration warranted selection for inclusion in the news, whether their presentation and contextualization was appropriate and whether the journalistic narrative contributed to a better public understanding of the situation and its implications. The incendiary potential of the abuse, as well as the protesters' chants, by contrast, remain the responsibility of the respective protagonists.

In order to examine the specific contribution of journalists, we conducted an in-depth comparative case study of the news covering the abduction and murder of four teenagers, three Israeli and one Palestinian, leading up to the 2014 Gaza war. Departing from 150 news items relating to these events in three Israeli, three Palestinian, and two each of German, British and US-based news outlets, we compared the resulting news coverage to the contents of the 22 most influential source texts (11 by Israeli and 11 by Palestinian sources) used therein. Thereby, we aimed to understand not only how journalists selected relevant source documents, but also how they selected specific contents within these documents and transformed and presented them in their coverage. Following our analysis, we identified five key journalistic transformations – evaluative, political, cultural, emotive and professional – through which journalists profoundly shaped the contents and narratives in the news (for details, see Tenenboim-Weinblatt & Baden, 2016). Focusing on what they perceived as the most newsworthy contents of sources' statements, and fitting them within a coherent news narrative, journalists substantively reframed – or, in the view of sources, possibly distorted (Wolfsfeld, this volume) – the contents of available information (for a discussion of journalistic reframing practices, see Baden & Tenenboim-Weinblatt, 2018b). Importantly, these transformations mostly followed, but at times also interacted with the selection of specific sources and input for use in the news. Together, the selection of input and specific contents, as well as their transformation and presentation, constitute the main stages of the distinct journalistic contribution to shaping the news.

Journalistic Selection

Concerning the selection of newsworthy information, many scholars in conflict news research have lamented journalists' tendency to preferentially cover violent events, incendiary statements and other manifestations of conflict. Also our own investigation corroborates this concern: Media attention culminated around the main eruptions of violence – the abduction and murder of three Israeli teenagers by Hamas operatives, the abduction and revenge murder of one Palestinian teenager by Jewish extremists and the build-up to the military confrontation. Among the statements issued by various officials, those including threats or calls for forceful action received most coverage; and also within selected statements, journalists reliably represented their evocative, controversial elements. Conciliatory statements and efforts at conflict management were comparatively rare to begin, covered with less emphasis, and even within these, some media chose to focus on the more contested claims. There is little doubt that journalistic practice is geared toward covering conflict and threats, while peace – as Wolfsfeld (2004) aptly had it – is structurally incompatible with news journalism. However, while the critique of news values privileging conflict appears valid, it does not necessarily follow that such practice constitutes journalistic failure. Given journalism's public function, not informing the public about violent events, political threats and escalation is hardly an alternative. Journalists might have dedicated more space to covering efforts at de-escalation, but even so there was only limited newsworthy material to be covered. As information spread rapidly via social media and word of mouth, fanned by political actors' heated commentary, engaging that debate and putting it into perspective clearly falls within those tasks legitimately expected from journalists.

Journalistic Transformation

Regarding journalists' transformations applied to selected, newsworthy contents, our analysis distinguished five common practices, each of which addresses salient journalistic functions. Journalists apply (1) professional transformations, checking the validity of selected contents and putting these into perspective, aiming to construct coverage that complies with professional balance and objectivity norms and can therefore claim authority and trustworthiness, (2) evaluative transformations serve to clarify the public relevance and historical significance of covered events, while (3) political transformations pass normative judgment and provide political orientation, (4) cultural transformations anchor reported news within the audiences' life worlds and render it relevant to 'us' as a community and (5) emotive transformations engage readers and viewers by enabling them to empathize and thus relive important events (Tenenboim-Weinblatt & Baden, 2016). These intended transformations contrast against several recurrent criticisms launched against journalists' presentation of conflict-related news in the literature. Critically, conflict news is said to frequently contain uncorrected falsehoods, apply double standards, stoke up emotions and promote an ethnocentric, self-righteous perspective. While the first criticism, where validated, amounts to a failure of journalistic professional transformations, the other three points may be considered possible outcomes of an excess of cultural, political and emotive transformations, or problematic side effects of, at least in principle, legitimate practices.

Professional Transformation

In our study, we indeed found several instances of failed professional transformation, some of which resulted in the misrepresentation of known facts. However, these distortions were rather unevenly distributed and originated partly from journalists and partly from the cited sources. For instance, Israeli PM Netanyahu was cited falsely claiming a rise of terrorist violence in the West Bank, justifying his dismissal of the existing security coordination with the Palestinian Authority. However, this statement was immediately challenged by the reporting *New York Times*, citing statistical evidence as well as inside sources to the contrary. Especially, broadsheet sources routinely challenged sources' factual statements, criticizing authorities for stating as certain what could merely be suspected, or for refusing to back up claims with appropriate evidence. Only infrequently did we find distortions inserted by journalists themselves – most notably, in those media controlled by specific conflict parties. For instance, the Hamas-controlled paper *Felesteen* incorrectly described the murdered teenagers as soldiers gone missing. Major transgressions by independent journalists – such as the German tabloid *Bild*, which edited one victim's yarmulke out of his picture, hiding his religious Jewish identity – were rare, mostly hiding or suggesting details needed to sustain culturally resonant, politically opportune news narratives (discussed below). A much more common failure of professional transformations concerned journalists' suggestion of professional efforts at balancing and fact-checking reports without actually doing it (e.g. Israeli free daily right-wing tabloid *Israel Hayom*'s report on a scandal cited various government-affiliated sources but failed to establish a meaningful balance of views). In sum, thus, while resulting news coverage occasionally suggested more professionalism and verified accuracy than the report redeemed, most major falsifications originated from sources and were duly challenged by journalists. Even if journalists surely missed additional distortions, and there is much to improve in journalists' implementation of ethical norms, most professional transformations arguably added to the quality of the news.

Cultural, Emotive and Political Transformation

Concerning journalists' tendency to generate politically biased and ethnocentric narratives, our analysis shows a more ambivalent picture. Most journalists not only relied preferentially on sources identified with or culturally close to the in-group, but they also treated out-group source with considerable suspicion and distance. Within Israeli and Palestinian media, the respective out-group leaders were regularly questioned, if not attacked or diminished when cited (e.g. *Israel Hayom* commented on Palestinian President Abbas' complaint about Hamas' destructive policies by adding a highlight stating "finally, he gets it!"; 19.6.2014 at front page). Out-groups were mostly presented as monolithic, while the domestic political controversy was covered in some detail. Furthermore, journalists regularly mobilized cultural narratives and collective memories of the in-group to make sense of the news (e.g. analogies with prior abductions, their political and public trauma and their pop-cultural representation in the Israeli TV series *Hatufim*, visual frames alluding to Palestinian everyday experiences with Israeli occupation). Where the news amplified the emotional experience of in-group members, fostering empathy with the respective victims' families and generating public outrage, the same was rarely true for the perspective of out-groups. In the foreign coverage, the input of Israeli and Palestinian sources remained subordinated to the narratives and verdicts of domestic elites as experts and commentators or to the journalists themselves. Such coverage tended to contrast the analysis and sound morality of outside observers against a somewhat patronizing depiction of either the culturally less similar, or both parties in the conflict as irrational, vengeful and irresponsible. Consequently, political endorsements and criticisms also favoured in-group policies and norms. However, at least in the Israeli media, this did not result in journalists' sweeping, uncritical support of government policies; rather, different media assumed different stances, with both the oppositional *Haaretz* and the centrist *Yedioth Ahronot* at times fiercely challenging government policies. Embracing the perceived needs and sentiments of the in-group – for example, by citing the relations of the victims or simply anxious citizens affected by the escalation – led journalists to position themselves sometimes in support, but often also in opposition to executive agendas. And even if journalists' political transformations mostly focused on domestic politics (e.g. conflict policies in Israeli and Palestinian media, foreign policy involvements in the international news), outside and even enemy voices were regularly cited in the debate. Only among the Palestinian media, political endorsements were largely determined by Hamas' and the Palestinian Authority's ownership and control of *Felesteen* and *Al Hayat Al Jadidah*, leaving only the resource-poor East Jerusalem broadsheet *Al Quds* in a position to develop its own editorial line.

Through their markedly ethnocentric presentation of the news, journalists regularly validated each groups' feelings of victimization and righteous anger, obstructed an understanding of out-groups' perspectives and thus arguably contributed to the rise of hostility and escalation. At the same time, the privileged attention to in-group concerns is not entirely dysfunctional, neither in the given situation nor *per se*. As journalists interpret current news to explicate what it means for their respective audiences, events – especially in conflict – inevitably have different implications for different groups. Political controversies among domestic parties, who are elected and mandated by popular vote, are more pertinent than the political struggles among significant out-groups, where the most immediate concern is what policies will likely prevail. In their efforts to render news meaningful, journalists necessarily mobilize culturally shared symbols and narratives of the in-group, constructing shared experiences and emotions. In that sense, news featuring no ethnocentric perspective at all – stripped of cultural references and discussions of implications for the community and domestic politics – presents an unreasonable standard for journalistic performance. At the same time, the de-contextualization and belittling of out-group perspectives, the lack of empathy and consideration for their needs validates the complaint of countless scholars studying conflict news. In addtion to the active role of political sources and public sentiment for stoking up ethnocentric agendas, also journalistic transformations contribute to aggravating polarization in the conflict.

In sum, even if there is often little doubt about the incendiary nature of conflict news, condemning the performance of the journalists responsible for the news is not quite so easy. Through their selection and transformation routines, journalists indeed tend to generate ethnocentric news narratives, illuminating the grievances and reasons of in-groups at the expense of others' outside perspectives. The popular critique of journalists rallying blindly in support of government agendas, distorting facts and amplifying propaganda, may be grossly overstated – but clearly, journalists' political and professional transformation practices regularly contribute to escalation. At the same time, (especially broadsheet) journalists do present a corrective to elites' distortions and continue to challenge executive agendas, especially where they perceive these to be in conflict with the needs of the people. Through their insertion of outside voices, and their provision of analysis and commentary, journalists introduce additional perspectives to the debate that would not be otherwise heard. Even when cultural and emotive transformation mobilizes collective identities and emphasizes antagonism, these practices are often better understood as excesses arising from otherwise legitimate journalistic functions.

Situation-Dependent Journalistic Contributions

In the ample scholarship on conflict news, especially moments of escalation are firmly associated with the failure of journalistic standards. Unlike routine phases, mounting pressures during escalation from elites as well as audiences, severe information asymmetries and the rapid pace of events are said to fatally compromise journalistic practices. Indeed, there is substantial evidence to support a wide range of escalation-related interferences with ethical, professional journalism. Concerning professional transformations, restricted access to information and the sites of events, manipulated and contested data, as well as the plain absence of verifiable knowledge severely constrain journalists' ability to ascertain reported facts. Some sources' efforts at propaganda and media management contrast against the decreased availability and cooperation of other sources, and the executive style of crisis politics limits the ability of competing elites to provide relevant commentary. Lagging behind rapidly unfolding events, oppositional groups provide little input for journalists' political transformations, while executives' ability to provide constant action and drama captures the public's as well as the media's attention. Concerning cultural and emotive transformations, escalation primarily affects journalistic practices by incentivizing them to construct dramatic, ethnocentric news. On the one hand, conflict situations lend themselves unlike others to the production of mythical narratives. Existential threats, violent action and suffering provide ample material for emotional presentations and evoke cultural myths of heroism and righteousness. On the other hand, journalists perceive themselves as members of the national communities in conflict, threatened by hostile action and enmeshed in the collective struggle. Finally, the mobilization of public outrage also rewards journalists for composing ethnocentric news and imposes severe sanctions on coverage perceived as unpatriotic.

In short, both constraints and incentives shaping the coverage of conflict sustain the expectation that journalistic practices might be markedly compromised during escalation (see Zandberg & Neiger, 2005).

To examine this possibility, we conducted several diachronically comparative analyses of conflict news coverage, in both domestic and foreign media and across all six considered conflicts. Based on publicly available casualties' data, we identified 26 escalation phases – 10 from the Israeli–Palestinian conflict, 4 each from Syria and Macedonia, 3 from DRC and Burundi and 2 in Kosovo. For each of these moments, we searched for characteristic changes in the journalistic coverage, identifying both consistent changes found across different escalations and conflicts, and specific shifts related to the nature of particular crises.

Given the critical role of ethnocentric news narratives for mobilizing public enmity, a first study examined journalists' uses of culture-specific collective memories. Following the argument that journalists tend to 'rally round the flag' during conflict (Baum, 2002), we expected a systematic increase in references to in-groups' national (and cultural, ethnic and religious) identities, forging a strong collective sense of community. However, our findings suggest that there are no major shifts in the prevalence and use of in-group collective memories during escalation. Instead, what we find is that journalists' use of out-group memories undergoes radical change. During phases of relative calm, some constructive engagement with out-group memories can also be found – for instance, Israeli media occasionally discussed whether the Nakba, the Palestinian displacement connected to the foundation of Israel, should become part of school curricula, and Palestinian media featured a similar debate about the Holocaust. During escalation, however, out-group memories became repurposed to denounce the immorality of out-group actions: In Israeli media, the Nakba served to postulate a collective, hateful revisionism uniting Palestinians against the very existence of Israel, and Palestinian media decried a modern 'holocaust' committed by Israel in Gaza (see Figure 2.1). In almost all cases examined, such weaponization of collective memories was fuelled equally by political sources mobilizing support for hawkish policies and journalists' efforts to transform current reports into culturally resonant news narratives.

To widen the scope of our analysis, we traced a range of indicators that capture the amount of ethnocentrism, as well as other escalation-related practices, across these moments of escalation. Besides the amount of attention dedicated to the conflict as a whole, we traced the prominence of in-group and out-group voices cited in the news, and measured the specific sentiment attached to both in- and out-group references. In addition, we gauged the relative attention dedicated to the coverage of violence and victimization, conflict management and non-violence/peace, and determined the prevalence of doubt and uncertainty expressed in

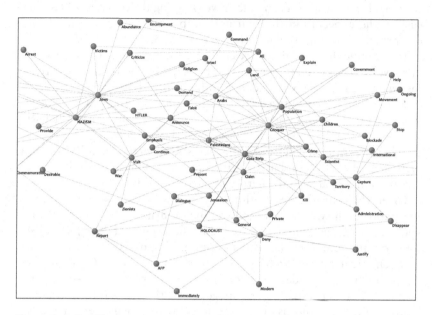

Figure 2.1 Significant associates of 'Holocaust', 'Nazism' and 'Hitler' in Palestinian news during escalation.

the news (for more details, see Baden & Tenenboim-Weinblatt, 2018a). While our analysis confirms that journalistic practices tend to change as conflict escalates, the specific nature of changes is highly context-specific. For instance, escalation following unilateral acts of violence – terrorism, murders, etc. – against the in-group tended to be accompanied by a sudden surge of journalistic attention to involved out-groups and a temporary improvement in the in-group's self-evaluation. Among media on the side of the perpetrators, by contrast, few notable changes were registered. By contrast, two-sided military escalation tended to generate more negative coverage about both in- and out-groups. Only in the conflict in Kosovo did we find the expected pattern of improved in-group evaluations and mirroring, deteriorated out-group evaluations (see Figure 2.2). While each pattern indicates a relevant, possibly problematic form of biased cultural and emotive transformation, escalation does not appear to prompt uniform journalistic responses, but invites different, context-sensitive adjustments in journalistic storytelling. Concerning the possible breakdown of professional transformations and critical distance, our analysis shows only a slight, not particularly consistent tendency toward reduced doubt during escalation. The mostly higher levels of scepticism expressed in foreign media suggest that critical reporting is easier from a distance than from within heated conflict; however, there is no indication of an alleged breakdown of professional distance at any time in our data.

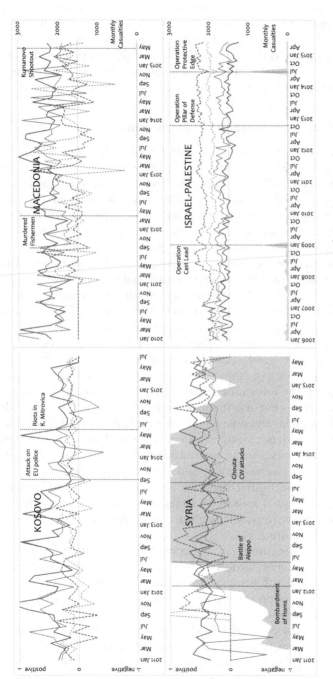

Figure 2.2 In-group- (bold) and out-group (thin) evaluations in opposing parties' domestic coverage.

Note: Dashed lines: evaluations by Albanian (top left and right), Syrian Rebel (bottom left) and Palestinian media (bottom right); full lines: evaluations by Serbian (top left), Macedonian (top right), Syrian regime (top right), Syrian regime (bottom left) and Israeli media (bottom right) (left axis); shaded areas: monthly casualties (right axis).

Note: Black lines: share of articles referring to violence; dark grey lines: victimhood; middle grey lines: negotiation; light grey lines: peace (left axis); shaded areas: monthly casualties (right axis).

Overall, our analysis thus confirms that escalation has the power to alter journalistic practices, but calls into question conventional wisdom about a sweeping failure of journalistic norms and practices. Both the contingency of journalistic adaptations and the mostly modest scale of observed changes suggest that journalists also remain very much in control of their work during escalation and continue making their independent contributions, for better or worse.

Persistent Patterns in Journalistic Transformation

At this point, it makes sense to examine a rival, radical position in the scholarship on conflict news, which holds that journalistic practices are generally rigged toward fostering conflict and violence. At a first glance, our data provides support for some of the underlying claims. For instance, our analysis shows a nearly constant, very high salience of violence, victimization and suffering in the coverage of all six conflicts, both during escalation and mostly calm phases (see Figure 2.3).

This holds true even for the coverage of the conflicts in Kosovo and Macedonia, which involve very little actual violence and suffering by comparison (<1 conflict-related death per month, compared to about 9 in Burundi, 30 in Israel and the Palestinian Territories, 125 in DRC and around 2,500 in Syria). In all six conflicts, there is far less attention to negotiated conflict management than to both violence and victimization, and only in the Israeli–Palestinian conflict news is there a consistent, notable discussion of non-violence and peace. Violence orientation is even higher in the foreign news, where many non-violent events are simply not reported – but also in the domestic news, between two-thirds (Burundi, Macedonia) and nine-tenths (Syria) of all conflict-related coverage contains a reference to some form of violence. Also, ethnocentrism is prevalent at all times, during and outside escalation, both in the preferential coverage of in-group voices and in their more positive presentation. At the same time, differences in evaluation are much smaller than one might expect, and at least in the Israeli media, domestic controversy actually engenders more negativity toward in-group sources than toward Palestinians (see Figure 2.2).

In order to further investigate the contribution of journalism to the creation of ethnocentric, distortive news, we conducted a large-scale comparative analysis of news on the Israeli–Palestinian conflict over time. In place of the prevalence of specific contents or patterns, this time we were interested in the extent to which different media in different countries provide similar or dissimilar news of the same events (Baden & Tenenboim-Weinblatt, 2017). Given the far-reaching, deeply entrenched polarization of positions in this exceptionally long-standing and controversial conflict, we expected any failure in journalistic ethics

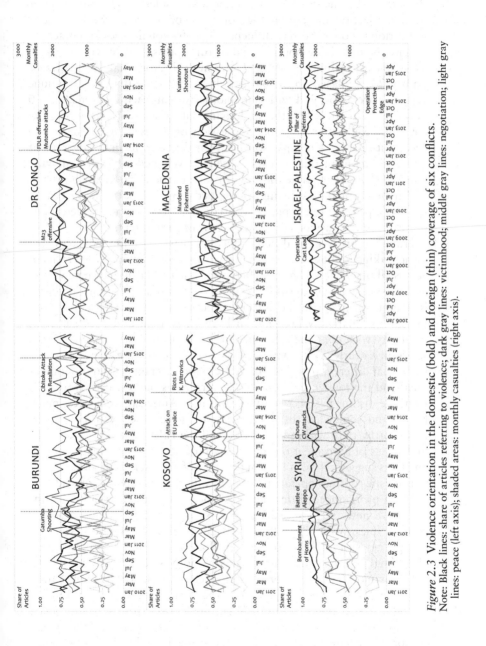

Figure 2.3 Violence orientation in the domestic (bold) and foreign (thin) coverage of six conflicts.
Note: Black lines: share of articles referring to violence; dark gray lines: victimhood; middle gray lines: negotiation; light gray lines: peace (left axis); shaded areas: monthly casualties (right axis).

to result in systematic and persistent differences between the news catering to Israeli and Palestinian, Western and Arab publics. Inversely,
the extent to which even media on opposing sides of the conflict agree
in their selection and presentation of newsworthy events can serve as an
indication for the persistent influence of professional ethics and practices
despite the polarizing political and cultural pressures. For this analysis,
we employ a technique called Evolutionary Factor Analysis (Motta &
Baden, 2013). Based on the patterns by which more than 3,700 unique
concepts are associated with one another within each of over 200,000
news texts, it identifies the underlying latent factors structuring the
coverage. Reflecting the rapid succession of different news items and
events, it enables a comparison between different media's coverage at
any given moment that focuses those relatively enduring, slow-moving
patterns that characterize the news of each particular outlet. The analysis furthermore allows distinguishing between each outlet's selection of
specific reported events, places, sources and facts, and the wider, interpretive frames constructed to make sense of the conflict.

From the analysis of different media's news selection practices, the
most striking finding concerns the very consistent, high level of agreement
across all surveyed media. Even between Israeli and Palestinian news outlets, news selection patterns correlated in excess of $r = 0.7$. This similarity
is roughly on par with the agreement between Israeli and Anglo-Saxon
media, and markedly higher than both Palestinian and Israeli media's
similarity with non-Anglo-Saxon European media. Consistency in news
selection is nearly perfect within the same language community, while two
somewhat different patterns emerge from the coverage within the conflict
area, and the foreign coverage of Western news outlets. Unsurprisingly,
from the distant perspective of European or American audiences, much
fewer, and somewhat different events in the conflict were considered
newsworthy than within both Israel and the Palestinian territories. The
high levels of agreement on the selection of newsworthy events, sources
and facts suggests that, at least in the stage of news selection, professional
journalistic routines operate powerfully and consistently on both sides.

More pronounced differences become visible in the analysis of interpretive news frames (see Figure 2.4). Agreement is reduced across
conflict lines (around $r = 0.5$)[5] as well as between the domestic and
foreign news, and the respective ideological alignments are recognizable (Anglo-Saxon media are markedly more similar to Israeli than to
Palestinian outlets; *Al Jazeera* is slightly closer to the Palestinian than to
the Israeli perspective). Importantly, the analysis shows major shifts in
the interpretive alignment of different media over time. However, even
though major wars and escalation moments contribute to the polarization of interpretive perspectives, agreement reaches its lowest point
(around $r = 0.4$) only after prolonged phases of mutual distrust and

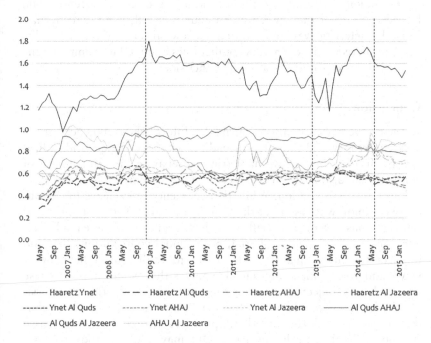

Figure 2.4 Frame similarity between Israeli and Palestinian media and *Al Jazeera*.

failed reconciliation. Considering the vastly different political, ideological, cultural and emotive positions and experiences in the conflict, persistent and medium-sized similarities in the framing of Palestinian and Israeli news still attest to the continuing presence of some harmonizing journalistic practices.

In sum, even if journalists interpret events differently (e.g. citing partial elites, following culturally tinted perceptions and catering to audiences hostile toward other views), they are still interpreting, to a large extent, the same events and available facts. Especially the similar news selections between media on opposing sides attest to the presence of fairly stable news values and professional routines, which can be bent only to a limited extent by conflict-related biases. This appears to be true even for the two comparatively less professionalized Palestinian outlets included in the analysis, as well as those outlets controlled by owners involved in the conflict (*Al Hayat Al Jadidah* belongs to the Palestinian Authority, *Israel Hayom* to a US billionaire strongly supportive of the Israeli Prime Minister). While possibly problematic in their focus on violent and threatening events, at the very least, journalists ensure that audiences everywhere are aware of roughly the same conflict reality. Moreover, this similarity even includes some similarities in interpretation. Besides justly lamenting the often ethnocentric and biased framing of the news, we can equally validly note that journalism's characteristic ways of narrating the news also result in certain edits that are shared by media across conflict lines and tend to counteract the one-sidedness of sources' frames on either side.

Conclusion

In their coverage of conflict, journalists inform their audiences about a violent reality and the often-incendiary views of leaders and radical groups. In this chapter, we have tried to separate the grim subject of conflict-related news from the specific ways in which journalists contribute to its presentation. While there is plenty of evidence to corroborate common worries about the fallible, biased, violence-oriented and self-righteous coverage of conflict, we have argued that these tendencies exist on top of a range of shared, professional contributions that add important, valuable qualities to the news. Journalists assemble relevant views and voices, including outside sources that would not otherwise be heard, and subject their claims to professional evaluation and possible challenge. Also, while there are many failures and excesses in conflict news, many of the underlying practices also serve a constructive function if applied in due measure. One may argue that journalism's important function of alerting societies to possible threats and dangers comes with detrimental side effects or becomes dysfunctional in certain situations or quantities. Likewise, it remains an open, normative question when legitimate involvement with the concerns and interests of a community turns into dangerous ethnocentrism. For a realistic appraisal of journalism's contribution to the coverage of conflict, it is necessary to confront these underlying normative questions and weigh the damage done by salient transgressions against the often less salient, but nevertheless important contributions to improving audiences' grasp of the conflict.

Especially in the present environment, where journalism is under pressure both economically and politically, it is important to consider its specific contribution in comparison to other channels available to convey conflict-related news. With the advent of digital communication technologies, and social media in particular, both strategic actors and audiences have considerably expanded their ability to circumvent journalistic mediation. Audiences can directly access uploaded footage and first-hand commentary on current conflict events, and follow the contributions of political leaders without the intervention and possible distortion by media professionals (see also Wolfsfeld & Tsifroni, this volume). Also challenges and critiques directed at sources' claims, and more generally the expression of public opinion no longer depend necessarily on their representation in the news. Political actors can enter into direct communication with their electorate, and the people can speak directly to those in power. However, especially in conflict, public anxiety typically incentivizes political leaders to advocate 'tough' positions; their tendency to distort or falsify claims and evidence in conflict is amply documented (Robinson, Goddard, Parry, Murray, & Taylor, 2010); and the dynamics of social media ensure that it is primarily the most outrageous, spectacular voices that are heard, while those advocating patience, measure and de-escalation are drowned out (Wolfsfeld, 2018). Also among online publics, radical and hostile attitudes motivate a much more active participation in social media debates than others' preference for calm and accommodation (Ben-David & Matamoros-Fernandez, 2016) and, while much knowledge is posted in online forums, they are outmatched by even more falsehoods and unwarranted claims – and there is no simple way to tell one from the other. Over the past decades, NGOs have increasingly stepped in as providers of trusted information and analysis, presenting both their reports and calls for action online, in their own publications, and by reaching out to journalists (see also Meyer & Sangar, this volume). However, only few select NGOs obtain sufficient visibility to assume a media-like role, and even their reach is limited. Despite their important role in conflict mediation and humanitarian work, not all NGOs advocate moderation and de-escalation; in addition, NGOs' perspectives remain interest-guided and fragmentary. Where digital media thus serve as powerful, highly heterogeneous platforms for the verbalization of all kinds of concerns, opinions and information, they tend to primarily amplify the propaganda activities of powerful elites as well as the hateful commentary of radicalized lay publics. While other voices exist plentifully on the web, their contributions are found only by those searching for them. In consequence, digital media critically lack the capacity for integrating and professionally evaluating the posted content and enabling a focused public debate (see also Dimitrakopoulou & Lenis, this volume).

By contrast, the integration and evaluation of information against a widely understood notion of what it means 'for us' is exactly one key sense in which journalism transforms the available input. Despite all of its failures and problems, journalism upholds a critical public debate that seeks to establish what is known and moderates competing claims and views, enabling the formation of shared preferences and a political agenda. Even if conflict journalism, for the most part, continues to produce predominantly bad news, this news is endowed with important qualities that are conducive to an informed debate – and as such, may be not quite so bad after all.

Appendix: Tables 1 and 2

Table 2.1 Sample of domestic conflict news coverage

Conflict	Origin	Outlet	Content	Language	Time range	N
Kosovo Jan. 2010–Jun. 2015	Kosovo	Gazeta Express	Online	Albanian	Feb. 2014–	1,345
		Koha Ditore	Online	Albanian	Feb. 2014–	4,160
		Telegrafi	Online	Albanian	Full	14,542[c]
		RTK1	Online	Albanian	Jul. 2014–	2,804
		RTK2	Online	Albanian	Jun. 2011–[a]	1,087
	Serbia	B92	Online	Serbian	Full[b]	289
		Politika	Online	Serbian	Full[b]	3,988
		Vecernje Novosti	Online	Serbian	Full[b]	6,379
Macedonia Jan. 2010–Jun. 2015	Macedonia	Utrinski Vesnik	Online	Macedonian	Full	3,812
		Dnevnik	Online	Macedonian	Full	4,817
		Vecher	Online	Macedonian	Full	2,623
		Koha	Online	Albanian	Feb. 2012–	1,819
Burundi Jan. 2010–Jun. 2015	Burundi	Arib	Online	French	Full	3,805
		Iwacu	Print	French	Full	2,296
		Le Renouveau	Online	French	May 2014–	227
		Net Press	Online	French	full	2,939
		Actualité Burundaise	Summaries	French	Oct. 2010–[d]	1,315
		Bonesha FM	Summaries	French	Oct. 2010–[d]	207
		Radio Insanganiro	Online/Sum.	French	Oct. 2010–[d]	1,083
		RNTB	Summaries	French	Oct. 2010–[d]	125
		RPA	Summaries	French	Oct. 2010–[d]	522
		Rema FM	Summaries	French	Oct. 2010–[d]	47
DR Congo Jan. 2011–Jun. 2015	DR Congo	Le Phare	Online	French	Full	2,704
		Le Potentiel	Print	French	Jan. 2012–	6,374
		Groupe L'Avenir	Online	French	Mar. 2015–	281
		Congo Tribune	Online	French	Full	718
		Digital Congo	Online	French	Full	11,402
		Media Congo	Online	French	Oct. 2013–	3,180
		Radio Kivu 1	Online	French	Oct. 2013–	658

Israel/Palestinian Territories Jan. 2006–Jun. 2015	Israel	Haaretz	Online	Hebrew	Full	19,269
		Israel Hayom	Online	Hebrew	Jul. 2007–	5,892
		Ynet	Online	Hebrew	Full	61,942
	Palestinian Territories	Arab48	Online	Arabic	Full	20,972
		Al Hayat Al Jadidah	Online	Arabic	Full	65,326
		Al Quds	Print	Arabic	Full	29,432
		Al Resalah	Online	Arabic	Aug. 2009–	14,098
		Felesteen	Print	Arabic	Jun. 2012–	13,345
		Ma'an	Newswire	Arabic	Aug. 2013–	12,219
		WAFA	Newswire	Arabic	Mar. 2011–	13,825
Syria Jan. 2011–Jun. 2015	Syria	Tishreen	Print	Arabic	Full	18,691
		DP News	Online	Arabic	Full	19,651
		Baladna	Print	Arabic	Oct. 2011–	2,881
		Enab Baladi	Print/Online	Arabic	Jan. 2012–	2,910
		Souriatna	Print/Online	Arabic	Sep. 2011–	2,638
		Hibr	Online	Arabic	Nov. 2014–	145
		Halab News	Online	Arabic	Sep. 2012–	3,889
		SANA	Newswire	Arabic	Apr. 2011–	8,711

a Data available only until March 2015.
b Data available only until May 2015.
c Including 3,342 texts reproduced from other sources.
d Data available only until December 2014.

Table 2.2 Sample of foreign conflict news coverage

Coverage of the conflict in:			Kosovo	Macedonia		Burundi		DR Congo		Israel/Palest.		Syria		
Sampled period:			Jan. 10–Jun. 2015	Jan. 10–Jun. 2015		Jan. 10–Jun. 2015		Jan. 11–Jun. 2015		Jan. 6–Jun. 2015		Jan. 11–Jun. 2015		
Outlet	Content	Language	Time range	N	Time range	N	Time range	N	Time range	N	Time range	N	Time range	N
...France: national media														
Le Monde	Print	French	Full	568	Full	135	Full	139	Jan. 12–	435	Full	4,510	Full	4,593
Le Figaro	Print	French	Full	531	Full	110	Full	132	Jan. 12–	262	Full	5,383	Full	5,849
L'Express	Online	French	Full	108	Full	31	Full	31	Full	130	Full	2,303	Full	1,230
...Germany: national media														
Süddeutsche Zeitung	Print	German	Full	1,346	Full	872	Full	157	Full	201	Full	5,856	Full	6,524
Die Welt	Print	German	Full	729	Full	1	Full	69	Jan. 12–	116	Full	4,296	Full	4,232
Der Spiegel	Print	German	Full	182	Full	54	Full	26	Jan. 12–	36	Full	810	Full	1,094
...UK: national media														
The Guardian	Print	English	Full	745	Full	466	Full	272	Jan. 12–	913	Full	6,279	Full	8,071
The Daily Telegraph	Print	English	Full	413	Full	401	Full	127	Jan. 12–	355	Full	2,534	Full	5,607
The Daily Mail	Print	English	Full	200	Full	160	Full	19	Full	183	Full	1,273	Full	1,898
...transnational media														
The New York Times	Print	English	Full	550	Full	224	Full	212	Jan. 12–	578	Full	7,818	Full	8,965
Financial Times	Print	English	Full	357	Full	105	Full	84	Jan. 12–	341	Full	3,373	Full	3,927
The Economist	Online	English	Aug. 12–	58	Aug. 12–	23	Aug. 12–	19	Aug. 12–	61	Aug. 12–	306	Aug. 12–	675

															Total
RFI	Online	French	Full	508	Full	316	Full	1,573	Full	4,374	Oct. 09–	4,135	Full	5,102
Deutsche Welle	Online	German	Full	397	Full	222	Full	104	Full	441	Full	5,663	Full	4,251
BBC World Service	Online	English	Aug. 12–	331	Aug. 12–	192	Aug. 12–	295	Full	978	May 10–	2,081	Full	7,756
Euronews TV	Transcripts	English	Full	127	Full	26	Full	14	Jan. 12–	104	Full	1,286	Full	2,221
CNN International	Transcripts	English	Full	95	Full	32	Full	33	Jan. 12–	89	Full	666	Full	2,673
Al Jazeera	Online	Arabic	Full	180	Full	1	Full	100	Full	56	Full	8,514	Full	16,779
…Global news agencies														
AFP	Newswire	French	Full	3,744	Full	1,540	Full	2,123	Jan. 12–	5,477	Full	38,128	Full	43,620
AP	Newswire	English	Full	846	Full	479	Full	480	Jan. 12–	364	Full	14,095	Full	13,072
Xinhua	Newswire	English	Full	895	Full	786	Full	1,748	Jan. 12–	1,818	Full	41,004	Full	23,255

Notes

1 For encompassing reviews of the expansive literature, see Carruthers (2000) and Cottle (2006). Arguments about the failure of journalism in conflict situations have been advanced, among others, by Bennett, Lawrence and Livingston (2008), Galtung (2006), Robinson, Goddard, Parry, Murray and Taylor (2010), and Wolfsfeld, Frosh and Awadby (2008).
2 For details on the rationale behind this selection of cases, as well as the covered time ranges, please refer to Romy Fröhlich's introduction to this volume.
3 The methodological strategy and choices are discussed in detail in INFO-CORE Working Paper 2015/10 (Baden & Stalpouskaya, 2015).
4 For the Balkan conflicts, we used data gathered by the Uppsala Conflict Data Program (UCDP); for the African conflicts, we used the Armed Conflict Location & Event Data Project (ACLED); for the Israeli–Palestinian conflict, we obtained data from the UN Office for the Coordination of Humanitarian Affairs (OCHA); and for Syria, we used the Syrian Revolution Martyr Database, which we validated against multiple other data sources to ascertain that, while the exact figures differ between sources, the overall shape and temporal distribution of data agree.
5 Values are slightly inflated because of possible correlations among those factors expressing different frames in the coverage of the same outlet, so the decrease in similarity compared to the news selection is more pronounced than the coefficients suggest.

References

Althaus, S. L., Edy, J. A., Entman, R. M., & Phalen, P. (1996). Revising the indexing hypothesis: Officials, media, and the Libya Crisis. *Political Communication, 13*, 407–421.

Baden, C., & Stalpouskaya, K. (2015). *Common methodological framework: Content analysis. A mixed-methods strategy for comparatively, diachronically analyzing conflict discourse.* INFOCORE Working Paper 2015/10. Online available at www.infocore.eu/results/working-papers/

Baden, C., & Tenenboim-Weinblatt, K. (2017). Convergent news? A longitudinal study of similarity and dissimilarity in the domestic and global coverage of the Israeli-Palestinian conflict. *Journal of Communication, 67*, 1–25.

Baden, C., & Tenenboim-Weinblatt, K. (2018a). The search for common ground in conflict news research: Comparing the coverage of six current conflicts in domestic and international media over time. *Media, War & Conflict, 11*, 22–45.

Baden, C., & Tenenboim-Weinblatt, K. (2018b). Viewpoint, testimony, action: How journalists reposition source frames within news frames. *Journalism Studies, 19*, 143–161.

Baum, M. (2002). The constituent foundations of the rally-round-the-flag phenomenon. *International Studies Quarterly, 46*, 263–298.

Ben-David, A., & Matamoros-Fernandez, A. (2016). Hate speech and covert discrimination on social media: Monitoring the Facebook pages of extreme-right political parties in Spain. *International Journal of Communication, 10*, 1167–1193.

Bennett, W. L., Lawrence, R. G., & Livingston, S. (2006). None dare call it torture: Indexing and the limits of press independence in the Abu Ghraib scandal. *Journal of Communication, 56*, 467–485.

Bennett, W. L., Lawrence, R. G., & Livingston, S. (2008). *When the press fails: Political power and the news media from Iraq to Katrina.* Chicago, IL: University of Chicago Press.

Boesman, J., d'Haenens, L., & van Gorp, B. (2016). Between silence and salience: A multimethod model to study frame building from a journalistic perspective. *Communication Methods & Measures, 10*, 233–247.

Carruthers, S. L. (2000). *The media at war. Communication and conflict in the twentieth century.* Basingstoke, UK: Macmillan.

Clausen, L. (2004). Localizing the global: 'Domestication' processes in international news production. *Media, Culture & Society, 26*, 25–44.

Cottle, S. (2006). *Mediatized conflict: Developments in media and conflict studies.* New York, NY: Open University Press.

Galtung, J. (2006). Peace journalism as an ethical challenge. *Global Media Journal: Mediterranean Edition, 1*(2), 1–5.

Motta, G., & Baden, C. (2013). Evolutionary factor analysis of the dynamics of frames: Introducing a method for analyzing high-dimensional semantic data with time-changing structure. *Communication Methods and Measures, 7*, 48–84.

Robinson, P., Goddard, P., Parry, K., Murray, C., & Taylor, P. M. (2010). *Pockets of resistance: British news media, war and theory in the 2003 invasion of Iraq.* Manchester, UK: Manchester University Press.

Tenenboim-Weinblatt, K., & Baden, C. (2016). Journalistic transformation: How source texts are turned into news stories. *Journalism, 19*, 481–499.

Wolfsfeld, G. (2004). *Media and the path to peace.* Cambridge, UK: Cambridge University Press.

Wolfsfeld, G. (2018). The role of media in violent conflicts in the digital age: Israeli and Palestinian leaders' perceptions. *Media, War & Conflict, 11*, 107–124.

Wolfsfeld, G., Frosh, P., & Awadby, M. T. (2008). Covering death in conflicts: Coverage of the second intifada on Israeli and Palestinian television. *Journal of Peace Research, 45*, 401–417.

Zandberg, E., & Neiger, M. (2005). Between the nation and the profession: Journalists as members of contradicting communities. *Media Culture & Society, 27*, 131–141.

3 The Dynamics of Strategic Communication Over Time

Patterns of Persuasive Communication and Its Relevance for the Construction of Discourse on War and Conflict

Romy Fröhlich and Marc Jungblut

Introduction

Research on political communication indicates that there is a relationship between the persuasive content distributed by strategic communicators and the way media coverage characterizes events and discusses issues. More specifically, there is profound evidence that at times strategic persuasive communication has the power to determine the news content (Bennett, 1990; Entman, 2003). Whether as an information source or a communicative tool, *strategic persuasive communications*[1] are of profound importance to the political sphere in general and to scenarios of war and armed conflict in particular (cf. Briant, 2015; Hayden, 2016; Ringsmose & Borgeson, 2011; Robinson, 2015; Snow & Taylor, 2006; Taylor, 2002). Even more, the accusation stands that during war and armed conflicts, war reporting is particularly prone to persuasive messages from strategic actors in the field of PR, information warfare and propaganda. It is no wonder, then, that interest in the analysis of strategic communication during war and armed conflict has been gradually growing. Still, there is a lack of comparative *quantitative empirical* research on strategic persuasive conflict communication. The majority of academic works in this area are based on case-specific *theoretical* and/or *qualitative* analysis (e.g. Miller, Robinson, & Bakir, 2016; Nohrstedt & Ottosen, 2008). Furthermore, only very few of these works examine strategic, persuasive conflict communication on its own. What is particularly lacking are empirical, large-scale studies looking across time and conflict cases that use content analysis with quantitative methods on large numbers of strategic and persuasive messages on war and conflict. That is why the question about the type and content of persuasive communication materials in the media's (strategic and persuasive) sources on war and armed conflict has remained largely unanswered until the present.

This is surprising, as the question has grown substantially in relevance over the course of the last decade. After all, new (digital) media especially social media in Web 2.0 – have fundamentally changed the conditions for the production and distribution of strategic persuasive messages. These circumstances[2] do not make simple forms of communicative persuasion any easier. Still, this trend seems to be in decline as the recent phenomena of post-truth might indicate. It is therefore no surprise that, especially in this day and age, strategic communicators and actors are applying ever more sophisticated forms of communication for their persuasive messages. This also applies to strategic persuasive communication in the context of wars and armed conflicts. It is now considered a truism that, in addition to so-called hard-power skills (e.g. military power), an increasing role is played by political actors' soft-power skills, that is, their ability to steer such conflicts with *communicative* methods (to fuel them, pacify them, solve them diplomatically or militarily, etc.).

With this background, 'strategic narratives' have been growing in importance for the strategic persuasive communication of international politics – especially in times of war and conflict. Be it public diplomacy (PD), information warfare, targeted communication campaigns, political speeches or messages disseminated on occasion at press conferences, it is said that strategic narratives in particular have strong effects on intended target groups (e.g. De Graaf, Dimitriu, & Ringsmose, 2015; O'Loughlin, Miskimmon, & Roselle, 2017). By analysing strategic narratives, a better understanding of the development, course, escalation or de-escalation of a war or armed conflict can be generated. Miskimmon, O'Loughlin and Roselle (2013) even go so far as to say: "(...) [S]trategic narrative analysis offers a way to understand the full context of war and conflict" (p. 182).

As a result, our contribution puts *strategic narratives* into the focus of empirical investigation into strategic persuasive conflict communication. We want to examine the question of which strategic communicators/ actors work communicatively at which times in a specific conflict with which type of persuasive tactics and with which strategic narratives. We are thus following a call from Miskimmon et al. (2013), who define "a need for empirical studies on how actors operationalize strategic narrative in international relations" (p. 184). In doing so, the study at hand aims to contribute to a better understanding of the role and contribution of strategic persuasive communication to peace-building and conflict resolution – or to the contrary. Before we make our interest more specific and then describe how we preceded methodologically, we will first very briefly discuss the theoretical underpinnings in the following. This includes our particular understanding of strategic narratives as semantic constructs in public discourse, of narratives as particular patterns of persuasive strategic communications on war and of strategic communicators in scenarios of armed conflict.

Strategic Narratives as Persuasive Means of Political Communication

To accentuate the *political* role of strategic persuasive communication especially in times of conflict, we define it with Daymon and Demetrious (2013) as "a communicative activity (…) to intervene socially in and between competing discourses in order to facilitate a favourable position within a globalized context" (p. 3). Against this backdrop and based on the definition from Miskimmon et al. (2013, pp. 105, 176), we regard strategic narratives as communicative means for political actors to construct a specific meaning of the past, present and future of a particular issue, topic, policy, etc., in order to shape the opinions and behaviour of relevant domestic and international actors. Strategic narratives are crafted and projected by political actors in order to give meaning to their decisions, their 'agendas for action' (Stalpouskaya & Baden, 2015; see also Baden and Meyer in this volume), their understanding and interpretation of an issue, etc., in a way that gives them a strategic benefit. Strategic narratives are not fictitious, unrealistic perspectives on an event. As Freedman (2006) correctly recognized, narratives do not arise spontaneously or coincidentally but are the result of deliberation: "Narratives are designed or nurtured with the intention of structuring the responses of others to developing events" (p. 22). They can only have strategic effects because their meaning is anchored in the real world or, as Freedman (2006) stated: "An effective narrative will work not only because it appeals to the values, interests and prejudices of the intended audience but also because it is not going to be exposed by later information and events" (p. 23). It is precisely this intention that gives narratives their strategic character. Fröhlich and Jungblut (2018) were able to demonstrate empirically what Miskimmon et al. (2013, pp. 112–114) suspected: that is, the particularly convincing and effective narratives are those that have a minimum of epistemological status. At this point, the question of the difference between 'narrative' and 'frame' arises.

Strategic Narratives and Frames as Semantic Constructs in Public Discourse

Strategic narratives can be part of different types of strategic communication activities (see Miller et al., 2016), including PD[3] and information warfare.[4] Strategic narratives are therefore elements of public and/or non-public discourses. In the context of this contribution, we are only interested in the *public* discourse, as non-public discourses largely elude access in the field and it is therefore difficult or even impossible to include them in research. Miskimmon et al. (2013, pp. 16–17) describe discourses as communicative acts that "are never quite fixed" and thus create "space for politics and contestation". Consequently, Fröhlich and Jungblut (2018) characterize discourse as "competitive communication environments where strategic communicators compete for sovereignty over (problem/issue) definitions and resolution" (p. 87). Within this competition, narratives and frames play a crucial role.

In agreement with Miskimmon et al. (2013, p. 181), we view the two constructs as separate and assume that a narrative in general has a more comprehensive structure than a frame. In contrast to Miskimmon et al., however, we see the relationship between frames and narratives as hierarchical. According to our understanding, a frame[5] is a component of a narrative and not another semantic construct posing an alternative to the narrative.[6] As we see it, a narrative can therefore be made up of specifically framed events, actors, contexts, etc. Again in contrast to Miskimmon et al., we assume that frames (and not only the superordinate narratives) can enclose temporal, spatial and diagnostic dimensions – at least *implicitly*: Frames, for instance, refer to selected antecedents (past) and causes (diagnosis) of a respective event and/or they include "suggested treatments" (future) "as coherent, logical consequences" (diagnosis) "from a presented situation" (Baden, 2015, pp. 1–2).

According to our understanding, a frame represents a particular interpretation of an event, actor, context, etc., whereas a narrative consists of a series of frames (framed actors, events, etc.) that each relate to each other and form a consistent idea of an internally coherent and causally linked past, present and future (the story). With Miskimmon et al. (2013, pp. 4–12), we assume that a narrative makes a causal statement about how this event, actor, context, etc., is linked to particular outcomes. For this purpose, a narrative *explicitly* puts particular interpretations (frames) of an event, actor, context, etc., in a specific temporal order to demonstrate the past, present and future principles of the promoted outcome. Furthermore, narratives construct causality by offering particular descriptions of how an event, actor, context, etc., has been transformed from one status to another.

To our understanding, a frame is a more or less static, single attribution of (a) particular characteristic(s) to an event, actor, context, etc., whereas a narrative is a multifaceted construction of a story(line), which uses frames for this construction. As components of narratives, frames are connected to each other in a particular manner; the respective narrative provides the semantic framework, which gives a particular meaning to the connection between the frames. As we will later show in the methods section, this (hierarchical) relationship between frame and narrative plays a role in the operationalization of our specific research questions (see "Methodology" further below).

Narratives as Particular Patterns of Persuasive Strategic Communications on War and Armed Conflict

We assume that within competitive communication environments, strategic narratives have great importance for the establishment of specific perspectives on certain wars and armed conflicts. For example, theoretical-qualitative research describes strategic persuasive conflict communication as being primarily escalative (cf. Angstrom & Honig, 2012; Bennett, Lawrence, & Livingston, 2006; Brown, 2005). With the aim of establishing a specific perspective, strategic narratives can, for instance, include a certain self-presentation (e.g. (self-)defence) by the sender/author or create (strategically useful) images of other actors (for example, of opposing combatants, organizations such as NGOs, governments, individual politicians or intergovernmental organizations such as the UN). Besides people or institutions, strategic narratives can also cast events in a certain light; they can interpret the actions and behaviour of organizations and institutions in a specific way depending on their intentions, or they can attribute a specific meaning to commonly shared values (e.g. responsibility to protect, or R2P).

Narratives do not only have the function of working persuasively, that is, convincing others of something or affecting something. Narratives can also be used to structure the spectrum of an actor's perspectives and actions (Miskimmon et al., 2013, p. 13). In our view, this function of narratives contributes to reducing complexity, which is not to say, however, that a reduction in complexity cannot also be used to pursue persuasive intentions. It is not decisive for our study whether the affected strategic communicators/actors are actually pursuing a persuasive goal or not, though. The focus of our interest is solely on the question of which communicators/actors in which conflicts use what type of (strategic) narratives at which times and on which occasions.

For the most part, it has been authors and works from the field of international relations that have thus far looked closely at strategic narratives in the specific case of communication during war (e.g. Freedman, 2006; Miller et al., 2016; Miskimmon et al. 2013). Here, a series of strategic narratives are described that are deemed typical for strategic persuasive communication. According to these works, strategic narratives in favour of war – we call them escalative narratives – can, for instance, consist of 'reasonable' and 'rational' argumentation (Ringsmose & Borgesen, 2011) such as the *horror of enemy atrocities* or *intelligence-based allegations*. Typical tactics here are 'testimony' (for instance, the Hill & Knowlton PR-campaign in the case of the US intervention in Kuwait; MacArthur, 2004, pp. 37–77) and 'valiant rescue' (for instance, the case of US soldier Jessica Lynch in Iraq; Martyn, 2008). Escalative narratives can also consist of 'emotional' argumentation such as *appeals to patriotism* and/or *appeals to the responsibility to protect* (UN doctrine R2P).

Strategic narratives against war – we call them de-escalative narratives – can consist of *non-coercive and non-military semantic concepts* typical for the PD approach (for instance, thinking positively about another country/government/actor). How we understand and operationalize semantic concepts will be explained in the "Methodology" section.

Strategic Communicators

Political communication on war and armed conflict is not only engaged in by governments and political decision makers (presidents, ministers, etc.) in the narrow sense. Especially in the case of wars and armed conflicts, other strategic actors outside of the specific, closely defined policy areas also play a large role. Besides the military, this includes in particular NGOs. For NGOs, one can generally assume a persuasive intention in their communication for two reasons: First, they conduct persuasive communication with an eye to their donors, to whom they are accountable and who secure their existence with financial resources; second, they engage in persuasive communication in regard to their respective mission, realizing this mission is the purpose of their organization. They must therefore provide continual communication with proof that they are fulfilling that mission. Their persuasive communicative power is comparatively high because, in contrast to political players and the military, they typically enjoy a high degree of credibility both in the policy area as well as with domestic and international audiences and citizens (see, for instance, Sangar and Meyer in this volume).

With this background, NGOs today behave like professional information brokers: They have their own, sometimes even exclusive, sources and intelligence tools, they have a great deal of experience in dealing with people and informants on-site and they produce highly effective communication, sometimes simulating journalism – for example, in their own publications (cf. Fröhlich & Jungblut, 2018). NGOs must therefore be viewed as significant actors in conflict-related discourses. Smith and Ferguson (2001) refer to them as issue managers. Together with political decision makers in a narrower sense, they play a key role in the formation of public communication about war and armed conflicts (Van Leuven, Heinrich, & Deprez, 2015). That is why our study focuses on the analysis of narratives in strategic communications about war and armed conflict by (1) political decision makers and (2) NGOs.[7]

Focus of Research, Objective and Research Questions

For our content analysis, we concentrate on the strategic communications of political decision makers and NGOs in the context of six specific armed conflicts in three different world regions as included in the INFOCORE project (see introduction to this volume). Our research interest is derived from two questions that Miskimmon et al. (2013) believe are key for researching strategic narratives in political communication: "(...) [H]ow actors use their agency, within specific situations and historical relationships, (...) in order to steer other actors toward certain behaviour (behavioural power)" (p. 16) and under which conditions and in which moments "strategic narratives play different roles, or are used differently (...)" (p. 183). Additionally, we believe that conflict phases of often longer endurance as well as short-lived relative escalation and de-escalation hold an impact on the application and relevance of specific conflict narratives (cf. Frère & Wilen, 2015). Following a call by Miskimmon et al. (2013, p. 5), we also look at the conflict context and conflict developments across time for each of the conflicts analysed.

Since our focus is on the variation in strategic narratives in relation to contextual factors and variances in the conflict, the question of the actual effects of strategic narratives on wars and armed conflicts must be excluded from our analysis. Our aim is to analyse the narrative density – the relative importance of one narrative as compared to others – of strategic-persuasive conflict communication in favour of or against war and international (military and non-military) intervention over time and across different conflicts. In doing so, we concentrate on strategic narratives in the strategic-persuasive communication of important political decision-makers in Europe (namely the EU and selected European national governments) and of important/relevant NGOs that focus on conflict (prevention, resolution, professional war reporting, etc.). The analysis of certain narratives may reveal particular strategies of communication that can then be interpreted within the given social, (geo) political, historic, etc., context of a conflict.

Our analysis of occurrence and co-occurrence of narratives in strategic communication aims to reveal, for example, the shares of escalative and de-escalative narratives (in favour of or against war including types of frames oriented on classic de-escalation like, for instance, peace talks, and diplomacy) as well as non-coercive and non-military concepts. Our aim is to identify possible patterns of reoccurring strategic narratives in the persuasive communication of the two kinds of actors during different conflicts. These patterns of strategic narratives can be understood as relevant re-appearing strategic conflict narratives typical for conflicts and their respective mixture of strategic actors outside the conflict region.

In our study, we differentiate between *strategic narratives* with which conflicts are described, interpreted and characterized, on the one hand, and *conflict measures*, on the other hand. We understand conflict measures as suggestions or demands from the communicators we analyse on the question of how to react to the conflict, how it can be resolved, etc. Conflict measures constitute what Stalpouskaya and Baden (2015) and Baden and Meyer in this volume describe as "agendas for action" – for example, demands for military intervention, diplomatic activities or providing security for a population. However, we see measures as specific, not necessarily programmatic ('agenda') proposed interventions. It should be noted that various strategic communicators (can) certainly use the same narrative, on the basis of which they might then, however, demand differing or even completely contradictory (escalative and/or de-escalative) measures as agendas for action.

On the basis of these explications and with the theoretical background described above, we can formulate the following overarching question to investigate our research interest as described above: What does the narrative density of strategic persuasive conflict communication in favour of or against war and international (military and non-military) intervention look like, how does it develop under which conditions and in which moments over a certain period of time and across various wars and armed conflicts? From this overarching question, we derive the following four research questions:

RQ1: How do different strategic communicators use strategic narratives in their persuasive communication material in general and across time and conflicts?

RQ2: Which agendas for action do different strategic communicators refer to in their persuasive communication material in general and across time and conflicts?

RQ3: How did narratives and agendas for action co-occur in general and across different conflicts?

RQ4: How did narratives and agendas for action co-occur with conflict casualties (escalation/de-escalation)?

Following Miskimmon et al. (2013), our goal is to be able to make initial statements as to under which conditions and in which moments "strategic narratives play different roles, or are used differently (...)" (p. 183).

Methodology

To answer the research questions, we investigate the occurrences of strategic narratives in communication materials from various strategic actors using concept counts. We will later describe the selection of these concepts and how they were found. The occurrences of identified narratives will be mapped across time and over the six conflicts (see introduction to this volume). In doing so, we point towards the relevance of conflict contexts when explaining the differences in the relative relevance of narratives in each conflict discourse. Also, we examine the relative importance of narratives across time, highlighting how applied narratives changed before, during and after relevant conflict events (RQ1). In a second step, we analyse the relevance of different conflict measures. Following a similar logic as for narratives, we differentiate between escalative, de-escalative and non-violent agendas for action. Each of these three categories is again operationalized on the basis of a list of concepts that is provided below. The relevance of different measures is then again compared across conflicts on an aggregated basis and across time to indicate the relevance of conflict contexts (RQ2).

To examine which type of narratives are used to advocate or push for which kind of measure/action, we will analyse significant co-occurrences between different types of strategic *narratives* and conflict *measures* (see above). This will enable us to obtain a more detailed perspective of *how* strategic narratives were applied by strategic communicators/actors in different conflicts when suggesting agendas of action to solve the conflict or to deal with it. To exemplify this, looking at the significant co-correlations between, for example, the strategic narrative 'R2P' and particular conflict measures will enable us to identify things like what the principles around particular conflict measures are or who establishes those principles under what conditions (conflict context, conflict phase, etc.) (RQ3).

Finally, we compare the results from RQ1 and RQ2 to the number of conflict casualties per month in each conflict. In doing so, we seek to unravel the relationship between dominant narratives, their underlying agendas for action and the degree of relative escalation. We see the numbers of conflict casualties as indicators of phases of escalation (or de-escalation) of conflict events. By cross-referencing vertexes in the occurrence of strategic narratives *over time* with relevant conflict *events* and the *estimated number of conflict casualties,* we identify relevant conflict *phases*. In doing so, we will be able to determine whether specific (kinds of) strategic narratives are used more (or less) often before, during or after specific (kinds of) conflict events (RQ4).

How do we understand *semantic concepts?* Semantic concepts are the basis for operationalizing different strategic narratives in persuasive communication from the selected strategic actors. Semantic concepts can be a variety of different things: people, organizations, places, semantics, events, etc. In a first analytical step, we measure the *occurrence of particular strategic narratives* in the persuasive communication material of selected actors. The narrative 'R2P', for example, can then be identified by counting the share of texts that refer to semantic concepts such as 'rape', 'ethnic violence', 'ethnic cleansing', etc.

Our study analyses the application of strategic narratives and agendas for action (including conflict measures) in six conflicts in three different world regions between 2012 and 2014: Burundi and the Democratic Republic of Congo (DRC) in the African Great Lakes area, Kosovo and Macedonia in the Western Balkans as well as Syria and the Israeli–Palestinian conflict in the Middle East. This case selection and the specific sample period investigated offer a variety of conflict phases and conflict intensity (Frère & Wilen, 2015) that allows us to compare all six conflicts with each other. Since it is our aim to analyse the narrative density of strategic persuasive conflict communication in favour of or against international (military and non-military) intervention, we selected those four political decision makers in Europe that have a leading role in European political discourse on war and armed conflict: the German, British and French governments[8] and the European Union.[9] For instance, the EU has been engaged in crisis management operations in Africa and the Balkans since the Treaty of Nice. The selection of NGOs was done using two criteria: (1) for the purpose of the data analysis, they were to be large, transnational organizations that distribute a relatively *continual* and *sufficiently large number* of persuasive strategic communications on these conflicts, and (2) for the purpose of comparability, they were to be organizations that are relevant for all six conflicts. The three NGOs *Reporters sans Frontières, Search for Common Ground* and *Human Rights Watch* all fulfilled these criteria.

The applied sample of texts consists of the publicly available strategic communication activities – press releases, interviews, speeches and other forms of publications – by the selected communicators/actors. For all conflicts, we sampled all communicated texts on the conflicts that were published between 2012 and 2014.[10] Overall, we therefore used a sample of 5,738 texts (see Table 3.1).

To answer our research questions (RQ1–RQ4), we conducted an automated content analysis based on JAmCAT and Python-scripts (Baden & Stalpouskaya, 2015). We used the INFOCORE dictionary to operationalize the different strategic narratives and conflict measures. This dictionary identifies around 3,800 semantic concepts in eight different languages; for the analysis at hand, we dealt with English and French texts and thus used the English and French version of the dictionary. We combined inductive and deductive approaches: (1) First, we annotated a text corpus to identify different narratives in the texts and then (2) completed the selection of narratives based on theoretical considerations.

Table 3.1 Sample

Conflict	Communicator					
	EU	German Gov.	British Gov.	French Gov.	NGOs	Total
Macedonia	113	39	16	7	25	200
Kosovo	288	237	132	32	39	728
DRC	154	55	492	71	336	1108
Burundi	4	4	6	14	98	126
Israel/ Palestine	354	439	339	73	63	1268
Syria	549	626	683	100	350	2308

The same strategy was applied to identify conflict measures. Afterwards, we collected all concepts from the dictionary that hint at a reliance on the different narratives and measures.[11] A narrative or a measure is regarded as being present if any of the respectively ascribed semantic concepts appears in a given text. This decision is based on the assumption that narratives and agendas for action are (mostly) well-known and established re-occurring patterns and/or consist of the respective (mostly well-known and established) frames.

Based on previous theoretical research on strategic narratives of persuasive conflict communication, we differentiate between two opposing groups of strategic narratives: (1) escalative vs. (2) de-escalative narratives. Within the groups, we investigate six typical, specific strategic narratives of persuasive communication in war and conflict that have repeatedly been deemed to be almost classic by previous literature. In the group of escalative narratives, they are 'Ethnocentrism/Patriotism/Religious Superiority', 'R2P' and '(Self-)Defence'. In the group of de-escalative narratives, they are 'Moral Values', 'Economic Necessity for Peace' and 'Last Resort/ No Other Way than Peace'. All six of these narratives could in turn be made up of various sub-narratives. The following figure visualizes the structure of our analysis of strategic narratives for publicly disseminated persuasive conflict communication (Figure 3.1).

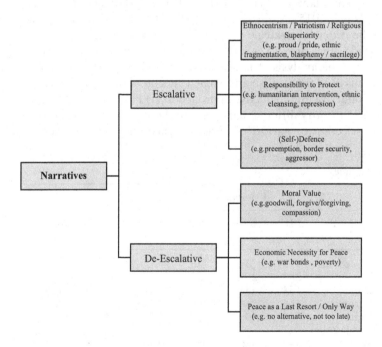

Figure 3.1 Analysis structure for strategic narratives.

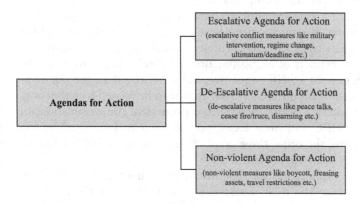

Figure 3.2 Analysis structure for agendas for action.

We proceeded in a similar manner with the agendas for action. Here, we differentiated among three main groups of agendas for action: (1) escalative, (2) de-escalative and (3) non-violent escalative. The following figure shows the make-up of these three types of agendas for action used in our analysis (Figure 3.2).

The number of conflict casualties was taken from different sources: The Uppsala Conflict Data Program (Croicu & Sundberg, 2015) was used for the Israeli–Palestinian conflict; data from the Violation's Documentation Center[12] in Syria was used for the Syrian conflict; whereas casualty data for Burundi and the DRC were taken from the Armed Conflict Location & Event Data Project (Raleigh, Linke, Hegre, & Karlsen, 2010). It is noteworthy that the measurement of conflict casualties is a much debated procedure with no exact measurement being possible. Still, since the variance in casualties is solely regarded within each conflict, any consistent measure provides meaningful insights (Baden & Tenenboim-Weinblatt, 2018). Finally, we enriched the resulting data with conflict context derived from detailed analyses by INFOCORE conflict experts,[13] its associated stakeholder network[14] and its advisory board[15] as well as from the BBC conflict timelines.[16] In doing so, we were able to make sense of the developments over time and differences in the relevance of narratives between conflicts.

Results

Analysis of Narratives

Overall, escalative narratives appear more often than de-escalative narratives in the persuasive texts of all strategic communicators – both the selected political actors and the selected NGOs. This holds true across all conflicts and across time. Our quantitative findings thereby give initial confirmation of a long-standing accusation from theoretical-qualitative research directed at strategic persuasive conflict communication, which the research describes as being primarily escalative (e.g. Angstrom & Honig, 2012; Bennett et al., 2006; Brown, 2005). When focusing on the most dominant specific narrative, however, the data for our conflicts show significant differences that appear to be related to differences in conflict contexts. While the strategic persuasive communication on Burundi, the DRC and (to a lesser extent) Syria is dominated by the 'R2P' narrative, the other three conflict cases show a much more balanced narrative structure (Table 3.2).

A potential explanation for this difference is that the three conflicts that heavily rely on the 'R2P' narrative also show the highest level of constant ongoing violence between 2012 and 2014. Kosovo and Macedonia are both in a situation of a somewhat unstable peace or a post-conflict situation. The conflict in Israel and Palestine, on the other hand, shows patterns of short phases with strong violent outbursts followed by longer periods of fragile peace. As a result, the constant violence in Burundi, DRC and Syria – including high numbers of refugees (!) – might have led to a high prevalence of the 'R2P' narrative.

A comparison of political communication and NGO communication reveals relevant differences in the application of escalative narratives. Whereas political actors use all three escalative narratives with nearly equal frequency, NGO communication puts a very strong emphasis on the 'R2P' narrative. While this narrative occurs in 48% of political communication (and thereby is still the most frequently used narrative in this sub-sample), it is used in 96% of NGO texts ($\chi^2 = 716.153$, p < 0.001, Phi = 0.35).

Combining the insights about the differences in the applied narratives across conflicts with the differences between political communicators and NGOs found above, one can assume that the relative composition of the sub-samples also has an effect on the overall relevance of the different narratives. This is especially true for the case of Burundi (Table 3.2). Whereas the 'R2P' narrative is the most important in political communication as well as NGO communication for DRC and Syria, the overall high relevance of this narrative in the discourse on Burundi stems mostly from the NGO texts.

When focusing on the reliance on de-escalative narratives, the data show that the 'Moral Values' narrative and the 'Last Resort/No Other Way' narrative are the most important de-escalative narratives for most cases. The 'Economic Necessity for Peace' narrative is generally used less often. Explaining the necessity of peace, for instance, with moral standards might be more appealing to the media and potential adherents than giving a high significance to the economic causes and/or consequences of war. Professional strategic communicators obviously consider

Table 3.2 Share of texts of all communicators/actors with references to strategic narratives per conflict (multiple answers set)

	Burundi (n = 126)	DRC (n = 1,108)	Israel/ Palestine (n = 1,268)	Syria (n = 2,308)	Kosovo (n = 728)	Macedonia (n = 200)	Total (n = 5.738)
Ethnocentrism/ Patriotism/ Religious	45%	42%	46%	44%	39%	31%	43%
Responsibility to protect R2P	83%	73%	44%	59%	39%	37%	56%
(Self-)Defence	64%	59%	50%	46%	52%	41%	50%
Moral Values	44%	28%	36%	37%	35%	17%	34%
Economic Necessity	21%	26%	22%	30%	22%	15%	26%
Last Resort/No Other Way	50%	39%	30%	29%	30%	18%	32%

this. However, Syria is an exception here (Table 3.2). This might be due to the particular fact that various direct and indirect economic effects of the Syrian war (further) facilitated the advance of the so-called Islamic State – a prominent and important topic of the international discourse concerning the violent crisis in Levant and Middle East. A further (economic) factor which might explain the particularity of the analysed strategic communication in the case of Syrian is the comprehensive international sanctions since 2011 (including those of the EU). Abboud (2017) refers to additional factors: (1) the intense mutual dependence within the state–business relations in Syria, (2) the deep factionalization of Syria's business elites, which are understood as agents who fuel Syria's violence and (3) the economic contraction experienced throughout the course of the conflict, which causes the actual geography of the Syrian conflict (pp. 6–13).

The stronger the competition among different narratives, that is, the higher the number of different or even contradictory narratives, the higher the leeway powerful actors and players are very likely to have for their actual political actions. Our findings suggest that in Burundi, Israel and Syria, the competition among dominating narratives is higher than in the other conflict cases (more variance on a relatively high level of shares).

Narratives Across Time

Since escalative narratives are the most dominant across all conflicts, we restrict our analysis of the application of narratives across time to the three escalative narratives. Overall, the conflicts show significant variance in the pattern of those narratives (Figure 3.3). In the discourse on Burundi, the 'R2P' narrative is dominant during most of the investigated months. The first moment that shows a deviant narrative structure is April 2013. This month is the only point in time in which the '(Self-) Defence' narrative is more prevalent than the other narratives. A possible explanation: In April 2013, the government of Burundi started to discuss a media law that was widely regarded as a restriction of press freedom. Still, we see an exceptional domination of the '(Self-)Defence' narrative over the 'R2P' narrative. This reveals that the specific circumstances of a violent or armed conflict are important criteria for the respective interpretative reaction of strategic communicators and need detailed consideration. In this case, after the new media law was introduced, Burundian journalists took to the streets and protested the law. As a result, the international communicators framed the conflict between journalists and the government as an act of journalistic self-defence against press restriction.

A significant highpoint in the reliance on strategic escalative narratives in the case of Burundi occurred in September 2014 when all three escalative narratives reached their highest shares overall. We argue that this can be related to one event of significant international importance that happened on the ground: Three Italian nuns were murdered in Burundi. This brutal incident obviously triggered all three types of escalative narratives in the persuasive communication of the strategic communicators analysed (political actors and NGOs). Incidents like this give strategic communicators (outside the conflict zone) a good reason to use the whole range of escalative strategic communication and thus to strongly trigger any escalative narrative no matter what the kind.

For Syria and the DRC, the 'R2P' narrative is the dominant narrative across the complete time frame. In both conflicts, the number of communicated texts along with the reliance on the 'R2P' narrative increased during relevant violent conflict events. In Syria, for example, both the number of communicated texts and the 'R2P' narrative increased in September 2013 after UN inspectors concluded that chemical weapons had been used in Ghouta. Similarly, in the DRC in November 2012 when M23 rebel groups entered Goma, the number of texts as well as the reliance on escalative narratives increased significantly.

The conflict between Israel and Palestine shows a much more fragmented and unsteady narrative structure. There is no single narrative that clearly dominates overall. During violent outbursts like Operation Pillar of Defense (November 2012) and Operation Protective Edge (July and August 2014), the '(Self-)Defence' narrative increased in significance and dominated the discourse. This reflects both predominant perspectives of the conflict: The Israeli self-defence against terrorism and the Palestinian self-defence against presumed Israeli suppression.

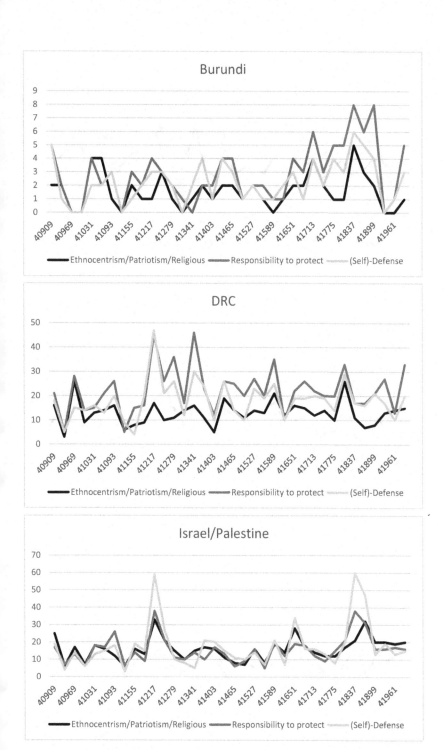

Figure 3.3 Number of texts with references to escalative narratives across time by conflict.

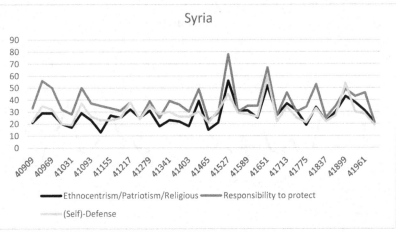

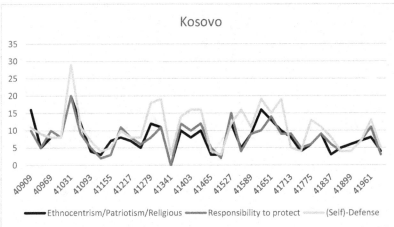

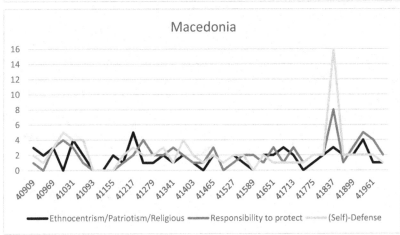

Figure 3.3 (Continued).

The conflict in Kosovo has '(Self-)Defence' as its dominant narrative throughout most of the time line. Similar to the Israeli–Palestinian conflict, it gained further significance during relevant conflict events like the Kosovar local elections that led to high tension between Kosovar Albanians and the Serbian ethnic minority in Northern Kosovo in October and November 2013. Again, the reliance on the '(Self-)Defence' narrative reflected Kosovo's position towards Serbia as well as that of the Serbian minority toward Kosovar Albanians. With these two results for the Israeli–Palestinian and the Kosovo conflict, we can confirm the assumption of Miskimmon et al. (2013, pp. 119–126) that long-lasting conflicts are predominantly characterized by narratives, which derive from long-established discourses of local, national and international provenance. These established narratives are predominantly escalative ones, making it harder to credibly apply de-escalative narratives in an attempt to advocate for reconciliation and peace building.

The discourse on Macedonia has a very fragmented narrative structure. Throughout most of the conflict, the different narratives had equal importance. Only in July 2014 did the '(Self-)Defence' narrative gain tremendous importance. At that time, Macedonian policemen fired teargas against 2,000 ethnic Albanians who were protesting against the imprisonment of six Albanians for murder and terrorism. Again, the '(Self-)Defence' narrative accompanies moments of (potential) escalation and reflects the occurrences on the ground. And again, after a relative moderate usage of all three types of escalative narratives between March and June 2014, this incident seemed to give all strategic communicators the opportunity to make use of more than only one particular escalative narrative.

Analysis of Agendas for Action (Conflict Measures)

Contrary to the dominance of escalative narratives, our analysis of the conflict measures demanded shows that, in all conflicts, *de-escalative* measures are called for more often than escalative measures and non-violent escalative measures (Table 3.3). Political Communicators and NGOs again show slightly different patterns in their communication. While both most often make use of de-escalative measures (67% of NGO texts and 74% of political communicators' texts), political communicators do so significantly more often ($\chi^2 = 22.215$, p < .001, Phi = 0.06). NGOs, on the other hand, significantly more often demand escalative measures (59% as compared to 32% of texts, $\chi^2 = 238.11$, p < .001, Phi = 0.2) and non-violent escalative measures ($\chi^2 = 35.983$, p < 0.001, Phi = 0.08).

Across time, the importance of conflict context again appears to have a significant impact on the relevance of the different conflict measures

Table 3.3 Share of texts with references to conflict measures per conflict (multiple answers set)

	Burundi (n = 126)	DRC (n = 1,108)	Israel/ Palestine (n = 1,268)	Syria (n = 2,308)	Kosovo (n = 728)	Macedonia (n = 200)	Total (n = 5.738)
Escalative Measures	48%	40%	37%	35%	34%	32%	37%
De-escalative Measures	63%	70%	79%	69%	84%	66%	73%
Non-violent Escalative Measures	17%	14%	19%	21%	16%	7%	18%

(Figure 3.4). Here, as well, the discourses on Kosovo, Israel/Palestine, Syria and the DRC show a similar pattern. References to de-escalative measures increase significantly during relevant conflict events. In Kosovo, this was the case, for example, in April and June 2013 during the negotiation and ratification of the Brussels agreement between Kosovo and Serbia. In the discourse on Israel/Palestine, the call for de-escalative measures increased during Operation Pillar of Defense (November 2012) and Operation Protective Edge (July–August 2014). In Syria, the general level of referenced de-escalative measures is significantly higher than the level of escalative measures. Still, both lines deviate even more from one another during relevant conflict events like the bombardment of Homs (February 2012), the UN conclusion that chemical weapons had been used in Ghouta (September 2013), and the failed peace talks in Geneva (January–February 2014). In the discourse on the DRC, the lines for escalative and de-escalative measures align closely, only deviating from another during relevant conflict events. When M23 rebel groups entered Goma in November 2012, for example, the discourse shows an increasing relevance of de-escalative measures.

The discourse on Burundi generally shows the same pattern as above: Relevant conflict events like the government's efforts to block a report by Human Rights Watch on the current Human Rights situation in Burundi (May 2012), the increase in the imprisonment of activists and journalists (June–July 2012), the returning of 35,000 Burundian refugees from Tanzania, and looting in Western Burundi by the rebel group "FPM-Abatabazi" (both October–December 2012) created an increasing relevance of de-escalative measures. However, unlike in the above-mentioned discourses, the discourse on Burundi has particular moments in which the relevance of escalative measures bypassed the relevance of de-escalative ones. This is the case, for instance, in January 2013. Interestingly, however, it appears not to be rooted in what happened on the ground. Rather, it reflects the published country reports,

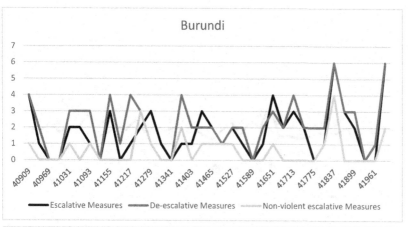

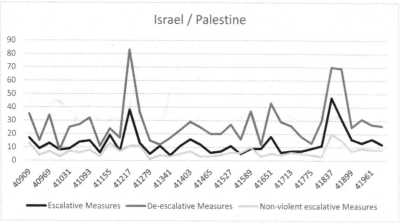

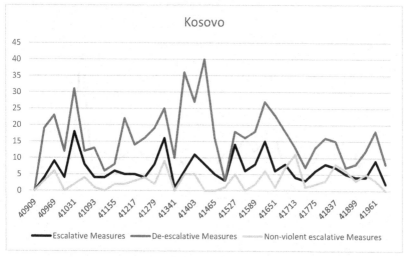

Figure 3.4 Number of texts with references to agendas for action across time by conflict.

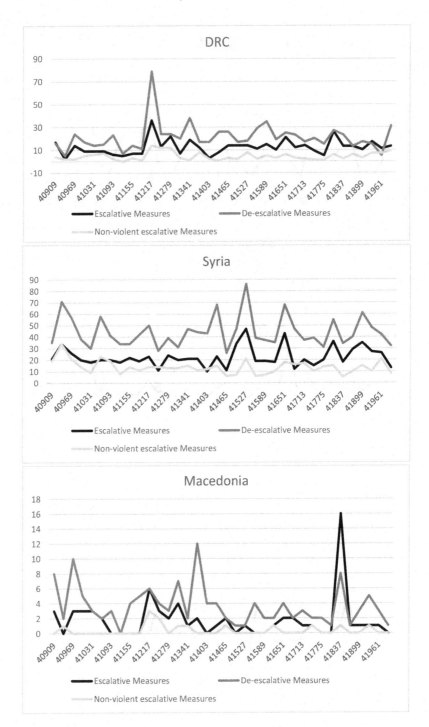

Figure 3.4 (Continued).

which are usually issued by NGOs at the beginning of each year reflecting on what happened the year before.

Macedonia shows a pattern similar to Burundi. During most phases, escalative and de-escalative measures aligned. As in all other cases, during some relevant conflict events, de-escalative measures increased in overall importance and deviated from escalative measures. This was the case, for example, in March 2012 when clashes between ethnic Macedonians and Albanians took place and after the release of Johan Tarculovski in April 2013, who was sentenced by the International Criminal Tribunal for the former Yugoslavia (ICTY) in The Hague for war crimes against ethnic Albanians. Similarly to Burundi, the discourse on Macedonia showed one moment where escalative measures gained more significance than de-escalative ones: In July 2014, parallel to the rise of the '(Self-)Defence' narrative, escalative measures were called upon very dominantly. As described above, this can be linked to Macedonian policemen clashing with ethnic Albanian protesters.

Correlation Between Narratives and Agendas for Action

In a next step, we correlated the occurrence of narratives and measures within the texts both for the complete dataset and for each conflict separately. Since the presence of a narrative as well as a measure is affected by the number of communicated texts, we applied partial correlations controlling for the number of texts communicated in each month (see Table 3.4).

For the complete dataset, the analysis reveals that the occurrence of escalative measures correlates significantly positively with all narratives except the 'Economic Necessity' narrative. To get a more nuanced picture, we created 95%-confidence intervals around the correlation coefficients using 1,000 bootstrap samples. This enables us to identify significant differences in the strength of correlations. If two confidence intervals do not overlap, then we can assume that both correlation coefficients differ significantly. The analysis of correlations with escalative measures reveals that the 'R2P' narrative and the '(Self-)Defence' narrative have a significantly stronger positive correlation with escalative measures than the 'Ethnocentrism/Patriotism/Religious Superiority', the 'Moral Values' and the 'Economic Necessity' narratives. The 'Economic' narrative shows a significantly stronger negative correlation with escalative measures than all other narratives.

Even though the correlations across all conflicts show strong differences that can be attributed to conflict contexts, the correlations with escalative measures reveal a similar picture as the one described above. Escalative measures show the highest number of significant correlations with the '(Self-)Defence' and 'Last Resort' narratives (five of six), followed by the 'R2P' narrative (four of six). The significant negative

Table 3.4 Partial correlations between conflict narratives and measures (per actor, per month, controlled for the number of texts ($n_{Burundi} = 52$; $n_{DRC} = 157$; $n_{Israel} = 162$; $n_{Syria} = 175$; $n_{Kosovo} = 139$; $n_{Macedonia} = 88$, $n_{total} = 773$)

		Escalative Measures	De-escalative Measures	Non-violent Escalative Measures
Ethnocentrism/ Patriotism/ Religious Superiority/	Burundi	0.387*	0.432*	0.320*
	DRC	0.454*	0.077	0.193*
	Israel/Palestine	−0.094	−0.106	0.162*
	Syria	0.042	−0.374*	−0.057
	Kosovo	0.496*	−0.042	0.256*
	Macedonia	−0.101	0.168	0.270*
	All conflicts	0.158*	−0.148*	0.154*
Responsibility to Protect	Burundi	0.226	0.347*	0.202
	DRC	0.533*	−0.127	0.414*
	Israel/Palestine	0.261*	0.176	0.341*
	Syria	0.406*	0.084	0.450*
	Kosovo	0.517*	0.098	0.354*
	Macedonia	0.110	−092	0.235*
	All conflicts	0.378*	−0.073*	0.328*
(Self-)Defence	Burundi	0.194	0.344*	0.399*
	DRC	0.465*	−0.022	0.355*
	Israel/Palestine	0.261*	0.336*	0.131
	Syria	0.420*	0.316*	0.115
	Kosovo	0.263*	−0.270*	−0.024
	Macedonia	0.665*	−0.647*	0.030
	All conflicts	0.378*	0.167*	0.091*
Moral Values	Burundi	0.299*	0.466*	0.281*
	DRC	0.546*	−0.162*	0.358*
	Israel/Palestine	−0.037	−0.111	0.352*
	Syria	−0.037	−0.205*	0.275*
	Kosovo	0.256*	−0.024	0.131
	Macedonia	0.070	0.125	0.251*
	All conflicts	0.091*	−0.120*	0.345*
Economic Necessity	Burundi	0.213	0.357*	0.167
	DRC	−0.004	−0.203*	0.164*
	Israel/Palestine	−0.132	−0.259*	0.063
	Syria	−0.278*	−0.369*	−0.037
	Kosovo	0.272*	0.018	0.270*
	Macedonia	0.011	−0.053	0.100
	All conflicts	−0.139*	−0.287*	0.124*
Last Resort	Burundi	0.280*	0.274	0.233
	DRC	0.545*	−0.149	0.403*
	Israel/Palestine	0.040	0.066	0.295*
	Syria	0.257*	0.278*	0.474*
	Kosovo	0.374*	0.201*	0.252*
	Macedonia	0.266*	−0.029	0.414*

correlation with the 'Economic Necessity' narrative found in the complete model, however, is not a general trend and can mostly be attributed to the Syrian conflict. All in all, the correlations show a trend towards the co-occurrence of escalative measures, on the one hand, and the 'R2P', '(Self-)Defence' and 'Last Resort' narrative, on the other hand. This means that a call for violent acts is often justified by emphasizing a potential responsibility to protect civilians or a form of unavoidability in terms of (self-)defence. Alternative narratives that emphasize ethnocentrism or in-group superiority are used less often. Violence is thus justified through the proactive application of specific escalative narratives that contain a specific degree of legitimacy.

For the complete model, an analysis of partial correlations with de-escalative measures shows that all narratives but the '(Self-)Defence' and 'Last Resort' narratives show significant negative correlations with these measures, with the latter two having a significant but weakly positive correlation with de-escalative measures. Based on confidence intervals created through bootstrapping, we were able to find out that the 'Economic Necessity' narrative has a stronger significantly negative correlation with de-escalative measures than all other narratives. Also, the correlation coefficients for the 'Last Resort' and 'R2P' narratives show significant differences from all other narratives.

Across conflicts, de-escalative measures have the highest number of negative correlations with narratives (nine of 36) with the 'Economic Necessity' narrative showing negative correlations for DRC, Israel/Palestine and Syria. Whereas the general trend of a strong negative relationship between the 'Economic Necessity' narrative and de-escalative measures can partly be demonstrated across conflicts, the positive correlation between the '(Self-)Defence' and 'Last Resort' narratives, on the one hand, and de-escalative measures, on the other hand, which was found in the complete model, cannot be shown across conflicts. Here, the different conflicts offer a more fractured picture with the overall positive correlation mostly stemming from a few very strongly positive correlations. Overall, calls for de-escalation appear to be justified in a very case- and context-specific manner through the reliance on very specific strategic narratives.

Finally, non-violent escalative measures correlate significantly positively with all narratives in the complete model. Confidence intervals do not reveal any significantly stronger correlation with specific narratives. These patterns also hold true across conflicts. There is no single significant, negative correlation with any narrative for any conflict. The highest number of significantly positive correlations across conflicts can be observed for the 'Last Resort', 'Moral Values', 'R2P', and 'Ethnocentrism/Patriotism/Religious Superiority' narratives. Similarly to de-escalative agendas for action, non-violent escalative agendas for action are justified with the help of case- and context-specific narratives. Overall, this means that while the call for these two forms of agendas for action appears to be mostly driven by the conflict and the specific conflict situation, calls for violence are more consistent in their narrative structure. This might indicate a more strategic and persuasive approach in the justification of violence. Instead of relying on narratives that are the best fit for the specific conflict situation, strategic communicators consistently and across different conflict contexts rely on the same set of narratives to justify violent acts.

Analysis of Conflict Casualties

To answer the final research question, we compare the relevance of references to escalative narratives (as a summed score), references to de-escalative narratives and the number of conflict casualties (Figure 3.5). Since the conflicts in the Western Balkans did not show a significant number of casualties for the analysed period of time, these cases are omitted from this analytical step.

The relationship between discourses and conflict casualties again demonstrates the relevance of conflict context (Figure 3.3). The discourse on the Israeli–Palestinian conflict was very much in sync with the number of casualties: When heavy violence took place, escalative narratives and de-escalative measures showed significant peaks. This might be a consequence of the nature of the conflict and the particular consideration of the situation of Israel and the Palestinian people – at least by the (Western) political actors analysed in our study.[17] It is a (very) long-lasting and established conflict with a constant high degree of international attention. Consequently, the strategic communicators analysed and their communication on the conflict might follow professional *routine* with recurring routine answers to the always same old conflict situations and even to new ones. This routine strategy, however, can contribute to a general sense of fatigue with human conflict and violence (also on the part of media), further intensifying a focus on violent phases and human suffering.

The African conflicts displayed greater differences between the development of the discourse and conflict casualties. Here, escalative narratives partly increased before the number of casualties rose. This can be interpreted as international (early) warning in moments of potential escalation and tension. In addition, there were points in the time line where the discourse reacted to conflict casualties with delay. This either suggests that information takes longer to reach the West from Africa (lower number and regional density of foreign correspondents, etc.) or is a result of the African conflicts having a lower priority on the communicators' international agenda.

In Syria, finally, the discourse seemed to be completely detached from the development of the number of conflict casualties on the ground. Again, we have two assumptions on why this might be: The first is the high degree of uncertainty. Since the conflict zone in Syria was not easily

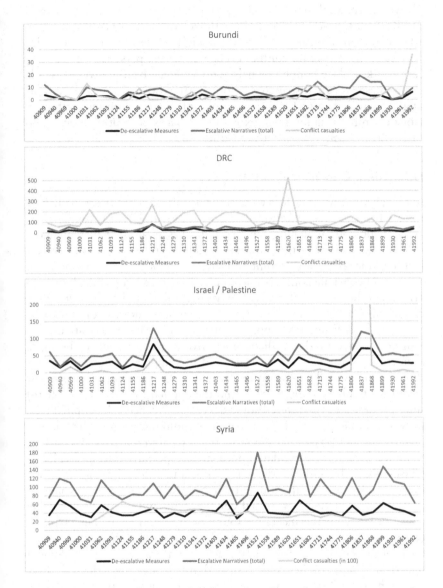

Figure 3.5 Number of texts with references to de-escalative measures, escalative narratives and conflict casualties across time per conflict.

accessible during our study's timeframe (and this is still the case), credible information on what was going on was rare. Secondly and connected to this, the independence of discourse and (high and low) numbers of casualties might also be a reflection of the high level of propaganda that is being distributed on the Syrian conflict. Since escalative narratives do not necessarily reflect actual escalations, they might at times be based on incorrect claims or rumours.

Overall, the analysis of the relationship between conflict casualties and escalative narrative again underlines the relevance of conflict context. In addition, there appear to be different kinds of temporal relationships between narratives and conflict events: At times, persuasive communication takes place simultaneously with violence on the ground, while sometimes texts are distributed before or after violence takes place. This might be an indicator for different roles of strategic communicators in violent conflict ranging from explaining what is currently going on, to early warning and retrospective justification.

Discussion, Conclusion and Prospects

In this chapter, we have looked into the use and content of strategic narratives from diverse (external) political actors and NGOs (understood as strategic communicators) in selected crisis regions. It was our goal to provide answers to the question of how political actors and NGOs in their role as strategic communicators use their agency in order to define and construe conflicts and to plead for measures to deal with an armed conflict or to solve it. We have been able to show under which conditions and in which moments the communicators/actors analysed in our study (differently) apply what kind of strategic narratives. We found that, across all conflicts, escalative narratives tend to be more important than de-escalative ones, and this applies to both groups of actors – political decision makers and NGOs. This might be a result of our particular conflict sample and the applied timeline (2012–2014) since all of the cases suffered some degree of violence. The applied narratives thus might differ from persuasive communication applied in pre- or post-conflict phases. At the same time, we found across all conflicts a higher focus on de-escalative measures, especially during escalative phases. Does this indicate that the NGOs and political actors analysed in this study do after all assume their particular de-escalative role and responsibility in times of armed conflicts? We will come back to this question later. Furthermore, we found high variations in the narrative patterns. These can be attributed to different conflict contexts, mainly the overall level of violence, and the degree of the actual epistemological uncertainty of a conflict. Our results show, for example, that conflicts with a high level of violence and a high epistemological uncertainty – expressed by propaganda distributed by combatants and/or due to restricted access to reliable intelligence or sources – are more likely to be discussed with the 'R2P' narrative.

Our correlation analysis shows that almost every narrative can appear with all three groups of measures. This narrative flexibility demonstrates that the theoretical differentiation between measures and narratives makes sense. Narratives therefore can be regarded as a particular form of persuasive advocacy that can be used to call for a variety of measures. A specific narrative thus does not automatically indicate one (and only one) specific measure. Rather, one must regard narratives as different semantic constructs that can appear in various combinations. A narrative describes a conflict by framing different conflict actors and events. This persuasive description then indicates what must be done to improve the current situation calling for a specific measure.

Finally, the correlation analyses show that even though there is a certain degree of narrative flexibility, there are some re-occurring persuasive patterns. The "(Self-) Defence" narrative, for example, shows a very strong relation with escalative measures. Similarly, the "Moral Values"-narrative often co-occurs with a call for non-violent escalative measures.

Our results may contribute to the development of a broader understanding of global/international strategic communication in times of violent conflict and of more democratic forms of persuasion as well as of the potential of PR for peace building and conflict resolution (or to the contrary!) like it is outlined in the work of Somerville, Hargie, Taylor and Toledano (2017). As a start, the study at hand allows for the following tentative deductions: The fact that not only the strategic persuasive communication of NGOs but surprisingly also that of the particular political decision makers of this study generally places a higher focus on escalative narratives (especially when conflicts escalate!) puts the de-escalative attitude of European politics/political institutions – often postulated from a normative point of view – to the test. Obviously, however, this escalative attitude has its limits, namely when it comes to particular appeals for actual conflict measures. Here, the higher focus on de-escalative measures (again: especially during escalative phases) indicates that the respective actors – political ones and NGOs – assume their particular de-escalative role and responsibility in times of armed conflicts better than when using and communicating via (more broad and less binding) narratives. Besides the narrative flexibility mentioned above, this is another indicator which demonstrates that our theoretical differentiation between measures and narratives makes sense.

Interesting are the partially different communicational strategies of political communicators and NGOs: While the former remarkably often call for agendas for action, which foster peace and negotiation (de-escalative measures) and also remarkably often combine this call with mostly escalative narratives, the latter call for escalative measures in combination with escalative narratives and in general also more often advocate for both kinds of escalative measures. In addition, when considering the important role of the R2P narrative for NGOs, our results could indicate that the communication strategy of the particular NGOs analysed in our study exhibits a "humanitarian intervention" emphasis.

Miskimmon et al. (2013) state that an academic analysis of the effects and success of strategic narratives is nearly impossible – especially in the context of international conflicts, foreign policy, PD and international relations. This is the reason why we, too, did not focus on the effects and success of strategic narratives on war and armed conflicts. Chapter 2 in this volume, however, revealed that escalative narratives also dominate the media coverage on war and armed conflicts. With all due caution, this provides ground for concluding that strategic narratives successfully make it into the media coverage and, once there, within particular pro-fessional journalistic routines probably contribute to the general "con-sonance of escalation" – as we put it – in media coverage on war and armed conflict.

Our study does not provide answers to other important questions which need further investigation in future research. For instance, it could be interesting to differentiate between short-term and long-term narratives and their strategic use in particular crisis contexts. Future research should also investigate the question whether the narratives in strategic communication can also be found in media coverage and, if so, in which form (for instance, edited and adapted to news factors)? Or: In which form are persuasive narratives and their ability to assert themselves dependent on the "agentic capacity" (Coole, 2005, p. 142) of the respective strategic actor/communicator? And finally, what role do strategic narratives play in legitimizing political, military, humanitarian, etc., decisions/interventions?

Appendix

Table A Concepts used for the escalative "Ethnocentrism/Patriotism/Religious Superiority" narrative

Dehumanize/Dehumanization (INCL common labels: Pigs, Rats, etc.)	Clan/Tribe
Immigrate/Immigrant/Come Into/ Come to	Ethnicity/Ethnic/Inter-Ethnic
Ethnic Fragmentation	Homeland/Home/Heartland/Sense of Place
Mixed Ethnicity (NOT Multiethnic)	Name of Macedonia
Patriotism/Patriot	Greater Albania
Proud/Pride	Greater Macedonia
Siege Mentality	Republic of Ilirida
Blasphemy/Sacrilege	Panarabism
Greater Israel	Kosovo autonomous region/non-recognized state within Serbia
Palestinian Unity	Nakba/Displacement
Kurdish State/Kurdish Autonomy	Believers/Worshippers/Worship/Faith
Recognition/Statehood of Palestine	Brothers In Faith
Custom/Customs/Rituals/Rites/ Cultural Practices (NOT Duties)	Unbelievers/Heretics
Apartheid	
National Unity/Unity Government	Indigenous/Autochthonous Martyrs
Ancestors/Ancestry/Our Blood	

Table B Concepts used for the escalative "Responsibility to Protect" narrative (R2P)

Media Blackout/Censorship/ Repression of Free Speech/Press Repression/Blocking URLs	Torture
Misuse of Power	Human Rights
Repression	Responsibility to Protect
Suppression/Crackdown	Forced Labour/Labour Camp
Hate Crimes/Pogroms	Red Line
Collective Punishment	Interventionism
War Crimes	Mass Grave
Flee/Escape/Take Refuge	Political Prisoners/Prisoners of Conscience
Humanitarian Intervention	Serbian Ethnic Cleansing in Kosovo 1998
Ethnic Cleansing	Genocide in Rwanda 1994
Ethnic Violence	Srebrenica 1995
Genocide	Holocaust
Mass Murder	Ex-Dictator Hitler
Massacre	Victims
Raid	Widow
Rape	Military Regime

Table C Concepts used for the escalative "(Self-)Defence" narrative

Defence	Infiltration Tunnels (Israel–Palestine)
Pre-emptive Strike/Pre-emption	Rocket Fire (Israel–Palestine)
Self-Defence	Border Security
Israel's Right to Exist	Aggressors
Right to Self-Defence	

Table D Concepts used for de-escalative "Moral Values" narrative

Forgive/Forgiving	Trustworthy/Honest
Humanize/Are Humans Too	Moral/Humane/Right Thing To Do
Appeasing/Appeasers/Doves	Common Fate
Coexistence/Cohabitation/Symbiosis	Good Will
Dignity/Honour	Solidarity/Compassion
Merciful/Grace	

Table E Concepts used for the de-escalative "Economic Necessity" narrative

Inflation/Hyperinflation	Rationing/Food Stamps
War Effort/War Bonds Poverty/ Subsistence	Recession
Debt/Deficit	Unemployment
Poverty/Subsistence	

Table F Concepts used for the de-escalative "Last Resort/No Other Way than Peace" narrative

Standstill/Gridlock/Ground to a Halt	Only Way/No Alternative
Surrender	Superiority (military)
Not Too Late	Weak/Inferior (military)
Last Resort	Survival
No Return/No Way Back/Bridges Burnt/Irrevocable	

Table G Concepts used for "Escalative" conflict measures

Regime Change	Mobilization
Restore Government Control	Air Strikes
Ground Offensive/Ground Forces	Attack/Offensive
Military Intervention	Ultimatum/Deadline

Table H Concepts used for "De-Escalative" conflict measures

Build Relationship/Build Trust	Disarming
Peace Talks	Pacification
Dialogue/Talks/Debate	Peacebuilding
Diplomacy	Peacekeeping
Negotiate/Negotiations	Resolution/Treaty/Contract/Agreement (NOT In Agreement)
Ceasefire/Truce	Peace
De-Escalation	Peace Process
Demilitarization	Peace Proposals

Table I Concepts used for "Non-Violent Escalative" conflict measures

No Fly Zone	Freezing Assets
Arms Embargo/Arms Control	Sanctions/Embargo/Trade Blockade
Boycott	Travel Restrictions

Acknowledgment

We thank Christian Baden for his very valuable comments on an earlier draft of this chapter.

Notes

1 Definition within the context of this contribution: "(...) the practice of deliberate and purposive communication that a communication agent enacts in the public sphere on behalf of a communicative entity to reach set goals" (Holtzhausen & Zerfass, 2013, p. 74).
2 For instance, global connectivity of audiences and content producers; classic professional media is increasingly losing its monopoly as a gatekeeper; as a result, strategic communicators are less dependent on the intermediary

role of mass media; globalization trends and the resulting growth in value pluralism; the increase in the international mobility of people, ideas and discourses; increasing formal education and people's interest in transparent and clear communication.

3 Understood as strategic communication that applies non-coercive and non-military approaches to projecting power and influence in the world; for instance, encouraging people to think positively about another country.

4 Understood as battlefield communication as a particular form of public communication (for instance, US strategy in Iraq: establishment of democracy; US strategy in Afghanistan: support for government of Karzai and continued presence of NATO and ISAF (Miller et al., 2016); also NATO newspaper Sada-e Azadi in Afghanistan).

5 For INFOCORE's definition of 'interpretative frame', see Baden (2015).

6 Tenenboim-Weinblatt, Hanitzsch and Nagar (2016) argue down a rather similar line.

7 Both groups are not understood as one 'collective agent' but as groups of different competing agents with different agentic capacities.

8 Germany: Federal Government and the two Ministries of Foreign Affairs and of Defence; UK: Prime Minister's Office, Home Office, Ministry of Defence, Department for International Development, Foreign Affairs Office; France: the two Ministères des Affaires Étrangères and de la Défense.

9 The European Council, the European Commission and its Directorate-General for European Civil Protection and Humanitarian Aid Operations, the European Union's diplomatic service European External Action Service and the European Parliament as well as its committee AFET (Foreign Affairs, Human Rights, Common Foreign and Security Policy, and the European Security and Defence Policy) and AFET's subcommittees on Security and Defence (SEDE) and on Human Rights (DROI).

10 For more details concerning the full methodological approach, see Fröhlich and Jungblut (2014).

11 The concepts that were used to identify the different research categories can be seen in the Appendix. The actual operationalization of each concept (strategic (sub)narratives and conflict measures; see Appendix) can be provided upon request.

12 http://vdc-sy.net/en/

13 www.infocore.eu/expert-directory/

14 www.infocore.eu/consortium/associated-stakeholder-network/

15 www.infocore.eu/consortium/advisory-board/

16 www.bbc.com/news/world-europe-18331273; www.bbc.com/news/world-europe-17553072; www.bbc.com/news/world-africa-13087604; www.bbc.com/news/world-africa-13286306; www.bbc.com/news/world-middle-east-29123668; www.bbc.com/news/world-middle-east-14703995

17 For instance: UN partition plan from 1947; the region's Cold War hot spot in the early 1960s; UN Security Council Resolution 242 (1967); diverse particular wars and occupied territories; first (1987) and second Intifada (2000); the Oslo accords (1993); Arab Peace Plan and 'Road Map' (2002–2004); Palestine's 'non-member observer state' status in the UN (2012); the majority (71%) of the UN member states recognized the State of Palestine as sovereign over both West Bank and the Gaza Strip.

References

Abboud, S. (2017). *The economics of war and peace in Syria. Stratification and factionalization in the business community.* Report Arab politics beyond the

108 *Romy Fröhlich and Marc Jungblut*

uprisings. The Century Foundation. Available online at https://s3-us-west-2.
amazonaws.com/production.tcf.org/app/uploads/2017/01/31110253/the-
economics-of-war-and-peace-in-syria.pdf

Angstrom, J., & Honig, J. W. (2012). Regaining strategy: Small powers, strategic culture, and escalation in Afghanistan. *The Journal of Strategic Studies*,
35, 663–687.

Baden, C. (2015). *INFOCORE definitions: "Interpretative Frame"*. Jerusalem,
Israel: The Hebrew University of Jerusalem. Available online at www.info-
core.eu/wp-content/uploads/2016/02/def_interpretative_frame.pdf

Baden, C., & Stalpouskaya, K. (2015). *Common methodological framework: Content Analysis. A mixed-methods strategy or comparatively,
diachronically analyzing conflict discourse*. INFOCORE Working Paper
2015/10. Available online at www.infocore.eu/wp-content/uploads/2016/02/
Methodological-Paper-MWG-CA_final.pdf

Baden, C., & Tenenboim-Weinblatt, K. (2018). The search for common ground in
conflict news research: Comparing the coverage of six current conflicts in domestic and international media over time. *Media, War & Conflict, 11*, 22–45.

Bennett, W. L. (1990). Toward a theory of press-state relations in the United
States. *Journal of Communication, 40*, 103–127.

Bennett, W. L., Lawrence, R. G., & Livingston, S. (2006). None dare call it
torture: Indexing and the limits of press independence in the Abu Ghraib
Scandal's. *Journal of Communication, 56*, 467–485.

Briant, E. (2015). Allies and audiences: Evolving strategies in defense and intelligence propaganda. *International Journal of Press/Politics, 20*, 145–165.

Brown, R. (2005). Getting to war: Communication and mobilization in the
2002–2003 Iraq Crisis. In P. Seib (Ed.), *Media and conflict in the twenty-first
century* (pp. 57–82). New York, NY: Palgrave.

Coole, D. (2005). Rethinking agency: A phenomenological approach to embod-
iment and agentic capacities. *Political Studies, 42*, 124–142.

Croicu, M., & Sundberg, R. (2015). UCDP GED Codebook version 2.0.
Department of Peace and Conflict Research, Uppsala University. Available
online at http://ucdp.uu.se/downloads/ged/ucdp-ged-50-codebook.pdf

Daymon, C., & Demetrious, K. (2013). Introduction: Gender and public relations:
Making meaning, challenging assumptions. In C. Daymon, & K. Demetrious
(Eds.), *Gender and public relations: Critical perspectives on voice, image and
identity* (pp. 1–19). Abingdon, UK: Routledge.

De Graaf, B., Dimitriu, G., & Ringsmose, J. (2015). *Strategic narratives, public
opinion and war. Winning domestic support for the Afghan war*. London,
UK: Routledge.

Entman, R. (2003). Cascading activation: Contesting the White House's frame
after 9/11. *Political Communication, 20*, 415–432.

Freedman, L. (2006). *Networks, culture and narratives*. Adelphi Papers Series 45, No. 379, 11–26. Available online at http://dx.doi.
org/10.1080/05679320600661640

Frère, M. S., & Wilen, N. (2015). *INFOCORE Definitions: "Conflict"*. Bruxelles, Belgium: ULB. Available online at www.infocore.eu/results/definitions/

Fröhlich, R., & Jungblut, M. (2014). *Development, structure and context of frames – The analysis of verbal communication material of strategic communicators in PR and Propaganda*. INFOCORE Methodological

Framework Paper, Work Package No. 6 "Strategic Communication". Available online at www.infocore.eu/wp-content/uploads/2016/02/INFOCORE_Methodological-Framework-WP6.pdf

Fröhlich, R., & Jungblut, M. (2018). Between factoids and facts: The application of 'evidence' in NGO strategic communication on war and armed conflict. *Media, War and Conflict, 11,* 85–106.

Hayden, C. (2016). Public diplomacy: Managing narratives versus building relations. In P. Robinson, P. Seib, & R. Fröhlich (Eds.), *Routledge handbook of media, conflict and security* (pp. 142–155). London, UK: Routledge.

Holtzhausen, D. R., & Zerfass, A. (2013). Strategic communication – Pillars and perspectives on an al-ternate paradigm. In K. Sriramesh, A. Zerfass, A., & J.-N Kim (Eds.), *Current trends and emerging topics in public relations and communication management* (pp. 283–302). New York, NY: Routledge.

MacArthur, J. R. (2004). *Second front: Censorship and propaganda in the 1991 Gulf War.* Berkeley: University of California Press.

Martyn, P. H. (2008). Lynch mob: Pack journalism and how the Jessica Lynch story became propaganda. *The Canadian Journal of Media Studies, 4,* 124–164.

Miller, D., Robinson, P., & Bakir, V. (2016). Propaganda and persuasion in contemporary conflict. In P. Robinson, P. Seib, & R. Fröhlich (Eds.), *Routledge handbook of media, conflict and security* (pp. 308–320). London, UK: Routledge.

Miskimmon, A., O'Loughlin, B., & Roselle, L. (2013). *Strategic narratives: Communication power and the new world order.* London, UK: Routledge.

Nohrstedt, S. A., & Ottosen, R. (2008). War journalism in the threat society: Peace journalism as a strategy for challenging the mediated culture of fear? *Conflict & Communication Online, 7*(2).

O'Loughlin, B., Miskimmon, A., & Roselle, L. (2017). Strategic narratives. Methods and ethics. In A. Miskimmon, B. O'Loughlin, & L. Roselle (Eds.), *Forging the world. Strategic narratives and international relations* (pp. 23–55). Ann Arbor: University of Michigan Press.

Raleigh, C., Linke, A., Hegre, H., & Karlsen, J. (2010). Introducing ACLED: An armed conflict location and event dataset. *Journal of Peace Research, 47,* 651–660.

Ringsmose, J., & Borgesen, B. K. (2011). Shaping public attitudes towards the deployment of military power: NATO, Afghanistan and the use of strategic narratives. *European Security, 20,* 505–528.

Robinson, P. (2014). News media, communications and the limits of perception management during military operations. In R. Johnson, & T. Clack (Eds.), *At the end of military intervention: Historical, theoretical and applied approaches to transition, handover and withdrawal* (pp. 271–291). Oxford, UK: University of Oxford Press.

Smith, M. F., & Ferguson, D. P. (2001). Activism. In R. L. Heath (Ed.), *Handbook of public relations* (pp. 291–300). Thousand Oaks, CA: Sage.

Snow, N., & Taylor, P. M. (2006). The revival of the propaganda state: US propaganda at home and abroad since 9/11. *International Communication Gazette, 68,* 398–407.

Somerville, I., Hargie, O., Taylor, M., & Toledano, M. (2017). *International public relations: Perspectives from deeply divided societies.* London, UK: Routledge.

Stalpouskaya, K., & Baden, C. (2015). To do or not to do: The role of agendas for action in analyzing news coverage of violent conflict. *Proceedings of the First Workshop on Computing News Storylines*, 21–29. Association for Computational Linguistics & The Asian Federation of Natural Language Processing, Beijing, China. Available online at www.aclweb.org/anthology/W15-4504

Taylor, P. M. (2002). Perception management and the 'war' against terrorism. *Journal of Information Warfare, 1*(3), 16–29.

Tenenboim-Weinblatt, K., Hanitzsch, T., & Nagar, R. (2016). Beyond peace journalism. Reclassifying conflict narratives in the Israeli news media. *Journal of Peace Research, 53*, 151–165.

Van Leuven, S., Heinrich, A., & Deprez, A (2015). Foreign reporting and sourcing practices in the network sphere: A quantitative content analysis of the Arab Spring in Belgian news media. *New Media & Society, 17*, 573–591.

4 The Dynamics of Parliamentary Debates on War and Conflict

Assessing the Impact and Role of the Media on the Political Agenda

Rosa Berganza, Beatriz Herrero-Jiménez and Adolfo Carratalá

Introduction: The Role of the Media in Setting the Political Agenda

Research on political agenda setting has long been a contentious issue in communication studies. However, in recent years, researchers have attempted to determine whether the (traditional) mass media or the politicians come first in creating such agendas. The conflicting results (Walgrave & Van Aelst, 2006) obtained from the studies suggest that political actors and the media (Davis, 2007; Vliegenthart et al., 2016) influence each other mutually. Broadly speaking, the ways politicians react to mass media discourses can be explained by several factors, including the novelty or negativity of the topics being addressed and the international nature of the coverage (Vliegenthart et al., 2016; Walgrave, Soroka, & Nuytemans, 2008). Accordingly, it is logical to conclude that mass media have a powerful impact on political debates, especially on agendas for action proposed by Members of Parliaments (MPs), which are privileged discursive constructions particularly relevant during violent conflicts.

While traditional mass media's influence on parliamentary debates has been proved to be an essential factor to understand how political agendas are built, the influence of social media on this process has not yet been scientifically explored. Thus, the aim of our study is to investigate first, whether social media play a role in the discussions of violent conflicts in parliament and, if yes, to what extent; and second, what is, on the other hand, the role of traditional mass media in such discussions. We aim to answer these questions by mapping the references to traditional and social media in debates that discuss the Syrian Civil War in British, French, German and EU parliaments between 2011 and 2015. In doing so, we applied a computer-assisted *quantitative* content analysis (for more details, see "Method" section) of parliamentary minutes. Moreover, we put a particular emphasis on the Chemical Weapons (CW) crisis in 2013. We will later show that the CW crisis was a crucial moment in the history of the Syrian conflict. Concerning the CW crisis, we carried out a *qualitative* content analysis of the respective parliamentary debates.

Our study centres around the particular role(s) that (traditional) media play in these debates compared to the role(s) social media play (e.g. if they appear as channels for politicians/MPs to *express their views* to the public or as key informative channels used to *support their arguments*). Finally, we examine whether traditional and social media were used as a discursive support to propose agendas for action (Baden & Tenenboim-Weinblatt, 2015).[1]

The Conflict in Syria: The International Response and Media Impact

From the Revolution to the Civil War: The Historical and Political Background

The series of revolutions collectively known as the Arab Spring began in December of 2010 when a Tunisian citizen, Mohamed Bouazizi, immolated himself in front of a municipal building (Bleek & Kramer, 2016). The protests in the country against the Ben Ali regime that ensued in the aftermath of this episode provided a template that would soon be followed in other nearby states. The conflict unleashed in Syria in March of 2011 also took its inspiration from the uprising in Tunisia (Dandashly, 2016). Nevertheless, the Syrian conflict developed according to a different pattern than witnessed in other countries in the region. This is due to the inner differences among the opponents of the regime as well as the role that Jihadists and Islamists played in the escalating conflict (Cozma & Kozman, 2015). Furthermore, Bashar al-Assad's aggressive response to the early protests plunged the country into a spiral of violence that would eventually lead to civil war.

The conflict soon turned into a quandary that aroused the concern and interest of principal international actors, who saw the confrontation from opposing perspectives. While the US and Europe have lent support to the moderate opposition, other key countries such as Russia have aligned themselves with the al-Assad government. A chemical weapons attack that took place on August 21, 2013, underscored the discrepancy among these policies. The US, convinced that the regime was responsible for the attack, threatened to spearhead a military intervention involving aerial bombardments, but Russia managed to prevent this from happening when it proposed to Syria that the latter join the Chemical Weapons Convention, an idea to which the al-Assad government readily assented

(Blake & Mahmud, 2013). This shift in Syrian policy paved the way for a relatively successful chemical weapons disarmament process, implicitly giving legitimacy to the regime (Makdisi & Pison Hindawi, 2017). The conflict did not end, however, in the wake of this disarmament. When ISIS[2] entered the fray in 2013, it further complicated the overall situation and distribution of forces in the territory, increasing the likelihood the Western democracies would favour a military intervention (Geis & Schlag, 2017).

Nonetheless, the countries of Western Europe did not initiate military operations in the region until 2015, once it had become inescapably obvious to them that their own security was also being threatened. Until then, the European Union's response to the Syrian conflict had been limited to sanctions. Although the speed and reach of these sanctions were unprecedented (Portela, 2012), they only had any effect on the Damascus regime between May of 2011 and June of 2012, given that afterward European policy prioritized the country's security by easing the sanctions (Seeberg, 2015). According to some authors, the European response to the Syrian crisis was indecisive, incoherent and weak, especially when compared to actors such as Russia (Dandashly, 2016). According to other studies (Portela, 2012), the EU's policy, developed in parallel with that of the US, has been undermined by other states, including Russia, which have prevented it from being implemented during meetings of the United Nations Security Council (UNSC), where resolutions invoking the 'Responsibility to Protect' principle (R2P), the same principle used to intervene in the Libyan crisis, have been repeatedly blocked.

During the Libyan crisis, the European Parliament acted as moral tribune rather than simply a forum for politically inconsequential debate, making it the European institution most critical of Muammar al-Gaddafi's regime and confirming its increasingly important role as an international actor (Stavridis & Fernández Molina, 2013). Its action in this case was thereafter framed within the growing global "parliamentarisation of international affairs" phenomenon. It includes dimensions such as the control exerted by an external police force as well as the exercise of parliamentary diplomacy, especially oriented toward the prevention and resolution of conflicts (Stavridis & Pace, 2011). This practice gives a clear moral dimension to international politics and it is materialized in the support shown by parliaments toward promoting democracy and human rights (Beetham, 2006).

In this context, the Arab Spring uprisings constituted a foreign policy priority for the European Parliament from the very beginning. The House accepted the legitimacy of the uprisings in numerous resolutions and initiated such measures as the suspension of Libya's role as observer and Syria's membership in the Parliamentary Assembly of the Union for the Mediterranean (UfM PA), as Cofelice (2016) points out. Still, the reaction to the Syrian crisis was not as forceful as it had been during the crisis confronting Gaddafi's regime. In the case of Syria, the European Parliament passed resolutions, which demanded responses from the members of the UNSC, but it made no appeals that they should act on the basis of R2P given that the situation failed to meet two essential criteria: The existence of agreement within the UN and a reasonable expectation of success (Stavridis, 2016a).

According to Dandashly (2016), the EU's attitude toward Syria was also affected by the general agreement among the distinct member states. Unlike other countries, France, Germany and the UK were decidedly in favour of intervening in the Syrian crisis by imposing sanctions and by passing a resolution within the framework of the UN (Blake & Mahmud, 2013). Moreover, these three countries represented 65% of the total defence budget from the then 27 states, which formed the EU in 2010, meaning that they were the three key actors involved in international defence (Stavridis, 2016b). Despite these nations' agreement on the issue, their parliaments played different roles as the political response toward to the Syrian Civil War developed.

The British Parliament has gained previously unimaginable power over the last few decades (Norton, 2017), coming into its own as an institution with an increasing capacity to impact politics (Russell & Cowley, 2016) and foreign affairs, especially when large military deployments are at issue (Strong, 2015b). Although it is the prerogative of the Prime Minister to deploy armed forces abroad, the parliamentary vote that Blair convened in March of 2003 in order to garner support for troop deployment to Iraq set a precedent that Cameron would act on, when eight years later he called for a vote to gain the House's backing for a military operation in Libya (Kaarbo & Kenealy, 2017; Mello, 2017; Norton, 2017).

With the chemical weapons attack in August of 2013, the al-Assad regime crossed the 'red line' that the leaders of the US, the UK and France had for months warned was inviolable, the ignoring of which would trigger a military intervention (Blake & Mahmud, 2013; Strong, 2015b). In response, Cameron went to Parliament with a proposal to deploy the army. This was ultimately rejected, with 285 nay votes to 272 yea votes, during a historic session held on August 29. During this meeting, the British Parliament made use of a power that it, strictly speaking, does not possess (Mello, 2017), thereby setting a precedent from which there was no turning back: "No future government will be able to deploy British forces without MPs' express support" (Strong, 2015b, p. 618). Indeed, the importance given to MPs has become nearly as great as that given by the German legal system to the Bundestag. By law, the German Parliament must authorize the army's participation in operations taking place under the auspices of the UN, NATO or any other coalition (Peifer, 2016), which, in fact, it did when its country's armed forces intervened militarily against ISIS.

In France, on the other hand, foreign policy is configured much like it is in the UK, where it is traditionally considered an area reserved for the president. Still, in 2008, a constitutional reform strengthened the role of parliament in matters of foreign policy. Since then, the government must inform the latter when any armed forces are deployed abroad within the first three days of the operation and obtain its approval if the intervention exceeds four months. As for the Syrian conflict, the National Assembly highlighted the need to respect, defend and promote the international treaty that prohibits the use of chemical weapon, thereby clearly acting as a moral tribune defending the rights of minorities, especially religious ones (Stavridis, 2016b). Nonetheless, during the CW crisis of 2013, despite the decisive position taken by Hollande, the British Parliament's nay vote along with Obama's about-face led France to view itself as clearly irrelevant and internationally isolated (Gaffney, 2014).

The behaviour of parliamentary assemblies is usually multi-causal and is affected, as we have seen, by factors specific to each country. Thus, for example, given the precedent of military operations with unexpected results (Iraq, Libya) and partisan politics (Kaarbo & Kenealy, 2014; Mello, 2017; Strong, 2015b), the debate that Cameron lost in the British Parliament in 2013 was also heavily influenced by public opinion. Aware that the debate centred around an institution that British citizens widely distrusted (Norton, 2017), the parliamentarians made continual mention of the prevailing mood and of surveys – 61% of those consulted said that in case of military intervention, it should have the approval of the parliament – in order to justify their vote against Cameron's proposal (Kaarbo & Kenealy, 2017). In the case of France as well, 64% of its citizens were against military intervention in Syria, as was revealed in a survey published in *L'Express* on August 31, 2013 (Gaffney, 2014). In Germany, 58% backed the executive's plan, approved in December of 2015, to participate in an operation against ISIS, even though two-thirds opposed an active role in the aerial bombardments (Peifer, 2016). In both cases, the impact of public opinion on political strategy proved decisive.

Covering the Syrian Conflict: A Threat for Traditional Media, an Opportunity for Social Media

The demonstrable impact of traditional mass media on citizens with respect to matters of foreign affairs (Soroka, 2003) increases in cases of violent conflict. The coverage of traditional and social media makes increasingly impossible to ignore the kinds of atrocities committed in all wars, and it has put pressure on democratic governments to respond (Geis & Schlag, 2017). During the Arab Spring uprisings, traditional media played an essential role, giving prominence to the events on the international stage and helping to garner support from Western societies and governments (Rane & Salem, 2012).

However, in the case of Syria, traditional media's reach was limited by the difficulties and risks posed to journalists working in the country (Geis & Schlag, 2017; Mast & Hanegreefs, 2015). In fact, *Reporters Without Borders* claimed in their 2016 report on freedom of the press that for the third year in a row Syria was the most dangerous country in the world for journalists. Arab satellite television channels played a very important role in keeping refugees up-to-date on the war's evolution (Rohde et al. 2016). The international press reports were also crucial during such episodes as the chemical weapons attack in Ghouta (Cozma & Kozman, 2015). In spite of those facts, coverage of the Syrian conflict has fallen, above all, to social media, often through images taken by opponents of the regime and disseminated by activists from outside the country (Andén-Papadopoulos & Pantti, 2013).

Indeed, social media played such a key role during the Arab Spring (Geis & Schlag, 2017) that the latter has often been referred to as the 'Facebook and Twitter revolutions'. In Syria, the combination of a media system that was under the control of or allied with the government (Harkin, 2013) and the risk that the region posed to international journalists (Kase, Bowman, Al Amin, & Abdelzaher, 2014) caused the distribution of information about the conflict to the outside world to be channelled via the Internet: "Syria's has been the most socially mediated civil conflict in history. Compared with others before it, an exceptional amount of what the outside world knows – or thinks it knows – about Syria's nearly three-year-old conflict has come from videos, analysis, and commentary circulated through social networks" (Lynch, Freelon, & Aday, 2014, p. 5).

Although it was launched in 1997, it was not until 2002 that the Internet became widely available to the public in general (Harkin, 2013). According to the Dubai School of Government, in 2010, Facebook was being used by 1% of the Syrian population, or 241,859 users. The beginning of the uprisings in 2011 coincided with an increase in online activity by Syrians, despite obstruction from the government. That year, 20% of the population was connected to the web. 200,000 fans followed the page 'Syrian Revolution 2011' (Rane & Salem, 2012) and more than 400 groups were affiliated with this social site, dedicated to tackling issues facing the country (Harkin, 2013). These facts offer a testimony of the central role that the social networks acquired, frequently used to organize protests (Rohde et al., 2016). For its part, Twitter ended up becoming the most popular application due to its ease of use, low cost and capacity to include text, image and links to other sites, in addition to the fact that it required little infrastructure to connect to it (Klausen, 2015). Although each of the parties involved in the war have utilized social media, the use made of it by ISIS has attracted the most attention because it successfully exploited the possibilities for dissemination and propaganda offered by applications like YouTube (Larsen, 2017; Lieber & Reiley, 2016; Veilleux-Lepage, 2016).

Social and traditional media interacted, then, in a fully symbiotic manner. The former was the tool with which diverse actors in the conflict insinuated themselves into the discourse on traditional media, spreading their messages and influence worldwide (Kase et al., 2014; Rane & Salem, 2012). For traditional media, social networks became content providers with which they could add to, in graphic detail, their coverage of the region (Harkin, 2013; Klausen, 2015), despite the unreliability of the material (Kase et al., 2014; Klausen, 2015; Mast & Hanegreefs, 2015). The massacre in Ghouta perfectly exemplified this convergence of interests. The first reports appeared with videos recorded on mobile phones that had been uploaded to YouTube. Traditional media like *The New York Times*, the *BBC* and *Al Jazeera* used those clips in their coverage, given the lack of professional images. As Geis and Schlag (2017, p. 7) have claimed: "It was the distributive power of social networks that turned the attention of the international community to the human suffering in Syria, and that called for an urgent political reaction."

The Impact of Traditional and Social Media on Parliamentary Debates About Violent Conflicts

Information found on social networks suggests a direct line of communication with a distant reality impossible to witness first hand, whether the goal is journalistic, academic (Harkin, 2013; Larsen, 2017), intelligence gathering (Lieber & Reiley, 2016) or even militaristic (Kase et al., 2014). In addition, it offers very useful and attractive material to add to the media's narratives since photos and videos recorded by citizens usually involve explicit representations of human suffering and death. They often also include elements that are taboo in journalistic discourse such as images of minors (Andén-Papadopoulos & Pantti, 2013; Mast & Hanegreefs, 2015).

Making political decisions often involves this sort of strategic use: "Media have the potential to impact on foreign policy" (Cozma & Kozman, 2015, p. 669). Media coverage of events affects different aspects of life (Couldry, 2008) and, in the political realm, obliges the relevant actors to act increasingly according to the media logic (Davis, 2007; Strömbäck, 2011). This influence draws our attention to the impact that traditional and especially social media has had on the European political debate about Syria. Although research into the traditional media's influence on parliaments has offered ambivalent results (Walgrave & van Aelst, 2006), recent work has demonstrated the impact that traditional and social media have on parliamentary debate when it involves violent conflicts in other countries (Herrero-Jiménez, Arcila Calderón, Carratalá, & Berganza, 2018; Jungblut, Carratalá, & Herrero, 2017).

In the case of Syria, studying the distinct narratives according to which Russian and Western newspapers covered the attack in Ghouta allows for an understanding of the different political postures assumed by each country (Brown, 2015). Media pressure has also proven essential to the way teams from the UN conducted investigations on chemical weapons (Makdisi & Pison Hindawi, 2017) and was instrumental in sowing doubt about the potential efficacy of a military intervention in Syria, especially in light of earlier unsatisfactory actions of the sort in Afghanistan and Libya (Strong, 2015a). In the new media environment, working together with traditional media, "digital media and social networks play an important role when massive human rights violations are documented" (Geis & Schlag, 2017, p. 13). This was revealed in a study on the effects on US senators when watching 12 videos on YouTube containing images of the chemical attack in Ghouta. The ISIS videos on YouTube also proved key during the votes in the British Parliament in September 2014 (Strong, 2015a) and December 2015 (Rashed, 2016).

This chapter evaluates the impact of traditional and social media on European parliamentary debates about Syria between 2011 and 2015, especially during the CW crisis. Taking into account what we have addressed so far, we have formulated the following research questions:

RQ1: How significant was the presence of traditional and social media as well as public opinion in influencing the group of parliaments studied and each one in particular?
RQ2: Has there been a trend indicating the presence of traditional and social media in parliamentary discourse throughout the period studied?
RQ3: Which media appear more frequently in the parliaments analysed?
RQ4: What function did traditional and social media have in parliamentary interventions following the chemical attack in Goutha? Can any relationship be found between the mention of traditional and social media and the formulation of agendas for action made by MPs?

Method

Sample and Procedure[3]

3,076 minutes from debates related to the Syrian conflict (from January 2011 to June 2015) were subjected to a content analysis. These debates were held in the European Parliament (n = 720), the Bundestag of Germany (n = 1,113), the House of Commons of the UK (n = 1,034) and the Assemblée Nationale of France (n = 209).[4] The debates were

downloaded from the official websites of the parliaments in their original languages (the only exception was the European Parliament's texts,
for which official English translations were chosen whenever possible).
Two researchers were trained for this purpose between June and July of
2015. Different types of minutes were collected (Parliamentary Debates,
Westminster Hall[5] debates and Oral and Written Questions and Answers) using a Boolean Search whenever these documents included at
least one mention (across the different languages) to Syria.

We web scraped texts in HTML and PDF formats that included metadata (Parliament, Type of Document and Date) in their titles. All these
files were automatically transformed to TXT (UTF-8) using specific
scripts designed in Python 2.7, which allowed for the implementation
of this procedure in batches. By using another automated Python script,
metadata were extracted from titles and included as tags at the beginning of each document (Herrero-Jiménez et al., 2018). Due to the nature
of the parliamentary work, the surveyed minutes, especially the debates,
were usually long and in most cases covered different topics (not related
to the Syrian Civil War). To exclude this extra information and make
the text analysis more accurate, we manually filtered the text, removing
those paragraphs that did not address the various ramifications of the
Syrian conflict. With this procedure, we obtained the filtered files.

All the documents were uploaded and stored in the Jerusalem Server
of the *Amsterdam Content Analysis Toolkit* (JAmCAT)[6], where all the
necessary scripts for the content analysis and computed initial indicators
were run.[7]

Measure

The dictionary created by the INFOCORE team and adapted to the
analysis of media and violent conflicts contained 3,738 entities. It includes *semantics*, *actors*, *places* and *events*, and it was translated into
the eight languages used in the project. For this chapter, we selected
entities for three constructed concepts. Reliability was analysed to obtain internal consistency. These constructed concepts were the mean of
the entities' appearance frequency. They measured the presence of traditional and social media and references to public opinion through specific
indicators. Specifically, we measured:

- *(Traditional) media presence* (α_C = 0.69). This indicator groups
  terms related to generic and specific traditional media quoted in
  parliamentary documents. It includes 29 entities including 'media',
  'press media', 'broadcast media', 'Syrian media' or 'war reporter'
  (generic); and 'BBC', 'CNN' or '*L'Express*' (specific).
- *Social media presence* (α_C = 0.75). This indicator groups terms related to generic and specific social media quoted in parliamentary

documents. It includes four entities: 'social media' and 'social network' (generic); and 'Facebook', 'Twitter' and 'YouTube' (specific).[8]

• *Public opinion presence* (α_C = 0.65). This indicator groups terms
  related to the generic concept of public opinion and includes three
  entities: 'public opinion/opinion polls', 'voters' and 'public'.

Furthermore, we created new variables that grouped specific and generic
references to traditional media outlets with respect to their nationality
(i.e. "British Media"). In this case, we proceeded by adding their frequencies to a new variable. This way, for each document, we got the
summation (and not the average) of the appearance of Syrian media,
Russian media, French media, British media, German media, US media,
Turkish media, Middle Eastern media, as well as European media.[9]

Finally, in order to conduct the analysis on the CW crisis, we selected
those minutes in which the dictionary concept "Chemical Weapons"
was present. We filtered them based on a date range. We selected parliamentary documents published between August 21, 2013 (the day when
the Ghouta Chemical Weapons Attack took place), and September 30,
2013, once the diplomatic solution to the crisis was agreed on between
the parties. Table 4.1 shows the distribution of the parliamentary documents used for the qualitative analysis.

Analysis

In order to answer our research questions, we conducted exploratory and
descriptive analyses. We ran independent and paired sample t-tests and
one-way and within-participants analyses of variance to compare differences between the groups. We also created a timeline with the average
presence grouped by months in the social media and (traditional) media
index. Finally, in order to conduct the in-depth analysis, we worked with
the 49 selected documents and extracted all the direct and indirect references to (traditional) media and social media and the context in which

Table 4.1 Distributions of the parliamentary minutes concerning CW crisis
and analysed in-depth (frequencies)

	European Parliament	German Parliament	British Parliament	French Parliament	N
Oral Answers	–	–	19	–	19
Parliamentary Debates	5	1	4	1	12
Westminster Hall	–	–	2	–	2
Written Answers	7	3	6	1	17
TOTAL	**12**	**4**	**31**	**2**	**49**

they were mentioned by the MPs. Once all the references were extracted, we formulated an exhaustive classification scheme according to the actors mentioned and the purpose for which they were incorporated.

Findings

The results derived from the analysis of 3,076 documents confirm that there are significant differences [$\lambda_W = 0.985$; $F (2, 3074) = 7.925$; $p < .001$; η^2 partial $= 0.005$] in the average presence of social media (M = 0.0127, SD = 0.1378), (traditional) media (M = 0.0176, SD = 0.0782) and references to public opinion (M = 0.0468, SD = 0.4818) in parliamentary debates concerning the Syrian Civil War (RQ1). In particular, public opinion had a higher presence in parliamentary discussions (Table 4.2). Thus, the analysis revealed that there are significant differences [$t(3075) = 3.55$, $p < 0.001$, $d = 0.085$] between the indicator for public opinion and the indicator for (traditional) media, even if the size of the effect can be considered *small* (Cohen, 1988). Additionally, concerning the presence of (traditional) media and social media, the differences between these two indicators approached significance [$t(3075) = -1.857$, $p = .063$].

Furthermore, we found that attention given to media [$F (3, 859.192) = 22.227$, $p < 0.001$] and to public opinion [$F (3, 1573.033) = 8,421$, $p < 0.001$] varies significantly depending on which parliament is under consideration (Table 4.3). This variation has not been found for attention given to social media [$F (3, 3072) = 0.462$, $p > 0.05$]. Specifically, regarding traditional media, Dunnett's T3 post hoc test shows that the European Parliament exhibits significant differences from the other three parliaments and that the largest difference is found when it is compared to the German Parliament [$t_{media}(1042.035) = 8.003$, $p < .001$, $d = 0.403$]. The size of this difference can be considered *medium* (Cohen, 1988). For public opinion, we have found that the largest difference exists between the European Parliament and, in this case, the French Parliament [$t_{publicopinion}(512.179) = 3.294$, $p = 0.001$, $d = 0.2$]. Here, the effect size can be considered *small* (Cohen, 1998).

As for the presence of (traditional) media and social media in parliamentary minutes specifically, our findings reveal that differences deepened as the Syrian conflict evolved (RQ2). To address this issue,

Table 4.2 Descriptive measures for the indicators of social media, media and public opinion presence

INDEX	M	SD
Social Media Presence	0.0127	0.1378
Media Presence	0.0176	0.0782
Public Opinion Presence	0.0468	0.4818

Table 4.3 Averages and standard deviations of the indicators for the presence of traditional media, social media and public opinion in parliamentary debates

	Media		Social Media		Public Opinion	
	M	SD	M	SD	M	SD
PARLIAMENT						
EU	0.034	0.077	0.014	0.089	0.066	0.380
Germany	0.009	0.045	0.012	0.133	0.041	0.231
UK	0.016	0.105	0.011	0.169	0.047	0.729
France	0.019	0.051	0.023	0.124	0.011	0.060
Total	0.018	0.078	0.013	0.138	0.047	0.070

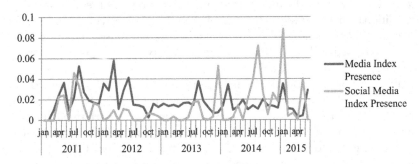

Figure 4.1 Presence of traditional media and social media in the European parliamentary debates concerning the Syrian conflict.

we designed a time series graph. Figure 4.1 includes the variation in media and social media throughout the period investigated. Both indexes exhibit different peaks as the conflict developed. However, one can also observe that, while at the beginning of the conflict traditional media presence was higher than social media presence, as the conflict evolved into its later stages social media assumed comparatively greater importance.[10]

As shown in Figure 4.1, one of the steepest peaks in traditional media presence (and to a lesser extent in social media presence) appeared in August 2013, a pivotal moment in international politics regarding the Syrian Civil War due to the Ghouta attack. How media and social media were integrated into parliamentary discourse will be examined below.

In order to deepen our understanding of the attention paid to media in parliaments, we analysed the most cited media according to their national origin (RQ3). Our results confirm that there are significant differences [$\lambda_W = 0.959$; $F(8, 3068) = 16.294$; $p < 0.001$; η^2 partial = 0.041] in the national origin of the traditional media, which is most often quoted

Table 4.4 Averages and standard deviations of the summation of the media presence with respect to nationality in parliamentary debates

	EU Parliament		German Parliament		British Parliament		French Parliament		All Parliaments	
	M	SD	M	SD	M	SD	M	SD	M	SD
Syrian Media	0.09	0.35	0.01	0.16	0.02	0.18	0.06	0.26	0.04	0.23
British Media	0.04	0.263	0.01	0.10	0.08	0.63	0.01	0.10	0.04	0.39
German Media	0.01	0.12	0.05	0.28	0.00	0.00	0.00	0.07	0.02	0.18
French Media	0.03	0.21	0.00	0.05	0.00	0.04	0.00	0.00	0.01	0.11
US Media	0.03	0.22	0.01	0.11	0.01	0.14	0.01	0.10	0.02	0.15
European Media*	0.04	0.20	0.01	0.09	0.00	0.00	0.04	0.20	0.01	0.12
Middle East Media	0.02	0.13	0.01	0.08	0.00	0.06	0.02	0.14	0.01	0.10
Turkish Media	0.02	0.20	0.01	0.12	0.00	0.08	0.00	0.00	0.01	0.13
Total	0.28	0.76	0.11	0.46	0.13	0.78	0.15	0.44	0.16	0.66

* 'European Media' refers to Media from all European countries except Germany, France, the UK and Greece.

in parliaments (Table 4.4). Syrian media (M = 0.04, SD = 0.23) and British Media (M = 0.04, SD = 0.39) received the most attention.

In the specific cases of the German and the British Parliaments, it is interesting to note that the media mentioned most often were those of domestic origin, which was not so in the case of the French Parliament. The National Assembly of France and the European Parliament paid more attention to media from the country where the conflict was taking place. In particular, taking into account the Syrian media quoted, we have found significant differences [F (3, 796.793) = 11.221, $p < 0.001$] among the four parliaments studied. Dunnett's T3 post hoc test revealed that the European Parliament maintains significant differences with the Bundestag and the House of Commons (not with the National Assembly of France), and that the largest differences appeared when comparing the European Parliament with the Bundestag [$t_{SyrianMedia}$(899.591) = 5.385, $p < 0.001$, $d = 0.29$]. The size of this difference can be understood as medium.

The European Parliament paid attention to media of all national origins. But this was not the case for the other parliaments under consideration. Thus, the British Parliament only quoted Syrian, British and US media. And neither the British, French, nor German Parliament made any explicit mention of French media. Russian media is one of the most significant absences (M = 0.0, SD = 0.04) from the four Parliaments studied, especially when taking into consideration how important this international actor has been to the development of the Syrian Civil War. Finally, it is worth noting that BBC is the most cited specific media (M = 0.01, SD = 0.169).

Before describing the results of the qualitative analysis we carried out concerning the media presence during the Syrian conflict's CW crisis and how these mentions are related to the creation of agendas for action (RQ4), it is revealing to examine the documents in question quantitatively. To begin with, the parliament that presents the most minutes during the dates under consideration is the British (63%), followed by the European Parliament (24%). The British Parliament was also the first to convene a debate on the chemical weapons crisis (on August 29, 2013). Thus, with respect to the others: The debate on the situation in Syria in the post-CW crisis period took place on September 3 in the Bundestag (although it was not exclusively devoted to this issue); on September 4 in the French National Assembly; and on September 11 in the European Parliament. Although it is true that, due to the nature of parliamentary work and the summer recess, these dates do not a priori demonstrate the relative significance of the issue in each of the parliaments analysed, the urgency with which the British Prime Minister convened the House of Commons is revealing, especially since the MPs had to return from their summer holiday early.

Of the 49 documents selected, 24 (49%) lacked any direct or indirect reference to traditional or social media. As for traditional media (without taking into account explicit allusions to images, photographs or videos with no mention of the channel or media on which they were viewed), we found 48 references. In comparative terms, if we consider each of the parliaments studied during their first debate on the CW crisis, we can see that the average presence index of traditional media during the acts is markedly higher in the House of Commons (M = 1.28), the first to host such a debate, than it is in the European Parliament (M = 0.34), the French National Assembly (M = 0.1) or the Bundestag (M = 0.0).

With respect to the function that media performed in these debates, we found that it fulfilled two principle purposes. The first (43.75%) of these was to serve as a source of information on the conflict. Media are configured as actors, on the ground offering information about remote places to which MPs have no direct access and serving as investigative journalists, publishing leaks and even, by means of so-called thematic framing, helping to contextualize information at their disposal, thereby revealing to MPs information of which they would otherwise be unaware.

Willy Meyer (European Parliament, 2013–09–11): *And it is also necessary to keep in mind the journalists who are there, on the* ground. *You do not read what the journalists write because you are not interested, but there are journalists, including journalists from the BBC, who say they have met with victims, families, and that they have said: 'They gave us chemical substances from the Saudi Arabian intelligence agencies.'*[11]

Mr. Andrew Mitchell (House of Commons, 2013–08–29): *There are allegations in the press today about US intercepts of communications between members of the regime. As much of that evidence as possible should be exposed to give our constituents confidence in the Government's position.*

As for this role, it is significant that MPs lacked first-hand information, especially since that situation was worsened by the patent distrust which a sizeable number of MPs hold toward their intelligence services and the information that the latter provides them. The origins of the distrust can be found, as the MPs themselves have pointed out, in the information about the supposed weapons of mass destruction that led to the military intervention in Iraq, weapons which of course were never found.

Richard Ottaway (House of Commons, 2013–08–29): *On the intelligence, those of us who were here in 2003, at the time of the Iraq war, felt they had their fingers burnt. The case for war was made and Parliament was briefed on the intelligence, but we were given only part of the story and, in some cases, an inaccurate story.*

The second role (41.66%) that the communication media fulfils in these debates is to provide a public space where politicians can express their points of view and observe those of their colleagues and adversaries as they compete to shape public opinion. Drawing upon those interventions, MPs can consider other points of view as well as gather information provided by other politicians to the media, whether to strengthen their own ideas or to distance themselves from them. What appears certain is that communications media provide an important forum for political dialogue, thereby transcending linguistic, procedural and territorial borders.

Mr. Davis (House of Commons, 2013–08–29): *That brings me to the Deputy Prime Minister on the "Today" programme this morning, talking about chemical weapons and saying – let me quote him exactly – that it is "the first time in close to a century" that we have seen – in Syria, he means – "the ever more frequent use of chemical weapons." I recommend that he speaks to our American allies. The CIA has recently declassified and published its information on Iraq's use of chemical weapons in the Iran-Iraq war [...]. How will our stance now be seen on the Iranian street?*

M. Jean-Marc Ayrault, Prime Minister (National Assembly of France, 2013-09-04): *Many speakers have reminded us that France has a special responsibility [...]. This morning, I was reading an interview with one of my predecessors, Mr. Édouard Balladur, who was at this level, in a great tradition that is not a hawkish or adventurous one, but who wants us to defend our values [...] with the will to convince the French people to assume their responsibilities. Ladies and gentlemen, we must assume our responsibilities.*[12]

In any case, in their role as both an information source and a public space where political dialogue receives feedback, the media help MPs create the first element in those formulations known as 'agendas for action' or prospective discursive constructions that postulate specific goals which must still be achieved (Tenenboim-Weinblatt, 2013). Thus, a completed agenda for action construction consists of three elements: "A presentation of the present state or dynamic that cannot justifiably be left to itself; a future state that is desirable and attainable; and a set of more or less specific courses of action suitable to progress from the lamentable or precarious current to the desirable future state." (Baden & Tenenboim-Weinblatt, 2015, p. 2)

> Mark Simmonds (Westminster Hall, 2013-09-10): *My hon. Friend the Member for Stone made a powerful point about other countries around the world that are not signatories to the Rome statute, and the terrible atrocities in Syria, which we have seen on our television screens. I am sure that he is aware of the UK Government's position: those who perpetrated those horrific crimes should face justice.*

Furthermore, communications media also appear in acts of Parliament, to a lesser degree, as unreliable sources that offer biased information and leave out large swathes of reality, but also actors whose freedom of expression is under threat in countries experiencing conflict. Equally interesting in themselves are those interventions through which MPs express awareness of the impact that coverage has on political dynamics, expressing their interest in the ways the media reflect their actions or their concerns about how those same media have altered the terms of the debate.

> Sir Gerald Howarth (House of Commons, 2013-08-29): *Our long debate today has served two valuable purposes. First, it has served to underline the huge complexity of the issues before the House and the country. As one who came to the debate as a sceptic about military intervention, I have found it extremely useful and I hope that*

the country and the newspapers will have observed that Parliament is taking this issue very seriously.

M. Bruno Le Roux (National Assembly of France, 2013–09-04): *Finally, this debate, which is a valuable one, makes it possible to escape the frenzy of media time, its brevity, its shocks, its volatility, and return to political time. Yes, this time of debate allows us to ask complex questions, exchange our points of view and reflect together [...].*[13]

On the other hand, few direct mentions of social media were found in debates on the CW crisis. Only three interventions mentioned YouTube and only one social media in general. However, indirect allusions to numerous videos uploaded to the Internet thanks to social networks were mentioned a greater number of times (n = 12). Of these, in six interventions the videos are taken as irrefutable proof of the events and their authorship, while in the others mention is made of the verification exercises carried out by the intelligence services.

M. Jean-Marc Ayrault, Prime Minister (National Assembly of France, 2013–09-04: *Mr President, ladies and gentlemen, in the early hours of 21 August, a few kilometres from the centre of Damascus, nearly 1,500 civilians, including hundreds of children, died of asphyxiation as they slept. They were assassinated by the Syrian regime in what constitutes, at the beginning of the century, a most massive and terrifying use of chemical weapons. Each of us was able to discover these facts almost immediately after this drama with dozens of videos. Videos shot by doctors, neighbours, parents, both terrified and conscious of their duty to inform the world about the horror of what had just happened.*[14]

Mr. Newmark (House of Commons, 2013–08-29): *That chemical weapons have been used in Syria is in no doubt. The question is whether the regime itself delivered them. My understanding is that the intelligence drawn from eye-witness statements, video footage and electronic intercepts is extremely compelling.*

Relatedly, if we regard the mentions of videos, pictures and images (n = 31) as a whole, it would appear that references made about the emotions of the person behind the camera as well as others addressing those of their interlocutors (61.29%) are quite frequent, thus confirming the distinctly affective nature of this material.

Rainer Brüderle (Bundestag, 2013–09-03): *Other pictures of what happened in Syria are not published for good reasons. These pictures are more than depressing: They are nightmarish, they leave you unable to breathe.*[15]

> Mr. David Lammy (House of Commons, 2013–08–29): *A few days ago, I found myself rushing to switch off the television because my five and seven-year-old boys were in front of the news when it was showing images of men, women and children who had been gassed and were lying on the floor dead – they were in front of our eyes. It is impossible to have watched events unfold in Syria in the past few years and to have thought anything other than, 'If not now, when?' It is impossible to have watched the footage in the past week and not to have felt the instincts of liberal interventionism pulsating in our consciences.*

This high emotional pitch, as witnessed in the last example, can lead to the complete formulation of an agenda for action, or, in other words, to the enunciation of procedures to be used to improve the present situation (Baden & Tenenboim-Weinblatt, 2015). However, in general terms, the mentions of images and videos which appear in parliamentary debates contribute mainly to the exposure of a current unacceptable situation in the world or, in other words, they form the foundation upon which agendas for action are constructed.

> The Prime Minister, Mr. David Cameron (House of Commons, 2013–08–29): *The evidence that the Syrian regime has used these weapons, in the early hours of 21 August, is right in front of our eyes. We have multiple eye-witness accounts of chemical-filled rockets being used against opposition-controlled areas. We have thousands of social media reports and at least 95 different videos – horrific videos – documenting the evidence.*

Conclusions

The results of this investigation reveal that public opinion is mentioned more often than communication media and social networks in parliamentary debates, a fact that seems to correspond with the idea that parliaments are chosen directly by their constituents, to whom they are held accountable. In fact, in those parliamentary minutes involving the CW crisis, one can observe that MPs make several direct references to letters they have received from citizens and which even, on some occasions, serve as sources of information by means of which their constituents keep them abreast of the news.

As for traditional and social media, we observed that the former has a greater presence than the latter, although the differences between the two are only tendential. This suggests that, while MPs still place more trust in traditional media, new social media, as has been pointed out in previous studies, acquired great importance throughout the course of the conflict in Syria, in particular. This becomes equally clear after examining the diachronic evolution of the presence of traditional and social media in the conflict throughout the phase under consideration (January 2011–June 2015). Thus, during the early stages of the conflict, until the end of 2013, the results indicated how traditional media maintained a greater presence than social media in parliamentary debates, a hegemony that it lost after that period. The increasing danger to journalists posed by the Syrian War as it intensified over time and the use of social networks as propaganda tools by the Islamic State, which entered the fray in 2013, are both reasons for the heightened presence of social media in parliamentary debates. This is a matter of concern for future research.

The results obtained suggest that there are significant differences between the attention paid to traditional media and public opinion by the parliaments studied. However, this is not so in the case of social media, the presence of which is similar in all four houses. The fact that the European Parliament paid the most attention to both media and public opinion might be a sign that the institution was interested in those countries that played the leading role during the Arab Spring, but it also reveals a lack of consensus among member countries as to which policy they should adopt. This may have led MPs to search for greater support for their arguments by turning to the media and public opinion, by means of which they could also increase the scant interest that their institution arouses among European citizens (Scherpereel, Wohlgemuth, & Schmelzinger, 2017).

The diversity of the communications media referred to in the European Parliament also testifies to its supranational character. Conversely, the only media mentioned in the British Parliament were those originating in the country of conflict, in addition to national and American media, which reflects both the political orbit within which this house operates and the fact that it has no need to transcend that orbit, given the worldwide hegemony of English as a key instrument in international relations and global media. Here, too, it is notable that the media outlet that the group of parliaments mentioned most often was the BBC. On the other hand, that the French Parliament had the lowest number of references to public opinion may be due to the fact that matters of international politics are the responsibility of the President of the Republic and that French MPs therefore feel no need to render accounts on the topic to their constituents or shoulder the burden of socially controversial decisions, such as the kind of support for the intervention in Iraq given by their British counterparts in 2003.

One matter that proved especially interesting was the absence of Russian media from the European parliamentary debates we examined. As we have seen with respect to the CW crisis, the Russian press offered a completely different perspective to the one adopted by the countries of Western Europe and the US, both with respect to the authorship and dimensions of the Ghouta massacre. Russia, moreover, continues to support a Syrian regime that is perceived to be harmful to Western countries. The absence of any mention of Russian media thus constitutes an important strategic vacuum in the way European MPs gather and frame information, probably because MPs largely use communications media to support their arguments during debates.

This is precisely one of the conclusions we reached thanks to the qualitative analysis that was performed on parliamentary debates during the CW crisis. Communications media serve two main purposes when they are mentioned in debates; they are both sources of information about the conflict and they represent a communicative forum, where political and public dialogue about the issue take place. On the one hand, this makes it clear that MPs lack first-hand information and, on the other, it reveals the absence of direct channels of communication between politicians of both the country in question and the international scene, making it necessary to rely on these indirect pathways to exchange their points of view. The cognitive and relational dependence that MPs have on traditional communications media is clear evidence of the mediatization of the political actors and institutions.

As for the number of communications media mentioned during this phase of the conflict, we could confirm that traditional media had a greater presence and that this presence was more notable in the debate in the House of Commons, most likely because of the proximity of the chemical attack, the absence of contrasting information and a general uncertainty about how events would unfold at the international level. Once the British Parliament decided against a military intervention in the conflict – a clear demonstration of how important the parliamentarization of international affairs has now become – the impact on debates in the French Parliament and the Bundestag became more pronounced. References observed in these houses regarding not only the vote itself but also the type of decision made reveal that parliamentary agendas are also influenced by other parliaments in a feedback loop of forces which other essays should analyse.

Social networks doubtlessly had a strong influence during the CW crisis as well, especially YouTube, which hosted videos showing images of the attack, and to a lesser degree, Facebook and Twitter. Even though reference to these videos often gave speeches made by MPs greater emotional resonance, it cannot be concluded that this resonance led to the formulation of complete agendas for action. As in the case of traditional media, social networks contributed to the formulation of the first element in agendas for action, that is, to the presentation of a situation understood as unacceptable, without that necessarily being followed up by specific proposals for intervention. A deeper analysis of the issue, dealing with the conflict over a longer time span, would permit a more rigorous conclusion on the issue.

Notes

1 For a detailed description about how the concept of 'agendas for action' (e.g. demands for military intervention, diplomatic activities, or providing security for a population) has been understood within INFOCORE, see also Baden and Meyer in this volume and Stalpouskaya and Baden (2015).

2 The Islamic State of Iraq and Syria (designated a terrorist organization by the United Nations) https://en.wikipedia.org/wiki/Islamic_State_of_Iraq_and_the_Levant

3 This research was developed within the framework of the EU research project INFOCORE and received additional financial support from Spain's Ministry on Economy and Competitiveness (CSO2016-78187-R).

4 We analysed fewer texts in this chapter than were analysed in previous papers (see Herrero-Jiménez et al., 2018). This is because, as has been previously explained, the parliamentary documents in this case were filtered manually instead of automatically to ensure quality and the data's relevance to the object being analysed.

5 Westminster Hall's texts belong to the House of Commons. The former is an additional room inside the House of Commons where MPs spend extra time debating issues that matter to them.

6 http://jamcat.mscc.huji.ac.il/accounts/login/?next=/

7 The authors of this paper want to thank Christian Baden for developing the scripts and for his assistance with the analysis.

8 To accomplish the specific goals of this chapter, we did not just select the index terms based on an *a priori* categorization, but decided to use more specific terms and clean the *a priori* categorization terms from the dictionary for the sake of conceptual coherence. We also took the specific details of the conflict under consideration. As can be observed, the internal consistency of this indicator is also higher than it was in previous work (see Herrero-Jiménez et al., 2018). This is also due to the fact that the texts analysed were filtered manually, so the batches that underwent Cronbach's alpha analysis were slightly different.

9 European Media collects references to media from Italy, the Netherlands, Spain, Belgium, Portugal, Ireland, Luxembourg, Sweden, Norway, Finland, Estonia, Latvia, Lithuania, Poland, the Czech Republic, Slovakia, Slovenia, Hungary, Austria, Switzerland, Romania, Bulgaria, Cyprus and Malta. Media from Germany, the UK, France and Greece have their own entity in the dictionary.

10 We found different peaks and processes of evolution in the social media presence studied here compared to that found in previous work (see Herrero-Jiménez et al., 2018), especially during the early phase of the Syrian conflict. These differences result mainly from the fact that we manually filtered parliamentary documents to obtain more consistent data on the specific object of analysis.

11 Translation from Spanish by the authors. Text in its original language: *Y también hay que tener en cuenta a los periodistas que están allí, sobre el terreno. Ustedes no leen a los periodistas porque no les interesa, y hay periodistas, incluso periodistas de la BBC, que dicen que se han entrevistado con las víctimas, con las familias, y que estas han dicho: "nos entregaron unas sustancias químicas de parte de los servicios de inteligencia de Arabia Saudí".*

12 Translation from French by the authors. Text in its original language: *Beaucoup d'orateurs l'ont rappelé: la France a une responsabilité particulière [...]. Je lisais ce matin l'interview de l'un de mes prédécesseurs, M. Édouard Balladur, qui se situait à ce niveau, s'inscrivant dans une grande tradition*

qui n'a rien de belliciste ou d'aventurière, mais qui veut que nous défendi-
ons nos valeurs [...] avec la volonté de convaincre le peuple français d'as-
sumer ses responsabilités. Mesdames, messieurs les députés, nous devons
assumer nos responsabilités.

13 Translation from French by the authors. Text in its original language: *Enfin,*
ce débat, chose précieuse, permet d'échapper à la frénésie du temps média-
tique, à sa brièveté, à ses à-coups, à sa volatilité, pour revenir au temps du
politique. Oui, ce temps de débat permet de poser des questions complexes,
d'échanger nos points de vue et de réfléchir ensemble [...].

14 Translation from French by the authors. Text in its original language:
Monsieur le président, mesdames et messieurs les députés, aux premières
heures du 21 août, à quelques kilomètres du centre de Damas, près de 1
500 civils, dont des centaines d'enfants, sont morts asphyxiés dans leur
sommeil. Assassinés par le régime syrien dans ce qui constitue, en ce début
de siècle, le plus massif et le plus terrifiant usage de l'arme chimique. Ces
faits, chacun d'entre nous a pu les découvrir, presque immédiatement après
ce drame, sur des dizaines de vidéos. Des vidéos tournées par des médecins,
des voisins, des parents, à la fois terrifiés et conscients du devoir d'informer
le monde sur l'horreur de ce qui venait de se produire.

15 Translation from German by the authors. Text in its original language:
Andere Bilder von dem, was in Syrien geschehen ist, werden aus guten
Gründen nicht veröffentlicht. Diese Bilder sind mehr als bedrückend: Sie
sind beklemmend, sie nehmen einem die Luft weg.

References

Andén-Papadopoulos, K., & Pantti, M. (2013). The media work of Syrian diaspora activists: Brokering between the protest and mainstream media. *International Journal of Communication, 7,* 2185–2206.

Baden, C., & Tenenboim-Weinblatt, K. (2015). *INFOCORE definitions:*
"Agenda for Action". Jerusalem, Israel: The Hebrew University of Jerusalem.
Available online at www.infocore.eu/results/definitions/

Beetham, D. (2006). *Parliament and democracy in the twenty-first century: A*
guide to good practice. Geneva, Switzerland: Interparliamentary Union.

Blake, J., & Mahmud, A. (2013). A legal "red line"? Syria and the use of
chemical weapons in civil conflict. *UCLA Law Review Discourse, 61,*
244–260.

Bleek, P. C., & Kramer, N. J. (2016). Eliminating Syria's chemical weapons:
Implications for addressing nuclear, biological, and chemical threats. *The
Nonproliferation Review, 23,* 197–230.

Brown, J. D. (2015). "A nightmare painted by Goya": Russian media coverage
of the Syrian chemical weapons attacks in comparative perspective. *Problems
of Post-Communism, 62,* 236–246.

Cofelice, A. (2016). Parliamentary diplomacy and the Arab spring: Evidence
from the parliamentary assembly of the Mediterranean and the European
parliament. *Mediterranean Quarterly, 27,* 100–118.

Cohen, J. (1988). *Statistical power analysis for the behavioural sciences.* Hillsdale,
MI: Erlbaum.

Couldry, N. (2008). Mediatization or mediation? Alternative understandings
of the emergent space of digital storytelling. *New Media & Society, 10,*
373–391.

Cozma, R., & Kozman, C. (2015). The Syrian crisis in the news: How the United States' elite newspapers framed the international reaction to Syria's use of chemical weapons. *Journalism Practice, 9,* 669–686.

Dandashly, A. (2016). The European Union's response to the Syrian conflict. Too little, too late.... *Global Affairs, 2,* 397–400.

Davis, A. (2007). Investigating journalist influences on political issue agendas at Westminster. *Political Communication, 24,* 181–199.

Gaffney, J. (2014). Political leadership and the politics of performance: France, Syria and the chemical weapons crisis of 2013. *French Politics, 12,* 218–234.

Geis, A., & Schlag, G. (2017). 'The facts cannot be denied': Legitimacy, war and the use of chemical weapons in Syria. *Global Discourse, 7,* 285–303.

Harkin, J. (2013). Is it possible to understand the Syrian revolution through the prism of social media? *Westminster Papers in Communication and Culture, 9*(2), 93–112.

Herrero-Jiménez, B., Arcila Calderón, C., Carratalá, A., & Berganza, R. (2018). The impact of media and NGOs on four European parliament discourses about conflicts in the Middle East. *Media, War & Conflict, 11,* 65–84.

Jungblut, M., Carratalá, A., & Herrero, B. (2017). Media, parliaments and NGOs in the Israeli-Palestinian conflict. In C. George (Ed.), *Communicating with power* (pp. 46–66). New York, NY: Peter Lang.

Kaarbo, J., & Kenealy, D. (2014). *The House of Commons' vote on British intervention in Syria.* ISPI Studies. Available online at www.ispionline.it/sites/default/files/pubblicazioni/analysis_228_2013.pdf

Kaarbo, J., & Kenealy, D. (2017). Precedents, parliaments, and foreign policy: Historical analogy in the House of Commons vote on Syria. *West European Politics, 40,* 62–79.

Kase, S. E., Bowman, E. K., Al Amin, T., & Abdelzaher, T. (2014). *Exploiting social media for army operations: Syrian civil war use case.* Army Research Laboratory. Available online at www.dtic.mil/get-tr-doc/pdf?AD=ADA603685

Klausen, J. (2015). Tweeting the Jihad: Social media networks of Western foreign fighters in Syria and Iraq. *Studies in Conflict & Terrorism, 38,* 1–22.

Larsen, A. G. (2017). Investigative reporting in the networked media environment: Journalists' use of social media in reporting violent extremism. *Journalism Practice, 11,* 1198–1215.

Lieber, P. S., & Reiley, P. J. (2016). Countering ISIS's social media influence. *Special Operations Journal, 2,* 47–57.

Lynch, M., Freelon, D., & Aday, S. (2014). Syria's socially mediated civil war. *United States Institute of Peace, 91,* 1–35.

Makdisi, K., & Pison Hindawi, C. (2017). The Syrian chemical weapons disarmament process in context: Narratives of coercion, consent, and everything in between. *Third World Quarterly, 38*(8), 1–19.

Mast, J., & Hanegreefs, S. (2015). When news media turn to citizen-generated images of war: Transparency and graphicness in the visual coverage of the Syrian conflict. *Digital Journalism, 3,* 594–614.

Mello, P. A. (2017). Curbing the royal prerogative to use military force: The British House of Commons and the conflicts in Libya and Syria. *West European Politics, 40,* 80–100.

Norton, P. (2017). Speaking for parliament. *Parliamentary Affairs, 70*, 191–206.

Peifer, D. (2016). Why Germany won't be dropping bombs on Syria, Iraq or Mali. *Orbis, 60*, 266–278.

Portela, C. (2012). *The EU's sanctions against Syria: Conflict management by other means.* Security Policy Brief No. 38. Available online at http://aei.pitt.edu/39406/1/SPB38

Rane, H., & Salem, S. (2012). Social media, social movements and the diffusion of ideas in the Arab uprisings. *Journal of International Communication, 18*, 97–111.

Rashed, H. (2016). UK parliamentary debate analysis: Bombing ISIL in Syria. *Medicine, Conflict and Survival, 32*, 93–111.

Rohde, M., Aal, K., Misaki, K., Randall, D., Weibert, A., & Wulf, V. (2016). Out of Syria: Mobile media in use at the time of civil war. *International Journal of Human-Computer Interaction, 32*, 515–531.

Russell, M., & Cowley, P. (2016). The policy power of the Westminster parliament: The "Parliamentary State" and the empirical evidence. *Governance, 29*, 121–137.

Scherpereel, J. A., Wohlgemuth, J., & Schmelzinger, M. (2017). The adoption and use of twitter as a representational tool among members of the European Parliament. *European Politics and Society, 18*, 111–127.

Seeberg, P. (2015). The EU and the Syrian crisis: The use of sanctions and the regime's strategy for survival. *Mediterranean Politics, 20*, 18–35.

Soroka, S. N. (2003). Media, public opinion, and foreign policy. *The International Journal of Press/Politics, 8*, 27–48.

Stalpouskaya, K., & Baden, C. (2015). *To do or not to do: The role of agendas for action in analyzing news coverage of violent conflict.* In ACL-IJCNLP Annual Meeting 2015. Beijing, China. Available online at www.aclweb.org/anthology/W15-4504

Stavridis, S. (2016a). The European Parliament's contribution to the R2P debate: Lessons from the Libyan and Syrian conflicts. *Global Affairs, 2*, 187–201.

Stavridis, S. (2016b). The French parliament and the conflicts in Libya and Syria. *Mediterranean Quarterly, 27*(4), 21–41.

Stavridis, S., & Molina, I. F. (2013). The European parliament and the conflict in Libya (2011): An efficient moral platform? *Revista CIDOB d'Afers Internacionals, 153*(101), 153–176.

Stavridis, S., & Pace, R. (2011). Assessing the impact of the EMPA's parliamentary diplomacy in international conflicts: Contribution or obstacle? In G. Garzón Clariana (Ed.), *La asamblea Euromediterránea – The Euro-Mediterranean assembly – L'assemblée Euro-Mediterranéenne* (pp. 59–105). Madrid, Spain: Marcial Pons.

Strömbäck, J. (2011). Mediatization of politics: Towards a conceptual framework of comparative research. In E. P. Bucy & R. L. Holbert (Eds.), *Sourcebook for political communication research: Methods, measures, and analytical techniques* (pp. 367–382). New York, NY: Routledge.

Strong, J. (2015a). Interpreting the Syria vote: Parliament and British foreign policy. *International Affairs, 91*, 1123–1139.

Strong, J. (2015b). Why parliament now decides on war: Tracing the growth of the parliamentary prerogative through Syria, Libya and Iraq. *The British Journal of Politics and International Relations, 17*, 604–622.

Tenenboim-Weinblatt, K. (2013). Bridging collective memories and public agendas: Toward a theory of mediated prospective memory. *Communication Theory, 23*, 91–111.

Veilleux-Lepage, Y. (2016). Retweeting the Caliphate: The role of soft sympathizers in the Islamic State's social media strategy. *Turkish Journal of Security Studies, 18*, 53–69.

Vliegenthart, R., Walgrave, S., Baumgartner, F. R., Bevan, S., Breunig, C., Brouard, S. et al. (2016). Do the media set the parliamentary agenda? A comparative study in seven countries. *European Journal of Political Research, 55*, 283–301.

Walgrave, S., Soroka S., & Nuytemans, M. (2008). The mass media's political agenda-setting power: A longitudinal analysis of media, parliament, and government in Belgium (1993 to 2000). *Comparative Political Studies, 41*, 814–836.

Walgrave, S., & Van Aelst, P. (2006). The contingency of the mass media's political agenda setting power: Toward a preliminary theory. *Journal of Communication, 56*, 88–109.

5 #iProtest

The Case of the *Colourful Revolution* in Macedonia

Dimitra Dimitrakopoulou and Sergios Lenis

Introduction

Social media are transforming how people transmit and share information, while at the same time providing the tools for building innovative structures and organizing and mobilizing different actors. These sweeping shifts have intensified the discussion of the actual role of social media in contemporary conflict-ridden societies, particularly after the protests in Iran (2009), Tunisia (2010) and Egypt (2011), as well as the subsequent Arab Spring movements. Changing dynamics between political actors, journalists and citizens, mainly through social networking platforms, have stimulated several claims for the transformation of these actors' relations as well as for the facilitation of new forms of political participation. While the actual impact of social media on the transformation of politics remains debatable, the unquestionable massive popularity of social networks in modern societies and the profound changes in information flows via online social media are challenging the timelines of mediated political participation in the globalized contemporary world.

In our analysis, we highlight a series of technological, organizational and communication shifts that have influenced information and communication flows and structures, as well as interrelations and interactions between different actors (politicians and political groups, journalists, users/audiences, NGOs) who were until recently heavily reliant on the mediating role of journalists and the media. In this chapter, we focus on social media and networks and their role in societies during times of social and political unrest by examining the *Colourful Revolution*, a social movement that was triggered during the ongoing political crisis in Macedonia that has swept through the country since 2015. The case of the 2016 Macedonian protests has been chosen as an example of the manifestation of a social protest that engaged a large number of active citizens and was extensively mediated and remediated through social media. In what follows, we provide a theoretical overview of the role of social networks in contemporary social movements and conflict-ridden societies, illustrating a typology of social media and networks that focuses on their dynamic functions on the levels of dissemination, diffusion and organization. The next sections, on the one hand, describe the current state of social media use in the country and, on the other, provide a framework for conceptualizing and understanding the development of the studied social movement in the country, both offline and online. The research design and methodology are explicitly described in the respective section, while the following section on results and findings elaborates on the selected case study. The chapter is concluded with a detailed discussion contextualizing the use of social media in the selected social movement while also illustrating the emerging patterns associated with the study of social movements at the global level, aiming to investigate their performance in the digital ecosystem.

Social Networks in Conflictual Collective Allotments

In the last few years, we have witnessed an increasingly heated debate among scholars, politicians and journalists regarding the role of the Internet in contemporary social movements and conflict-affected societies. Social media appear to be ideal tools for the creation of new opportunities for social movements. Social networking platforms allow protestors to collaborate easily, which enables them to quickly organize and disseminate messages across the globe. By enabling fast, easy and low-cost diffusion of protest ideas, tactics and strategies, social media and networks allow social movements to overcome problems historically associated with collective mobilization (Ayres, 1999).

Particularly after 2009 and the revolutionary wave of the Arab Spring, there has been considerable evidence advocating the empowering, liberating and yet engaging potential of online social media and networks (Cardwell, 2009; Christensen, 2009; Cohen, 2009; Schectman, 2009). Social media and networks are built on a pattern of online communities of people who may be driven by collective action or interacting/debating on a shared topic of interest or conflict.[1] Within digital networks, 'networked publics' (Ito, 2008) act, interact and react, forming emerging publics who create powerful communities in order to resist hegemonic publics. Powerful communities emerge, particularly when audiences come together around shared understandings of the world (Boyd, 2014). In conflict-afflicted societies, social media can prove vital for communication among the actors involved, as in the case of the Arab Spring where social media were of great significance for the coordination, scheduling and communication of demonstrations against authoritarian leaders. The dynamics of social networks highlight the possibilities provided through the multimodal networking function of social movements, which include social networks online and offline, as well as pre-existing social networks, and networks formed during the actions of the movement (Castells, 2012).

The following sections illustrate a typology of social media and networks focusing on their possible mechanisms within the "collective allotment" (Gauntlett, 2011, p. 4) on three distinct, yet interconnected, levels: (1) dissemination: alternative information providers/sources; (2) diffusion: direct and interactive communication channels; and (3) organization: self-organized participatory networks for mobilization purposes. The selected case of the *Colourful Revolution* in Macedonia will be studied against the typology employed and further analysed in light of the concept of digitally networked action (DNA) and connective action, as introduced by Bennett and Segerberg (2012) and further elaborated by Papacharissi (2015).

Dissemination Mechanism: Alternative Information Providers/Sources

Social media have substantially increased levels of information dissemination in all contexts of conflict. In a conflict environment, individuals or collective groups can act as on-the-spot reporters and first-hand witnesses capable of producing their own news stories, thus bypassing the mediating role of journalists. The example of the Syrian Civil War, which has been illustrated as the most socially mediated conflict in history, is indicative of the fact that social media not only kept citizens in the rest of the world informed about the latest developments in the country; they also provided crucial knowledge to foreign governments concerning the actors on the ground (Aday, Farrell, Lynch, Sides, & Freelon, 2012).

News is transformed into a participatory activity to which people can contribute their own stories and experiences and their reactions to events; the fact that such items can be directly transmitted through available online tools turns them into alternative and first-hand sources for professional journalists. In this manner, the public becomes involved in determining (and configuring) the news agenda, not only by producing original content, but also by making critical contributions to the definition of the news agenda set by mainstream media. The transformation of interactions among political actors, journalists and citizens through new technologies has created conditions conducive to the emergence of a distinct form of professional journalism, also known as citizen, participatory or alternative journalism. Citizen journalism can be of vital importance for conflict-ridden societies, particularly in countries with undemocratic regimes and few civil liberties (Bock, 2012). It puts forward a different model for selecting and using sources, as it involves a reallocation of power – power that does not come exclusively from official, conventional institutions. At the same time, it proposes an alternative use of sources, as individuals are in a position to directly describe their first-hand experiences, thus challenging professional journalistic standards of detached and objective reporting (Atton, 2009). While mainstream media rely extensively on elite groups, alternative media can offer a wider range of "voices" wanting to be heard.

Citizen reporting may prove very effective in cases of exposing oppression by governments or broadcasting violence between groups of different identities, as well as during conflict escalation cases, where extreme measures of censorship may be imposed by totalitarian regimes. Social media add capacity to social movements and allow protesters to communicate and coordinate in ways that were not possible before (Bock, 2012). While social media appear in specific cases and conflict environments and are influential in terms of a shift towards citizen power, the extent of their influence remains an issue worth exploring (Seib, 2012). Bock (2012) is a helpful resource in this context, as it provides an overview of the use of social media in the creation of 'smart crowds' and their effectiveness in conflict early warning and early response, especially when combined with building trust networks, community organizing and bounded crowd feeding.

Diffusion Mechanism: Direct and Interactive Communication Channels

The distributed, dynamic and fluid structure of social media enables users to circumvent professional and political restrictions on news production (Wolfsfeld, Segev, & Sheafer, 2013) and allows direct communication between political and social actors and citizens, free from the norms and structural constraints of conventional journalism (Stromer-Galley & Jamieson, 2001). This revolutionary transgression of mediation reallocates power from the exclusive information and communication function of journalists and the media into the hands of ordinary people. The role of social media in providing exclusive and unfiltered content during protests or riots validates their value as direct and interactive communication channels, e.g. by connecting Western and Arab individuals to participants in the case of the Arab uprisings, identifying protestors in Tahrir Square in Cairo, Egypt, or watching horrific videos of civilians murdered in Syria and Libya (Aday et al., 2012).

Social media have created new, direct and interactive communication channels that can bypass the hierarchical filters of the traditional mass media, which used to heavily rely on established institutions and authority figures for information, and create direct and influential linkages between single and anonymous users or organized citizen groups and mainstream mass media. In this manner, the gatekeeping function of the mass media is challenged as new players enter the field, players who are potentially capable of making direct contact with interested political and social actors. At the same time, mainstream media increasingly broadcast online videos produced by citizen journalists rather than their own correspondents for real-time and on-the-ground reporting of the protests in Tunisia and Egypt (Khamis & Vaughn, 2011). Hence, social media may directly provide, through their own channels, unfiltered and unmediated original content that is not only shared between protestors and civilians in respective countries, but with the international community as well.

Organization Mechanism: Connective Action Platforms

Social media platforms have taken on a leading role as communication and mobilization tools in the development and coordination of contemporary social movements in conflict-ridden societies.[2] Social media appear as aspiring tools for the creation of new opportunities for social movements and self-organized protest networks by offering low-cost forms of participation, promoting collective identity and creating a sense of community (Garrett, 2006). In many conflict cases, digital media tools are integral to the operations of activists and combatants, being used to organize and mobilize forces and demonstrations and to create media content so as to influence the outcome of conflict. Social networking platforms allow political action to be organized on a scale and at a rapidity never before possible. By enabling the fast, easy and low-cost diffusion of protest ideas, tactics and strategies, as well as by facilitating group formation, recruitment and retention and by improving group efficiency, social media and networks allow social movements to overcome problems historically associated with collective mobilization (Ayres, 1999).

The organizational potential of social movements through online networks should be critically studied through their collective and connective action. While connective action captures the dynamic and fluid relations of interconnected crowds, which may form temporary links in the virtual online sphere (Papacharissi, 2015), it is also vital for fulfilling the movement's objectives in serving a certain cause and achieving collective impact. In this light, it is important to discern between movements that utilize social networks into tools that: (1) help mobilization and interaction in cases where no other infrastructure is possible; (2) are used only temporarily just to push a specific agenda forward and (3) are used in parallel to their acts/mobilization on the ground.

The concept of DNA, as articulated by Bennett and Segerberg (2012), works well in understanding contemporary networks at the scale of contentious political action and can be further employed to interpret the two inherent logics of collective action and connective action. While the former is a well-established approach of the organizational structures of contentious politics, the latter remains a less familiar concept that proves increasingly relevant and suitable for the study of large-scale protests based on personalized content production and sharing through social networks and networking dynamics that keep accelerating. Connective action is fundamentally built on personalized reactions to political issues, whether old or new, which are then transformed into broader topics disseminated and shared via personal communication technologies (Papacharissi, 2015). The next section focuses on the use of social media and networks in the country under study.

Social Networking Performance in Macedonia

In a country where the media have been at the heart of acute political instability in recent years, the rise of the Internet as a primary news source has expanded the range and scope of media/public voices, while the rapid growth of broadband connections has accelerated social networking activity in the country; this has resulted in an increase in the number and range of available news sources, particularly international ones, and in issues that are generally neglected or underreported in Macedonian media outlets (Belicanec & Ricliev, 2012). Internet penetration in Macedonia is 72.16%, while mobile use is also high at 98.52%, thus enabling the extensive use of social media (International Communications Union, 2016). Given the respective percentages in neighbouring Balkan countries and the fragile domestic political and economic conditions, the figures on Internet and mobile use and connectivity are quite high.

In a study conducted in Macedonia in 2015 led by INFOCORE's principal researcher, Snezana Trpevska and Anke Fiedler (2016), with a sample of 923 participants, content posted on social media is the third most used source of information (41.1%) for local audiences (Table 5.1). According to Trpevska & Fiedler, social networks and news websites are among the most used sources of information about conflict events in countries where Internet technology has reached high penetration. It seems that, at times of uncertainty, audiences tend to check the information received from traditional media, these being the most frequently used sources (television or radio, respectively). People compare different sources whenever possible, and, in fact, read or rely on what their friends post or comment on social networks about recent events.

Information received from social networks is considered quite reliable, since one in three participants (33.5%) considers online content "quite credible". In the very fragmented media landscape of Macedonia, in times of tension, traditional media (Table 5.2) are sought less frequently than social networks since the former may be perceived as politically manipulated and often inaccessible to the public (Trpevska & Fiedler, 2016). Although later in the year the country was associated with the massive production of fake news on social media, which mostly favoured the Republican candidate for US President Donald Trump, our study monitored a much earlier period of this phenomenon. In what follows, we provide a detailed contextual information on the rise and evolvement of the *Colourful Revolution* in Macedonia.

Table 5.1 Media activities on a daily basis

Every and almost every day (N = 923)	%
News on TV channels from Macedonia	74.5
Discuss with different people (relatives, friends, etc.)	57.5
News and comments written by my friends on social networks	41.1
News websites (including news aggregators)	31.5
News from links I found on social networks	31.3
News on regional TV channels and TV channels from neighbouring countries	15.1
News on the radio	14.3
Newspapers	10.2
News watched on international TV channels (CNN, BBC, DW)	4.7

Table 5.2 Interaction with media on a weekly basis

1-3 times/week (N = 923)	%
Comments posted on social networks	10.9
Share information on SN	16.2
Comments posted on news websites	7.2
Participate in call-in shows on TV or radio	1.0
Talk with friends and colleagues	68.0
Send letters to newsrooms	1.0

'I Protest' for Justice, Freedom and Democracy

The *Colourful Revolution* is rooted in the political crisis that arose in the country in May 2015, when protests began in Skopje, the capital of Macedonia, against the Prime Minister, Nikola Gruevski, and his government, who were being accused of having wiretapped over 20,000 people, while there was also evidence of corruption scandals involving ministers, mayors and other persons and a cover-up of a young man's murder by the police in 2011. In the months that followed, several ministers resigned during the protests, a transitional government was formed in October 2015 and Gruevski, finally, resigned in January 2016. After six months of turmoil, the country reached a point of equilibrium with the introduction of the Pržino Agreement, which was reached between the main political parties in the Republic of Macedonia, with mediation by the European Union. The main objectives of the Pržino Agreement were the participation of the Opposition party, *SDSM*, in some ministries, the early resignation of Prime Minister Nikola Gruevski in January 2016, a caretaker government to lead the country until general elections in June 2016, as well as a special prosecutor to lead investigations into crimes highlighted by the wiretapping scandal.[3]

Protests, however, were sparked off again in early April 2016 against the President, Gjorgje Ivanov, and the government led by interim Prime

Minister Emil Dimitriev, from the ruling *VMRO-DPMNE* party, after the controversial decision taken by President Gjorge Ivanov to par-
don 56 politicians and businessmen, most of whom were connected
with the ruling party and facing corruption charges. Dubbed the
'*I Protest*' movement on social media, thousands of demonstrators
marched against political corruption, the government's wire-tapping
scandal and presidential pardons. The country entered a second year
in turmoil. Demonstrations were organized by '*Protestiram*' (I protest) and supported by a coalition led by the *Social Democratic Union
of Macedonia* and other opposition parties. Further events included
the newly formed *Levica* (The Left) demanding the government's
resignation, the formation of a technical government and cancella-
tion of the parliamentary elections planned for June 5, 2016 on the
grounds that the conditions for free and transparent elections were
not in place. The government and its supporters, who had organized
pro-government rallies, claimed that the June 5 elections were the
only solution to the political crisis. Initially taking place in Skopje,
the capital, both anti- and pro-government protests were held across
the country, in Bitola, Kicevo, Strumica, Kumanovo and Tetovo. The
European Union and the US criticized the government of Macedonia
for pardoning politicians and stated that Macedonia's prospects of
becoming a member of the EU and NATO were under threat because
of this act.[4]

The *Colourful Revolution* belongs to the category of the so-called
'colour revolutions' that have mostly used non-violence; they are also
called civil resistance, employing protest methods such as demonstrations, strikes and urban interventions. Such movements strongly oppose
corrupt or authoritarian governments and strive to advocate democracy
and the need for change; they usually employ colour as a symbol, as
seen in the *Yellow Revolution* (Philippines, 1986), *Orange Revolution*
(Ukraine, 2004–2005) and *Green Revolution* (Iran, 2009–2010). In the
case of the *Colourful Revolution*, there is also a clear reference to activists' splattering paint on government buildings and state-funded statues
that they regard as symbols of widespread corruption.[5]

The current case study was selected for this edited volume due to its
role in the political and institutional stability of a Balkan country that
has long suffered interethnic conflict. While the utilization of social media in social movements and violent conflicts in the Middle East (e.g.
Syria, Egypt, Israel) has been extensively studied, the Balkans remain
a rather understudied area. Our aim in this chapter is to investigate the
role of social media and networks in the case of Macedonia and to analyse the power of networks within the specific conflictual context. Twitter
is selected as an ambient, dynamic – in terms of social connectivity –
platform and a hybrid information ecosystem that "discursively actu-
alises as an electronic one elsewhere" (Papacharissi, 2015, p. 70). As
Bennett, Segerberg and Walker (2014) argue, Twitter has developed

stitching mechanisms that connect different networks into coherent organizations though peer production, curation and dynamic integration of various types of information content and other resources that become distributed and utilized across the crowd.

Research Design and Methodology

To monitor the full development of the *Colourful Revolution* movement, we followed the Twitter stream for over three and a half months, while the movement lasted (see Figure 5.1 for a step-by-step presentation of the analytical process). First, we started by studying printed and broadcast news material in both local and international media reporting on the protests. At the same time, we followed the development of the conflict on Twitter by identifying trending hashtags that emerged during the events. Both processes enabled us to identify a curated list of prominent hashtags (#шаренареволуција, #Шаренатареволуција, #colourfulrevolution, #colorfulrevolution, #skopje, #Macedonia, #Македонија, #protest, #Iprotest and #ШарамПравдаБарам) and keywords (Zaev, SDSM, Ivanov, VMRO-DPMNE, Skopje, Bitola, Strumica, Kumanovo, Prilep, Kočani, Stip, Tetovo, Gruevski, Заев, Иванов, Скопје, Битола, Струмица, Куманово, Прилеп, Кочани, Штип, Тетово, Груевски), which were associated with the protests and the specific period of unrest, namely from April 12, 2016 to July 27, 2016. To be exact, the collection of tweets was performed following a two-pronged approach. At first, tweet IDs were collected directly through Twitter's front-end search function. Then we collected the full tweets using Twitter's API for these tweet IDs.

Data collected resulted in a total set of 141,648 tweets. At this stage, it was important for our analysis to carefully 'clean' our dataset of irrelevant content. Such content may emerge from Internet bots or spamming users that try to manipulate trending hashtags and distract attention from what is really important and relevant in a Twitter thread. For the filtering part of our process, we produced lists of: (1) most used keywords in the dataset; (2) most important users in terms of tweeting frequency and volume and (3) most mentioned users. After extensive manual checking of the relevance of keywords to the conflict studied, as well as employing a detailed qualitative user identification process, we used programming scripts to remove irrelevant content and resulted in a narrower but targeted dataset of approximately 89,706 tweets, which were further analysed using content and frequency analysis.

The textual content of the filtered dataset was transcribed into coded text, using a computer-assisted dictionary-based approach, comprising more than 3,700 unique concepts, ranging from actors, places and events to activities, objects, relations and qualities (Baden, 2014).[6] Using topic modelling analysis, we used the dictionary as a library to trace prominent keywords, which were organized in clusters so as to identify key

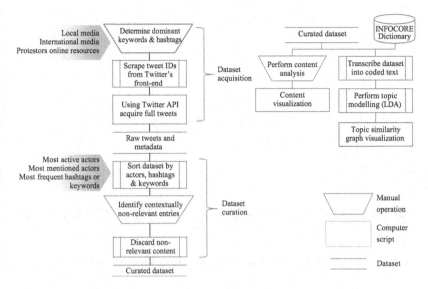

Figure 5.1 Flow chart of the steps of the study.

concepts in the Twitter debate. Latent Dirichlet allocation[7] was applied indicating the five most prominent topics. Finally, the model was visualized as a graph connecting tweet-related topics with tweet-hashtags based on topic similarity. In short, for every tweet, keywords were represented as the topic to which they belonged and connected to hashtags belonging to that tweet. This way we were able to identify the co-occurring keywords that emerged from the debate within the timeline studied, group them into clustered and coherent topics and, ultimately, link them to their corresponding hashtags.

Results and Findings

The first step in our analysis consisted of identifying and monitoring prominent trends in the stream by following leading hashtags in the Twitter debate. First, the data were analysed in order to study content evolving online as visible spikes in its production. The content was further collated with a detailed timeline of events in the country, which resulted after systematic monitoring of media content and audio-visual material released during the Macedonian protests (Figure 5.2).

Demonstrations began on April 12, 2016, triggering a debate on Twitter.[8] More actions occurred on April 14, when five police officers were injured by people throwing rocks at them and one protestor was detained. This is the first visible spike in the stream, followed by a second spike on April 18, when it was reported that more than 10,000 people

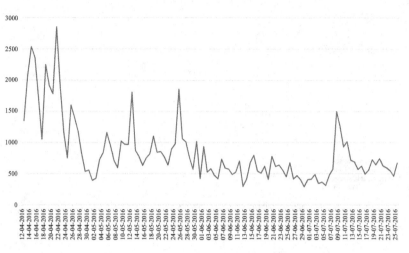

Figure 5.2 Time series of total tweets between April 12, 2016 and July 27, 2016.

took part in demonstrations in Skopje, with protests also being held in other cities of Macedonia, such as Bitola, Strumica and Veles. The protest on April 19 began in front of the special prosecutor's office, proceeded to Parliament and was stopped by police before reaching the EU mission. Several thousand people turned out for demonstrations on the eighth day of the protest, April 20. At this point, splattering coloured paints[9] at various governmental buildings and monuments of the Skopje 2014 project had become a regular feature of protests,[10] and the term '*Colourful Revolution*' gained popularity among protesters and on social media.[11] After eight days of protests, journalists began referring to such events as the '*Colourful Revolution*', Kristina Ozimec's article for *Deutsche Welle* being the first one to use the term.[12]

On April 21, two rallies took place near each other in Skopje, each attended by thousands of people. One was an anti-government event, organized by the *SDSM* and the *Protestiram* ('I Protest') organization, while the second one was organized by *Citizens' Movement for Defence of Macedonia* (GDOM, in Macedonian), supported by the ruling *VMRO* party. That was the day when the debate peaked in the stream, attracting increasing attention on social media and indicating two clashing rallies. The anti-government protest started in front of the special prosecutor's building, where protestors shouted, "No Justice No Peace" and "Support the SJO" (special prosecution). The pro-government protestors shouted, "No one can harm you, Nikola" and carried anti-NATO banners.

On April 23, anti-government protests continued in several cities in the country. The next day, Zdravko Saveski, a member of the collective presidency of the left-wing party *Levica* (the Left), and another member of the same party were placed under house arrest. The protests organized by *Protestiram* ('I Protest') and supported by the opposition and non-governmental organizations continued in several cities, and between 15,000 and 20,000 demonstrators in Skopje protested in front of the Parliament and several government ministries.

On April 25, a large pro-government rally occurred in Bitola, organized by *Citizens' Movement for Defence of Macedonia* (GDOM in Macedonian), with thousands in attendance. They rallied in support of the parliamentary elections scheduled for June 5. On that day (April 25), the stream started to abate. In the following days, several anti-government protests began in several other Macedonian cities.

On May 12, demonstrators protested in various cities across the country and the debate started to peak again.[13] In Skopje, thousands of demonstrators protested[14] in front of the home of the former prime minister and the leader of *VMRO-DPMNE*. The anti-government protests continued, and on May 14, there were anti-government protests in 12 cities. May 25 was the last visible peak in the debate. On May 26, the Macedonian media released news that the next day, in Parliament, a procedure would begin to impeach President Ivanov; this was supported by the main Opposition party, *SDSM*, and other parties from the Opposition coalition. From that point on, and towards the final phase of the conflict, the discussion reached moderate levels and then started to gain visibility in early July, when political negotiations started, ending on July 20 and August 31, 2016, with an agreement of the four largest political parties in Macedonia to hold early elections on December 11, 2016, under a deal brokered by the European Union and the US so as to resolve the political crisis.[15]

The frequency analysis captured 89,706 multilingual tweets, Macedonian and English being the most frequently used languages. The analysis traced what was being tweeted when and monitored the unfolding online debate during the time period examined. While the distribution of languages is not surprising, monitoring the languages across the timeline studied reveals an interesting pattern. In the beginning of the upheaval, the leading language was Macedonian, as expected, followed by English. This trend started during the first days of the uprising and then peaked on April 21, when the two rallies were held near each other in Skopje, one anti-governmental, organized by the *SDSM* and the *Protestiram* ('I Protest') organization, the other supported by the ruling *VMRO* party and organized by the *Citizens for Macedonian Defense*. However, in early May the debate balanced between Macedonian and English and then shifted towards English on May 12, when demonstrations swept through the country and protests started attracting greater international attention (Figure 5.3).

Figure 5.4 records the 30 most active users, that is, those who tweeted most frequently during the timeline studied. A systematic examination of

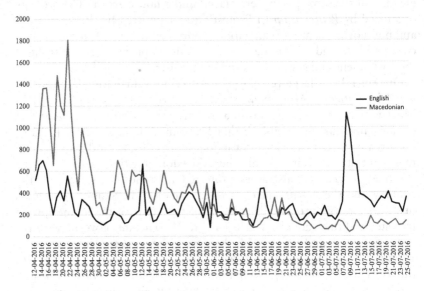

Figure 5.3 Timeline of used languages.

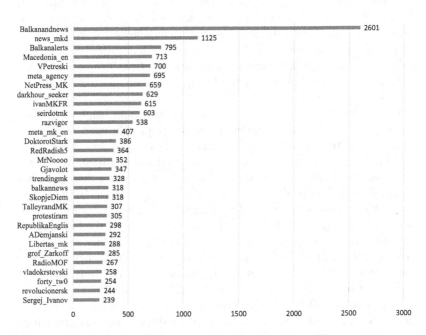

Figure 5.4 Most active users (tweeted most during the studied timeline).

their profiles on Twitter revealed several formal and institutional media and political organizations, groups of protesters, bloggers and activists reporting on events, and people following the events at the national or international level and expressing solidarity with protestors. Statistics reveal two main clusters of users: (1) domestic or regional media reporting or commenting on an event (e.g. Balkanandnews, Balkanalerts, NET_PressMK, balkannews) and (2) citizens/activists taking part in the movement or sharing information about the events (e.g. darkhour_seeker, razvigor, Gjavolot, TalleyrandMK). Interestingly enough, no political actors are found among the top 30 users, indicating a lack of engagement by politicians in commenting on events or addressing some of the major political issues at stake during this event-packed time period.

However, the order of actors changed when proceeding with identifying the most frequently referred to users and those that emerged as more visible during the period studied (Table 5.3). In contrast to the previous ranking, actors associated with the ongoing events rank high in the list. Three main clusters of actors involved can be traced here: (1) activists/citizens and blogs reporting on the protests; (2) domestic and foreign media, the latter being most mentioned and (3) political actors ranging from national political actors to EU actors. Reference to specific political actors mainly concerned addressing those actively involved in the events and seen as the protagonists or attributing political accountability.

Table 5.3 List of most mentioned users (@)

	Users	Times mentioned	Role
1	RedRadish5	457	activist/blogger
2	nedavimobgd	191	blog
3	AmbBaily	181	political actor
4	JHahnEU	178	EU actor
5	dwnews	173	media
6	SDSMakedonija	170	political party
7	protestiram	152	movement
8	Zoran_Zaev	146	political actor
9	VMRO_DPMNE	144	political party
10	FedericaMog	123	EU actor
11	SPIEGELONLINE	110	media
12	usembassymkd	97	political actor
13	BalkanInsight	94	media
14	Gjavolot	87	citizen
15	Libertas_mk	82	blog
16	AmbassadorEU	81	EU actor
17	Kaliopi_KMP	80	citizen
18	Portalbmk	75	media
19	BritAmbCGarrett	74	political actor
20	darkhour_seeker	73	citizen
21	BBCWorld	71	media
22	dw_macedonian	66	media
23	MKColorful	65	movement

(Continued)

	Users	Times mentioned	Role
24	CNN	63	media
25	realDonaldTrump	60	political actor
26	razvigor	51	citizen
27	LOshGZE	49	citizen
28	GruevskiNikola	47	politician
29	VlatkoVasilj	46	citizen
30	mindplumber	44	citizen
31	filippetrovski	41	activist
32	NikolaPoposki	41	political actor
33	kopukot	39	citizen

The step that ensued was network analysis to monitor the patterns of interaction between the most prominent actors within the debate and to illustrate the leading actors who were most frequently referred to. This analysis enabled us to detect who they were communicating and interacting with and to what extent, and it informed our findings about the form and density of interaction while also contributing to our understanding of developing interconnected actions between users. An interaction map was developed by tracking all users mentioned in the Twitter debate studied (Figure 5.5). Interpretation of the network map of the most influential users on topics mentioned and referred to most frequently reflects different relations: (1) expressions of solidarity with protesters and activists on the ground; (2) attribution of accountability or blame to specific politicians or political parties/entities and (3) a strategy of capturing the attention of specific political actors and addressing specific content to them. The following network graph demonstrates dense interactions. Many clusters are formed in the visualized network, indicating that there are a lot of two-way communication patterns between users where they mention other users while also being mentioned by them.

A closer look at the network, presented in Figure 5.6, filtered to indicate the most strongly interconnected users reveals a more targeted subgroup consisting of interacting citizens/activists. This network is indicative of the major interactions that take place between activists for information and communication purposes, not involving any media or political actors in the process.

Working further with network analysis, we were able to monitor users' positions in the network and provide a series of indicators of how influential they were. According to the degree centrality (Tables 5.4 and 5.5), the users with the highest number of interactions are mainly citizens and activists, indicating dense interactions between them, while domestic and international political actors rank quite low in the overall classification. This changes, however, when we rank users according to *PageRank*, which evaluates the influence of each user taking into account

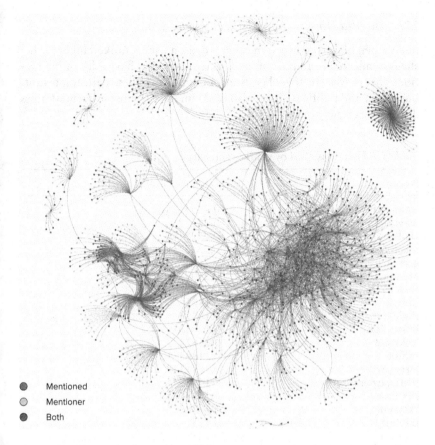

Mentioned

Mentioner

Both

Figure 5.5 Network of mentions (@) between users.

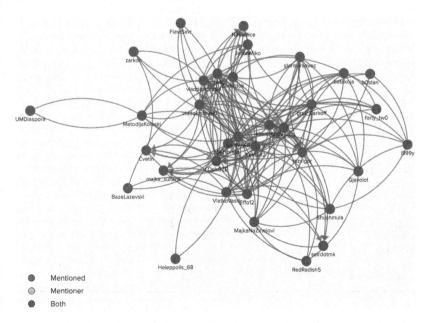

Mentioned

Mentioner

Both

Figure 5.6 Strongly connected users (@).

his/her neighbouring users; in other words, a user is ranked higher if he/she is connected to important and active users that have a lot of interactions themselves. In this classification, activists still remain important, but media and political actors also rank among the most influential users during the events studied (Tables 5.4 and 5.5).

Table 5.4 Users classified by degree centrality

Node	Degree centralities
ivanMKFR	0.4453125
razvigor	0.328125
vladpandovski	0.2421875
thedjmkd	0.234375
grof_Zarkoff	0.2265625
MetodijaKoloski	0.2109375
ebiveterebi	0.203125
Effo12	0.1875
vladokrstevski	0.1875
LOshGZE	0.1796875
Kokran2	0.15625
zarkoh	0.1484375
forty_tw0	0.1484375
UMDiaspora	0.140625
kopukot	0.1328125
SkHornet	0.1328125
JHahnEU	0.125
Gjavolot	0.125
JasonMiko	0.125
VPetreski	0.1171875
starmarsovec	0.1171875
Cvetin	0.109375
Shushmula	0.109375
AmbBaily	0.1015625
protestiram	0.1015625
batakoja	0.1015625
darkhour_seeker	0.09375
ZaraIstok	0.09375
richardhowitt	0.09375
VlatkoVasilj	0.0859375
Zoran_Zaev	0.0859375
MajkaNaZmejovi	0.0859375
meta_agency	0.0859375
peter_vanhoutte	0.078125
AmbassadorEU	0.078125
Nacalnice	0.0703125
BritAmbCGarrett	0.0703125
seirdotmk	0.0703125
MKColorful	0.0625
majka_sultana	0.0625
usembassymkd	0.0625

Table 5.5 Users classified by page rank

Node	Page Rank
CivilMacedonia	0.048620674
dw_macedonian	0.032191067
KMahoski	0.02981193
SATodayNews	0.026471019
aa_macedonian	0.026471019
Shushmula	0.023804035
Gjavolot	0.019225291
richardhowitt	0.01636979
JHahnEU	0.016286981
SkHornet	0.015803034
YouTube	0.015347859
Zoran_Zaev	0.014730902
StateDept	0.013973074
MajkaNaZmejovi	0.012496889
protestiram	0.01203303
RedRadish5	0.012009846
Effo12	0.011785169
FedericaMog	0.011602642
VMRO_DPMNE	0.011171746
AmbBaily	0.01088246
NikolaPoposki	0.0102147
darkhour_seeker	0.010132547
AmbassadorEU	0.009960456
Portalbmk	0.009946359
VlatkoVasilj	0.009937234
mindplumber	0.009830173
Hedera_Genus	0.00962072
LOshGZE	0.009459857
MKColorful	0.009375689
Libertas_mk	0.009238312
ivanMKFR	0.008930149
S_J_O_	0.008898505
razvigor	0.008805194
i999y	0.008789415
GruevskiNikola	0.008657439
Sekerinska	0.008645745
BritAmbCGarrett	0.008541499
Kokran2	0.008483665
SDSMakedonija	0.008260405

When working with community detection, three main components were traced in the hashtags narrative. Following the different partitions in Figure 5.7, we identified one community formed around the protests in the country, mentioning: (1) the different cities where demonstrations mostly took place; (2) the prominent political actors that were held accountable and (3) the emerging topic of the refugee crisis that

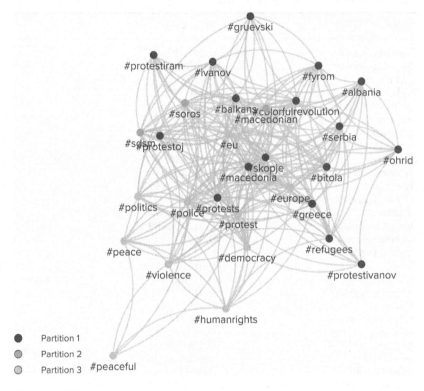

Figure 5.7 Hashtags community detection.

became a heated issue during the same period as the protests and affected the country's relationship to the neighbouring country of Greece. This was actually the most visible community that illustrated the main geolocations where the protests took place as well as the leading political figures associated with the events. The second community formed around a counter-narrative that emerged during the protests, linking the President of the Opposition party of the *Social Democratic Union of Macedonia* (SDSM), Zoran Zaev, with funding received by the *Open Society Foundations* of George Soros[16]; Zaev was accused of orchestrating efforts to organize the protests and cause instability in the country. Pro-governmental supporters deployed the narrative that *SDSM* and activists supported by the *Open Society Foundations* were responsible for violent incidents that occurred during the protests and led to clashes with the police. The third community was associated with the protests, once again, but traced two prevalent features of the events: The first, the use of coloured paints splashed on governmental and public buildings, was linked to the peaceful profile of the revolution and indicated the movement's objectives (peace, democracy and human rights); and the second was the reactions of certain activists in the movement, who were portrayed as the young and innocent voices against the authoritarian police force. A vivid example is the case of "Macedonia's lipstick protester", Jasmina Golubovska, a young woman who was photographed applying her lipstick, staring straight into the reflective plastic police shield in front of her. As the policemen moved forward, later photos showed that one shield had the mark of a crimson kiss. The woman was used by the movement as a symbol to demonstrate her calm defiance during the anti-government demonstrations and was shared widely on Facebook and Twitter, first by young Macedonians and then around the world.[17]

To further our analysis, we implemented topic modelling analysis to trace the emerging and most prominent events in the timeline studied via a quantitative approach and without the subjective limitations of manual coding, but, rather, with a need for critical interpretation and analysis. Topic modelling analysis allows us to identify the details of an event that are summarized more appropriately with a list of associated words (Figure 5.8).

The first list of concepts (Topic 1) links the *Colourful Revolution* with peaceful protests, which then clashed with the police, while the location of the event in Skopje, Macedonia was also highlighted. In the next emerging cluster (Topic 2), the timeline of the protests coincides with the refugee crisis Greece was experiencing, while it grew as a heated issue all over the Balkans. The next topic (Topic 3) highlights the protests that appeared in various cities across the country and identifies the protesters/activists as prominent actors in the events. The most relevant topic to the events studied is Topic 4, which associates the protesters in Macedonia with their means of demonstrating against the government, namely the protests outside the parliament and the throwing of paint at governmental buildings and public statues. For the first time, the President of Macedonia, Gjorge Ivanov, is visible in the analysis. He is the central political actor deemed important for the events, as he was the one who decided to stop the investigation against former Prime Minister Nikola Gruevski and dozens of politicians who were allegedly involved in a wire-tapping scandal; his decision triggered the ensuing upheavals in the country. Another important development in the course of the protests emerged, namely the proceedings initiated in Parliament for the impeachment of Gjorgje Ivanov by *SDSM*, the main oppositional party that led the protests. This is linked to the next topic (Topic 5) that refers to one of the main pursued objectives of the protests, namely the postponement of the early parliament elections scheduled for June 5. In the following topic (Topic 6), two main themes emerge: Various arrests of protesters by the police, and relations of Macedonia to the EU, which were endangered by the ongoing crisis in the country. The last topic

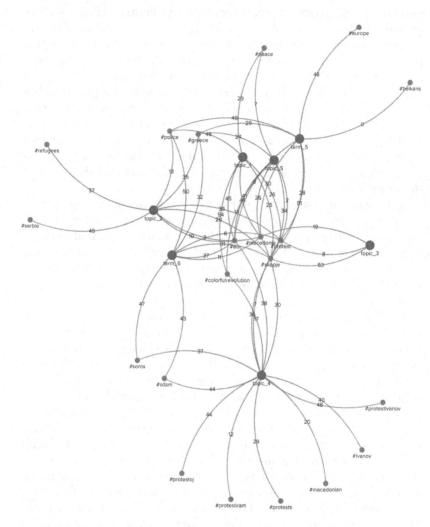

Figure 5.8 Topic modelling.

traced (Topic 7) captures various arrests by the police as well as shooting incidents. The concept of victims entered the debate, although no casualties had been reported during the events apart from injuries among policemen and protesters.

Contextualizing the Performance of Social Media and Networks During the *Colourful Revolution*

Interpreting the data analysis presented in the previous section, we further aim to investigate how the movement operated within the broader political crisis that has been fuelling the interethnic conflict since 2015. We have placed particular emphasis on the prominent actors that led the Twitter debate, as well as on unfolding patterns of communication, so as to comprehend the different political and social narratives as they evolve online. Our aim is to study the extent to which Twitter may facilitate "the burgeoning of alternative space for grassroots political activism during times of heightened political and economic crisis" (Papacharissi, 2015, p. 69).

The results of our research are further supported and contextualized through diverse resources gathered and studied by the authors; they ranged from news articles covering the protests in the national and international press, visual and video material uploaded by Macedonian citizens participating in the movement or shared by geographically distant supporters, witnessing posts on Twitter and Facebook traced through relevant hashtags, to various websites associated with the movement.

Digitally mediated collective formations tend to scale up faster and, as demonstrated in our data, this is reflected by the actual velocity of Twitter activity. Communicating short and simple political messages to domestic/national audiences (for informational and/or organizational purposes) and to international audiences (mostly for informational purposes) is also remarkably effective. These messages, tailored to Twitter's textual and spatial affordances (e.g. slogan-like content, 140 characters, upload of visual/video material) and fitting well into the media logic, got easily picked up by journalists.

The *Colourful Revolution* stands as a case that accords with the connective action logic. The movement was largely organized through protests sweeping the country in a united manner under the hashtag #Protestiram (I protest), a keyword that marked not only all digital communication around the development of the protests, but also the movement as a whole. Recognizing digital media as organizing agents lies at the core of the connective logic (Bennett & Segerberg, 2012, p. 752) and, in the case of Protestiram, participants were sharing their organizational tactics across social networks encouraging others to join in. The protests were organized horizontally by a loose network of activists, members of some opposition parties and individual citizens without any central or 'leading' organizational actors. In the case of the *Colourful Revolution*, as with the case of *The Indignants (Los Indignados)*[18], conventional organizations kept to the periphery (Bennett & Segerberg, 2012). The common principles of the *Colourful Revolution* were systematically articulated through social networks using infographics like the one illustrated below (see Figure 5.9) titled *"Why do I protest, and what is the Colorful Revolution?"*

The movement also demonstrated an underlying economic logic of digitally mediated social networks, as elucidated by Benkler (2006) and further elaborated by Bennett and Segenberg (2012). According to these

Шарена Револуција
@MKColorful

Follow

Зошто #протестирам и што е #ШаренаРеволуција

🌐 Translate from Russian

Figure 5.9 Infographic posted on Twitter on April 25, 2016 (@Mkcolorful).

authors, "participation becomes self-motivating as personally expressive content is shared with and recognized by others, who, in turn, repeat these networked activities" (Bennett & Segenberg, 2012, p. 752). When social networking involves co-production and sharing, and people often work collectively for free, participation in a public action becomes part of one's personal expression, and self-validation is achieved though sharing ideas and actions in trusted relationships. Analogous actions were prominent among protesters who wore T-shirts with custom-made logos that were uploaded online by designers for people to download and share and make their own T-shirts, banners, badges, stickers and flags. All paraphernalia were self-financed by protesters (Figure 5.10).

Twitter was further used as an action-dynamic platform that incorporated the dense protest activities of the movement (Figure 5.11) from information sharing, event coordination and instruction-based videos (e.g. how to make balloons filled with paint and sand to throw onto public buildings) to organizational connectors and legal information about citizens' rights in case people were detained or arrested. The transcendence of temporal and geographical boundaries that social networks allow was

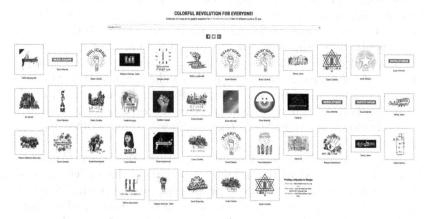

Figure 5.10 Screenshot of digital collection of a total of 41 graphic materials for #ColourfulRevolution.

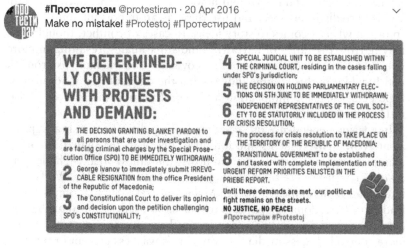

Figure 5.11 Infographic posted on Twitter on April 20, 2016 (@Protestiram).

also recorded by posting relevant infographics and audio-visual material. Protest activities were systematically recorded on Twitter through photographs, mobile phone videos and textual references.

Discussion

Our quantitative analysis revealed a versatile group of active, heavily tweeting actors. Consistent with similar findings from other conflicts (Dimitrakopoulou, Boukala, & Lenis, 2016), the Macedonian case reveals two major categories of actors: An elite group (Papacharissi, 2015) tweeting on the conflict and consisting of mainstream media and prominent political actors, and a grassroots pool of participating citizens, bloggers, activists and intellectuals actively participating in the protests and regularly tweeting while on the ground or in reaction to unfolding events. Addressivity and connectivity markers further enhance communication between participants, "by enabling phatic conventions of information sharing and comprise the socio-informatic backbone of Twitter" (Papacharissi, 2015, p. 35). Mentions may address a specific individual or institution, but also include a response to something another user has posted.

Research on citizens in Macedonia regarding their participation in collective action reveals that an increasing part of the audience (15%) belongs to an informal group of people that engages with the media and social networks in order to advance their own agenda and promote collectively constructed values (Trpevska & Fiedler, 2016). The usage of social media is also embedded in journalistic work: According to Hoxha and Hanitzsch (2018), journalists have reported that they often go through social media and news first thing in the morning, in an almost ritualistic manner, and use these as an important source of inspiration when it comes to story ideas. In cases of conflict, though, this may narrow the range of narratives and story angles, resulting in more homogenous and consonant conflict coverage – all the more as Fröhlich and Jungblut in this volume showed that the range of narratives in strategic persuasive communication material of journalistic sources is also rather narrow.

Increasing dependence on social media by political actors is also prevalent. While governments and militaries find it increasingly difficult to maintain control over information flows, they allow weaker challengers an opportunity to get their messages out (Wolfsfeld, 2016). Wolfsfeld's interviews with political actors in Macedonia revealed that oppositional leaders in Macedonia, in particular, are heavy users of social media and depend on social media as a way to get their messages out and bypass more controlled mass media. However, this was less evident in the case of the *Colourful Revolution*, since the content produced for dissemination on Twitter heavily relied on activists and citizens participating in the protests on the ground.

In the case of the *Colourful Revolution* studied, our results demonstrate mechanisms within the social networking arena at all three levels reviewed: (1) dissemination, (2) diffusion and (3) organization. As evident in various social movements around the world that have emerged as a result of social, political and financial indignation, social constellations that get heated up to form rebellious protests are built on social networks whether online or offline. Castells argues that "networking technologies are meaningful because they provide the platform for this continuing, expansive networking practice that evolves with the changing shape of the movement" (2012, p. 221). Expanding like a network of networks, both on the ground and online, allows movements to thrive without any central structure or formal leadership. At the same time, the horizontality and multimodality of networks allows and promotes cooperation and solidarity (Castells, 2012), which are both essential for the formation of movements inspired more by a feeling of togetherness and less by the common values of a community.

At the core of these formations lies information that is constantly produced and shared. At the same time, information appears to be disruptive to the prevailing political and media narratives and brings to the fore under-represented ideas and standpoints. This feeds an "ambient, always-on environment, supportive of social and peripheral awareness for the people and publics connected" (Papacharissi, 2015, p. 129). Building on connective action and resembling traditional/conventional forms of collective action, protesting groups become increasingly mobilized via online networks. Papacharissi's concept of 'affective publics' is a perfectly fitting way to describe networked public formations mobilized and connected or disconnected through expressions of sentiment and forming an imagined collective through their interaction via networked technologies. Because affective publics leave distinct digital footprints, we can trace and follow them long after their formation or even their existence. Social movements that emerged and were maintained online retain a historical visibility and an unprecedented archival functionality.

Concluding Remarks

Going beyond the mere distinction of whether contemporary social movements formed online or supported by social networking are deemed as more or less successful, this chapter aspires to focus on a movement that has attracted less visibility in academic research and places the Balkan region onto the global network protest map. Whatever the outcome of these collective actions, the lifespan of which varies as opposed to more traditional forms of protest historically, digital connectivity and digital networked action are interwoven into the fabric of modern social movements and revolutions. Networked social movements may well be presented as new forms of democratic movements that restructure the public sphere in a virtual forum of autonomy built around the interaction of urban spaces and online networks (Castells, 2012). That said, research shows that although social media may trigger and encourage feelings of connectivity and engagement (Dean, 2010; Karatzogianni & Kuntsman, 2012; Van Dijk, 2012) and, thus, activate and sustain latent ties that may prove crucial to the mobilization of networked publics (Papacharissi, 2015), online presence is not directly linked to either the impact of a movement or to the fulfilment of its objectives.

The study of contemporary social movements around the globe reveals an emerging pattern: First of all, such movements utilize digital technologies to arouse and attract attention both locally and globally and craft an alternative agenda that challenges traditional and mainstream agendas in the realms of mass media and politics. Second, they employ direct and interactive communication channels that help their members connect, address broader publics and amplify their own narrative. Finally, these movements manage to organize at viral speed, mobilize through the use of digital tools and resources and resist, thus leaving their own trajectories with shorter or longer life spans.

Digital tools have altered the narrative, disruptive and electoral/ institutional capacities of movements and the ways in which they can reveal these capacities, resulting in strengths, weaknesses and complexities (Tufekci, 2017). However, investigating the performance of social movements in the digital ecosystem does not guarantee that their challenges and opportunities can be easily comprehended. Within the sphere of everyday political and social activities, online activity may connect disorganized crowds and enable the formation of networked publics around communities, whether actual and imagined (e.g. Howard & Hussain, 2011). Media (traditional and new), social networking platforms and political and civil society institutions all play their part in articulating demands, mobilizing on-the-ground/networked publics and engaging in collective/connective action. As our experiences become progressively mediated, (social) "media converge, reproduce and become a part of the sociocultural habitus that we reference in defining ourselves" (Papacharissi, 2015, p. 31). Studying the impact of digital technologies on social movements calls for the consideration of multiple dynamics that we are only just trying to experience and explore.

Notes

1 Boyd and Ellison (2007, p. 211) provide a robust and articulate definition of social networking sites (SNS), describing them as "web-based services that allow individuals to (1) construct a public or semi-public profile within a bounded system; (2) articulate a list of other users with whom they share a connection, and (3) view and traverse their list of connections and those made by others within the system".

2 See, for example, the protests in the Philippines/2001, Lebanon/2006, Pakistan/2007, Kenya and Georgia/both 2008, Moldova/2009, Iran/2009, the Arab Spring/2010-2013, and Syria/2012 to date.

3 www.euractiv.com/section/enlargement/news/commission-hammers-out-macedonia-compromise

4 www.euractiv.com/section/enlargement/news/tusk-says-macedonias-eu-and-nato-future-at-risk

5 www.aljazeera.com/news/2016/06/macedonia-protest-demonstrators-160604153228127.html

6 For further details, see the "Introduction" in this volume by Romy Fröhlich.

7 For details, see Blei, Ng and Jordan (2003) www.jmlr.org/papers/volume3/blei03a/blei03a.pdf
8 www.nytimes.com/2016/04/13/world/europe/macedonia-gjorge-ivanov-wiretapping-corruption-investigation.html?partner=IFTTT
9 www.bbc.com/news/world-europe-36440895
10 www.dw.com/en/macedonia-a-colorful-revolution-paint-bombs-the-regime/a-19211904
11 www.dw.com/en/protesters-hit-macedonias-capital-with-paint-balls-and-soap-suds-in-a-colorful-revolution/a-19201617
12 www.dw.com/mk/%D0%BE%D1%81%D0%BC%D0%B8-%D0%B4%D0%B5%D0%BD-%D0%BE%D0%B4-%D1%88%D0%B0%D1%80%D0%B5%D0%BD%D0%B0%D1%82%D0%B0-%D0%BC%D0%B0%D0%BA%D0%B5%D0%B4%D0%BE%D0%BD%D1%81%D0%BA%D0%B0-%D1%80%D0%B5%D0%B2%D0%BE%D0%BB%D1%83%D1%86%D0%B8%D1%98%D0%B0/a-19199808?maca=maz-rss-maz-pol_makedonija_timemk-4727-xml-mrss
13 www.aljazeera.com/news/2016/06/macedonia-colourful-revolution-issues-ultimatum-160606192016686.html
14 www.aljazeera.com/news/2016/06/macedonia-protest-demonstrators-160604153228127.html
15 www.nytimes.com/2016/07/22/world/europe/macedonias-political-parties-reach-deal-to-end-crisis.html?_r=0, http://ec.europa.eu/enlargement/pdf/key_documents/2016/20161109_report_the_former_yugoslav_republic_of_macedonia.pdf
16 Hungarian-American investor, business magnate, philanthropist, and political activist.
17 www.theguardian.com/world/2015/may/13/macedonia-lipstick-protester-jasmina-golubovska
18 The anti-austerity movement in Spain that sparked back in 2011.

References

Aday, S., Farrell, H., Lynch, M., Sides, J., & Freelon, D. (2012). *Blogs and bullets II: New media and conflict after the Arab Spring.* United States Institute of Peace. Available online at www.usip.org/publications/blogs-and-bullets-ii-new-media-and-conflict-after-the-arab-spring
Atton, C. (2009). Why alternative journalism matters. *Journalism, 10,* 283–285.
Ayres, J. M. (1999). From the streets to the internet: The cyber-diffusion of contention. *The ANNALS of the American Academy of Political and Social Science, 566,* 132–143.
Baden, C. (2014). *Constructions of violent conflict in public discourse: Conceptual framework for the content & discourse analytic perspective (within WP5, WP6, WP7, & WP8).* INFOCORE Working Paper 2014/10. Available online at http://www.infocore.eu/wp-content/uploads/2016/02/Conceptual-Paper-MWG-CA_final.pdf
Belicanec, R., & Ricliev, Z. (2012). *Mapping digital media: Macedonia.* Open Society Foundations. Available online at www.opensocietyfoundations.org/sites/default/files/mapping-digital-media-macedonia-20120625.pdf
Benkler, Y. (2006). *The wealth of networks: How social production transforms markets and freedom.* News Haven, CT: Yale University Press.

Bennett, W. L., & Segerberg, A. (2012). The logic of connective action. *Information, Communication & Society, 15,* 739–768.

Bennett, W. L., Segerberg, A., & Walker, S. (2014). Organization in the crowd: Peer production in large-scale networked protests. *Information, Communication & Society, 17,* 232–260.

Blei, D. M., Ng, A. Y., & Jordan, M. I. (2003). Latent Dirichlet allocation. *Journal of Machine Learning Research, 3,* 993–1022.

Bock, J. G. (2012). *The technology of nonviolence: Social media and violence prevention.* Cambridge, MA: The MIT Press.

Boyd, D. M. (2014). *It's complicated: The social lives of networked teens.* New Haven, CT: Yale University Press. Available online at http://www.danah.org/books/ItsComplicated.pdf

Boyd, D. M., & Ellison, N. B. (2007). Social network sites: Definition, history, and scholarship. *Journal of Computer-Mediated Communication, 13,* 210–230.

Cardwell, S. (2009, June 26). A Twitter timeline of the Iran election. *Newsweek.* Available online at www.newsweek.com/2009/06/25/a-twitter-timeline-of-the-iran-election.html

Castells, M. (2012). *Networks of outrage and hope: Social movements in the internet age.* Cambridge, UK: Polity.

Christensen, C. (2009, July 1). Iran: Networked dissent. *Le Monde Diplomatique.* Available online at http://mondediplo.com/blogs/iran-networked-dissent

Cohen, N. (2009, June 21). Twitter on the barricades: Six lessons learned. *The New York Times.* Available online at www.nytimes.com/2009/06/21/weekinreview/21cohenweb.html

Dean, J. (2010). Affective networks. *Media Tropes Journal, 2,* 19–44.

Dimitrakopoulou, D., Boukala, S., & Lenis, S. (2016). *Building on an interdisciplinary approach for the study of social media during violent conflicts.* Paper presented at the final INFOCORE conference, 17. November 2016, Brussels.

Garrett, R. K. (2006). Protest in an information society: A review of literature on social movements and new ICTs. *Information, Communication and Society, 9,* 202–224.

Gauntlett, D. (2011). *Making is connecting: The social meaning of creativity, from DIY and knitting to YouTube and Web 2.0.* Cambridge, UK: Polity Press.

Howard, N. P., & Hussain, M. M. (2011). The role of social media. *Journal of Democracy, 22,* 35–48.

Hoxha, A., & Hanitzsch, T. (2018). How conflict news comes into being: Reconstructing "reality" through telling stories. *Media, War & Conflict, 11,* 46–64.

International Telecommunications Union (ITU). (2016). *ICT Statistics, Data for TFYR Macedonia.* Available online at www.itu.int/en/ITU-D/Statistics/Pages/stat/default.aspx

Ito, M. (2008). Introduction. In K. Vernelis (Ed.), *Networked publics* (pp. 1–14). Cambridge, MA: MIT Press.

Karatzogianni, A., & Kuntsman, A. (2012). *Digital cultures and the politics of emotion: Feelings, affect and technological change.* London, UK: Palgrave Macmillan.

Khamis, S., & Vaughn, K. (2011). Cyberactivism in the Egyptian revolution: How civic engagement and citizen journalism tilted the balance. *Arab Media and Society*, 13. Available online at www.arabmediasociety.com/?article=769

Papacharissi, Z. (2015). *Affective publics: Sentiment, technology, and politics.* Oxford, UK: Oxford University Press.

Schectman, J. (2009, June 17). Iran's Twitter Revolution? Maybe not yet. *Business-Week*. Available online at www.bloomberg.com/news/articles/2009-06-17/irans-twitter-revolution-maybe-not-yet

Seib, P. (2012). *Real-time diplomacy: Politics and power in the social media era.* New York, NY: Palgrave Macmillan.

Stromer-Galley, J., & Jamieson, K. (2001). The transformation of political leadership? In B. Axford, & R. Huggins (Eds.), *New media and politics* (pp. 172–191). London, UK: Sage.

Trpevska, S., & Fiedler, A. (2016). *Audiences and publics in times of conflict: Sources of information, perceptions and interaction with the media?* Paper presented at the Final INFOCORE conference, 17. November 2016, Brussels.

Tufekci, Z. (2017). *Twittter and tear gas. The power and fragility of networked protest.* New Haven: Yale University Press.

Van Dijk, J. (2012). *The network society.* London, UK: Sage.

Wolfsfeld, G. (2016, July). *Political leaders, asymmetrical conflicts, and the media: The case of Macedonia.* Paper presented at the INFOCORE Stakeholders Workshop, 1–3 July, Ohrid, Macedonia.

Wolfsfeld, G., Segev, E., & Sheafer, T. (2013). Politics comes first: Social media and the Arab Spring. *International Journal of Press/Politics 18*, 115–137.

Part III

The Dynamics of Conflict News Production as a Social Process

Key Actors' (Changing) Roles and Their Interrelations

6 Journalism of War and Conflict

Generic and Conflict-Related Influences on News Production

Thomas Hanitzsch and Abit Hoxha

Introduction

It belongs to common wisdom that journalists write the first draft of history. This is particularly true for journalists reporting on conflict and violence. They provide their audiences with an immediate account of events as they unfold in places to which most members of their audience often have very limited access. It is for this reason that conflict journalists assume significant discursive authority in shaping public perceptions of conflicts. This goes for both the war correspondent reporting from conflicts overseas and for the local reporter covering a conflict in his or her own community.

What both types of conflict journalists have in common is that they have limited freedom to exercise their journalistic duties. Their work is constrained by a number of forces, both internal and external. Internally, the process of news production is typically shaped by organizational structures, news-making routines and access to editorial resources. In addition, conflict journalists have to deal with many, often incommensurate, external pressures emanating from individuals and institutions having a stake in the conflict, such as political and military actors, non-governmental organizations and the proponents of rivalling groups broadly speaking. Given the discursive power journalists have in driving public consciousness about a given conflict, it is crucial to understand how the news about conflicts comes into being.

Communication and media scholarship have a long tradition of looking into the relationship between journalism, war and conflict. Journalists' tendency to rely on official and elite sources, for instance, has been found to be more pronounced in times of war and conflict (Bennett & Cropper, 1990; Gans, 1979). Official sources and frames substantively dominate in news coverage of conflicts around the world (Bennett, Lawrence, & Livingston, 2007; Robinson, Goddard, Parry, & Murray, 2009). Contradicting professional aspirations can pull journalists in different directions especially when trying to serve two masters: the standards of their profession and the expectations of their audience. As Zandberg and Neiger

(2005) demonstrate for the Israeli–Palestinian conflict, professional aspirations emphasize objectivity, neutrality and balance, while audiences may demand patriotism and solidarity. In another study, Tumber and Palmer (2004) revealed how the US military, during the 2003 Iraq campaign, co-opted journalists by embedding them in combat units, enveloping them into an unfamiliar occupational world of the military from which there was no chance of distancing themselves. Markham (2011), more recently, established that the professional community continuously reproduces and naturalizes journalistic norms and practices of war reporting, dismissing its negative fallout through irony and cynicism.

In addition, war reporters constantly face tensions between the highest professional aspirations on the one hand and military imperatives, censorship, public relations and propaganda, technological pressures, and heightened competition between media outlets on the other. Often it is easier for reporters "to tell stories of global conflict between military and economic superpowers, or a worldwide alliance against terrorism and extremism, than to explain much more complex and uncertain realities" (McLaughlin, 2016, p. 217). Wolfsfeld (2004) makes a similar point, arguing that there is a fundamental contradiction between the nature of a peace process and news media logic. When the news media focus on immediacy, drama, sensation, simplicity and ethnocentrism, journalists are more likely to amplify conflict and violence rather than contribute to peaceful settlement.

This cursory review of the literature does certainly not do justice to the breadth and wealth of studies in the area of journalism, war and conflict (see also Chapter 2). As we have argued elsewhere (Hoxha & Hanitzsch, 2018), research so far has looked at either conflict news content or war journalists' perceptions of influence. Both perspectives have greatly contributed to the literature; however, a separation of these approaches bears an epistemological problem: On the one hand, studies of news content treat the news production process as a black box; little is known about how the content has actually come into being and what specific considerations have informed journalists' editorial decisions. Studies of conflict journalists' perceptions and values, on the other hand, run the danger of getting caught in social desirability. The interview responses of journalists may then reflect the predominant occupational ideology and journalistic aspirations rather than real news practice. As journalists are professionally socialized into the corporate view, problematic aspects of their work may become normalized to the extent that external influence on conflict news production appears to be the 'natural' way of making news. Furthermore, professional ideology and occupational self-consciousness may call upon journalists to deny the importance of some of these factors and cast their practice in rather idealistic terms.

The study reported in this chapter tries to overcome these problems by proposing a refined conceptual approach to the analysis of conflict news production and by applying it to capturing the empirical realities of journalists reporting on a variety of conflicts. We have explored the panoply of influences on conflict news with regard to three stages in the production process: ideation, narration and presentation. We studied those influences using retrospective reconstructive interviews conducted with 215 conflict journalists reporting on a variety of conflicts. Altogether, we have reconstructed 314 news accounts of the Israeli–Palestinian conflict, the civil war in Syria, the ethnic violence in Burundi and the rebellion in the Democratic Republic of Congo (DRC) as well as the post-war situation in the Western Balkans (Kosovo and Macedonia). The technique of retrospective reconstruction enabled us to explore the genesis of news through journalists' recollections of the concrete choices and considerations made in the process of news production (Brüggemann, 2013; Reich, 2006). By forensically reconstructing editorial decisions, we believe we can arrive at a better and more nuanced understanding of the processes and routines by which journalists habitually make decisions about conflict news – working in a hectic organizational environment that leaves them with little time for reflection and introspection.

Mapping Influences on News Production

As noted above, this chapter aims at mapping out the various sources of influence conflict journalists face in the process of news production. Studies of news influences have a long tradition in journalism research. Early studies have tended to emphasize the editorial autonomy of journalists as gatekeepers, while more recent work suggests that journalists' freedoms are severely constrained by forces operating at multiple levels of influence (Ettema, Whitney, & Wackman 1987; Whitney, Sumpter, & McQuail 2004). The perhaps most widely known conceptual framework of news influences is Shoemaker and Reese's (2013) now updated hierarchy-of-influences approach, which organizes sources of influence into five hierarchically nested layers: the individual, routine practices, media organization, social institutions and social systems.

While a growing scholarly consensus toward a common classification of influences echoes Shoemaker and Reese's work, there is little agreement on the relative importance of these levels. Early gatekeeping research suggested that individual factors reign supreme in the process of news production (Flegel & Chaffee, 1971; White, 1950), while more recent evidence points to a rather modest influence of journalists' individual predispositions (Kepplinger, Brosius, & Staab, 1991; Patterson & Donsbach, 1996). Organizational factors were found to shape news production mostly through ownership, editorial supervision, decision-making and management routines, news routines, and the allocation of time and editorial resources (Altheide & Rasmussen, 1976; Breed, 1955; Gans, 1979; Schlesinger, 1987; Tuchman, 1978). In addition, a number of studies have found the newsroom environment to act as an important source of influence (Shoemaker, Eichholz, Kim, & Wrigley, 2001; Weaver, Beam, Brownlee, Voakes, & Wilhoit, 2007). At the same time, researchers and journalists have long recognized the power of political factors, economic imperatives and media structures (Bagdikian, 1983; Hallin & Mancini 2004; Preston & Metykova, 2009; Whitney et al., 2004). In the area of conflict news, studies – such as the ones mentioned in the introduction – tend to take the above opportunity structures for granted, while there are few attempts to systematically classify sources of influence taking account of the fact that conflict journalists are often operating under conditions different from other journalistic beats.

For the purpose of this study, we have therefore conceptualized two general domains of influences on news production, generic influences and conflict-related influences. Generic influences generally apply to all forms of journalism, while conflict-related influences are specifically relevant for news about conflicts. Furthermore, in line with the literature on the multilevel nature of news influences, we distinguish between three levels of influences depending on where the influences emanate from: the level of society/community, the level of organization and the individual level.

Table 6.1 provides an overview of the main sources of generic influences on the news. Here, we further distinguish between five subdomains of influence. One of these areas is sociocultural identity, as journalism usually operates within an existing set of social-cultural value systems. These value systems find expression on three levels – on the level of society/community in the form of normative expectations as to the role of journalism in society, on the level of organization in the shape of newsroom culture and on the individual level in the form of the cultural beliefs and identities of journalists.

Table 6.1 Generic influences on news production

Subdomain	Level of society/ community	Level of organization	Level of individual
Sociocultural identity	Social/cultural values	Organizational culture	Personal values and beliefs
Political influence	Government intervention	Editorial policy	Political stance
Economic imperatives	Structure of media market	Business models/ editorial resources	Salaries, pay
Institutional arrangement	Professional conventions	Editorial structures	Editorial autonomy
Reference groups	Audiences	Competing media	Colleagues, sources

Political influence is typically exercised by authorities through means of censorship, press bans or, more indirectly, by intimidating journalists. On the organizational level, political influence is often channelled through editorial policy, which requires journalists to frame their stories within a certain political ideology. This ideology may or may not be in line with the journalists' own political stance. Economic imperatives emanate from the structure of a given media market (e.g. concentration, availability of advertisement) and, on the organizational level, from the news media organization's business model and allocation of editorial resources to the news desk.

The institutional arrangement, on the societal level, encompasses a shared sense of desirable occupational practice, usually enshrined in professional codes of conduct. On the level of the organization, newsrooms are coping with the increased complexity of news work through managerial and editorial regimes (of decision-making, supervision, fact-checking, etc.), which together form an opportunity structure facilitating and restraining journalists' autonomy. Reference groups, finally, involve significant groups of social actors who typically serve as a point of reference for journalists' editorial decisions. The taste and desires of audiences are often invoked in journalists' justifications of story selection. At the same time, news media companies compete with other news organizations for attention and audience shares, and journalists compete with other journalists for recognition and reputation. As a result, journalism is a highly self-referential enterprise; hence, excellence in journalism is less dependent on what the audience thinks and more on how a journalist and a news organization is recognized by other actors in the field.

The above opportunity structure is typically found in newsrooms around the world, regardless of the kind of stories journalists are covering. For the area of conflict news, however, we believe that there is another set of conflict-related influences that deserves specific attention. As a consequence, the way a given conflict is covered by the news media also depends on the properties of the conflict itself, notably the nature and salience of the conflict. The major argument we would like to advance is that the properties of the conflict have important consequences for the way generic news influences come to bear on news production.

One of these domains of influence is the nature of the conflict, which relates to the properties of the conflict itself. The literature traditionally distinguishes between several types of conflicts, such as interstate conflicts, extra-state conflicts (between a state and a non-state group outside its boundaries), internationalized internal conflicts (between a state and internal opposition groups with intervention from other states), and internal conflicts (Small & Singer, 1982). Lee and Maslog (2005), for instance, have shown that interstate conflicts, such as the one between India and Pakistan, triggered more war-oriented news coverage than did other conflicts they investigated. Another important marker of differences between conflicts is the issues of dispute, or the question of what the conflict is about. Research has shown that disputes in which territorial issues are at stake tend to be much more escalatory – and hence generate intensified news coverage – than disputes over less salient issues, such as conflicts about natural resources (Hensel, 1996). Finally, the intensity of a conflict, typically classified into "dispute", "non-violent crisis", "violent crisis", "limited war" and "war" (Heidelberg Institute for International Conflict Research, 2011) is known to heavily drive the media's news agenda (Galtung & Ruge, 1965; Harcup & O'Neill, 2001).

The salience of a conflict is a second area; it relates to the subjective importance of the conflict for the journalists. We believe that salience of conflict importantly shapes the production of conflict news. Arguably, journalists report differently when they are involved in the conflict they are covering. When governments are marching to war, journalists are expected to act as patriots and defend the interests of their nation (Ginosar, 2015). In other types of conflicts, notably internal or intrastate conflicts, journalists likely belong to one of the rivalling groups (often ethnic or religious communities), which raises the issue of split loyalties (Zandberg & Neiger, 2005). However, even when journalists, or societies as a whole, have no stakes in a given conflict, events may become salient to them. Studies have demonstrated that journalists are likely to report more, more often, and differently about conflicts in world regions that are geographically closer to them and with which they share similarities in terms of history, political systems, cultural values and religious affiliations (Galtung & Ruge, 1965; Harcup & O'Neill, 2001).

The nature and salience of a conflict, we argue, have important consequences for the way generic influences come to bear on the news production process. Two areas are particularly interesting in this regard: the extent to which journalists have access to a given conflict and the degree to which journalists are facing intimidation and threats to their security. Reporters Without Borders has reported at least 780 journalists were killed in connection with their work between 2006 and 2016.[1] Delivering the news from conflict zones, reporters may be accidentally hit in a gunfight, but often, however, they become targets of deliberate killings. In many civil wars, the ethnic or religious affiliation of a journalist may incidentally decide over his or her life if caught by the wrong group in the wrong place (Hanitzsch, 2004).

At the same time, strategic communication actors have learned that media coverage can be an essential resource in a conflict. Political and military actors have considerable leverage to restrict media access to information, sources and conflict spots, and they make extensive use of it – sometimes vigorously through censorship and press bans, other times with greater sophistication through embedding journalists in combat units (see above). Furthermore, strategic communication has become

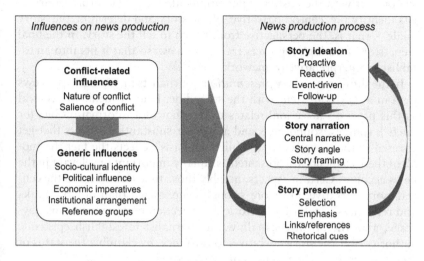

Figure 6.1 Influences on news production.

substantially professionalized and well equipped, while newsrooms have to manage with fewer resources. This situation makes it increasingly difficult for journalists to cope with sophisticated and subtle approaches to information warfare through targeted disinformation and fake news.

In our study, we have looked into journalists' recollections of news influences with regard to three essential stages in the process of conflict news production: story ideation, story narration and story presentation (see also Hoxha & Hanitzsch, 2018). The three stages build on the work Domingo et al. (2008) and develop it further. Figure 6.1 provides an illustration of the overall model, including the stages of news production and news influences.

The first stage in the news production model we call *story ideation*, borrowing from Bantz, McCorkle and Baade (1980), is key to the generation and development of the story idea. There are four modes through which a story can be ideated: 'proactively' by the journalist herself, or 'reactively', when a story is initiated by a person or an institution outside journalism (press release, leaked information, etc.). In the 'follow-up' mode, journalists become aware of a potential story by observing other media outlets coverage or by revisiting an issue previously reported by themselves, their own news organization, or other media outlets. In addition, story ideation can also be 'event-driven', for there are events that do not leave journalists and the media a choice but to report on them.

Story narration refers to the development of the story narrative as well as its narrative context. In this stage of the news production cycle, journalists put information into an established narrative that connects the present with the past, and potentially also with the future. Journalists identify the 'central narrative' of the story and determine the 'story angle' – that is, the perspective from which to tell the story. In the final step, 'story framing', reporters frame the news so that it fits into an established interpretative framework.

In the third stage, *story presentation*, journalists finally build the news item in a way consistent with the story line. Four elements are central in this process: 'Selection' relates to the choice of information bits (or 'facts'), sources, sound bites and any other substantive aspects that get covered in the news account, while 'emphasis' reflects the fact that not all of these elements are presented as equally important or relevant in the news account. Certain aspects, notably those that speak best to the central story narrative, are more strongly emphasized than others. 'Links and references' establish a rhetorical connection to previous media coverage, and 'rhetorical cues' allow the journalist to establish epistemic authority over the story narrative, for instance, by claiming the status of an eye witness or using sources of high credibility.

Notably, the three stages appear in a linear sequence in Figure 6.1, while in fact they are recursively interrelated. News production is a non-linear process in which journalists often move back and forth until they feel they arrive at the optimal outcome. At times, news accounts may undergo several iterations of the above production cycle before they are deemed worthy of publication. The central narrative, angle and framing of a story may well change when facts do not support it. Also, the narrative may also change in response to the coverage of other, notably competing, news media. Furthermore, the above process of news production does not end with the story presentation; rather, it continues its life cycle into distribution and delivery of news to the audience, potentially leading to media effects and triggering user and audience feedback, which in turn may influence and shape conflict coverage.

In the following section, we outline the methodological procedures we have used in order to capture influences of conflict news through forensic reconstructions of selected journalists' news accounts.

Methodology: Reconstructing Conflict News

In this study, we have investigated the influences on conflict news based on interviews with 215 journalists covering six different conflicts, including the war in Syria, the Israeli–Palestinian conflict, ethnic violence in the Great Lakes regions (Burundi and DRC) as well as in the Western Balkans (Kosovo and Macedonia). These interviews were conducted in the various native languages by field researchers from the country teams participating in the INFOCORE[2] project. After transcription, interviews were translated into English. The different types of conflicts (see 'Introduction'), we reasoned, likely produce differential conditions of journalistic work. In all these regions and countries, we conducted interviews with journalists who routinely covered these conflicts on the ground. In addition, we completed a number of interviews with journalists from leading media outlets in the European decision-making centres who reported on these conflicts to their European audiences back home. For this part of the study, we had selected journalists working for news media consumed by audiences working for the European Union in Brussels as well as news media organizations in France, Germany and the UK.

Our sample included journalists working for public service and private commercial media organizations as well as from pro-government, pro-opposition, community-based and independent media outlets. We deliberately selected journalists from media channels and outlets that presumably had the most significant impact on the national political and media agendas. In the European countries, this agenda-setting power was strongly exercised by national broadsheet newspapers (such as *Le Monde*, *The Guardian* and *Süddeutsche Zeitung*) along with public service broadcasting institutions (e.g. the *BBC*, *ARD* or *France Télévision*). In the African countries, on the other hand, the most powerful medium was radio due to regional limited media affordances and high illiteracy rates.

After selecting the media channels, we chose the relevant news accounts covering the above conflicts and identified the journalists who had authored these items. Only then did we establish contact with the journalists to schedule the interviews. The final sample consisted of 215 interviews and 314 reconstructed stories. Overall, we aimed at reconstructing two news stories per interview. Some technical limitations (e.g. no or incomplete archives of newscasts) prevented us from achieving this goal especially in the two African countries. Table 6.2 reports a full breakdown of the sample.

Table 6.2 Media sample distribution per conflict and country

Country	Number of interviews	Number of articles reconstructed
Macedonia	19	36
Kosovo	18	36
Israel	20	40
Palestine	15	30
Syria	25	50
Burundi	27	11
DR Congo	39	8
Germany	17	34
UK	9	18
France	16	32
Brussels	10	19
Total	215	314

The interviews consisted of two stages: In the first stage, we asked rather general questions about how journalists usually come across their stories, how much editorial freedom they have, how they choose among sources, their role perceptions as well as about perceived influences on their work and many other issues. The second phase of the interview was devoted to story reconstruction. Most of the time, we selected one very recent story and another one that had covered some kind of significant event in the more distant past.

Before the interview, the selected articles were forensically deconstructed into the relevant aspects based on a coding scheme. This deconstruction resulted in condensed article abstracts that identified the specific points the interviewer would raise in the story reconstruction. Article abstracts included, for instance, the main story narrative, the story angle, and the sources coded in the news item. Typically, the reconstruction of article 'biographies' was initiated with questions such as: 'What triggered this particular news story?', 'Why was it published at this particular time?' or 'What sources did you approach?'.

The major advantage of this study is that we did not only look into the news content produced by conflict reporters, but together with the journalists, we also reconstructed the editorial considerations and decisions through which the stories came into being. This technique was popularized in journalism research through the work of Reich (2006, 2009, 2011) and Brüggemann (2013). An important purpose of reconstructive retrospective interviews is to qualify journalists' interview responses against the backdrop of their own content. Hence, in the interview, we paid particular attention to instances in which journalists' interview responses contrasted with the actual content they produced. This technique helped us identify concrete cases in which journalists were not able, or unwilling, to fully comply with their high professional aspirations. It also pointed journalists' attention to news influences they are usually not aware of in their routine news work.

Findings

Studies have shown that journalists around the world enjoy considerable professional autonomy in their work (Reich & Hanitzsch, 2013; Weaver & Willnat, 2012). This could mean two things: Journalists are relatively independent of constraining forces when they produce news content, or they are not particularly good at recognizing those influences. Is it then possible that journalists have a tendency to overestimate the extent to which they are free to report on whatever they would like to write about? As we have noted above, journalistic reporting is constrained by a variety of factors, but many of these external influences may be absorbed and filtered by editorial management and subsequently translated into primarily institutional arrangements. As journalists have become socialized into the corporate view, they have learned to accept the presence of these influences, and their consequences in terms of restricted autonomy, as the natural way of doing news. Furthermore, professional autonomy is a hallmark of journalistic ideology, which makes it difficult for journalists to admit that they do not have full control over the content they produce.

Here, reconstructing the process of news production has been a valuable approach to unearthing the manifold constraints attached to the work of conflict journalists. When we asked the journalists to recall the decisions they made in the course of story production, we invited them to go beyond normative professional consciousness and remember the concrete considerations behind news decisions. It also helped excavate some instances of dissonance between journalists' normative aspirations and their actual practice, for instance when the politics of a conflict makes its way into news decisions in a subliminal fashion. For instance, one of the Palestinian journalists working for a news website covering Israeli affairs was very bold about the editorial autonomy he enjoys:

> There is relatively good freedom, which allows journalists to do their job in a professional and credible manner. I present the Israeli viewpoint, analyse what it says and publish along with it the Palestinian view or reaction. No restrictions impede my work.

Later in the reconstruction interview, he finally admitted the limitations of this freedom, which were mostly related to the difficulties of truly objective reporting in a heated political climate, especially when journalists are reporting to an audience not interested in editorial neutrality. This, according to the Palestinian reporter, does often lead to controversies in the newsroom:

> There are conflicting views on whether to report the full Israeli narrative of a certain story or on whether we should buy whatever it says. There is material that Palestinian media should not address, as it may sound aggressive against the Palestinians. Such issues need to be discussed with colleagues and editors.

The major observation threading through most of the interviews with conflict journalists is that, as we expected, the properties of the conflict itself have important consequences for the way generic news influences come to bear on news production. In the following analysis, we will thus refrain from emphasizing generic pressures on journalistic work; this area has been extensively researched already, as we have demonstrated in the above literature review. Rather, we will focus this analysis on the way contextual properties of conflicts – that is, the nature and salience of a conflict – are moulding the conditions in which conflict news is produced. And here, three major issues came out of the interviews: the major obstacles particularly pertinent to the coverage of violence, conflict and war are (1) access to information, (2) a lack of financial resources and (3) intimidation and threats to journalists' safety.

Access to Information, Sources and Locations

Access to information, actors and sites is a problem mentioned by almost all journalists interviewed for this study. The nature and salience of a given conflict is shaping the contextualities of journalists' work with regard to sociocultural identity, political influence, economic imperatives, institutional arrangements and the way journalists interact with reference groups.

For one, journalists are not necessarily predisposed to take side in a dispute, but when they belong to one of the communities affected by the conflict, their sociocultural identity – indexed with nationality, ethnicity or religious affiliation – inevitably matters. In Kosovo and Macedonia, for instance, depending on the ethnic group they belong to, journalists have restricted access to the "other side". Kosovar journalists usually do not have the same level of access to Serbian sources as do their colleagues from Serbia, while they have much better access to the Albanian-speaking community. In part, this challenge was overcome through collegial collaboration between journalists working for their respective communities.

Very similar obstacles are experienced by journalists reporting on the Israeli–Palestinian conflict. Access to information tends to be limited for journalists reporting from both sides of the conflict. A Ramallah Bureau Chief and TV Correspondent reported that due to the restricted access to certain material coming from Israel, some information will not reach Palestinian news media: "Sometimes, they require an official letter asking for a certain piece of information and this is time consuming process that by the time it is done, the story is too old to air."

Furthermore, Israeli authorities notoriously restrict Palestinian reporters' mobility. Most of the Palestinian journalists are not allowed to cross into Israel; those permits are difficult to get. Crossing check points is regularly a struggle for many of them, said one of our Palestinian respondents: "Whoever wants to cross from one part to the other of the village needs a permit from the Israeli authorities." As a consequence, journalists in Palestinian media organizations very much rely on what is published in the Israeli media. To be sure, access is also limited for Israeli journalists, who were not allowed to enter Gaza by the time we conducted the study.

Most of the journalists we interviewed felt committed to a particular side in the conflict, and that can lead to specific arrangements within the media organizations. Journalists reporting on ethnic violence in the DRC, for instance, were particularly cognizant of their ethnic belonging and the expectations of their respective audiences. As a result, the limited access to the other side in the conflict inevitably leads to coverage that lacks balance and impartiality. News coverage then tends to be rooted in a standpoint epistemology; journalists are reporting from a particular point of view dictated by the local communities to which they belong. Oftentimes, this is not quite a matter of choice but simply a way to stay alive. Refering to a training he received from a senior journalist when Radio Okapi was created, an experienced program director recalls that Burundi was taken as an example: "In Bujumbura, the people has for a long time been devided along ethnic lines. If something happens in a Hutu neighbourhood, whom do you send to the scene? Do you send a Hutu or a Tutsi journalist? A Tutsi in Hutu neighbourhood, there are too many risks."

In the interview, journalists also noted that political influence usually intensifies in times of conflict. Journalists often find themselves in the crossfire of political competition and battles. Many times, the news media are perceived, or cast, as the enemy by political actors. A Kosovar journalist working for a daily newspaper reported that certain political leaders in the region notoriously treat journalists as protesters even when they properly identified themselves as reporters. When covering protests and riots, political authorities and security forces often think that reporters are hindering their work. This is even more complicated in Syria, when journalists try to obtain information from conflicting parties. As direct communication with all conflict parties is very difficult, if not impossible, many Syrian journalists resorted to alternative ways of communicating by writing a post on Facebook and getting people to comment on it.

Although the news media industry around the world tends to be characterized by a high degree of competition, the demands of conflict reporting instigate, and sometimes necessitate, willingness to collaborate with other journalists. As an experienced male journalist from a prestigious newspaper in Israel explained: "I have friends, journalists, in nine countries here in the region, members of journalists I speak with them, some more often, sometimes more distant, but as if I can call them and send email, and coordinate what possible." Not rarely, this collaboration extends across competing conflict parties. This way, journalists manoeuvre around a lack of access to information, sources and places on the "other side" of the conflict.

Kosovar journalists, for instance, have established collegial relationships with their Serbian colleagues to exchange information about Serbian political leaders and get access to sites when it is impossible for an ethnic Albanian. A journalist working for a prominent Kosovar newspaper explained how he and his colleagues get over language, political and sociocultural barriers by creating a collaboration based on the interest for the stories with their colleagues from the "other side". This collaboration, he said, was "(...) very important, especially with the journalists in areas where we cannot cover, even across the border in Serbia, Montenegro, Macedonia". Contacts between journalists are often created and nurtured through professional trainings involving reporters from multiple regions. As another Kosovar journalist explained in the interview:

> *I have contact with Serbian colleagues, colleagues from Macedonia, from Serbia. We have been together in some trainings and workshops that have helped us a lot. Normally when you need information from their government, we require assistance and vice versa.*

Interestingly, journalists are more willing to collaborate with their peers on the other side if the salience of the conflict is rather low or receding, such as in post-conflict Kosovo. In protracted and still violent conflicts, such as the one involving Israel and Palestine, stakes and risks seem to be much higher, thus effectively hindering collaboration across conflict parties. In our study, we found Palestinian journalists to be not very eager to speak about the subject of cooperation with the Israeli journalists. In part, this has to do with the Palestinian Journalists Syndicate's own troubled history with press freedom as it has issued boycotts of Israeli journalists and news media in the past. In such a climate of heightened tensions, a Palestinian journalist would have to secretly collaborate with Israeli journalists in order to not expose herself to public outrage in parts of the Palestinian community.

Israeli journalists, on the other hand, said that they have good relations with Palestinian reporters, though it used to be better in the past. An Israeli radio journalist, who was reporting on Palestinian affairs, the West Bank, and Gaza for many years, explained that it was well known to every Israeli journalist that there was one Palestinian journalist in each town. Over the years, the number had grown, reaching tens in Ramallah alone. "For me, these journalists are a primary source", he said. However, if he gets contacted by a Palestinian journalist, the Israeli reporter continues, "I know I need to check what he said".

Lack of Economic Resources

One issue slightly underplayed in our theoretical considerations was the availability, or absence, of economic resources necessary to carry out conflict coverage. In Syria, as well as in large parts of Africa, for instance, journalists and media organizations typically work on very limited financial resources. This is particularly true for news media and reporters operating in conflict-ridden regions. In such an environment, journalism and news making is notably supported by local donors (such as the government or pressure groups) and by international organizations providing infrastructure, funding and trainings. In Burundi and DRC, especially, news media organizations heavily depend on subsidies from abroad. When violence broke out in Burundi in 2015, journalists had to flee the country and seek refuge in neighbouring Rwanda while facing an enormous economic fallout affecting the whole media industry. As a journalist, who left the country's capital Bujumbura, noted about the financial ramifications for his working as a journalist: "Many of our donors had suspended their partnerships and we were forced to reduce staff. When I arrived as director, the radio had no backers."

Ultimately depending on the importance of the conflict to the major funding institutions, many news media organizations in the region are supported mainly through foreign aid from the development agencies and international NGOs. In Burundi and the DRC, these media assistance programs are even crucial to the very existence of news media in the region. As a journalist from Burundi told us in the interview:

> *We then considered it necessary to find financial assistance for journalists because it was catastrophic. Initially, there was the Press House organization here which was set up by seeking money and renting a hotel. Journalists were housed and fed. They really helped us. But since it was time-consuming and the organization was short of money, we began to contact other associations such as IMS[3] and they began to support financially. There are other organizations that gave support to journalists including the European Union, just for subsistence.*

Many journalists from Burundi were exiled in Rwanda while we interviewed them. They received some support from Burundian diaspora organizations to fund travel and telephone credits. Apart from this little assistance, most of them have worked as volunteers hoping that one day, they would have sufficient funding. As a consequence, many Burundian reporters conceived of themselves as functioning in "survival mode", and receiving "donations" from political actors (e.g. the opposition) and from the international community was critical to their survival. And it is exactly here where many international organizations, which actively pursue a political agenda in the region, have become an important factor in the conflict itself. With foreign money arguably travels foreign political influence; however, journalists would rarely admit the influence explicitly in the interviews.

In Syria, too, international organizations and the media assistance community are playing an important role in shaping political discourse about the conflict. Oppositional journalists and media organizations, both inside Syria and in Turkish exile, operated on the basis of EU funding. A Syrian journalist working for a newspaper identified as a "pro-revolution" media outlet said that if it had not been for the EU, they would not be able to function like media:

> *When politicians know that we have European funding, they try to show that they are communicating with the media. Even the military in Kurdish areas did not use to give us the permission to distribute*

the newspaper and asked for many documents. However, when they knew that our funding is European, they accepted. That is why their concern about the media is not for the sake of the news but to improve their image in western eyes.

Safety Threats and Intimidation

For journalists, delivering the news from conflict zones often means working in hostile environments. Figures reported by the International Federation of Journalists suggest that, overall, 93 media professionals have been killed doing their job as a journalist in 2016 alone.[4] Foreign correspondents tend to be better protected, as it is much easier for them in making claims to their independence and impartiality in a conflict – perhaps with the exception of them being targeted by militant Islamists. In this regard, Syria is clearly different from the other conflict regions covered by the study, again pointing to the fact that the nature and salience of a conflict moulds the way the various sources and mechanisms of influence come to bear on the news production process. In the multi-faceted and complex conflict in Syria, it is impossible for any journalist to provide adequate coverage of all sides in the conflict. As a Syrian journalist stated in the interview, "[w]e are targeted by terrorist groups who succeeded many times at tarnishing our reputation. Rumours circulated about me in person, such as getting killed in Al-Qusayr".[5]

Threats to safety and experiences of violence are especially an issue for local journalists reporting from conflict zones where the ethnicity, religious identity or even political affiliation of a journalist may decide over his or her life if caught by the wrong group in the wrong place. Instances of death threats were reported particularly frequently by journalists from Burundi, where the reporter's ethnicity can easily make her or him a target of killings. A journalist who had to flee from Burundi when violence broke out had experienced one of the most frightening things that could happen to a person: "One day I came home with my family about 18:30, the thugs began to sing: 'We will kill you! We will kill you! We will kill you!'" Similarly, military and security personnel habitually threaten journalists at their workplaces, which is a very common experience of reporters in the region. After publishing a story about the 1993 assassination of then President Melchior Ndadaye, another journalist from Burundi received direct threats from the military, being told by a colonel: "If we find you, you will die."

In the DRC, a country with a long history of continued clashes between rivalling political fractions from both within and outside the country, journalists tend to be threatened in slightly different ways. Threats are usually not expressed in a direct fashion but are channelled through phone calls or are conveyed via messengers. A journalist from

Goma, a large city on the eastern border to Rwanda, reported that reporters often receive phone calls from the intelligence services asking them to "correct" the facts.

A commonality in the experience of journalists in Burundi and the DRC is that information is tightly controlled by the military and the political elite. Journalists in the DRC, as cynical as it may sound, are very much used to political instability caused by volatile political factions and coalitions as well as sometimes unpredictable hostilities between ever-changing groups. This conflict, in a country rich on natural resources, can best be understood in terms of a struggle over political dominance. This contrasts the DRC from Burundi, where clashes between the ethnic groups of Hutu and Tutsi, the origins of which date back to European colonial rule, resulted in a civil war killing approximately 300,000 people that lasted between 1993 and 2005.

The difference between the two conflicts – one being about political dominance, the other one about ethnic divisions – has obviously created very specific contexts for how influences come to bear on journalistic news production. In the DRC, journalists may not be entirely safe from becoming a target of violence, but most of the time, the various political groups seek to influence journalists – through means of intimidation – rather than to make them a subject of killings. In Burundi, on the other hand, the conflict went very much to the heart of people's ethnic identities. There is no viable middle ground for journalists in such a conflict; they are either Tutsi or Hutu.[6] If ethnic violence breaks out between the two groups, journalists are inevitably conceived of as enemies by the opposing group.

Although the situation has changed for the better since the end of the war in 2005, the country was drowning in violence again in spring 2015 after President Pierre Nkurunziza announced he would run for a third term in office, which critics feared could jeopardize the peace deal between the Hutu and the Tutsi ethnic groups. The protests, a failed military coup, and the ensuing government crackdown on its opponents and independent media have led to an exodus of more than 400,000 Burundians. Radio Publique Africaine, which was founded in 2001 with the goal of encouraging peace between the rivalling ethnic groups, was shut down by the government as part of this effort. This is how a Burundian radio journalist experienced the time following the failed coup on May 13, 2015:

> *That's when they began to destroy the media. First RPA and Radio Renaissance on the night of May 13 and the next day they started with Radio Bonesha. A colleague called me to tell me that his radio had been destroyed. I then ordered the technicians to put on music and leave. We closed all the studios and fled. People believed that journalists were there but had fled. In that day, uniformed men*

destroyed the radio. We were hiding in a nearby hotel close to the radio and we saw everything what was happening. On leaving, they even destroyed all the vehicles that were outside. They were uniformed officers jumping off pick-up trucks with police plates. They left after having destroyed everything. After that, we went to see the damage and turned off the machines, but these were severely damaged. They pointed their guns on the screen and we lost all our news items. Fortunately, I had foreseen how the situation would evolve and had saved some materials in an external hard drive kept out of the radio. That's how we were able to save some news items. But all programs that we had produced, all our archives were gone. No one went home and I rented a hotel for three days for the staff to see how the situation develops.

Returning to the Middle East, journalists there also face considerable safety threats and intimidation when covering the Israeli–Palestinian conflict, broadly speaking. This is particularly true for Palestinian journalists who are struggling with security constraints coming from multiple directions. On the one hand, they are threatened by the Israeli military and security apparatus, as we have illustrated earlier in this chapter. On the other hand, Palestinian journalists are facing pressures from either Hamas or Fatah or both at the same time (especially when they disagree). As a Palestinian reporter told us in the interview: "*I was threatened in a telephone conversation by a Hamas member in Gaza about a certain report I covered. He asked that I change my report as I was biased, according to him, to Fatah against Hamas.*"

Hence, Palestinian journalists are seemingly caught in multiple frontlines, but they are clearly not alone. Israeli journalists also face considerable strain when they visit the West Bank, especially as there are more and more voices of people who oppose normalization of Israeli–Palestinian relationships. The durable and deep-seating conflict has created a general sense of insecurity, as an Israeli journalist put it: "*The value of human life has become very cheap here. And injury to persons, and journalists in particular, has become something much more acceptable.*"

Conclusions

In this chapter, we have set out to understand the contextual forces shaping the production of news in times of conflict. We have put the journalist in the spotlight reasoning that they have significant discursive authority in shaping public perceptions of conflicts. In so doing, we believe the chapter makes a contribution to both the theoretical understanding of conflict news production and the empirical mapping of its contextualities. On the level of theory, we have proposed a heuristic model consisting of two parts, a process model accounting for the various stages in the news production process and a hierarchical model of influences charting the major factors driving those editorial processes.

On the empirical level, we have conducted retrospective reconstructive interviews with 215 conflict journalists reporting on a variety of conflicts, including the Israeli–Palestinian conflict, the civil war in Syria, the ethnic violence in Burundi and the DRC as well as the post-war situation in the Western Balkans (Kosovo and Macedonia). As part of these interviews, we forensically reconstructed 314 news accounts together with the journalists who authored them.

We found that the extent to which conflict journalists have access to important information, sources and locations is often contingent on their ethnic, religious or political affiliations. Depending on the group journalists belong to, they may or may not have access to the 'other side'. Sometimes, these problems can be overcome through collegial collaboration between journalists on both sides of the conflict. This collaboration is more likely to happen in conflicts of low or receding salience, while things are often more complicated in acute, violent and enduring conflicts. When journalists do not have access to all sides in a conflict, their coverage likely lacks balance and impartiality.

Furthermore, journalists, news organizations and the whole technical and economic media infrastructure are among the first victims of war. It is for this reason that in a number of conflicts, including several of those we investigated, journalists and media organizations often survive on financial support coming from foreign institutions, notably western governments and NGOs. Many of these institutions pursue a political agenda related to the conflict, thus creating a gateway to foreign influence.

Finally, our study shows that safety threats and intimidation are especially an issue for local reporters reporting from conflict zones where the ethnic or religious identity of a journalist may decide over his or her life if caught by the wrong group in the wrong place. The intensity of terror, broadly stretching from sinister telephone calls to assassinations of journalists, also varies quite a lot between conflicts, broadly depending on what the conflict is all about, the intensity of the conflict and the extent to which journalists' loyalties are at stake.

Hence, a major conclusion we can draw from the interviews with conflict journalists is that, as we have expected, the properties of the conflict have consequences for the way generic news influences come to bear on news production. The nature and salience of a conflict are meaningfully shaping the way journalists are covering them. This has important normative implications. Calling on reporters to produce more peace and less war journalism (Galtung, 2002; McGoldrick & Lynch, 2001), noble and well intended as it may be, likely overestimates journalists' autonomy in conflict reporting. Peace journalism trainings may help raise awareness among journalists, but they do not change the conditions of reporting. Many decisions conflict journalists are making in the course of news production are dictated less by their free will than they are by external constraints imposed on the reporter.

Notes

1 https://rsf.org/sites/default/files/rsf_2016-part_2-en.pdf
2 The fieldwork in Burundi, the DRC and Rwanda was conducted by Marie-Soleil Frère and Anke Fiedler (Université libre de Bruxelles); in Macedonia by Snezana Trpevska and Igor Micevski (School of Journalism and Public Relations); in Israel and Palestine by Gadi Wolfsfeld (Interdisciplinary Center Herzliya) and Keren Tenenboim-Weinblatt (Hebrew University of Jerusalem); in Kosovo and Germany by Abit Hoxha (LMU Munich); in the UK and France by Marga de Candia, Christoph Meyer, Eva Michaels and Eric Sangar (King's College) and in Syria by research assistants from LMU Munich.
3 International Media Support funded by the Danish Union of Journalists.
4 http://ifj-safety.org/assets/docs/197/232/a1957c5-19e2be8.pdf
5 A small city between Homs and the Lebanese border.
6 The third ethnic group, the indigenous Twa, make up only less than 1% of the country's population.

References

Altheide, D. L., & Rasmussen, P. K. (1976). Becoming news: A study of two newsrooms. *Sociology of Work and Occupations, 3*, 223–246.

Bagdikian, B. H. (1983). *Media monopoly.* Boston, MA: Beacon Press.

Bantz, C. R., McCorkle, S., & Baade, R. C. (1980). The news factory. *Communication Research, 7*, 45–68.

Bennett, P., & Cropper, S. (1990). Uncertainty and conflict: Combining conflict analysis and strategic choice. *Journal of Behavioral Decision Making, 3*, 29–45.

Bennett, W. L., Lawrence, R. G., & Livingston, S. (2007). *When the press fails: Political power and the news media from Iraq to Katrina.* Chicago, IL: University of Chicago Press.

Breed, W. (1955). Social control in the newsroom: A functional analysis. *Social Forces, 33*, 326–335.

Brüggemann, M. (2013) Transnational trigger constellations: Reconstructing the story behind the story. *Journalism, 14*, 401–418.

Domingo, D., Quandt, T., Heinonen, A., Paulussen, S., Singer, J. B., & Vujnovic, M. (2008). Participatory journalism practices in the media and beyond: An international comparative study of initiatives in online newspapers. *Journalism Practice, 2*, 326–342.

Ettema, J., Whitney, C., & Wackman, D. (1987). Professional Mass Communicators. In C. R. Berger, & S. H. Chaffee (Eds.), *Handbook of Communication Science* (pp. 747–780). Beverley Hills, CA: Sage.

Flegel, R. C., & Chaffee, S. H. (1971). Influences of editors, readers, and personal opinions on reporters. *Journalism & Mass Communication Quarterly, 48*, 645–651.

Galtung, J. (2002). Peace journalism — A challenge. In W. Kempf, & H. Luostarinen (Eds.), *Journalism and the new world order. Vol. 2: Studying war and the media* (pp. 259–272). Göteborg, Sweden: Nordicom.

Galtung, J., & Ruge, M. H. (1965). The structure of foreign news: The presentation of the Congo, Cuba and Cyprus crises in four Norwegian newspapers. *Journal of Peace Research, 2,* 64–90.

Gans, H. J. (1979). *Deciding what's news: A study of CBS evening news, NBC nightly news, Newsweek, and Time.* New York, NY: Pantheon Books.

Ginosar, A. (2015). Understanding patriotic journalism: Culture, ideology and professional behavior. *Journal of Media Ethics, 30,* 289–301.

Hallin, D. C., & Mancini, P. (2004). *Comparing media systems: Three models of media and politics.* Cambridge, UK: Cambridge University Press.

Hanitzsch, T. (2004). Journalists as peacekeeping force? Peace journalism and mass communication theory. *Journalism Studies, 5,* 483–495.

Harcup, T., & O'Neill, D. (2001). What is news? Galtung and Ruge revisited. *Journalism Studies, 2,* 261–280.

Heidelberg Institute for International Conflict Research. (2011). *Conflict Barometer 2011: Disputes, non-violent crises, violent crises, limited wars, wars.* Heidelberg, Germany: Heidelberg Institute for International Conflict Research.

Hensel, P. R. (1996). Charting a course to conflict: Territorial issues and interstate conflict, 1816–1992. *Conflict Management and Peace Science, 15,* 43–73.

Hoxha, A., & Hanitzsch, T. (2018). How conflict news comes into being: Reconstructing 'reality' through telling stories. *Media, War & Conflict, 11,* 46–64.

Kepplinger, H. M., Brosius, H.-B., & Staab, J. F. (1991). Instrumental actualization: A theory of mediated conflicts. *European Journal of Communication, 6,* 263–290.

Lee, S. T., & Maslog, C. C. (2005). War or peace journalism? Asian newspaper coverage of conflicts. *Journal of Communication, 55,* 311–329.

Markham, T. (2011). *The politics of war reporting: Authority, authenticity and morality.* Oxford, UK: Oxford University Press.

McGoldrick, A., & Lynch, J. (2001). What is peace journalism? *Activate, 4,* 6–9.

McLaughlin, G. (2016). *The war correspondent.* Chicago, IL: University of Chicago Press.

Patterson, T. E., & Donsbach, W. (1996). News decisions: Journalists as partisan actors. *Political Communication, 13,* 455–468.

Preston, P., & Metykova, M. (2009). From news to house rules: Organisational contexts. In P. Preston (Ed.), *Making the news: Journalism and news cultures in Europe* (pp. 72–91). London, UK: Routledge.

Reich, Z. (2006). The process model of news initiative: Sources lead first, reporters thereafter. *Journalism Studies, 7,* 497–514.

Reich, Z. (2009). *Sourcing the news: Key issues in journalism– an innovative study of the Israeli press.* New York, NY: Hampton.

Reich, Z. (2011). Source credibility and journalism: Between visceral and discretional judgment. *Journalism Practice, 5,* 51–67.

Reich, Z., & Hanitzsch, T. (2013). Determinants of journalists' professional autonomy: Individual and national level factors matter more than organizational ones. *Mass Communication and Society, 16,* 133–156

Robinson, P., Goddard, P., Parry, K., & Murray, C. (2009). Testing models of media performance in wartime: UK TV news and the 2003 invasion of Iraq. *Journal of Communication, 59*, 534–563.

Schlesinger, P. (1987). *Putting 'reality' together: BBC news.* New York, NY: Methuen.

Shoemaker, P. J., Eichholz, M., Kim, E., & Wrigley, B. (2001). Individual and routine forces in gatekeeping. *Journalism & Mass Communication Quarterly, 78*, 233–246.

Shoemaker, P. J., & Reese, S. D. (2013). *Mediating the message in the 21st century: A media sociology perspective.* New York, NY: Routledge.

Small, M., & Singer, J. D. (1982). *Resort to arms: International and civil wars, 1816–1980.* London, UK: Sage.

Tuchman, G. (1978). *Making news: A study in the construction of reality.* New York, NY: The Free Press.

Tumber, H., & Palmer, J. (2004). *Media at war: The Iraq crisis.* London, UK: Sage.

Weaver, D. H., Bream, R. A., Brownlee, B. J., Voakes, P. S., & Wilhoit, G. C. (2007): *The American journalist in the 21st century: U.S. news people at the dawn of a new millennium.* Mahwah, NJ: Erlbaum.

Weaver, D. H., & Willnat, L. (Eds). (2012). *The global journalist in the 21st century.* New York, NY: Routledge.

White, D. M. (1950). The "gate keeper": A case study in the selection of news. *Journalism Bulletin, 27*, 383–390.

Whitney, D. C., Sumpter, R. S., & McQuail, D. (2004). News media production: Individuals, organizations, and institutions. In J. D. H. Downing, D. McQuail, P. Schlesinger, & E. A. Wartella (Eds.), *The SAGE Handbook of Media Studies* (pp. 393–409). Thousand Oaks, CA: Sage.

Wolfsfeld, G. (2004). *Media and the Path to Peace.* Cambridge, UK: Cambridge University Press.

Zandberg, E., & Neiger, M. (2005). Between the nation and the profession: Journalists as members of contradicting communities. *Media, Culture & Society, 27*, 131–141.

7 The Enduring Value of Reliable Facts

Why NGOs Have Become More Influential in Conflict Discourse

Eric Sangar and Christoph O. Meyer

Introduction

Non-governmental organizations (NGOs) have been widely welcomed as an increasingly intrinsic and vital part of the evolving system of global governance after the end of the Cold War – a period associated with rising investment in development, humanitarian relief and a significant number of violent conflicts being brought to an end through a combination of peace-making, peacekeeping and peace-building activities (Pettersson & Wallensteen, 2015, p. 16). Unlike states, international organizations or armed groups, NGOs do not have coercive means at their disposal to influence conflict dynamics. Therefore, they need to rely on the power of ideas and discourses to make an impact on armed conflict. Since media discourses allow actors from different institutional and geographical backgrounds to shape interpretations of conflict and resulting decision-making (Baden & Meyer, 2016), influencing these discourses is therefore a central instrument used by NGOs to influence conflict dynamics. At the same time, news media may be reluctant to allow NGOs to influence their output as these organizations do not possess the same credibility, legitimacy and power as political or military actors.

So how do NGOs try to influence media discourses on armed conflict, and how successful are they in doing so? This question has received surprisingly little attention among a rich and varied literature on how NGOs influence and shape global politics (for exceptions focusing on NGOs as communicators, see Bob, 2005; Fenton, 2010; Powers, 2018). Existing studies focus mainly on advocacy strategies and media impact analysis without taking enough into account the specific media-sociological context of coverage of armed conflict. Furthermore, the media impact of local NGOs has remained largely unexplored, and therefore existing analysis of the impact of NGOs on media discourses on armed conflict suffers from a bias towards the 'usual suspects', such as *Amnesty International (AI)* or *Human Rights Watch (HRW)*. Last but not least, there is also a lack of systematic comparison of impact variation across the specific discourse contexts with varying degrees of media interest and violence intensity.

Combining content-analytic and interview-based research across six different conflicts, involving a team of geographical and thematic experts working in nine different institutions, INFOCORE provides a unique opportunity to collect and analyse the material required to understand if and under which circumstance NGOs have managed to gain visibility in a rapidly evolving media landscape.

The core of our theoretical proposition is the 'supply-and-demand model', which argues that NGOs have generally been more able to deliver relevant conflict media to news media, while the latter have increasingly relied on NGO information in order to compensate increasing financial and security constraints. We illustrate this argument using quantitative and qualitative results from across the six INFOCORE conflict cases.

This chapter proceeds in four steps: First, we briefly explain our definition of NGOs and explain why it is important to differentiate between different NGO activity profiles and communication strategies. Second, we present the main overall findings of our study, combining results of an automated content analysis and a qualitative media impact analysis. In the last part, we assess to what extent the increasing influence of NGOs is a burden or a bonus for evidence-based, multi-perspective conflict journalism.

Key Differences Between NGOs as Communicators

Much of the literature tends to treat NGOs as if they were a clearly identifiable and relatively homogenous actor class. In fact, most of the literature only talks about large International NGOs (INGOs) based in the Global North without paying enough attention to other NGOs as well as to the differences between these INGOs. While we agree that it is relevant to examine and measure the aggregate effects of NGOs on media contents related to conflict, understanding NGOs' concrete roles and impact in specific cases often does require us to be more specific and examine how and to what extent differences between NGOs matter. We are starting from the definition of NGOs as organizations that are formally and legally independent from government, with goals rooted in particularly values, ideas and issue objectives, and with a strong drive to reinvest all or most of any financial surpluses into the pursuit of these goals. However, our research confirms significant difference between NGOs as well as an increasing blurring of NGOs with either media organizations or indeed with political organizations. Differences among NGOs matter as they account for significant differences in their communication strategies, capacities as well as their media impact. We want to discuss briefly the major factors at play.

First of all, NGOs differ greatly in the resources they have at their disposal. Some NGOs, especially local NGOs in some of the poorest countries affected by conflict, are run on a shoestring by activists with limited capability of investing in specialized staff or technological equipment necessary to run sophisticated communication activities. The IT and communication revolution has levelled the playing field for these NGOs significantly, but there are still huge differences in the underlying resources among NGOs, if one just considers the overall income of major international humanitarian NGOs taken from the financial statements in their annual reports such as *Oxfam* (£414 million in 2016), *AI* (€279 million 2016), *HRW* ($78 million USD in 2014), *Doctors without Borders/Médecins Sans Frontières* (*DWB/MSF*) ($54 million USD 2016) and *International Crisis Group* (*ICG*) ($18 million USD 2015). This does not automatically translate proportionally into the size of their research, communication and advocacy divisions, but the larger organizations do employ large and highly sophisticated experts needed for such communication, and their ability to recruit former journalists into their teams gives them network power that allows them to pass through some of the typical media filters more easily than other NGOs.

Secondly, these NGOs often differ in terms of their funding structure, which can restrict in more or less subtle ways whom they can criticize in their public communication and influences which countries and issues they choose to focus on within their overall mandates. Some NGOs are dependent on one or a small number of funders whether they are governments, foundations or individuals. In the case of the ICG, funding comes from a small group of Western governments as well as some liberal foundations. *AI* receives 75% of its funding from donations by over two million individuals (AI Global Financial Report, 2016), whereas *HRW* received a significant part of its funding from its 100 million endowment, including annually 10 million from the *Soros Foundation* payable between 2011 and 2021 (BDO, 2016, p. 16). Some of the local NGOs in conflict regions are heavily dependent on foreign funding and/or on very few individual funding sources. Visibility in the media is seen as important for attracting individual donations, but perhaps even more so for showing relevance and impact for some of the donors according to our interviewers. Advocacy NGOs need the media to advance their objectives and influence public opinion in favour of their policy prescriptions. They tend to invest strongly in quality research and building their reputations as reliable, valuable and trustworthy providers of factual knowledge and analysis.

Thirdly, NGOs differ in terms of their mandates and their activity profiles. We follow here Gareth Evans, the former president of ICG, who broadly distinguished between talking, thinking and doing NGOs (Evans, 2011), although in reality we see variations and hybrid forms. The first are specializing in advocacy for human rights or other values; the second category is engaging in analysis and problem-solving such as warning for conflict prevention; and the third is helping to alleviate suffering on the ground by providing shelter, food and protection.

Doing NGOs are more reliant on donations from the general public as well as major international donors, so their communication needs to emphasize the impact they make, but they are typically also cautious in criticizing governments and International Organizations (IOs) as their major donors, unless they have a very diversified funding structure. International NGOs on the ground may also need to be more cautious with regard to what they say as they have the duty to protect their staff and citizens in their care. This is not necessarily true for some of the local NGOs who are prepared to run much higher risks for their (often volunteer) staff such as *Raqqa is Being Slaughtered Silently* (*RSS*) and the *Syrian Observatory of Human Rights*. *RSS* in particular saw some its members killed by *ISIS*. *RSS* also epitomizes the issue of blurring lines between an advocacy NGO and a new model of media organization based on citizens journalism recognized in the 2015 International Press Freedom Award.

Fourthly, we can distinguish between NGOs in terms of where they are headquartered and their geographical reach. On the one hand, we have the major Western-based INGOs who cater for an international audience and have a broad regional and often even global reach. On the other, we have local NGOs within conflict regions, some of whom may be tied in various ways to conflict parties or to international donors, others may be more strongly rooted in ethnic or religiously defined communities. In between we find NGOs that may appear to be either local or international, but which are in fact hybrids. Some may be headquartered outside of the conflict region in Western capitals, but have strong local roots and networks. Some may be staffed by citizens who have fled the country and are now organizing NGOs that operate from the neighbourhood or link up with diasporas in Western countries.

Finally, NGOs may differ in their organizational culture and internal composition. The organizational culture component shapes the extent to which communication is driven by funding imperatives, whether it is driven by research, expertise and methods, or whether it is driven by media impact. Some of the organizations do cultivate an atmosphere of vigorous internal discussion about what and how to communicate about a conflict; others are more hierarchically organized and strongly discourage challenges to the beliefs held by senior management. As a result, some organizations maintain a strong set of ideological beliefs that can shape what evidence is being collected, how it is analysed and, of course, whether and what kind of policy prescriptions are advanced – this does not necessarily mean the suppression and distortion of facts, but does create internal biases in information processing, sense-making and communication. NGOs differ in terms of the people they recruit, from which kind of disciplinary and professional background and indeed organizations. Some of the domestic NGOs may be exclusively or predominantly staffed by members from one ethnicity or nationality, which does not necessarily turn them into political activists or even conflict parties, but does blur some of the boundaries and can create significant differences in how conflicts are being framed and, crucially, how these NGOs are being perceived by other domestic actors, including local journalists.

Explaining the Growing Influence of NGOs on Conflict Discourse: The 'Supply and Demand Model'

We argue NGOs have gained in capacity to influence media discourse on armed conflict since the end of the Cold War, in terms of gaining access as a directly or indirectly referenced source but also in terms of shaping of media content along the three main dimensions of the INFOCORE project – evidential claims, frames and agendas for action as elaborated in Chapter 1. We are elaborating in the following the main factors behind this rise rooted in a supply–demand model of journalistic and organizational choice. Our argument does challenge some of the tenets of the 'classical' literature on the relationship between the media, politics and civil society, which tends to highlight the asymmetry of power relations as NGOs depend on the media to reach and mobilize key audiences for their organizational objectives (Gamson & Wolfsfeld, 1993, p. 116). Furthermore, it has been argued that 'politics comes first' with official government sources and political dynamics being the most influential determinants of media coverage far above civil society actors such as NGOs: Only recently, a study has demonstrated that "international news coverage, including international aid coverage, is dominated by authoritative sources and especially government sources" (Van Leuven & Joye, 2014, p. 162). Until the 1990s, the 'traditional' mass media can therefore be seen as gatekeepers who have the power to decide to what extent civil society actors are granted access to debates in the public sphere.

We argue, however, that since the early 2000s, the comparative disadvantage of NGOs has decreased because of two simultaneous processes: an increase in the value, timeliness and breadth of conflict-related information supplied by NGOs, and a relative decrease in journalists' independent capabilities to obtain such information from the ground. As a result, we expect NGOs to have become a more influential source of journalistic coverage at least for Western news media, giving them greater power to shape evidential beliefs, framing of conflict situations and indeed advocacy for specific forms of action in mediated discourse.

Improved Supply of NGO Information

We argue that NGOs – especially transnationally operating advocacy NGOs with professional communication departments – are increasingly well equipped to position themselves as media actors in their own right, being more able to engage with journalists of 'traditional' news media as well as directly with their target audiences through social media.

This is due to two advantages: First, to the extent that many NGOs are operating over the long term in close contact with local populations in periods before and during conflict escalation, they often have access to exclusive information from the ground that are not available for journalists or even official actors. Because NGOs are often the only 'foreign' actors present in civil wars, for some local conflict actors, such as insurgency movements striving to gain international recognition for their cause and thus access to legitimacy and external support, they have become essential gatekeepers for the access to international news media (Bob, 2005). Moreover, some NGOs have been able to hire country experts who are able to draw on knowledge, networks and access that most journalists do not have. They also have the time to invest in research. For instance, an *HRW* report will typically be based on around 100 interviews, sometimes more, allowing these organizations to triangulate and verify information in a way that most media organizations cannot afford anymore. Even smaller advocacy organizations, such as the French human rights organization *Action by Christians for the Abolition of Torture*, employ desk researchers and try to produce relevant analysis as a way to gain access to media and thus more prominence for their cause (personal interview, 2 March 2015).

Second, NGOs are more and more aware of this information advantage and many have made efforts to capitalize upon it more systematically. The largest transnational NGOs have hired communication professionals at all levels, including former journalists, to professionalize, diversify and tailor their external communication activities (Cottle & Nolan, 2007; Powers, 2018). These large NGOs are using the full spectrum of modern communication outlets (such as targeted social media campaigns, background talks with journalists, or self-produced video coverage). Particularly the well-resourced and respected Northern NGOs have increased their chances for their information not only to be mentioned in mainstream media coverage, but also to be used increasingly verbatim and with little editorial change (Fenton, 2010). A quintessential case for this influence is *HRW*, which has accumulated 3.5 million followers on Twitter and 2.4 million followers on Facebook, and this is just for English. In addition to the institutional account, 190 *HRW* staff also have their own accounts to tweet about their own areas and in their own languages, creating a large social media footprint for the organization, its content and messages (Interview with *HRW* Communication Director). But also, smaller as well as local NGOs can rely on social media to reach the general public directly and thus are increasingly able to 'bypass' the often strictly regulated national and local media environment in zones of conflict. In conflict zones such as Syria, NGOs often combine the benefits of social networks and their direct access to the population, as one interviewee described: "For the organization [of our] media advertising, we have a website, a page on

Facebook and a Twitter account. I guess the majority of organizations work this way. Marketing is happening now on the field. What do people know about us? Or how do they benefit from the organization? This is how marketing is done, through word of mouth" (personal interview with Syrian NGO *Maan*, conducted as part of the INFOCORE project, autumn 2015).

Third, the quick and reliable provision of factual information can be an asset for NGOs that can translate into better visibility for potential supporters in the domestic public, improved access to political actors and, last but not least, better credibility in the eyes of institutional donors. Improved recognition by and easier access to institutional actors can, in turn, enhance NGOs' credibility and relevance in the perception of journalists. Some advocacy NGOs, such as *AI* or *HRW*, have established communicative workflows through which information produced by researchers on the ground are fed rapidly to journalists, crisis management agencies and donors organizations. One concrete example of this was given to us by a communication officer of the French humanitarian NGO *Secours Islamique* (*SI*): Because *SI* was able to provide up-to-date information to the Crisis Management Cell of the French Foreign Ministry, the NGO could establish a personal contact and was subsequently able to secure funding from the French government to rehabilitate schools in the Palestinian territories (personal interview, 5 March 2015)

Increased Media Demand for NGO Information

In the second part of our theoretical argument, we argue that there is increasing demand for NGO conflict information from both local and international news media. This means that "NGOs can now offer international news that news organizations are no longer well placed to provide" (Fenton, 2010, p. 160). There are three arguments to support this claim.

First, the arrival of Internet-based news portals as well as social media has caused the increasing fragility of the business model of quality news media, in Western as well as in non-Western contexts. News media revenues have decreased due to a loss in advertising, declining subscription rates and increasing competition from non-traditional news providers (such as news blogs, aggregators and semi-official communication agencies). These trends have hit foreign affairs coverage particularly hard because its relevance to local audiences is more difficult to explain, whilst its output costs are higher due to expenses for travelling, equipment, local access and security. As a result, many media organizations decided to close their offices abroad, shift from high-status permanent foreign correspondents towards junior freelancers or local contractors, or indeed buy in content from news agencies (Otto & Meyer, 2012; Meyer, de Franco and Otto, under review). Such trends may increase a tendency even of large transnational news networks to rely on "parachute journalism" and neglect long-term research and reporting when covering violent conflict (Musa & Yusha'u, 2013). It is therefore not surprising that quantitative studies have overall confirmed that "the news outlets that dedicated the fewest resources to international newsgathering are most likely to mention NGOs" (Powers, 2016, p. 327).

Second, journalists are facing increasing security challenges when covering armed conflict from the ground. Especially the rise of more unpredictable and radical non-state actors has placed journalists at greater risk of being tortured, killed or abducted for either financial or propagandistic purposes. Whereas in the past, experienced correspondents could rely on their networks to navigate risk or seek authorization from local conflict leaders, such practices are increasingly challenged by constantly shifting alliances on the ground, as well as armed groups explicitly targeting foreign journalists. Ideological radicalization may play some role in this, but the primary cause is the changing media logic due to "relatively cheap broadcasting technology [that] have, to some degree, eliminated the need for a third-party intercessor like a journalist. Indeed, for some, the publicity gained by the act of kidnapping a journalist is more valuable than whatever avenues of communication that journalist offers" (Crawford & Davies, 2014, p. 8).

This increase in security hazards has led to an increase in financial costs for risk management procedures and a decreasing autonomy of conflict journalists to decide themselves where to travel and which sources to talk to. Thus, a British foreign correspondent of a major newspaper described this situation as follows:

> We've lost a reporter killed in Syria and another reporter kidnapped and almost killed. [...] And obviously everyone's seen what's happened to James Foley and Steve Sotloff and those other guys. [...] So it's pretty difficult to get an organisation to allow us to go into those kind of areas without very, very high level of preparation and security clearance. Any trip like that would have to be signed off at a very high level and there are a lot of new people in our organisation who are now employed explicitly to look at the security environment for us. It's much, much more restricted than it used to be. [...] Which means that we're now a very, very unwieldy organisation if you're trying to do that sort of operation.
>
> (interviewed in London, 21 July 2015)

Third, journalists may have become more sceptical of official sources of information as a result of more and more open attempts by governments to control and distort media coverage. In Western contexts, "as much as the post 9/11 environment has been witness to the ability of media to empower non-elites and challenge political elites, it is also the case that governments have become more organised and more adept at both managing and influencing the new media environment" (Robinson, 2014, p. 203).

Furthermore, a number of non-Western states established semi-official news outlets (such as Russia Today or al-Arabiya) to challenge independent news providers. Rightly or wrongly, NGOs with a reputation of being independent and at times critical of government therefore have a credibility bonus in the eyes of many journalists and amongst their audiences, even if they also pursue a particular, albeit not party-political agenda. Indeed, earlier research has found evidence that some transnational NGOs such as *DWB/MSF* adapt to the increased demand for NGO information by the media: *DWB/MSF* "distributes background reports about the settlement of international aid projects in different countries and regions throughout the year. From this authoritative position as an expert source on the ground, *DWB/MSF* is able to lever news attention to long-term disasters" (Van Leuven & Joye, 2014, p. 175).

Preliminary Results From the Quantitative Content Analysis and From the Qualitative Discourse Analysis

A Methodology Combining Quantitative and Qualitative Tools

In our empirical analysis, we combined a quantitative automated content analysis with a qualitative discourse analysis to assess both the diachronic evolution of NGO presence in media discourses on armed conflict and their qualitative influence (in terms of types of claims). For the latter analysis, we manually performed a qualitative analysis of news publications in periods of presence 'peaks' of three NGOs that are often considered as influence 'superpowers', namely *AI*, *HRW* and *ICG*.

With regard to the quantitative analysis, we present results from the automated content analysis based on INFOCORE's JAmCAT[1] interface. For this analysis, we define 'NGO presence' as the proportional frequency of references to NGOs in individual texts of sampled media articles that covered each INFOCORE conflict context over the period of January 1, 2010, to December 31, 2014 (see Table 7.1). Using JAmCAT, absolute and relative frequencies can be retrieved based on the number of their occurrences in individual articles. This approach enables us to observe important longitudinal and cross-conflict variation using the totality of the sampled material. The results were then aggregated according to the type of medium and time period.

We compiled for absolute and relative frequencies of articles mentioning at least one of the international NGOs and one of the respective local NGOs, and aggregated these figures for each month of the covered period. In the following charts, 'absolute frequencies' therefore represent always the number of articles of the respective period which contain at

Table 7.1 Number of identified NGOs and sampled articles

	Across all contexts	Serbia/ Kosovo	Macedonia	Israel/ Palestine	Syria	Burundi	DRC
Number of identifiable NGOs	55 international NGOs	25 local NGOs	31 local NGOs	30 local NGOs	11 local NGOs	20 local NGOs	12 loc NG
Total number of sampled articles	$\sum$ = 1,750,246	320,669	122,832	781,179	365,611	44,099	115,8

least one NGO reference; 'relative frequencies' point to the proportional share of articles with NGO references compared to the total number of sampled articles in the respective period.

For the quantitative analysis, we have examined the ways in which NGOs were used in media reports, focusing on three types of epistemic claims, each of them implying different typical target audiences, production and communication processes. The first layer could be described as factual information regarding the conflict reality on the ground, which is typically the object of major reports from NGOs similar to reports by official fact-finding missions or major in-depth news features. It can serve multiple purposes from enhancing situational awareness to collecting evidence of who is responsible for human rights violations or aggression. The second layer goes substantially beyond observable phenomena to analytical judgements about, for instance, the reason for why social tensions are rising or violence is escalating. This could be a simple matter of assessing actor's motivations and capabilities, but could also encompass more complex, structuralist or model-based explanations. Thirdly (and this is an element not all NGOs will openly pursue) is prescriptive or policy-related knowledge about what might work to achieve certain ends vis-à-vis a given conflict and which measures are politically feasible to implement in a given case and case as well as for a given actor.

Results Across all Conflict Cases

Figure 7.1 shows the aggregated relative frequencies of NGO occurrences across the six INFOCORE corpora. The intriguing peak in March 2012 coincides with an increase in quoted NGO references in the media coverage of the Syrian conflict, which represents the second-largest share of sampled articles for the INFOCORE corpus (see Table 7.1). In that period, the conflict in Syria was on the verge of escalation from a largely peaceful anti-government protest movement into a violent counter-insurgency campaign (for an in-depth analysis of NGO influence on coverage of the war in Syria, see Meyer, Sangar, & Michaels, 2018).

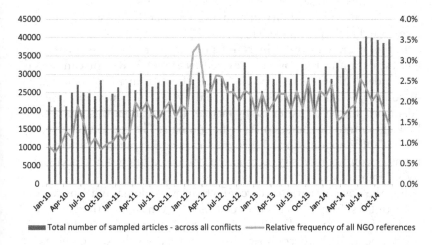

Figure 7.1 NGO occurrences across the six INFOCORE Conflict Contexts (Relative Frequencies).

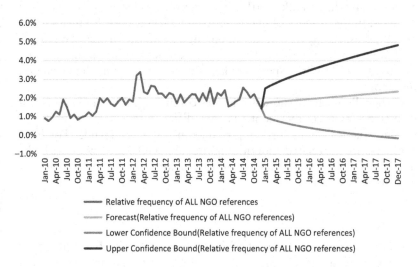

Figure 7.2 Forecast of NGO presence based on observed relative frequencies from 2010 to 2014.

Advocacy NGOs such as *AI* and *HRW* alerted against the increasingly violent repression of popular protests, and outside observers feared the outbreak of a full-scale civil war, as had happened previously in Libya.

But a closer look at the overall trend of NGO presence in media discourse reveals that within a period of only four years, the share of article quoting at least one NGO has nearly doubled. Figure 7.2 illustrates this trend with a linear forecast of NGO presence until the end of 2017.

Therefore, we can see that over the last four years, NGOs have gained slowly but steadily visibility in mediated conflict discourses, both in international and in local media.

Is this overall increase in NGO presence a result of growing violent escalation in the conflicts covered by INFOCORE, or can we say that indeed NGOs have become more effective in influencing media discourses – independently of external events that may increase the "demand" for NGO expertise by media? To find about this, we need to look closer into discourses on specific conflicts. The conflicts covered by INFOCORE not only include geographic variation but also difference in terms of conflict intensity, actors, general media interest and accessibility for journalists.

For the covered period, the conflicts in Macedonia and Kosovo did not exhibit substantial instances of violence even though there were episodes of significant political tension and some international diplomatic involvement. In both countries, we found extremely low numbers of articles referring to NGOs (between 0 and maximum 30 per month, representing between 0.0% and maximum 0.9% of the absolute coverage) – so low that it makes little sense to produce a descriptive statistical analysis. In the absence of major political violence, both countries made headlines especially as a result of corruption affairs in the covered period, and apparently NGOs focusing on conflict resolution, humanitarian and human rights issues were less able to influence media debate on these topics.

In the following, we show two figures coming from Burundi and Israel/Palestine – two conflict contexts that differ with regard to both the violence intensity and their importance in the news agenda. For both conflicts, we correlated monthly figures of NGO "presence" with the number of monthly aggregated conflict casualties as an indicator of conflict intensity.

Burundi

Until the outbreak of the latest crisis in Burundi in early 2015, the country had a relatively low priority on the global media agenda. During the analysed period between 2010 and 2014, there were no major humanitarian crises, which would have resulted in a large presence of international NGOs. Furthermore, until recently, Burundi did have a vibrant and relatively independent media system, heavily supported by international donors, as well as a relatively active civil society, with some prominent activists being routinely quoted by local and international media. In the absence of larger humanitarian crises or massive human rights violations, the country had a lower priority in the communication activities of transnational NGOs. As a result, we can see an extremely high share of local NGOs among the total number of media references to NGOs (Figure 7.3).

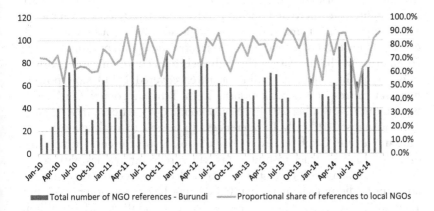

Figure 7.3 Absolute frequencies of NGO references and proportional share of references to local NGOs.

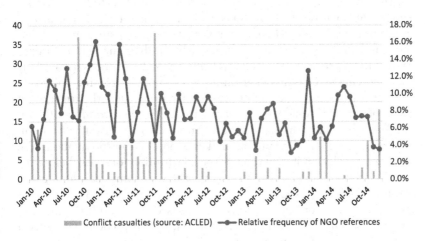

Figure 7.4 Relative frequencies of NGO references and monthly conflict casualties.

On average, 7.3% of all sampled articles (between 200 and 1000 per month) contained at least one NGO reference – higher than in all the other conflict contexts studied by INFOCORE.

To what extent did changes in conflict violence correlate with changes in the presence of NGO references? Figure 7.4 shows the available evidence. Using data from the Armed Conflict Location & Event Data Project to detect potential correlations between violence escalation and NGO impact, we found a very low correlation rate of only 0.02 between the relative frequency of NGO reference and the occurrence of deaths related to political violence (Figure 7.4).

These results strongly suggest that in the context of Burundi, local NGOs have been particularly successful in shaping media discourses independently of external events. In the absence of large-scale violence that might have increased the journalistic demand for transnational NGO expertise, Burundi might indeed be seen as a country in which especially local NGOs have become effective media actors, successfully stimulating media discourses through their own communication efforts.

What qualitative impact did the three covered NGO superpowers have in their respective 'peak months' in the Burundi context? In *HRW*'s peak month November 2010, we only counted 11 articles, in *AI*'s peak month August 2010 only 10 references. To be able to analyse a substantial sample of *ICG* references, we had to look across the entire timeframe of 2010–2014 in order to find at last three relevant articles with reference to this particular INGO. This may reflect the fact that this particular country did not see major conflict during the observation period, but also its relatively lower news priority due to its small size of 10 million vis-à-vis 80 million in DRC.

For *ICG*, we found the first reference in a *Xinhua* report of February 10, 2011, covering the Burundian government's reaction to ICG's "Africa Report 169", whose analytical insight is quoted as stating that "Burundi risks reversing the decade of progress it has enjoyed since its civil war ended unless the government resumes political dialogue with the opposition". In an article a year later, on February 8, 2012, the German daily *Die Welt* cites ICG as a background source about worsening politically motivated violence in the country to enrich a feature length article about child soldiers. The final piece referring to *ICG* in the *Guardian* of April 6, 2014, has again a human interest feature character as it talks about the President's football team, but makes a more serious point about him seeking a third term in violation of the constitution (one year before the actual outbreak of the current crisis for the very same reason), a claim that is backed up by *ICG*: "The result is 'the worst crisis in Burundi since the civil war', according to the Brussels based think tank the International Crisis Group."[2] As in other contexts, *ICG* is predominantly used as a source of impartial analysis, and its recommendations for action rather neglected.

AI is cited in the month of August 2010 largely as a result of a successful "push" action following the publication of detailed report on August 23 that documented human rights abuses such as torture committed by the intelligence services and the presidential police against opposition figures. The findings of the report were reported in *Radio France Internationale* (*RFI*) on August 24 and, interestingly, extensively and simultaneously also in local media such as *NETPRESS* (24 August) and *Association de Réflexion et d'Information sur le Burundi* (23 August). Both media provided a long summary of the report itself, including recommendations on how perpetrators should be brought to justice. No major international medium covered these reports, making this a largely "French-language" affair.

Finally, *HRW*'s peak month of November 2010 is highly interesting for underlying the highly salient role of the NGO in the domestic politics of the country. It starts with an article in the local *NETPRESS* dated November 12, which reports on the visit of US Senator Richard Luga, who reportedly demanded (and subsequently achieved) for *HRW* to be authorized to do a human rights investigation. Later that month, on November 23, *HRW* again creates a news effect by publishing the report "Des portes qui se ferment? Réduction de l'espace démocratique au Burundi"[3]. On November 25, *HRW* is cited in an *Agence France-Presse* (AFP, 2010) piece, this time in the context of a strongly worded reaction from a government spokesperson who described the report as an "act of revenge and frustration after findings (...) that the election process was successful".

Overall, Burundi demonstrates once again that advocacy organization such as *AI* and *HRW* are successful in 'pushing' media coverage through the publication of factual reports framed as condemnable violations of human rights. But the same NGOs exert limited control over the transformation of their agendas for action in local media discourse. They are being constructed without good justification – both by media's supporters and media opposing their claims – directly or indirectly as political actors, their legally driven advocacy being reinterpreted as a political rhetoric helping or destroying domestic political unity. This translates, at least for *HRW*, not only in perceived but very real influence in domestic politics, as the US-initiated invitation to *HRW* and the subsequent expulsion of their representative illustrate. *ICG* does not seem to cause such effects, or at least not as impulsive reactions, and this is probably more than anything else due to *ICG*'s focus on analysing and resolving conflict dynamics, rather than morally denouncing illegal acts committed by political actors.

Israel/Palestine

The conflict between Israel and Palestine is a conflict for which we might expect lower media demand for NGO information. Since the access for journalists is comparatively easy, the territory small and the conflict continuously high on the global media agenda, we could expect that mainstream media mostly rely on their own sources to cover major external events with news value during the conflict. At the same time, human rights but also conflict analysis NGOs, and even some humanitarian organizations focus on this conflict as a priority of their operations. Earlier studies have found for this context that publications by local and international NGOs have regularly sparked national and international debate, and that, as a result, NGOs have increasingly been drawn into conflict politics by the local conflict parties (Hallward, 2013; Kaufman, Salem, & Verhoeven, 2006; Ron, Ramos, & Rodgers,

2005; Steinberg, 2011). At the same time, this conflict is characterized by high degrees of volatility. During the covered period, the Gaza War in summer 2014 occurred, which sparked an intense international debate that also centred on allegations of human rights violation committed by the Israeli Defence Forces during the invasion of Gaza. During this war, due to the intensity of the fighting, journalists had little access to the Gaza territories, and media outlets therefore had to rely on other sources to provide insights on the effects of the fighting on civilians inside Gaza. We could therefore expect an increase in media demand for NGO information during that specific period.

Indeed, our analysis shows that there is an isolated peak of absolute numbers of NGO frequencies during the period of the Gaza War, which coincides with a drop in the share of references to local NGOs (Figure 7.5). We can presume that this is due to an increased demand for information by international humanitarian NGOs such as *DWB/MSF*, which were often the only civilian organizations able to communicate with the outside world from Gaza. In some of our interviews conducted with spokespeople of humanitarian NGOs, this war was indeed often quoted as an example when media turned toward humanitarian NGOs as a reliable source of evidence from the ground.

Looking at the relative frequency figures, we can indeed confirm the Gaza War seems to be associated with a spark in media demand for NGO information. While on average across the covered period, NGO references only occur in 1.4% of all sampled media material on the Israel/Palestine conflict (considerably lower than in the Burundi context), there is indeed a peak of 3.2% during the Gaza War (Figure 7.6):

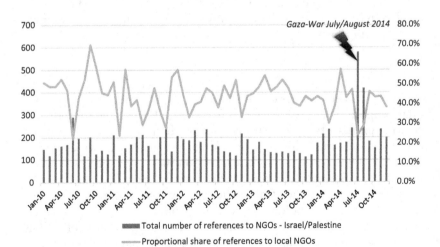

Figure 7.5 Absolute frequencies of NGO references and proportional share of references to local NGOs.

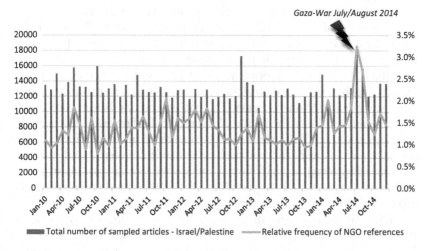

Figure 7.6 Total number of sampled articles and relative frequency of NGO references.

How were the three NGO 'superpowers' quoted in their respective peak months in the Israel/Palestine context? *ICG* was relatively speaking the least visible INGOs with nine references in its peak months of November 2012 in the context of the eight-day-long Israeli airstrikes starting on November 14 against militants of Hams launching rockets in Gaza during what Israel called 'Operation Pillar of Defence'. Relatively speaking, this case shows the highest relative visibility of *ICG* across the four cases and a majority of the references with a remarkable number of five references alone in the *New York Times* (*NYT*), but also one in the *Guardian*. *ICG* was quoted mainly as a source of conflict analysis and of recommendations for political action – in particular with regard to the diplomatic victory for Hamas in agreeing to a ceasefire and Egypt's help in this respect.

For the other two NGOs, we found 26 references to *HRW* in the peak month February 2011, and 22 for *AI* in the peak month February 2014. Compared to the other contexts, a smaller proportion of references were of factual nature, while there were more references used for interpretative or indeed prescriptive purposes.

AI was quoted 22 times in February 2014 – and here in this context we can see *AI*'s impact as a good example of a successful NGO 'push' onto the news agenda through the publication of new and therefore newsworthy facts with clear moral implications. Most of the coverage relates to a substantial report published by *AI*, which accuses, as the *NYT* reports on February 27, 2014: "Israeli forces of being 'trigger happy' and using excessive force in the West Bank. The human rights organization said it had documented the killings of 22 Palestinian civilians in the West Bank in 2013, a sharp rise from the previous two years. At least 14 of them were killed during protests, the group said, adding that in all the cases the Palestinians did not appear to have been posing a direct and immediate threat to life" (Kershner, 2014).

Remarkably, the *AI* report triggered also some coverage in news agencies such as *AFP* and *Xinhua*, but also coverage in the local Israeli newspaper *Haaretz* on February 27, that is, one day before the report was covered by the *NYT*. In the *Haaretz* article, however, *AI* credibility is questioned: While the article covers the core accusations of the report about disproportionate and indeed wilful violence and killings committed by Israeli security forces, the author also gave ample space to a source from the Israeli Foreign Ministry dismissing the report on the grounds that those who were killed were indeed a threat.

HRW was cited mostly in press agency reports such as *Associated Press* (*AP*) and *AFP*, but also in one article in the *Financial Times* (*FT*). Most of these publications related to the implications of the recent Egypt uprisings for Palestinian/Israeli security in February 2011. In the *FT* of February 10, 2012, *HRW* was quoted with factual evidence about the crack-down of Palestinian security services against protesters, but also with calls on the EU and other donors to stop funding for the Palestinian security services until they were held accountable for human rights violations.

Overall, in the Israeli–Palestinian case, the covered INGO references seem to be a result of communication activities by the three 'superpower' NGOs. It appears plausible that NGOs become more visible whenever they are able to create newsworthy stories by themselves (through the uncovering of new facts or, as in the case of *ICG*, through the provision of relevant and timely analysis). There is a clear tendency of local media to give ample voice to government sources describing NGOs as interest groups with more or less "hidden" political agendas, whereas international media seem to accept the three examined INGOs as trustworthy and impartial sources.

Discussion of the Findings of the Qualitative Analysis

When returning to our overarching question about cross-case patterns, three observations stand out. First, most of the coverage in the peak months of violence-intensive conflicts could be described as being 'pulled' by events on the ground, particularly, when there was renewed fighting as in Syria, Gaza or the DRC. 'Pull' effects imply that NGOs were being quoted as sources to complement already ongoing coverage of conflict. This needs to be qualified, however, by the observation that INGOs proactively contributed to stimulate demand for their knowledge by publishing reports, rather than just providing expert voices.

Another kind of pull factor that benefited particularly the *ICG* seemed to be major upcoming events or diplomatic initiatives that required media interpretation.

Especially in conflicts with a less high intensity of violence, we also found substantial evidence of NGO successfully 'pushing' media coverage. 'Pushing' implies here that NGOs were able to generate media coverage through their own initiative by publishing reports (e.g. containing new information and analysis on human rights violations or actors driving violent conflict) or holding press conferences that subsequently trigger media coverage in their own right, often with reactions from political actors. This contrasts with NGOs being sought out as sources by journalists for news stories generated originally from other actors or major events. Typically, many NGO reports did produce such effects, including from some local media who either endorsed or questioned them, or who provided local governments views. A rough estimate would be that around 25% of such references are 'push', which indicates the substantial impact that these INGOs have with news media in these country cases – although their agendas for action are often reframed by local media as political statements supporting or opposing partisan views. The figure is higher than the rough average of around 15% share of "NGO-driven" articles Powers found in his content analysis of US media outlets with respect to human rights and humanitarian NGOs (Powers, 2018).

Secondly, most of the coverage using INGO references (roughly 40–50%) is of a factual nature, providing evidence about victims and the nature of violence. Another 30–40% is interpretation and analysis about the conflict dynamics and positions of conflict parties, and another 20–30% are various calls for action. Some of those are relatively vague in nature containing warnings about future dynamics, but also more explicit calls on the international community to put pressure on certain actors, on local government to address impunity and show restraints, or more complex prescriptions to prevent or stop violence. But the impact on the individual conflict settings is not as clear-cut: Given that the factual evidence is about human rights violations, these citations imply already an implicit action frame and this is what triggers particularly local actors' reaction. It is clear that particularly in the cases of DRC and Burundi, especially *AI* and *HRW* reports seem to generate quite a lot of domestic political resonance and official government reaction, some of it accusing these INGOs of political biases and hidden agendas.

Thirdly, there are considerable differences regarding the question of which type of media reacts to INGO reports. Perhaps unsurprisingly, a large share of the references could be found in news agency reports, especially the *AFP* and *AP*. There was a clear "interest or proximity" bias relating to French-language media for the African cases. The Israel–Palestine case had the smallest number of press agency reports and the greatest number of articles in quality newspapers, especially *NYT*, *FT* and *Guardian*, but also local newspapers such as *Haaretz*. Overall, most of the audiences in the cases of Syria and Palestine/Israel were international, whereas there was greater local resonance in the two African cases, particularly, Burundi. Overall, local media tended to treat these INGO reports generally as influential, and there was also greater controversy reported regarding potential "political agendas", sparked both by local political actors and the local media themselves.

An analysis of the differences between the three NGOs is also instructive. On the whole, in quantitative terms, *AI* was most successful with 'push' citations in its peak months with *HRW* not too far behind, while *ICG* references were significantly more likely in pull dynamics. Overall, *AI* and *HRW* had a similar (and much higher) level of visibility in these peak months in marked contrast to *ICG*. We suggest that the reason can be found less in the fact that *ICG* has less resources available, but that *AI* and *HRW* provide more valued "raw material" for news about human rights and democracy violations. In fact, most of the *AI* citations were of a more factual nature with significantly less analysis and calls for actions than *HRW* and *ICG*. *HRW* and *AI* arguably benefited in media terms from HR violations being relatively simple to understand in their significance and could be immediately connected with critique and potential political consequences at domestic and international levels.

ICG is most in demand by the media when a conflict is already going on and diplomatic initiatives are planned or under way, demanding interpretation of actor motives and potential consequences of action. Interestingly, they are much less likely to have their normative recommendations reflected in the media than *HRW*, even though this is *ICG*'s main mandate. The frequent designation of *ICG* as a "think tank" rather than a conflict prevention or peace-building NGO illustrates this point further. What is interesting is that *HRW* seems to leverage quite successfully its human rights expertise to also provide conflict analysis to media (despite this not being their main expertise) and calls for actions such as sanctions (which may be counter-productive for agreeing ceasefires or stopping violence). *HRW* may thus be more successful in connecting with dominant liberal frames and news values than *ICG* is.

Assessing the Increasing NGO Influence on Media Debates on Armed Conflict

In the following, we provide a preliminary normative assessment of our findings primarily against the normative benchmark of NGOs as providers of accurate and transparent expert knowledge within the representative liberal tradition as identified by Powers (2017). Alternative models include advocacy roles as in participatory democracy, outreach roles engaging civil society or the voice of radical criticism for excluded constituencies. The communication activity of NGOs in the context of armed conflict has often been criticized for relying on appeals to emotion that mobilizes public empathy with 'weak' and 'innocent' victims, 'names and shames' perpetrators of violence and channels anger and outrage into support for outside intervention. Boltanski (1993) has analysed this as an effective communicative strategy to produce solidarity with distant suffering, while others have shown that this strategy has indeed been used by humanitarian NGOs in the past (Dogra, 2012; Nash, 2008). The downside comes not just from critiques of military intervention, but also that these moral frames and emotionalization hinder the identification of relevant knowledge and multiple perspectives needed for a more accurate analysis of the conflict and the rational weighting of policy options.

However, our research suggests that the emotionalization is less of a problem than portrayed, confirming the observation of the "emergence of a style of humanitarian appeal that departs from previous ones in terms of aesthetic quality, problematizing photorealism, and in terms of moral agency, breaking with the traditional registers of pity as motivations for action (guilt and indignation, empathy and gratitude)" (Chouliaraki, 2010, p. 114).

This evolution may be a result of internal or external criticism as "demands by communications, campaigns and advocacy professionals to eschew dehumanizing, stereotypical depictions of distant others are (at least partly) accepted" (Orgad, 2013, p. 310). We found that many NGOs themselves believe that over-emotionalized communication is potentially detrimental to their reputation as reliable, trustworthy actors (Motion & Weaver, 2005). NGOs have to anticipate not only 'empathy fatigue' within their audiences (Kinzey, 2013, p. 5), but also the risk of jeopardizing established relationship with journalists and institutional actors. This is why especially the largest transnational NGOs put strong emphasis on evidence-based reporting, citing multiple sources and emphasizing facts instead of emotions. Some NGOs have established fact-checking standards superior to journalistic standards, given that they are under less time pressure with more resources, put a premium on protecting their reputation from errors or need to reach evidential standards required by courts. Reliable facts (which, embedded in an appropriate narrative, may also stimulate audience anger or compassion) thus appear to be the key asset for NGOs to build sustainable relationships with individual supporters, journalists and political actors. *HRW*, but also smaller local NGOs have internalized this logic and adapted their research and communication output accordingly.

Although the resources of established transnational NGOs enable them to 'drive' media discourses more easily, in contexts of high violence and difficult security conditions for Western journalists, local NGOs can also sometimes succeed in giving voice to local populations in conflict zones. The media-ersatz function of NGOs appears even more important in times when political actors of diverse ideological background seek to control or even suppress independent media coverage from the ground, as can be observed in Burundi, Macedonia, Syria or Israel/Palestine. This suggests that journalists' reluctance to use NGO information because of potential 'hidden agendas' may be exaggerated, and that in times when news media increasingly depend on 'desk coverage', a (sensitive) reliance on factual reports produced by NGOs, ideally with different organizational causes and activity profiles, can effectively diversify and enrich journalistic stories – especially when official sources are the only alternative for obtaining information from the ground. We also found that local NGOs' influence can be considerable, especially in contexts of lower violence intensity, relatively low presence of international media and a diverse, yet under-funded local media environment. As the results for Burundi illustrate, local NGOs are able to outweigh communication activities of large transnational NGO 'superpowers'. In such contexts, in which neither international nor local journalists seem to have the means required for sufficient independent journalistic research, NGOs seem to be capable of driving media coverage on their own at times by producing newsworthy reports and disseminating needs and grievances of local populations. Without these efforts, many needs, grievances, but also political abuses would remain undiscovered, and the political costs of corruption and human rights violations would be substantially lower. Consequently, local NGOs can become a de facto opposition force, as they are the last remaining actor to be able and willing to challenge a government's conflict frames. This makes NGOs increasingly targets for government repression. In Israel, NGOs have been obliged to reveal any source of funding from abroad, a provision that has been criticized for targeting "groups that campaign for Palestinian rights while excluding rightwing pro-settlement NGOs, who will not be required to reveal their often opaque sources of foreign funding" (The Guardian, 2016). In Burundi, during the conflict on the extension of the presidential mandate, leaders of major local NGOs have been forced into exile since 2016, and new laws stipulate that NGOs need to obtain government authorisation prior to any public activity and to receiving funding from international donors (RFI, 2017).

As elaborated above, NGOs differ in the degree to which they manage to gain access to the news media and shape their content. This is partly due to the highly variable resources that NGOs have at their proposal and the reputation they have managed to build over many years. However, we have also observed differences across NGO mandates. The most frequently cited organizations are either those who specialize in defending human rights, such as *AI* and *HRW,* or those who are on the ground catering to humanitarian needs, such as *DWB/MSF* and the *Red Cross* organizations. By contrast, organizations promoting conflict mediation and understanding root causes of conflict (such as *ICG*) are less influential in terms of their media visibility, even if they may have considerable "behind-the-scenes" influence on policymakers. This may partially be due to differences in their ability to produce relevant and expert knowledge since the large human rights-based and humanitarian NGOs often have the necessary local presence and manpower to provide accurate, timely and reliable information as compared to the slower communication cycles of 'thinking' NGOs. Nevertheless, a result of this is that some analytical frames are more often disseminated than others, especially those denouncing human rights violations. Although not necessarily intended by these NGOs, in cases when journalists rely almost exclusively on a small number of NGOs as sources of conflict coverage, this may contribute to binary, moralist framings of armed conflict, with clearly identified 'victims' and 'perpetrators' – as we could show for the media framing in the early days of the Syrian conflict (Meyer et al., 2018).

Last but not least, a potential danger may arise if NGOs become more and more media actors on their own, while mainstream 'traditional media' become more and more platforms of disseminating knowledge from external producers. Especially transnational NGOs have easier access to conflict situations on the ground, but also more financial means to produce high-quality media content themselves, or to 'sponsor' such output through the provision of logistical support and financial incentives to freelance conflict journalists. Some transnational NGOs also offer much better working conditions than media organizations and hire country experts and former journalists into their ranks. In these conditions, media organizations are increasingly deciding against sending their own staff into conflict regions and rely instead on the professionally produced contents of NGOs either directly or indirectly through news agencies, to cover armed conflicts in non-strategically important regions at less cost and risk. Instead of hiring, retaining and training well-qualified foreign correspondents, they tend to rely on temporary, part-time, freelance or less experienced staff to save costs. The problematic issue here is not just a loss of country expertise and journalistic skills, but also a loss of journalistic independence in making choices about sources and analytical frames to use, as many of these journalists work for multiple organizations, including NGOs, PR companies or businesses. The danger is that especially in conflict areas where mainstream media refrain from providing any substantial coverage, NGOs come to absorb journalist functions. This would undermine the established professional deontology of journalists, gradually devalue independent journalistic research, decrease the plurality of stories disseminated in the public and lower the incentive for media organizations to invest in quality journalism.

Conclusion

The changing role of NGOs in the production of conflict knowledge and news discourses, as well as conflict management has long been neglected. In this chapter, we have focused on observing and explaining the increasing presence of NGOs in news discourses on conflicts covered by the INFOCORE project. While we provided mainly quantitative evidence for this growing importance, other members of INFOCORE working on the dynamics of news story construction have confirmed through qualitative interviews with journalists "that many stories had 'occurred' to them as a result of various external forces and influences, whether that was in the form of political leaders, non-governmental organizations or other media" (Hoxha & Hanitzsch, 2018, p. 54).

We have introduced the so-called 'supply-and-demand model' to explain why NGOs have become more attractive sources of news production. This is partly due to the reduced economic capacities of media organizations to conduct research in the increasingly risky conflicts. Both transnational and local NGOs have anticipated this demand and professionalized their information production and dissemination strategies using new IT technology and social media. The production and dissemination of evidential claims about conflict-related issues has become an essential asset in NGO communication strategies to bolster their reputation and to gain attention from journalists, political actors and the general public. However, not all NGOs are the same in how they communicate, on what and with what effectiveness. We have identified a number of key variables such as NGOs' budget resources, funding dependencies, activities profiles, local presence and organizational cultures that can explain why some NGOs are more visible in media discourse than others. Moreover, NGOs' influence varies greatly according to specific context. We have shown that in countries with a lower priority on the international news agenda and under-funded local media environment, NGOs can sometimes manage to initiate news debates. By contrast, in other contexts such as Israel–Palestine, an increase in NGO presence is linked to violent escalations such as during the 2014 Gaza War, when NGOs often were the only available source of information from the ground.

The normative implications are ambiguous from the liberal perspective of NGOs as providers of reliable and accurate expert knowledge. One could justify this rising influence with their ability to provide highly relevant, reliable and verifiable factual information about conflicts that are otherwise hard to come by, especially relating to less frequently covered countries (Meyer & Sangar, 2017). So, NGOs play today an indispensable part in providing citizens and policymakers with knowledge about conflicts and human rights abuses that would otherwise be noticed too late, not at all or be misunderstood. On the other hand, the growing influence of NGOs comes with a narrowing of conflict knowledge and perspectives, the risk of hollowing out of journalist functions and independence, and some instances of NGOs speaking outside of their expertise and influenced by funding interests. Media organizations need to step up their support for quality journalism and carefully consider in what ways collaboration with NGOs can help to advance rather than undermine public trust in journalism.

Notes

1 http://jamcat.mscc.huji.ac.il/navigator/ More methodological background information on JAmCAT can be found in Baden and Stalpouskaya (2015, p. 14).
2 Title: "Football-mad president plays on while Burundi fears the return of civil war" (*The Guardian*, 6 April 2014).
3 "Closing Doors: Reduction of Democratic Space in Burundi" (translation by authors).

References

AFP Report. (2010). *Burundi: Le rapport de HRW est un 'acte de vengeance' dit le gouvernement* [Burundi: The report of HRW is an 'act of vengeance', said the government]. Available online at www.arib.info/index.php?option=com_content&task=view&id=2804.

Amnesty International. (2016). *2016 global financial report*. Available online at www.amnesty.org/en/2016-global-financial-report/

Baden, C., & Meyer, C. O. (2016). *The INFOCORE approach to media influence on violent conflict*. INFOCORE working paper presented at International Studies Association Annual Convention, Atlanta, 16–19 March 2016.

Baden, C., & Stalpouskaya, K. (2015). *Common methodological framework: Content analysis. A mixed-methods strategy for comparatively, diachronically analyzing conflict discourse*. INFOCORE Working Paper 2015/10. Available online at www.infocore.eu/results/working-papers/

BDO. (2016). *Human Rights Watch Inc, Financial statements*. Available online at www.hrw.org/sites/default/files/supporting_resources/financial-statements-2016.pdf

Bob, C. (2005). *The marketing of rebellion: Insurgents, media and international activism*. Cambridge, UK: Cambridge University Press.

Boltanski, L. (1993). *La souffrance à distance: Morale humanitaire, médias et politique* [Distant suffering: Humanitarian moral, media and politics]. Paris, France: Editions Métailié.

Chouliaraki, L. (2010). Post-humanitarianism. Humanitarian communication beyond a politics of pity. *International Journal of Cultural Studies, 13*, 107–126.

Cottle, S., & Nolan, D. (2007). Global humanitarianism and the changing aid-media field. *Journalism Studies, 8*, 862–878.

Crawford, E., & Davies, K. (2014). The international protection of journalists in times of armed conflict: The campaign for a press emblem. *Wisconsin International Law Journal, 32*, 1–36.

Dogra, N. (2012). *Representations of global poverty: Aid, development and international NGOs*. London, UK: I.B. Tauris.

Evans, G. (2011). *Preventing violent conflict: What have we learned?* USIP second annual conference on preventing violent conflict. Available online at www.gevans.org/speeches/speech438.html

Fenton, N. (2010). NGOs, new media and the mainstream news: News from everywhere. In N. Fenton (Ed.), *New media, old news: Journalism and democracy in the digital age* (pp. 153–168). London, UK: SAGE.

Gamson, W. A., & Wolfsfeld, G. (1993). Movements and media as interacting systems. The *Annals of the American Academy of Political and Social Science, 528,* 114–125.

Hallward, M. C. (2013). *Transnational activism and the Israeli-Palestinian conflict.* New York, NY: Palgrave Macmillan.

Hoxha, A., & Hanitzsch, T. (2018). How conflict news comes into being: Reconstructing 'reality' through telling stories. *Media, War & Conflict, 11,* 46–64.

Kaufman, E., Salem, W., & Verhoeven, J. (2006). *Bridging the divide: Peacebuilding in the Israeli-Palestinian conflict.* Boulder, CO: Lynne Rienner.

Kershner, I. (2014). Palestinian Found Dead After Standoff With Israelis. *New York Times.* Available online at https://www.nytimes.com/2014/02/28/world/middleeast/palestinian-man-found-dead-after-standoff-with-israeli-forces.html.

Kinzey, R. E. (2013). *Promoting nonprofit organizations: A reputation management approach.* New York, NY: Routledge.

Meyer, C.O., de Franco, C., & Otto, F. (under review) *Heeding warnings about violent conflict: Persuasion in foreign policy.* Cambridge, UK: Cambridge University Press.

Meyer, C. O., & Sangar, E. (2017). As NGOs fill the gaps in conflict news, should we be worried? *New Europe,* 8 January, Available online at www.neweurope.eu/article/ngos-fill-gaps-conflict-news-worried/

Meyer, C. O., Sangar, E., & Michaels, E. (2018). How do non-governmental organizations influence media coverage of conflict? The case of the Syrian conflict, 2011–2014. *Media, War & Conflict, 11,* 149–171.

Motion, J., & Weaver, C. K. (2005). The epistemic struggle for credibility: Rethinking media relations. *Journal of Communication Management, 9,* 246–255.

Musa, A. O., & Yusha'u, M. J. (2013). Conflict reporting and parachute journalism in Africa: A study of CNN and Al Jazeera's coverage of the Boko Haram insurgency. *Journal of Arab & Muslim Media Research, 6,* 251–267.

Nash, K. (2008). Global citizenship as show business: The cultural politics of make poverty history. *Media, Culture & Society, 30,* 167–181.

Orgad, S. (2013). Visualizers of solidarity: Organizational politics in humanitarian and international development NGOs. *Visual Communication, 12,* 295–314.

Otto, F., & Meyer, C. O. (2012). Missing the story? Changes in foreign news reporting and their implications for conflict prevention, *Media, War & Conflict, 5,* 205–221.

Pettersson, T., & Wallensteen, P. (2015). Armed conflicts, 1946–2014. *Journal of Peace Research, 52,* 536–550.

Powers, M. (2016). Opening the news gates? Humanitarian and human rights NGOs in the US news media, 1990–2010. *Media, Culture & Society, 38,* 315–331.

Powers, M. (2017). Beyond boon or bane: Using normative theories to evaluate the newsmaking efforts of NGOs. *Journalism Studies, 18*, 1070–1086.

Powers, M. (2018) *NGOs as newsmakers: the changing landscape of international news*. New York, NY: Columbia University Press.

RFI (2017). *Burundi: l'ONU s'alarme de la répression contre les ONG* [Burundi: The UN warn againt the increasing repression of NGOs]. Available online at: http://www.rfi.fr/afrique/20170207-burundi-repression-ong-alerte-rapport-onu

Robinson, P. (2014). News media, war and world politics. In C. Reinemann (Ed.), *Political Communication* (volume 18 of the Handbooks of Communication (HOCS)) (pp. 187–210). Berlin, Germany: De Gruyter Mouton.

Ron, J., Ramos, H., & Rodgers, K. (2005). Transnational information politics: NGO human rights reporting, 1986–2000. *International Studies Quarterly, 49*, 557–588.

Steinberg, G. M. (2011). The politics of NGOs, human rights and the Arab-Israel conflict. *Israel Studies, 16*(2), 24–54.

The Guardian (2016). *Israel passes law to force NGOs to reveal foreign funding*. Available online at https://www.theguardian.com/world/2016/jul/12/israel-passes-law-to-force-ngos-to-reveal-foreign-funding

Van Leuven, S., & Joye, S. (2014). Civil society organizations at the gates? A gatekeeping study of news making efforts by NGOs and government institutions. *The International Journal of Press/Politics, 19*, 160–180.

8 Political Leaders, Media and Violent Conflict in the Digital Age

Gadi Wolfsfeld and Linor Tsifroni

This chapter is devoted to the topic of how political leaders mired in violent conflict deal with the media in the modern age of communication.[1] It is clear to even the most casual of observers that the dawn of the 'digital age' has led to major changes in the role the media play in such conflicts. The newer media provide political leaders, both in and out of power, with powerful new tools for waging war over national and international public opinion. A number of previous studies have dealt with the role of the newer media in the politics. This is one of the first, however, to look at the ways in which the new technology has provided both opportunities and threats for political leaders involved in conflict. It is also one of the only studies to look at the issue from a cross-cultural perspective.

This study is based on in-depth interviews conducted with government officials and members of the opposition from four entities involved in conflict: Israel, Palestine, Kosovo and Macedonia. The goal was to better understand how these leaders have adapted to the new realities brought about by the introduction of so many new forms of communication. It should be considered an exploratory study in that we intend to provide an initial list of the most important changes that emerged from these interviews.

Our argument is structured as follows. First, we will present some of the previous scientific literature on the topic, and then present some of the major theoretical arguments, followed by a brief description of the methodology employed for collecting the evidence and brief overviews of the conflicts that studied. Next, we will briefly summarize each of the conflicts. This is followed by the findings and discussion section, in which we use selected quotes from various interviewed leaders to demonstrate what we have learned. In the conclusion, we will summarize our findings and suggest future avenues for research.

Scientific Background

The role of the traditional media in conflict has received considerable attention in the scientific literature. A partial list of topics includes the role of the media in uprisings and revolutions (Aday et al., 2010; Cohen & Wolfsfeld, 1994; Popkin, 2015; Wolfsfeld, 1997; Wolfsfeld, Frosh, & Awabdy, 2008;), terrorism (Hess & Kalb, 2003; Liebes & Kampf, 2009; Norris, Kern, & Just, 2003; Yarchi, Wolfsfeld, Sheafer, & Shenhav, 2013) and wars (Aday, Livingston, & Herbert, 2005; Baum & Groeling, 2010; Bennett, Lawrence, & Livingston, 2007; Hoskins & O'Loughlin, 2010; Wolfsfeld 1997, 2004).[2] Other studies have investigated the role of the media in conflict resolution, especially the role of the media in peace processes (Hackett, 2006; Lynch & McGoldrick, 2005; Saleem & Hanan, 2014; Sheafer & Dvir-Gvirsman, 2010; Spencer, 2005; Wolfsfeld, 2004; Wolfsfeld, Alimi, & Kailani, 2007).

Although research on the role of the newer media and conflict is in its early stages, it is clear that interest in the field is growing.[3] Perhaps unsurprisingly, much of this research deals with how the new communication environment provides important opportunities to weaker challengers to mobilize supporters (Bennett & Segerberg, 2012; Bimber, 2014; Cable, 2017; Gohdes, 2015; Morozov, 2011; Youmans & York, 2012) and get their messages out to a variety of publics. There is also quite a bit of scholarly interest in the ways that terrorist organizations use the Internet and social media, both for recruitment and for sharing information (Klausen, 2015; Weimann 2015; Yarchi et al., 2013).

There has been less work put into adopting the perspective of political leaders, especially those who are in power or more established members of the opposition who are trying to replace them. According to Zeitzoff (2017), over 75% of world leaders have active Facebook and Twitter accounts. The newer media have become essential tools for leaders to communicate with both their own people and the world. This is especially true for those involved in violent conflicts, where the ability to mobilize local and international support can have a major impact on their levels of success (Wolfsfeld, 1997). As with any change in the communication environment, the advent of the digital age has brought both opportunities and threats to these leaders.

Given the goals of this chapter essay, we will focus specifically on the literature regarding leaders' use of the newer media in violent conflicts. It is noteworthy that the role of the newer media in one of the conflicts we studied *has* received a certain amount of scholarly attention. The use of the newer media in the Israel–Palestine conflict became especially salient during the last two wars in Gaza (Kwon, Oh, Agrawal, & Rao, 2012; Rapaport, 2010; Ward, 2009; Zeitzoff, 2011, 2017). In addition, some studies have looked more at the 'image war' as Israelis and Palestinians compete as each promotes their cause both locally and to the international community (Wolfsfeld, 2018; Yarchi, et al., 2013).

In the present study, we intend to expand the literature in three major ways. The first is to examine this issue specifically from the perspective of political leaders involved in violent conflict. As noted, this is an important and somewhat neglected perspective because so much of the literature on the newer media has dealt with either social movements or election campaigns. Secondly, we shall propose a more detailed list of the advantages and disadvantages for these leaders that can be linked to the modern media ecosystem. This should make a theoretical contribution to the literature in the field. Finally, we will deal with two new conflict areas that have been mostly ignored: Macedonia and Kosovo. The more conflicts that are studied, the more likely we will be in a position to understand cross-cultural commonalities and differences with regard to this issue. In this particular essay, the emphasis will be what these different leaders have in common. This will provide an opening for generalizing more than in previous studies, which have often focused on one country or conflict.

Theoretical Claims

It is important to begin this discussion by making two preliminary points. First, despite our focus on the newer media, the underlying assumption is that one cannot make a clear distinction between the various types of media that now exist. Chadwick (2013) describes these changes as a "hybrid media system". Chadwick's major point is that it is critical to see the new communication environment as one in which older and newer media not only feed off and influence each other, but also have an ongoing impact on the overall flow of information among citizens. As Chadwick notes: "Internet-driven norms of networking, flexibility, spontaneity, and ad-hoc organizing have started to diffuse into our politics and media, and these norms are generating new expectations about what counts as effective and worthwhile political action" (p. 210). Van Dijck and Poell (2013) make a similar point by noting: "Social media logic is increasingly becoming entangled with mass media logic" (p. 3). Modern political leaders have little choice but to adapt to this new hybrid media environment.

The second major point is that although this specific study focused on leaders involved in violent conflicts, there is every reason to believe that many of the principles discussed here can be applied more generally. While there are no doubt cross-cultural variations, Western leaders running for election or simply attempting to compete for political influence face similar opportunities and threats. While some of the points we make are more narrowly focused, researchers should attempt to think about which parts of the discussion could be applied to related areas of research.

The major theoretical claims we intend to make will only be *listed* in this section. The underlying rationale and empirical evidence in support of these claims will be presented in the findings section. The underlying question refers to the ways in which the ability of political leaders to

achieve their communication goals has become easier and/or more difficult in the digital age.

As noted, this should be considered an exploratory study. The purpose
is to create an initial list of changes that have taken place during the
digital era. The underlying assumption is that other studies and scholars
will add their own additions to this list and will contribute to our level
of cumulative knowledge on the topic. In addition, as we begin to examine this issue in an increasing number of cultural settings, countries and
circumstances, we will gain a better understanding of how the role of the
newer media varies. To put it differently, the opportunities and threats
detailed below should become the *dependent* variables in future studies.
We will discuss four opportunities and two threats.

The four opportunities are: (1) an increase in leaders' ability to bypass
the traditional media and communicate directly with various publics;
(2) the ability to use the newer media to generate news stories in the traditional media; (3) an increased ability to mobilize supporters for their
cause and (4) an enhanced ability to send messages to the international
community.

The two major threats to modern political leaders are: (1) the difficulties they face taking control over the flow of information about the
conflicts; and (2) the pressures leaders face to react much more quickly
than in the past to events as they erupt on the national and international
agenda.

Methodology

The data here is based on one specific dimension of the larger research
project focused on the ongoing interactions between political leaders and
the media. In this chapter, we will report on the results of interviews carried out in Israel (15), Palestine (15), Macedonia (10) and Kosovo (15).
In addition to those interviewees who were elected to their positions,
some were officials involved in diplomacy, while others were leaders of
political organizations. The major criteria for selection were that interviewees must be somehow involved in promoting a particular political
agenda concerning the conflict and had to have ongoing contact with the
media concerning this issue. All interviewees were promised anonymity,
so only a general description of their role and status is noted when they
are quoted below. The one-hour interviews were conducted in person in
2015, in the local language. They were recorded, transcribed and then
translated into English.

As is usually the case with research employing in-depth interviews, the
overall approach was mostly inductive rather than an attempt at hypothesis testing. We did have a number of theoretical expectations that were
based on previous research and our own observations of current events.
Nevertheless, the overall methodological plan was to listen and learn

and, based on these conversations, say something meaningful about political leaders and the new media.

Although the interviews covered a large number of topics, the core questions that are the most relevant to this chapter are presented below (some of the answers reported in the findings section were based on follow-up questions that varied among interviewees).

1   Can you tell me something about the amount of efforts and resources that you invest in attempting to communicate using the Internet in general and more specifically the social media?
2   Has this changed much in recent years?
3   Would you say you mostly use social media to communicate with various publics or more to attempt to interest journalists?
4   Do you sometimes exploit social media for sending messages to international audiences, including foreign leaders?
5   Can you please tell me something about the differences you find in using social media compared to traditional media?
6   Some leaders have argued that, in the last few years, the amount of time they have to react to events has become much shorter. Do you agree with this? If so, do you think it is a problem?
7   Many people have talked about the fact that people walking around with camera phones has changed the nature of the news, meaning much more stories start from the field. Do you think this new development has affected the news and the conflict itself?

The Conflicts: A Very Brief Summary

Israel–Palestine Conflict

While we assume that most readers know quite a bit about this conflict. Nevertheless, a short summary is in order.[4] The conflict, which started as a political and nationalist conflict over competing territorial ambitions, has shifted over the years from the large-scale regional Arab–Israeli conflict to the more specific Israeli–Palestinian conflict. Although there have been a number of clashes, a turning point was the 'Six-Day War' of 1967, which resulted in Israel taking over all of Jerusalem and capturing Gaza and the West Bank. The territories captured in 1967 (whose border is known today as the 'Green Line') remain one of the most contentious issues in the conflict.

The First Intifada (uprisings) began in December 1987. In 1993, when the violence declined, Israel and Palestinian officials signed a Declaration of Principles (the Oslo Accords) guiding the interim period of Palestinian self-rule. It was assumed that these accords would set the stage for a comprehensive peace agreement, but all subsequent attempts have ended in failure.

The Second Intifada broke out in September 2000. In contrast to the relatively low level of Palestinian violence of the First Intifada, the second uprising included guerilla warfare and a large number of terrorist attacks. Israel also used a considerable amount of force to put down the uprising, including targeted attacks on terrorist leaders.

In early 2006, the Islamic Resistance Movement, Hamas, won the Palestinian Legislative Council election and took control of the Palestinian Authority (PA) government. Attempts to form a unified government failed.[5] The status quo remains, with Hamas in control of the Gaza Strip and the PA governing the West Bank.

In 2008, in response to the ongoing rocket fire from the Gaza Strip to Israel, Israeli Prime Minister Ehud Olmert decided to conduct a military operation (known as the 'Gaza War'), which included airstrikes, naval operations and a ground invasion. The goal was to damage the Hamas infrastructure and to reduce the level of rocket fire aimed at Israel. Two other recent military operations in the Gaza Strip against Hamas were (to use the Israeli terms) Operation Pillar of Defense (2012) and Protective Edge (2014).

In 2016, the Freedom House (2016b) lowered the grade given to Israel from "Free" to "Partly Free", based on the following rationale: "Israel declined from Free to Partly Free due to the growing impact of *Israel Hayom*, whose owner-subsidized business model endangered the stability of other media outlets, and the unchecked expansion of paid content – some of it government funded – whose nature was not clearly identified to the public." As in other Western countries, there are often controversies in Israel regarding if and how social media should be regulated. However, for the most part, this form of communication remains open and free.

When it comes to the PA, the Freedom House makes a distinction between the West Bank, which is governed by *Fatach* and the Gaza Strip, which is ruled by Hamas. Nevertheless, both entities are considered "Not Free". Here is the explanation for that designation for the West Bank: The media are not free in the West Bank. Under a 1995 PA press law, journalists may be fined and jailed, and newspapers closed, for publishing 'secret information' on PA security forces or news that might harm national unity or incite violence. Media outlets are routinely pressured to provide favourable coverage of the PA and Fatah. Journalists who criticize the PA or Fatah face arbitrary arrests, threats and physical abuse. Reporters are also subject to administrative detention by Israeli forces (Freedom House, 2016a).

Freedom House (2017) describes the lack of press freedom in Gaza as follows: "The media are not free in Gaza. Following the 2007 schism, Hamas security forces closed down pro-Fatah media outlets and began exerting pressure on media critics, including through the use of arbitrary arrest, detention, beatings, and other tactics of intimidation (...). In 2012, Hamas's media office banned Palestinian journalists from giving interviews to or working with Israeli media. In 2016, foreign journalists reported various arbitrarily enforced restrictions on their work, including detentions and interrogations, excessive registration fees for vehicles, and unreasonable conditions attached to permits."

It is worth noting that when comparing the three antagonists involved in this conflict, with regard to the social media, Israelis have the most freedom, with the West Bank second, while in Gaza publishing oppositional material on the Internet can be considered a crime.

The Conflict in Macedonia

Macedonia is a country of about two million citizens and was the only entity to secede non-violently from Yugoslavia in 1991.[6] While relations between the Macedonian majority and the Albanian minority were historically peaceful, there were a number of events that led to tension and bloodshed. Significant violence broke out in 2001, including a number of violent events between local insurgents and the Macedonian government. One of the more important was the 'Aracinovo Crisis': On June 12, 2001, members of the Albanian National Liberation Army (NLA) took control of the ethnically mixed village of Aracinovo.[7] After attempts at negotiation and international intervention failed, the Macedonian government launched an attack on the NLA forces on June 21. Eventually, the insurgent forces were allowed to evacuate their positions. A ceasefire was declared on July 5. Nevertheless, there were a number of battles and other acts of violence in the months ahead.

In January of 2002, the two sides settled the Ohrid Agreement, in which, among other things, the Macedonian government agreed to improve the rights of the Albanian minority. The Albanian side gave up any demands for independence and agreed to recognize all Macedonian institutions. Even after the agreement, however, there were acts of violence. In October of 2014, NLA insurgents fired rocket-propelled grenades at a Skopje government facility and further violent confrontations occurred in April and May of 2015.[8]

When it comes to freedom of the press, Freedom House (2016c) gives Macedonia low grades. In fact, in 2016 the country moved from "Partly Free" to "Not Free", "due to revelations indicating large-scale and illegal government wiretapping of journalists, corrupt ties between officials and media owners, and an increase in threats and attacks on media workers". As discussed below, this lack of press freedom has significant ramifications for the use of social media by those in the opposition. The expression of oppositional views in the social media in Macedonia is relatively free, especially when compared to the traditional news media.

The Conflict in Kosovo

The conflict in Kosovo can be traced back to an historical dispute with roots in both Albanian and Serbian ethnic-nationalisms, each claiming rights to the area.[9] The Kosovo War took place from February of 1998 to June of 1999 between the Federal Republic of Yugoslavia (which, at the time, included the Republics of Montenegro and Serbia) and the Kosovo Liberation Army. It was also the first time NATO went to war, by providing air support for the Kosovo forces. The bombings continued until an agreement was reached, which led to the withdrawal of Yugoslavian troops from Kosovo and the establishment of the United Nations Interim Administration in Kosovo (UNMIK). In June 1999, the outline of a new Kosovo peace deal was announced and direct talks between Serbian and Kosovo Albanian leaders began in 2003. In 2004, following some years of tense peace, the worst clashes since 1999 between Serbs and ethnic Albanians erupted.

Direct talks between ethnic Serbia and Kosovo leaders on the future status of Kosovo started in 2006 and, at the end of that year, voters in a referendum in Serbia approved a new constitution declaring that Kosovo is an integral part of that country. Kosovo's Albanian majority boycotted that ballot (the Albanians are the largest ethnic group in Kosovo).

Kosovo authorities declared independence on February 17, 2008, and 110 UN members recognized Kosovo's independence. Traditional allies of Serbia, including Russia, China and Greece, refused to recognize the new state. Serbia protested the decision, issued a warrant for the arrest of Kosovo leaders for high treason and adopted an "action plan" that involved withdrawing its ambassadors from countries that recognized Kosovo.

Serbia and Kosovo began direct talks to try to end their dispute in March of 2011. The talks are referred to as the "Belgrade–Pristina Dialogue" (based on the names of the two capital cities) and were facilitated by the United Nations. These were the first talks between the two countries since Kosovo broke away from Serbia. The two sides made some progress, including an agreement to regulate border crossings between the two entities.

With regard to press freedom, Freedom House (2016c) gives Kosovo a grade of "Partly Free", with the following explanation: "Laws protecting press freedom are mostly in line with European Union (EU) standards, but their enforcement is inconsistent. While the media environment is diverse, many private outlets struggle financially, particularly those serving Kosovo's ethnic Serb population. The public broadcaster, *Radio*

Television of Kosovo (*RTK*), is funded through the state budget, leaving it vulnerable to politicization. Journalists continue to experience death threats and occasional physical attacks in connection with their work." As with Macedonia, the expression of dissident views in the social media in Kosovo is mostly free.

Political Leaders and the Newer Media:
Findings and Discussion

As discussed, the findings are based on what we learned from the interviews conducted with the four sets of leaders from the three conflicts. In this relatively early stage in the research, we focused on those opportunities and threats that were mentioned by many different leaders. While we will also allude to a few interesting differences, this will not be the major concern here. We start by discussing the ways in which the new technologies provided new opportunities to political leaders that were unavailable in the past.

Opportunities

As noted, the digital age provides a number of important opportunities for modern leaders that were previously unavailable. We focus on four major ways in which the newer media can serve the political leaders from both the government and the opposition. First, while political leaders are often frustrated by the coverage they receive in the traditional media (Street, 2012; Wolfsfeld, 2001, 2004; Wolfsfeld & Sheafer, 2006), they find the unfiltered nature of the new media to be a major advantage. President Trump's almost obsessive use of Twitter is the best-known example of this phenomenon (Barbaro, 2015; Ott, 2017), but the basic strategy is one that we found in all four of the conflict areas we studied.

As might be expected, oppositional leaders who found the mainstream media difficult to access were the most enthusiastic about the opportunities provided by the newer media. Oppositional leaders in Macedonia, for example, talked about their extensive use of the social media and argued that it was essential because all of the traditional outlets were owned by (what they called) government "cronies". A senior member of one of the oppositional parties echoed the sentiments of many of the interviewees about the newer media:

> *This is one powerful tool and we as a political party [...] are active in order to spread our ideas, because it is the cheapest way to convey certain positions to the public. And since we do not have access to the mainstream media, the social networks are very important.*
> (M6, 12/6/2015)[10]

The case of the Palestinian leaders is similar, but somewhat more complex. Unsurprisingly, they have no faith in the Hebrew press in Israel to convey their messages and many also feel the international media is against them.[11] Nevertheless, many leaders claimed that they also use the social media to bypass the mainstream media in Arabic because they are frustrated about how they are covered. As with many of the people we spoke to, Palestinian leaders emphasized the advantages of reaching various publics through an unfiltered medium. The comments by one of the Palestinian leaders were typical:

> *There are clear differences between messages that are published through social networks and messages put out via traditional media outlets. Social media publishes the messages fast and in a vital way that stays very close to the average citizen while using simple language and terminology.*
>
> (P4, 1/12/2015)

It is important to emphasize that those in power also find the social media an extremely useful tool for bypassing the mainstream media. President Trump is not the only powerful leader to feel the press is against him. The ability to talk *directly* to large audiences represents an extremely positive development for those both in and out of power.

Generating News Stories for the Traditional Media

The second opportunity for modern political leaders is the ability to use the newer media as a convenient tool for attracting interest from the traditional media. It may appear somewhat contradictory that modern political leaders want to both bypass the traditional media and exploit them. Thinking strategically however, it makes perfect sense.

All of the leaders we spoke to from the four entities were cognizant of the continuing importance of the traditional media for reaching a variety of audiences. It is no secret that many journalists invest time following leaders' social media tweets and Facebook posts to see if there is anything sufficiently interesting that they can turn into a news story. In some ways, this practice can be seen as the digital version of the traditional press conference or press release. Here is a typical comment about this from a political leader in Kosovo:

> *When I joined politics, Tim Juda, a journalist, recommended to me to start using Twitter on a daily basis. He is a friend of mine and he says that if a modern politician doesn't have a Twitter account, they don't have access to the world journalists' network as well. Nowadays, Facebook is not as helpful as Twitter is as a primary source of information for journalists in the world. Thus, I've been using it for*

> *five years now, and I can say that I consider myself as a source of information in the Balkans, for international journalists on Twitter, from Macedonia to Greece, and I am followed, perhaps, by thousands of journalists on my information network. I consider it an essential tool.*
>
> (K9, 22/12/2015)

This practice has other similarities to the traditional press release or conference. The most important is that, given the vast number of leaders in each of these conflict zones who use these tools, only a few can expect to have their stories turned into news. The rules of competition regarding whose tweets and posts are picked up by the news media remain the same as in the pre-digital era. The more powerful leaders are inherently more newsworthy and the weaker ones can only hope to gain access if their messages are especially provocative.

It is important to re-emphasize that it is not an 'either-or' type of situation for political leaders. The modern politician may use somewhat different strategies for sending messages through the traditional and newer media, but the ultimate goal is to exploit as many different communication channels as possible. As is the case more generally in public relations, there is a certain skill set that leaders and their staff need to develop in order to be successful in these efforts. One Israeli leader provided some useful insights about his strategy for exploiting the various forms of media:

> *Today in Israel, Twitter is better than other social media tools because there is an inner circle of journalists there. The distinction is different – we use social media when we want to stimulate interest among all journalists at once. Actually, we have two ways to access the media: I can penetrate a central media outlet, contact Amit Segal [an Israeli political journalist] and tell him: 'Amit I have a story just for you,' and then we both have a definite interest in the growth of the story because for him it's an exclusive, and for me because I want it to be a big story. The second way is to flood a post on Facebook and I know everyone will take it, but with less interest. It is a kind of negotiation that we do on a daily basis.*
>
> (I4, 27/5/2017)

Mobilizing Support for the Cause

If there is one indisputable advantage to using social media that has been discussed in previous research, it is the ability to mobilize supporters for one's cause (Bennett & Segerberg, 2013; Cable, 2017; Katz-Kimchi & Manosevitch, 2015; McCurdy, 2012; Youmans & York, 2012). It is unsurprising that much of this research focuses on social movements and other extra-parliamentary organizations. Here too, the weaker the political actor, the more difficult they find it to gain access to the traditional media (Wolfsfeld 1997, 2011).

Some leaders are popular enough on social media that they can reach audiences that are as large as, or even larger than, those they can contact via the 'mass' media. The following comments by a Kosovo political leader were representative of this understanding:

> *According to the British Council's survey that I just read today, this means that now we have a Kosovan population of over 70 percent using the Internet, either daily or few times a week. So, if you are not present on social networks, then you have a much narrower channel of information to the citizens.*
>
> (K12, 22/12/2015)

As discussed in the previous literature cited above, the social media also provides other extremely important advantages when communicating with supporters or potential supporters. Major advantages include being able to frame messages with no editorial filter, the ability to distribute multimedia types of content, quickly mobilizing supporters for public events, the ability to direct audiences to other supportive content and fundraising. Perhaps the most important advantage of all for political leaders is that the social media provide an ongoing *dialogue* with audiences that often leads to a greater level of engagement.

This is one reason why the newer media have become especially important in election campaigns (Gurevitch, Coleman, & Blumler, 2009; Trippi, 2013; Zurn, 2017). These newer media allow campaigners to turn their supporters into *activists* who can then mobilize others to the cause. While there has been less research on political leaders' ability to exploit the new media between elections, it is clear that the same principles apply. One Israeli political leader talked about his own extremely positive experience in building his political party by relying heavily on the social media:

> *When I founded the party, we had no money and no operations, so I did most through Facebook and that was how we gathered the people. The great ability of social media, as opposed to a newspaper or radio or television, is that they are bi-directional. In other words, they allow you to gather people around an idea. In the past, you had to be engaged intensively in doing segmentation and you had to go around the world looking for people interested in your idea. Today, you just launch it and it comes back to you with a pretty good segmentation of people who agree with you. Therefore, my initial effort was made through Facebook.*
>
> (I4 27/5/2015)

None of this enthusiasm for the newer media is meant to suggest that they are some form of magical wand that can bring success to all those who wave it. Every political leader has access to these tools. Their level of success in exploiting them is not just a matter of digital knowledge and experience; it rests on a more fundamental question about leaders' inherent popularity among various publics. As is the case with all forms of media, political success leads to success in the media (Wolfsfeld, 2011). This can be seen as a good example of the Politics–Media–Politics principle (Wolfsfeld, 2011, Wolfsfeld, Segev, & Sheafer, 2013). Here, variations in the political environment (the relative popularity of leaders and their messages) lead to variations in media performance (more people liking and sharing the leaders' political content), which can then lead to further variations in the political environment (higher levels of political support).

Sending Messages to the International Community

All the digital opportunities that have been discussed thus far are easily applied to political leaders of almost all Western democracies. The next point, however, can be linked more specifically to leaders involved in violent conflicts. While many political leaders often find themselves in need of international support, this need is especially strong for those involved in violent conflicts.

In an asymmetrical conflict, the weaker side is especially desperate for the rest of the world to intervene. Those who are able to enlist third parties onto their side have a better chance of surviving than those who find themselves isolated from the world (Wolfsfeld, 1997). This has always been the case with the traditional media and the social media now provides new opportunities to gain access to a global audience.

This point was made very forcibly by almost all of the Palestinian leaders who were interviewed. One argued that while the Israelis were in a better position to exploit the traditional media, Palestinians depended more on the social media to get their message out. Here is how one of the Palestinian leaders put it:

> With regard to sending out Palestinian and Israeli messages to European leaders, I say the Israelis use their media outlets as the main channel of sending their messages to European leaders whereby Palestinians rely more on Twitter, which has become the best tool for them to send out their messages.

(P1, 30/10/2015)

The Israelis have also invested a great deal of resources into harnessing the power of the social media in the battle over world opinion.

One of the more interesting comments on this issue came from a senior official in the Foreign Ministry, who talked about using social media to reach Arab audiences:

> *As soon as we talk about digital media, you have more tools to measure, and have more ability to keep track of things with hashtags, some kind of search or another. What we see at the micro-level is that we reach people. We see who is following us because these studies have showed that we are doing not bad. It's not just Israelis, and it is not only non-Israelis. We can see and identify information that goes away and really comes to other media outlets. Important examples come from those who are not considered pro-Israel. We see that the Arabic page, in terms of 'likes', is our most popular, with 320,000 likes.*

> (I11, 16/9/2015)

The problems facing political leaders in Macedonia and Kosovo are somewhat different. While the Israeli–Palestinian conflict is almost constantly on the international news agenda, leaders from these conflict areas are mostly ignored unless violence breaks out. Some of the leaders we spoke to in those countries talked about exploiting the new media to raise awareness about their problems.[12] One of the Kosovo leaders brought up an interesting example where Facebook became especially significant:

> *One concrete example was when Facebook recognized Kosovo as a region in the list of states, whose citizens are allowed to register. We also published a new item on social networks that Facebook recognizes Kosovo, given that the wording was unusual because it is the United Nations recognizing states and not social networks. But, on the other hand, it showed a new field of digital diplomacy. Then this news got the momentum, and at the end it reached the front page of the New York Times newspaper, Facebook recognizes Kosovo, on Washington Post, on BBC trending news, being one of the most clicked news of the day, on The Atlantic magazine, Slate magazine, and it was selected as one of 10 leading news of diplomacy for 2013.*

> (K4, 17/12/2015)

In order to summarize this section, it is perhaps best to think about the newer media as an additional communication tool that political leaders use in order to compete, both domestically and internationally. This list of functions is certainly not exhaustive, but it does provide some helpful insights about how the communication environment has changed in recent years. However, it is important to bear in mind that previous developments in communication have also led to significant changes in how political leaders operate. The invention of the telegraph, radio and television are three important examples. Whether the most recent changes represent a more revolutionary development remains an open question.

Threats

As is always the case, changes in communication technology represent a double-sided sword. They present both opportunities and threats for political leaders. The notion of threats refers to those aspects of the new communication environment that create difficulties and dangers for modern political leaders that their predecessors were less likely to face. While a number of threats emerged from the interviews, we will focus on two that are especially relevant to leaders involved in violent conflicts: (1) The difficulties they face taking control over the flow of information about the conflicts; and (2) the pressures leaders face to react much quicker than in the past to events as they erupt on the national and international agenda.

Lack of Control Over the Flow of Information

The most important negative change for political leaders involved in violent conflict, especially for those in power, is the difficulties they face in their attempts to take control of the flow of information. Here, the flow of information refers to everything that is "known" and seen concerning a particular conflict. We have put "known" in quotation marks because one of the problems with the digital age is that journalists and citizens find it increasingly difficult to make a clear distinction between facts, rumours, fake videos and outright lies. While traditional journalism was far from perfect, there was, at least among the most reputable news organs, a sense of professional responsibility for verifying the stories they produced.

At first glance, the very notion of 'taking control over information' may seem like an undemocratic approach to this issue. It certainly runs against the value of governmental transparency. For many, the difficulties modern leaders face in controlling the flow of information in the digital age should be seen as a blessing rather than a curse. Scholars studying this topic must bear this perspective in mind when thinking about this question.

However, our approach is somewhat different. We are quite consciously looking at the issue from the perspective of those who have the responsibility for governing. When these leaders are involved in violent conflicts, their ability to take control over the flow of information is likely to have an impact on their ability to succeed. The analysis intentionally leaves out questions concerning the best possible outcome for a given conflict. For those who are uncomfortable with this approach, it is worth remembering that there *are* circumstances, such as the war against terrorism, when the international community is relatively united in support of those attempting to defeat these enemies.

Two major aspects of this change are especially notable. The first is the widespread use of camera phones, which enable observers to instantly record, upload and disseminate conflict events as they take place. The second is the fact that governments find it extremely difficult to keep secrets. While there have always been leaks that embarrassed, endangered or reduced the legitimacy of those in power, the ability of individuals to gain access to classified information has grown enormously in recent years.

The ways in which the spread of camera phones has put political and military leaders on the defensive is apparent in the Israeli–Palestinian conflict. Many Palestinian and human rights activists have learned to use their phones to record any abuses by the Israeli security forces. This is good news for the Palestinians and bad news for the Israeli authorities. The comments by one Palestinian leader were typical of this phenomenon:

> *The people's media, so I call it, has a major influence on news and on the conflict itself through publishing live coverage from the site of events. This is more crucial in cases where journalists are not present while ordinary people with their smartphones are there to capture the scenes. People now use their smartphones and publish images almost instantly, causing a major echo and impact to what they do. This in itself is positive.*
>
> (P6, 11/1/2015)

The Israeli leaders who were interviewed considered their inability to take control over the flow of information to be a serious problem. Revealingly, some of the more serious problems in this area had to do with problems associated with their own troops going into battle with cell phones. This became especially apparent during the Second Lebanese War in 2006. The continual flow of bad news from the front coming from the troops themselves led to a significant change in policies when the Gaza War broke out in 2008. Among other things, the policies prohibited soldiers from taking their cell phones into battle and strictly controlling officers being allowed to give interviews to the press without prior authorization (Rappaport, 2010; Wolfsfeld, 2018).

Concern about how the lack of control over information, especially videos, is not limited to the Middle East. One leader from Kosovo talked about how information spread through the newer media, which is often picked up by the mainstream media, can make a bad situation even worse:

> *I have watched some sequences, and thanks to these video materials provided by some portals, I have been watching some materials of RTS [Radio Television of Serbia], which simply contributed to the spread of dissatisfaction among citizens, in the sense that this is what is really happening, KFOR [NATO] NMIK [United Nations] and EULEX [European] troops are having an impact on the citizens, or they are limiting citizens' freedom, which then affects in massiveness of demonstrators, protesters, which led to the burning of premises at the border points.*
>
> (K7, 21/7/2015)

Concerns about the media's effects on political violence are not new. In Northern Ireland, for example, a number of television stations made a conscious and mutual decision not to send cameras when violent protests would erupt (Wolfsfeld, 2004). In an unusual step, they decided that the presence of cameras could inflame an already volatile situation. One can only wonder whether such policies would be possible today. Given that anyone with a cell phone is in a position to both film and upload video clips of such events, few television stations can afford to ignore them. Even if they did, those who were interested in inflaming the situation could easily distribute the most sensational scenes to a large audience, even without any coverage in the mainstream media. A counter-argument could claim that the presence of large television cameras are more likely to inflame a volatile confrontation than a video clip taken with a cell phone.

A related issue is the difficulty that political and military leaders have in the modern age in keeping secrets. Again, we stress that although having secrets leaked can often bring positive results for a society, it does make it more difficult for modern leaders to govern. This problem arose quite often in the interviews with Israeli leaders, who were especially concerned about leaks concerning military operations. Here are the comments of one fairly senior political leader about this problem:

> *One day I saw during the operation ['Protective Edge'], a presentation the IDF [Israel Defence Forces] presented something in one of the meetings of the Cabinet. Someone leaked. I wanted to perform a polygraph test for everyone, but Netanyahu refused. This was an attempt to influence someone through the media on public opinion, in a certain way on the decision making as well. It teaches us that the walls of the meeting rooms are not sealed.*
>
> (I7, 8/8/2015)

The Instantaneous News Cycle

The other major problem that political leaders face in the digital age is the speed at which information and images spread around the globe. Virtually all of the political leaders we spoke to talked about how difficult it was to deal with the dramatic change in what is conventionally known as the 'news cycle'. In the digital age, political leaders have significantly less time to consider their options and respond. It is almost as if the entire political world has "Attention Deficit Hyperactivity Disorder". Here is how one Kosovo leader responded when asked about whether there had been a change in how quickly leaders were expected to react to breaking news:

> *Certainly yes. There is huge time difference. In the past, if you were able to wait for 24 hours for reaction, for example once the evening news were over, you were able to wait until the next evening news, because those were prime-time massive information news, now you cannot wait like that. Now, even in midnight you can tell your opinion which will be placed early in the morning.*
>
> (K2, 5/5/2015)

The problem is that the pressure to respond too quickly in times of crisis can be dangerous Here, again, it is hard not to think of the many times when President Trump has decided to tweet an ill-considered reaction to something he has heard or seen in the media. Most analysts believe that his aggressive rhetoric concerning North Korea in the summer of 2017 increased the probability of war between those two countries. Modern political leaders no longer have the luxury enjoyed by their predecessors of carefully gathering all of the facts and carefully considering their options before responding. Below is the way an Israeli leader formulated this concern when asked about the pressure to respond quickly:

> *This is true. The pace here is very quick. Once we could convene a meeting of consultants and think of what to say and what not to say and what and what not to initiate. Today the speed is high and need the ability to respond immediately and non-response has a meaning. That is why you see many more young men and women in new media.*
>
> [Interviewer: Do you think this does damage to leaders' decision making process?]
>
> *There is no doubt that when you need to respond quickly, the range of errors may grow. If you have to react to a specific event and a there are only a few hours, it is a problem. When the incident happened in the morning, you have until tonight to fix, to consider,*

> *delete, and if you have 15 minutes after the event to give a com-*
> *ment on a social network, which is viral and many people see it in*
> *seconds and minutes, there is no doubt that the number of mistakes*
> *is growing.*

> (I13, 19/4/2015)

Another leader from Kosovo made a similar point about the instantaneous news cycle:

> *This has happened gradually, and this process started two or three*
> *years ago. You get used to it, and it becomes an ordinary thing in*
> *life. So, the media pressure has started imposing on us another way*
> *of working, not as in the past. For example, you may be in your car*
> *and write your own opinion and post it, being aware that the media*
> *will take it immediately.*

> (P14, 5/5/2015)

The fact that modern leaders have to react quickly does not necessarily
mean that they have to change their actions or their policies. The more
perceptive and experienced leaders realize that the best course of action
is often to respond rhetorically rather than actually changing course.
However, when it comes to violent conflicts, ill-considered rhetoric can
certainly lead to some very dangerous consequences.[13]

Conclusion

The goal of this essay was to provide some details about the major opportunities and threats faced by modern political leaders involved in
violent conflicts as they enter the digital age. As with every new technology, the emergence of the Internet, and especially the social media, has
brought good and bad news for these leaders.

Four major changes were seen as good news for these leaders. The first
was an increased ability to use the newer media to bypass the traditional
media. The second was the ability of leaders to exploit the newer media
for generating news stories that the mainstream media would then pick
up and provide a much larger audience. Third, the dawn of the digital
age has provided political leaders, both those in government and those
in opposition, with a dramatically increased ability to mobilize support
for their causes. Finally, the change in the media environment has provided leaders with a much more effective means of communicating with
the international community. All of these changes are especially important for weaker challengers who are attempting to overcome the inherent
disadvantages they have always faced in their attempts to use the more
traditional media.

On the other hand, the threats that were discussed were especially likely to create difficulties for those in power. By far the most serious difficulty they face is their inability to maintain control over the flow of information and images concerning the conflict. It is not an exaggeration to suggest that the spread of cell phone cameras and the difficulties that leaders have in keeping secrets can be considered a revolutionary change in the ability of modern leaders to manage conflicts. As discussed, we are fully aware that this change also had positive ramifications because this has become a powerful weapon for those working on behalf of human rights. Nevertheless, not all official actions and plans are inherently evil, and some amount of secrecy is essential for governments to function.

The final threat has to do with the significant shortening of the traditional news cycle. All of the interviewed leaders from the four entities discussed this development and most saw it as a problem. Modern leaders are now expected to react immediately to every major event, and this new reality is unhealthy. As discussed, even when leaders confine themselves to rhetorical responses, such reactions have the potential to further inflame an already dangerous situation.

The way forward is clear. First, we need to expand the list of opportunities and threats that confront leaders in the digital age. As an example, we have not dealt with the fact that the Internet and social media have become much more powerful tools for spreading hate than for reconciliation.[14] However, this should also be considered as a new threat not only for leaders, but also for the entire world.

Second, we need to better understand cross-cultural differences in the use and abuse of the newer media in violent conflicts. As noted, the purpose of this article was to discuss the commonalities that were found by interviewing leaders from the four entities. We need to expand the number of conflicts being studied and to give more thought to those variables that are most likely to lead to variations in the role the newer media play in different conflicts.

One such cross-cultural difference was alluded to earlier. In a country such as Macedonia, where oppositional actors find it so difficult to gain access to the mainstream media, these leaders are much more dependent on the social media. It would also be a good idea to compare those societies where the vast majority of citizens have easy access to the Internet with those where citizens have little or no access. Yet another direction for future research along these lines would compare conflicts that are high on the international news agenda (such as the Israel–Palestinian conflict) with those that are rarely mentioned in international news (such as Macedonia and Kosovo). Clearly, this will have a major impact on the ability of leaders to exploit all forms of media for sending messages to the international community.

Finally, this paper has intentionally avoided thinking about policies that would lead to newer media playing a more constructive role in violent conflicts. This should be the ultimate goal for those who study this issue. Given our assumption about newer technology always being a double-edged sword, researchers and policymakers need to give some serious thought to how the new 'swords' can be used in ways that decrease the likelihood of bloodshed.

Notes

1 This research was conducted as part of INFOCORE, an international collaborative research project funded under the 7th European Framework Program of the European Commission.
2 None of these bibliographic lists is to be considered exhaustive. They are given as examples of some of the more noteworthy research in each of these fields.
3 A useful summary of much of this research can be found in Zeitzoff (2017).
4 Although a huge number of books and articles have been written about this conflict, we mention three of the more recent volumes: Bourke (2013), Bunton (2013), Shavit (2015).
5 At the time of this writing (fall 2017), there is a renewed attempt to form a unity government.
6 Those interested in learning more about the conflict in Macedonia should read Crighton (2003); Engström (2009); MacEvoy (2014); Micevski and Trpevska (2015).
7 See https://en.wikipedia.org/wiki/2001_insurgency_in_the_Republic_of_Macedonia #Ara.C4.8Dinovo_crisis, and www.crisisgroup.org/europe-central-asia/balkans/macedonia/macedonia-last-chance-peace
8 https://en.wikipedia.org/wiki/2001_insurgency_in_the_Republic_of_Macedonia #Ara.C4.8Dinovo_crisis. See also: www.bbc.com/news/world-europe-32674121. It is worth noting that the NLA eventually became a political party with many of the insurgents becoming politicians who were elected to office.
9 For more about the conflict, refer to Adams (2016), Judah (2002) and Webber (2009).
10 We will use the first letter of the entity to indicate where the interview was conducted (in this case, Macedonia) and the interview number we used when transcribing the interviews. We use the American system of writing the date of the interview (Month/Day/Year).
11 Most Israeli Jews feel that the international media are biased against *them*.
12 It should be remembered that, for some political leaders in these countries, especially those in power, 'no news is good news'. While all leaders have an interest in sending their messages to the global community when necessary, some would prefer to stay off the international news agenda. This is also true for the Israeli government, although given the number of journalists permanently stationed in the country, this is unlikely to happen very often.
13 Again, it is difficult not to think of Trump in this regard. Most analysts believe that his aggressive (and often immediate) rhetoric concerning North Korea in the summer of 2017 increased the probably of war between those two countries.
14 This issue was discussed in a previous article from this research project (Wolfsfeld, 2018).

References

Adams, E. (2016). *History of Kosovo and Conflict*. Seattle, WA: Amazon.

Aday, S., Farrell, H., Lynch, M., Sides, J., Kelly, J., & Zuckerman, E. (2010). *Blogs and bullets: New media in contentious politics*. Washington, DC: United States Institute of Peace.

Aday, S., Livingston, S., & Hebert, M. (2005). Embedding the truth a cross-cultural analysis of objectivity and television coverage of the Iraq War. *The Harvard International Journal of Press/Politics, 10*(1), 3–21.

Barbaro, M. (2015). Pithy, mean and powerful: How Donald Trump mastered Twitter for 2016. *International New York Times* (October 5th). Available online at www.nytimes.com/2015/10/06/us/politics/donald-trump-twitter-use-campaign-2016.html

Baum, M., & Groeling, T. (2010). *War stories*. Princeton, NJ: Princeton University Press.

Bennett, W. L., Lawrence, R. G., & Livingston, S. (2007). *When the press fails: Political power and the news media from Iraq to Katrina*. Chicago, IL: University Of Chicago Press.

Bennett, W. L., & Segerberg, A. (2012). The logic of connective action: Digital media and the personalization of contentious politics. *Information, Communication & Society, 15*, 739–768.

Bennett, W. L., & Segerberg, A. (2013). *The logic of connective action: Digital media and the personalization of contentious politics*. New York, NY: Cambridge University Press.

Bimber, B. (2014). What's next? Three challenges for the future of political communication research. In H. G. d. Zuniga Navajas (Ed.), *New technologies and civic engagement: New agendas in communication* (pp. 215–223). New York, NY: Routledge.

Bourke, D. H. (2013). *The Israeli–Palestinian conflict: Tough questions, direct answers (Skeptic's Guide)*. Westmont, IL: IVP Books.

Bunton, M. (2013). *The Palestinian–Israeli conflict: A very short introduction*. New York, NY: Oxford University Press.

Cable, J. (2017). Communication sciences and the study of social movements. In C. Roggeband, & B. Klandermans (Eds.), *Handbook of social movements across disciplines* (pp. 185–201). New York, NY: Springer.

Chadwick, A. (2013). *The hybrid media system: Politics and power*. Oxford, UK: Oxford University Press.

Cohen, A. A., & Wolfsfeld, G. (1994). *Framing the Intifada: People and media*. New York, NY: Preager.

Crighton, A. (2003) *Macedonia: The conflict and the media*. Skopje, Republic of Macedonia: Macedonian Institute for Media.

Engström, J. (2009). *Democratization and the prevention of violent conflict: Lessons learned from Bulgaria and Macedonia*. Burglington, VT: Ashgate Publishing.

Freedom House. (2016a). *Freedom in the World 2016 — West Bank*. Available online at https://freedomhouse.org/report/freedom-world/2016/west-bank

Freedom House. (2016b). *Freedom of the Press 2016 — Report on Israel*. Available online at https://freedomhouse.org/report/freedom-press/2016/israel

Freedom House. (2016c). *Freedom of the Press 2016 — Report on Kosovo.* Available online at https://freedomhouse.org/report/freedom-press/2016/kosovo

Freedom House. (2017). *Freedom in the World 2017 — Gaza Strip.* Available online at www.ecoi.net/local_link/341803/485122_de

Gohdes, A. R. (2015). Pulling the plug network disruptions and violence in civil conflict. *Journal of Peace Research, 52,* 352–367.

Gurevitch, M., Coleman, S., & Blumler, J. G. (2009). Political communication – Old and new media relationships. *The Annals of the American Academy of Political and Social Science, 625*(1), 164–181.

Hackett, R. A. (2006). Is peace journalism possible? Three frameworks for assessing structure and agency in news media. *Conflict & Communication online, 5,* 1–13.

Hess, S., & Kalb, M. L. (2003). *The media and the war on terrorism.* Washington, DC: Brookings Institution Press.

Hoskins, A., & O'Loughlin, B. (2010). *War and media.* Cambridge, UK: Polity.

Judah, T. (2002). *Kosovo: War and revenge.* New Haven, CT: Yale University Press.

Katz-Kimchi, M., & Manosevitch, I. (2015). Mobilizing Facebook users against Facebook's energy policy: The case of Greenpeace unfriend coal campaign. *Environmental Communication, 9,* 248–267.

Klausen, J. (2015). Tweeting the Jihad: Social media networks of Western foreign fighters in Syria and Iraq. *Studies in Conflict & Terrorism, 38,* 1–22.

Kwon, K. H., Oh, O., Agrawal, M., & Rao, H. R. (2012). Audience gatekeeping in the Twitter service: An investigation of tweets about the 2009 Gaza conflict. *AIS Transactions on Human–Computer Interaction, 4,* 212–229.

Liebes, T., & Kampf, Z. (2009). Performance journalism: The case of media's coverage of war and terror. *The Communication Review, 12,* 239–249.

Lynch, J., & McGoldrick, A. (2005). *Peace journalism.* Stroud, UK: Hawthorn Press Stroud.

MacEvoy, J. (2014). *Power-sharing executives: Governing in Bosnia, Macedonia, and Northern Ireland.* Philadelphia, PA: University of Pennsylvania Press.

McCurdy, P. (2012). Social movements, protest and mainstream media. *Sociology Compass, 6,* 244–255.

Micevski, I., & Trpevska, S. (2015). What the Macedonian phone-tapping scandal tells us about clientelism in the media. *International Journal of Digital Television, 6,* 319–326.

Morozov, E. (2011). *The net delusion: The dark side of internet freedom.* Jackson, TN: Public Affairs.

Norris, P., Kern, M., & Just, M. R. (2003). *Framing terrorism: The news media, the government, and the public.* New York, NY: Routledge.

Ott, B. L. (2017). The age of Twitter: Donald J. Trump and the politics of debasement. *Critical Studies in Media Communication, 34,* 59–68.

Popkin, J. D. (2015). *Media and revolution.* Lexington, KY: University Press of Kentucky.

Rapaport, A. 2010. *The IDF and the lessons of the second Lebanon War.* Ramat Gam, Israel: Begin-Sadat Center for Strategic Studies.

Saleem, N., & Hanan, M. A. (2014). Media and conflict resolution: Toward building a relationship model. *Journal of Political Studies, 21*, 179–198.

Shavit, A. (2015). *My promised land: The triumph and tragedy of Israel.* New York, NY: Spiegel & Grau.

Sheafer, T., & Dvir-Gvirsman, S. (2010). The spoiler effect: Framing attitudes and expectations toward peace. *Journal of Peace Research, 47*, 205–215.

Spencer, G. (2005). *The media and peace: From Vietnam to the 'war on terror'.* New York, NY: Palgrave Macmillan.

Street, J. (2012). Do celebrity politics and celebrity politicians matter? *The British Journal of Politics & International Relations, 14*, 346–356.

Trippi, J. (2013). How Technology has restored the soul of politics. *MIT Technology Review, 116*, 34–36.

Van Dijck, J., & Poell, T. (2013). Understanding social media logic. *Media and Communication, 1*, 2–14.

Ward, W. (2009). Social Media in the Gaza Conflict. *Arab Media & Society.* Available online at www.arabmediasociety.com/social-media-and-the-gaza-conflict/

Webber, M. (2009). The Kosovo war: A recapitulation. *International Affairs, 85*, 447–459.

Weimann, G. (2015). *Terrorism in cyberspace: The next generation.* New York, NY: Columbia University Press.

Wolfsfeld, G. (1997). *Media and political conflict: News from the Middle East.* Cambridge, UK: Cambridge University Press.

Wolfsfeld, G. (2001). The news media and the Second Intifada: Some initial lessons. *Harvard International Journal of Press/Politics, 6*, 113–111.

Wolfsfeld G. (2004). *Media and the path to peace.* Cambridge, UK: Cambridge University Press.

Wolfsfeld, G. (2011). *Making sense of media and politics: Five principles in political communication.* New York, NY: Routledge.

Wolfsfeld, G. (2018). The role of the media in violent conflicts in the digital age: Israeli and Palestinian leaders' perceptions. *Media, War & Conflict, 11*, 107–124.

Wolfsfeld, G., Alimi, E. Y., & Kailani, W. (2007). News media and peace building in asymmetrical conflicts: The flow of news between Jordan and Israel. *Political Studies, 56*, 374–398.

Wolfsfeld, G., Frosh, P., & Awabdy, M. T. (2008). Covering death in conflicts: Coverage of the Second Intifada on Israeli and Palestinian television. *Journal of Peace Research, 45*, 401–417.

Wolfsfeld, G., Segev, E., & Sheafer, T. (2013). Social media and the Arab Spring: Politics comes first. *The International Journal of Press/Politics, 18*, 115–137.

Wolfsfeld, G., & Sheafer, T. (2006). Competing actors and the construction of political news: The contest over waves in Israel. *Political Communication, 23*, 333–354.

Yarchi, M., Wolfsfeld, G., Sheafer, T., & Shenhav, S. R. (2013). Promoting stories about terrorism to the international news media: A study of public diplomacy. *Media, War & Conflict, 6*, 263–278.

Youmans, W. L., & York, J. C. (2012). Social Media and the activist toolkit: User agreements, corporate interests, and the information infrastructure of modern social movements. *Journal of Communication, 62*, 315–329.

Zeitzoff, T. (2011). Using social media to measure conflict dynamics: An application to the 2008–2009 Gaza conflict. *Journal of Conflict Resolution, 55,* 938–969.

Zeitzoff, T. (2017). How social media is changing conflict. *Journal of Conflict Resolution, 61,* 1970–1991.

Zurn, S. (2017). The digital battle. In D. W. Johnson, & L. M. Brown, (Eds.), *Campaigning for president 2016: Strategy and tactics* (pp129–144). New York, NY: Routledge.

9 A Game of Frames in Conflict Transformation

Mapping the Media-Active Publics' Nexus of Competing Conflict Frames

Igor Micevski and Snezana Trpevska

Introduction

Societies struggling to pledge to a democratic process, in their recovery from a violent conflict, tend to be multidirectionally pulled by competing conceptions about the 'nature' of past antagonism. Different groups tend to believe in different 'truths' about why violence occurred and consequently feel uncertain about whether the achieved peace is just and sustainable. The content, the character and the public current of these conceptions about the conflict, referred to as conflict frames (Baden, 2014; Bartholomé, Lecheler, & De Vreese, 2017; Semetko & Valkenburg, 2000)[1], are obviously a critical matter of concern regarding how complex the sociopolitical aspects of future conflict transformation and reconciliation will be[2] (Drake & Donohue, 1996; Galtung, 2000). This is because various types of conflict frames encapsulate certain power relations and as they are constructing frictional collective identities, their public flow may impact potential antagonists' positions in the prospective conflict developments (Wolfsfeld, 2004). By implication, just as they contribute to constructing frictional identities, publicly circulated conflict frames may also be important in constructing residual spaces of solidarity and alliances that cut across hitherto antagonistic lines, opening up spaces for new frictions. A greater understanding of this nexus of fluctuating lines of antagonism and solidarity is especially important for conflict transformation processes in the age of social media, where virtually anyone is able to contribute to the construction and dissemination of conflict frames, adding new qualities into the conflict dynamics.

The aim of this study,[3] therefore, is to identify the repertoires of these competing conflict frames in post-conflict societies and to better understand them by deconstructing each frame's potential to create future frictions, including the potentials to support relapses into violence. We consider comparatively two cases of violent conflicts on the Balkan Peninsula: Macedonia, a moderately violent conflict with ever-present post-conflict tensions; and Kosovo, a somewhat more severe conflict with ubiquitous presence of moderate post-conflict tensions.[4] They were chosen on the basis of the similarity of their political contexts, such as transposing from a single to a multiparty system (Ramet, 2002), suffering from failure of democratic institutions or state capture, ethnic complexity (Bieber, 2004), and a strengthened role of social media in thinking about public issues. The cases do have, some important differences, however, including the severity of hostilities and the international status of the polity (Weller, 2009). We map the varieties of existing competing conceptions about conflict manifestations, constructed and disseminated by what we call media-active publics, defined as members of recent protest movements in both societies that are active on social media. We then analyse the ways in which the competing conflict frames they construct support or challenge existing hegemonic lines of antagonism in these societies. We thus answer the questions, what types of conflict frames do media-active publics tend to reproduce through the social media, what is their operational rationale and how can they be utilized in conflict transformation processes?

In this chapter, we explore the idea that rather than pushing opposing conflict frames into alignment and consensus by all means, conflict transformation strategies, including media strategies, need to examine the possibility of embracing and supporting certain types of counter-hegemonic conflict frames to transfigure violent conflict into non-violent (or at least less violent) conflict outcomes. To arrive at our definition of conflict frames and framing interactions, we use Gamson's notion of 'collective action frames'. Using the MaxQDA software, we analyse transcripts from focus group interviews with media-active publics.

Theory

Since our approach necessitates interdisciplinary conceptual thinking, we need to define the general theoretical framework, briefly consider the conceptual tools important for understanding of our argument and explain how that is tied to our methodology and findings. In this section, we first identify Postmarxism[5] as our general theoretical framework, and then we elaborate on the concepts of 'conflict', 'conflict transformation', 'competing conflict frames', 'hegemony' and 'media-active publics', and link their substance to our goals.

Postmarxism in Conflict Transformation and Communication

It is clear thus far that this study presupposes the idea that conflict is constitutive of society (and democracy). This idea is central to the so-called agonistic notion of 'radical pluralist democracy' (Mouffe, 2000), which is theoretically rooted in the Postmarxist tradition.

Literature from peace and conflict studies has been flooded by normative ideas about preferred paths to conflict transformation. These ideas, widely accepted by practitioners and policymakers, tend to make readymade and often simplified propositions as to what construes a successful post-violent-conflict process (Little & Maddison, 2017, p. 146). They often advocate for the formation of overarching narratives that support 'common ground' ideologies, emphasizing "social harmony" and "overlapping consensus of community" (Hirsch, 2012, p. 2), working in the direction of de-escalation. Recently, however, a branch of reconciliation theory scholars have suggested that conflict transformation and reconciliation need to embrace struggle rather than to suffocate conflicting positions (Little, 2014; Schaap, 2006), and should acknowledge that these processes are to be regarded as flexible endeavours, performed in open and "new political spaces" (Maddison, 2017, p. 155). Advocates for agonistic pluralism in conflict transformation acknowledge that in volatile societies, the opening of new spaces may involve immensely greater risks than those encountered in more stable settings, but consider that risk as necessary in moving away from violence toward democratization.[6] In doing so, they do not engage in detailed analysis about how that approach would look in practice, and hence they leave a great deal of uncharted territory. One of the questions to ask would be, for example, what symbolic resources are readily available in the public or, in other words, what views, beliefs and attitudes circulate among various publics about the nature and causes of the conflict, the parties involved in the conflict situation and possibilities and directions of its resolution? Hence, the 'symbolic resources' here are envisaged as a discursive pool of ideas in the public realm that may be used to stop or perpetuate conflict. They may be used by lay publics, politicians or international community, in conflict transformation processes.

Unanswered questions aside, this agonistic pluralist turn makes an interesting argument, and since it is rooted in a Postmarxist standpoint (Harrison, 2014; Howson, 2017), it rests on at least three assumptions important for our analysis of competing conflict frames: It dismisses or it is greatly sceptical of the existence of non-adversarial types of politics; it rejects essentialism and it is anti-deterministic. The *first* claim implies that conflict *is* constitutive of society and democracy (Laclau & Mouffe, 2001). To Chantal Mouffe, for example, liberalism, and its quest for rational deliberation and consensus making, leads to political arrangements that may even pose a threat to democratic values. For her, pushing for non-adversarial consensus is just another "expression of hegemony and the crystallization of power relations" (Mouffe, 2000, p. 49). The *second* notion of concern, Postmarxism's anti-essentialism, has a constructionist trait. It necessitates the awareness that individuals and groups do not possess fixed identities and that "the 'social' represents the process of meaning construction" (Howson, 2017, p. 26).

These identities, then, are in constant antagonistic flux induced by the social processes of meaning construction, which operate both "within and across hegemony" (2017, p. 26). *Finally*, anti-determinism in Postmarxism marks the radical departure from Marxist deterministic ideas in which the final revolutionary transformation of society is an inevitable effect of history. Postmarxism, in contrast, claims that conflicts infuse risk in the "social", and therefore history must be envisaged as a multiplicity of *open* processes and systems that are "never complete" (Sim, 2013, p. 17).

The briefly elaborated Postmarxian framework provides this study with the political 'imagery' necessary to conceptualize open-ended political processes in which conflict is ubiquitous, constructed and perpetual. Our mapping of the competing conflict frames of media-active publics may be understood as repertoires of 'symbolic resources' in this 'imagery' that may be invoked in construction of new sociopolitical antagonisms. In the following section, it is important to elaborate on what is meant by *conflict, conflict transformation and competing conflict frames* in the context of this research.

Conflict Definition and Conflict Transformation

Conflicts may be understood in a variety of different ways relating to situations of friction between individuals, societies and states (Reuben, 2009, p. 49). They may be defined and classified in connection to the level of manifest violence, ranging from non-violent friction to full blown wars. They may be differentiated according to the types of antagonists involved or the frictional issue at their core – as interstate or intrastate, ethnic, religious or ideological conflicts (Frère & Wilen, 2015). Finally, multilayered definitions tend to combine variables such as time, level of intensity of violence and possible intervening strategies (Swanstrom & Weissmann, 2005) to land at more sophisticated typologies, differentiating between stable peace, unstable peace, open conflict, crisis and war.

Among the multiplicity of ways to define conflict, one stands especially relevant for our argument. 'Conflict' may be understood as a pervasive state of affairs and may be put in juxtaposition with the concept of 'dispute/escalation' in a way that the former consists of underlying frictional domains[7] knitted in social and political life, and the latter represents a particular manifestation of those frictional domains. Using the Macedonia conflict in 2001 as an example related to our comparative analysis: violence escalated in parts of the north-western regions of the country, the Macedonian police forces engaged with an armed group of Albanian rebels. The outbreak devastated the area and left a couple hundred military and civilian casualties behind. This episode may be considered a manifest escalation of a deeper conflict that includes broader issues concerning sovereignty and separatism, the relation between the state and existing ethnicities, the state legitimacy, claims of discrimination, criminality, corruption, etc. The underlying conflict thus contains the 'possibility of escalation', and the manifestation embodies that 'possibility'. This study analyses the available frames of the underlying conflict reproduced by media-active publics, and it considers conflict transformation to be a process of metamorphosis of violent conflict manifestations into non-violent but still adversarial outcomes/conflicts (Maddison, 2017).

Competing Conflict Frames and Framing Interactions

Studies of conflict framing adopt different types of definitions of conflict frames and framing (Bartholomé et al., 2017). Since the concept of framing is not a fixed one within communication literature, this section provides a definition applicable to this study and it is mostly based on the interactionist paradigm within framing theory.

The interactionist paradigm sees the symbolic discoursive currents on any issue in the public realm as a process of meaning creation through interactive co-construction. Framing in this sense is "a dynamic enactment and shaping of meaning in ongoing interactions" (Dewulf et al., 2009, p. 158). Frames are understood simply as interpretative cues that "[...] provide meaning to an unfolding strip of events" (Gamson & Modigliani, 1987, p. 143); they are keys within human interactions that signal how a situation is to be understood (Goffman, 1974). This approach is based on the proposition that people, through their interaction, are "co-constructing the meaning of their world", that this meaning is "located in the discourse", and that conflict framing may be understood as "an interactional process in which the meaning of the conflict situation is co-constructed through the meta-communicational aspects of discourse" (Dewulf et al., 2009, p. 163).

Expedient for our construction of the conflict frame definition are Gamson's interactionist collective action frame conceptions, which we use to come to the construction of our conflict frames and framing interactions. In *Talking Politics,* Gamson (1992, p. 7) claims that collective action frames consist of three components: injustice, agency and identity. Injustice, he argues, denotes "moral indignation expressed in the form of political conciseness". The agency refers to the idea that collective action might change political reality, and finally the identity component refers to the definition of some 'we', typically in opposition to some 'they'. His collective action frame contains a combination of references to injustice, a location of an adversary and support for collective action. Our conflict frames use Gamson's line of thought concerning the last two components, conflict frames and conflict framing interactions, which contain a definition of a certain *adversary* and *support collective action against that adversary*. We, however, additionally expand on the first component of his collective action frame, and in that we are informed by social psychology literature. Social psychology has suggested the existence of five beliefs that propel groups toward conflict: injustice, vulnerability, distrust, superiority and helplessness (Eidelson & Eidelson, 2003, pp. 182–192). In our analysis, these elements are a part of what we may call *frictional domain*, which is a sphere of friction envisaged as wider than the injustice frame in Gamson's sense. A frictional domain contains one or more of the five types of beliefs that Eidelson and Eidelson (2003) isolate from social psychology literature. The frictional domain is the location of antagonism because it expresses a relation between a realization of a displacement (dissatisfaction) in social reality and the implied urge for resolution of that displacement. Our conflict frame thus contains three elements: a frictional domain, an identification of an adversary (antagonist) and an implied antagonistic action.

Following from this argumentation, and following from the varieties of ways media-active publics in our study use conflict frames and participate in conflict framing interactions, we could extrapolate certain ways in which they ultimately define the underlying conflicts in the respective cases (the explanation of which may be found in the *Method* section). Here it suffices to say that some of these "definitions of the conflict" are opposed to others. For example, some of the interactions of media-active publics within the focus group interviews suggest that the underlying conflict is basically a conflict between two antagonizing ethnic groups, while other interactions would suggest that the *same* conflict is a result of an antagonism between the citizens and the hegemonic or authoritarian state. The first vectors the antagonism against an ethnocultural group, and the second vectors antagonism against a corrupt or authoritarian elite, despite both being considered *one and the same* conflict. We call these *competing conflict frames* because they compete for prominence in a variety of ways and are in opposition to one another. They may be viewed as *publicly available symbolic resources* that are used to legitimize or de-legitimize potential manifestations of collective action, leading to (or pulling away from) certain types of conflict manifestations. Some of these conflict frames support hegemonic discourses about conflict, and others are counter-hegemonic. Mapping the competing conflict frames of media-active publics and deconstructing their potential to create frictions between adversaries presupposes that antagonistic discourses opposing hegemony are useful for the process of conflict transformation. This requires discussion about the hegemony/counter-hegemony dichotomy.

Hegemony, Counter-hegemony and Conflict frames

In D'Angelo's (2002) 'research program', the constructionist and critical paradigms within framing theory are differentiated, in addition to the cognitive paradigm. He claims that the critical paradigm is putting emphasis on hegemony since scholars working within it theorize that "[f]rames that paradigmatically dominate news are also believed to dominate audiences" (D'Angelo, 2002, p. 876). The constructionist paradigm, on the other hand, is defined by what he calls a "paradigmatic image of co-optation", by which frames are understood as tool-kits from which "citizens *ought* to draw in order to form their opinions about issues" (2002, pp. 876–877). The difference between the two is the idea that the former is concerned with ideological and institutional mechanisms of frame construction, and the latter is interested in micro-sociological interactionism of interpretative 'keying'. However, as we claim in this study, these paradigms have more in common than has been suggested. Namely, since power in a Foucauldian sense is both constitutive and impersonally fluctuating in the social realm, the issue of hegemony is applicable to both. Systemic and ideological discursive strongholds are not (or not always) unilaterally formed – they too are interactional. But how are the concepts of hegemony and counter-hegemony understood in this study?

The competing conflict frames do not have equal weights. Some of them achieve cultural resonance for the wider population (Baden & David, 2017) or are being sponsored by powerful patrons such as corporate actors, state institutions, media or ruling political parties. Others exist on the margins of the public sphere,[8] struggling to get broader prominence. Some of them seem to be ubiquitous, while others are sporadic. The first type of conflict frames may be called *hegemonic* (Gramsci, 1995) because they tend to uphold a powerful sponsors' "interests by keeping the subaltern social groups fragmented and passive within civil society" (Howson & Smith, 2008, p. 5), and because they tend to construct a singularity around a certain definition of a conflict, fortifying existing cultural meanings and lines of antagonism. The second type may be called *counter-hegemonic,* because they are devices that tend to destabilize established hegemony and power relations by perpetually infusing 'risk' into the social order. This process of destabilization of hegemonic discourse is an important aspect of the agonistic theory of democracy to which our study subscribes, a theory which acknowledges conflict as a defining feature of any society, but which also, however, emphasizes the significance of opening political spaces where conflictual antagonism may be transformed into *agonistic pluralism*. Since the 'public sphere' or rather the 'public spheres' (Fraser, 1990) may be envisaged as a dynamic nexus of these competing fluctuating power encapsulators, and since the struggle for publicness of particular conflict frames is in fact a struggle for legitimization (or de-legitimization) of potential performances of collective action, it is important, in conflict transformation analysis to explore fluctuating conflict frames revealing their relations, their escalation vectors and the lines of antagonism they draw, and to establish whether they confront or justify hegemony.

The Subjectivity of Media-Active Publics

At the outset, we offered a short definition of the concept of *media-active publics*, and in this section, we provide a very brief theoretical justification for that definition. With the rise of social media, the importance of the wider audience has become pivotal when it comes to the production and public reproduction of conflict frames. The "lay" population has now become an important actor in conflict communication, so much so that some scholars claim that their activity through the Internet and the social media may be important when it comes to protest mobilization (Castells, 2015), or that the existence of Internet and social media may in fact hinder mobilization (Fuchs, 2007). Our definition of media-active publics rests on the notion that social media have enabled this transformation of audiences from receivers of news into active producers and reproducers of contents about social issues – they have in fact helped the transformation of audiences into lay publics. This stands, despite the fact that the 'online public sphere' is a contested conceptualization given the volatility of the platform discussions and the uncertainty over the Internet's capability to perform the "generalized functions of the public sphere" (Rauchfleisch & Kovic, 2016) in a sustainable fashion.

For us then, it is epistemologically of great importance to distinguish between the concepts of 'audiences' and 'publics', a distinction that is provided by communication literature (Dayan, 2005; Livingstone, 2005). Livingstone, for example, claims that audiences " ... sustain a modest and often ambivalent level of critical interpretation, drawing upon – and thereby reproducing – a somewhat ill-specified, at times inchoate or even contradictory sense of identity or belonging which motivates them towards, but does not wholly enable the kinds of collective and direct action expected of a public" (Livingstone, 2005, p. 31). Daniel Dayan (2005) shares Livingstone's position, and juxtaposes the 'publics' with other concepts resembling 'audiences' such as the spectators, crowds, communities and the like by emphasizing the issue of what he calls 'attention'. While audiences are, as he puts it, 'spectators in the plural', a public is "[...] a coherent entity whose nature is collective; an ensemble characterized by shared sociability, shared identity and a sense of that identity" (Dayan, 2005, p. 46). He emphasizes that there is a fundamental difference here in the style of attention, in that the attention of the spectators is 'floating' and 'undirected', and the attention of publics is 'issue driven', in addition to being focused.

On the basis of this discussion, we envisage media-active publics as lay communities[9] that are defined by their collective action, which is manifested through their activity on social media, where they tend to participate in debates on sociopolitical issues. As the most comprehensive way to identify media-active publics is to seek them in existing protest movements, this study takes that road (an additional explanation on this is provided in the *Method* section).

Method

Recruitment and Interviewing Strategy

We conducted 24 two-hour focus group interviews (FGIs) in three waves in Macedonia and Kosovo in April/May 2015, August/September 2015 and January/February 2016. Each focus group consisted of between seven and nine participants recruited from current protest movements in both societies. Three criteria were used in the recruitment process: (1) that they are part of the audience that have been active in protest movements in each society and that they have regular online and face-to-face communication with each other; (2) that they are active on social media participating in public discourse with politically and socially engaged content and (3) that they do not belong to governing state or party bodies, peace-building NGOs or media organizations. The rationale behind this recruitment was the greater likelihood that these media-active fragments of protest movements would be involved in the dynamic of possible conflicts, and that their 'laity', in the sense that they are not professional stakeholders in the conflict, allows the researcher to exclude professional motivations for their statements. The groups were ethnically homogenous consisting of Serbian-, Macedonian- and Albanian-speaking participants. They were also ideologically consistent, such as being participants from the 2014 University of Pristina students' movement who were not mixed with participants in the nationalist protest manifestations of the same period. Each FGI in one of the conflict cases has an equivalent in the other case. Participants were first asked to discuss the conflict in their respective societies in general. They were then presented with TV coverage of conflict escalations, adding a symbolic weight to their interaction. Ethnic conflict frames were deliberately dominant in the presented coverage: In Macedonia, TV coverage of the 'Kumanovo clash' on May 9, 2015, and the 'Xhaferi protests' in March 2013; in Kosovo, the Brussels agreement on April 19, 2013, and the Jarinje and Brnjak clashes in July 2011. The rationale behind the choice of ethnic conflict frames was the need to understand if and how media-active publics in Macedonia and Kosovo pose resistance to ethnic hegemony. The discussions were conducted by researchers speaking the mother tongue of the participants.

Coding and Validation

The focus group discussions were transcribed, coded, analysed and mapped in MaxQDA software. The coding procedure consisted of four steps. *First*, open coding: Two coders identified speech that indicates friction or antagonism between groups or individuals. The speech of every interlocutor, suggesting they were wronged, deprived, endangered and so on, was coded. In a second reading, the coders identified the presumed enemy or adversary that the interlocutors were blaming for the friction. Basic codes emerged from this process serving as indications of the existence of patterns, coded on the level of individual interlocutions.

Second, axial coding (a): In this stage, we grouped the detected elements of antagonistic friction, using the Eidelson and Eidelson (2003) conceptual framework. We organized the references into five friction domains, namely (1) injustice: a friction that is tied to the past in which "we" have been wronged, deprived or humiliated; (2) vulnerability: a friction that proscribes that the group is subject to immediate dangers, threats or hostility, and that there is great uncertainty about the future; (3) distrust: speech with references to the harmful intent of others; (4) superiority: references to ethno-centrism, ideological superiority or special destiny; and (5) helplessness: a sense of despair by members of the group. Then, we located the generic 'other' that occurred in the friction domains. We assembled these into two prominent adversarial clusters: (1) Political Actors as Adversaries (pa) and (2) Social Groups as Adversaries (sg).

Third, axial coding (b): The coders in this stage focused only on the individual interlocutor's speech junctions of co-occurrence between friction domain code and an adversary code. They identified why, within a certain frictional domain, a particular adversary was blamed. The answer to the question why enabled the identification of subcodes that were an indication of conflict framing. Four such delineations were identified: (1) ethno-nationalist, (2) civic-ideological, (3) institutional/constitutional and (4) manipulative/malicious interest conflict frames.

Fourth, selective coding: This last stage identified frames on the level of the group interaction – interactive framing processes. Thus far, the codes were identified on the level of individual interlocutors' speech. This last line of coding grouped these individual level codes into streams of conversations, which we called interaction units (IUs). Each IU was dominated by some idea about what the conflict was about – so the coders labelled each IU in the dominant frame. In each IU, both the frames and the framing process were recognized. Four types of framing interactions were identified in the IUs, corresponding with the demarcations from the axial coding (b) of stage 3.

Validity

The complete corpus of transcripts was in the first instance coded by one coder who performed a manual validation by reassessing the codes. Each stage was further checked and validated by a second coder who identified the potential points of disagreement. An inter-coder agreement test was performed in MaxQDA on the four IU codes (see Stage 4), using all focus group transcripts from Macedonia. The focus group 3–6 tests showed inter-coder agreement of between 90.9% and 93.3%. The rest of the tests showed agreement of 96% or higher.

Results

Framing Interactions, Frame Content and Antagonism Vectoring

The MaxQDA analysis enabled the identification of four types of IUs dominated by: (1) ethno-nationalist, (2) civic-ideological, (3) institutional/constitutional and (4) manipulative/malicious interest conflict frames. This means that the recruited media-active publics through their interactions co-defined the respective underlying conflicts in one of these four categories. When they were presented with actual media coverage of actual conflict manifestations (escalations), they tended to interpret the events through the same lenses they used to define the underlying conflict. If, for example, they used an ethnic frame to define the underlying conflict in the respective societies, they tended to use the same frame when they discussed a particular violent episode. Each of the isolated conflict framing interactions consists of an exchange of individual statements on which conflict frames are carried. This section provides an inventory and an elaboration of framing interactions and the individual level frames. They are also deconstructed with respect to their focus of antagonism; certain frames and framing interactions direct the focus of antagonism against different adversaries. As they suggest antagonism with a certain adversary, they simultaneously suggest possible alliances. It is within this dynamic that we claim the utility of our results for conflict transformation in the age of social media.

Ethno-nationalist Conflict Framing Interaction

These conflict framing interactions define the conflict as antagonism between ethno-nationally defined groups or between pseudo-monolithic ethno-cultural groups and the state. The references of 'Us' and 'Them' are always marked by ethnic identifiers. The ethno-nationalist conflict frame may be considered hegemonic in Kosovo and Macedonia. It tends to put virtually any manifestation of friction into the brackets of ethnicity. As it constructs antagonism along ethnic lines, it creates residual within-ethnic-group solidarity (see Table 9.1 at the end of this chapter). We isolated the following manifestations with respect to political actors (pa) and social groups (sg) as adversaries:

1   *The discriminatory/illegal state (pa); Their villain politicians (pa)* create an antagonism between the ethno-culturally defined minority group and the state. The state is typically viewed as 'their ethnic state' that is illegitimate or genocidal, and it is ruled by their kin politicians:

> *It's going to be even worse. There is a systematic attempt to annihilate the Serbs from Kosovo, the Serbs as people. This is a classic example of genocide against an ethnic group.*
>
> (FGI04Kosovo 27.06.2015)

2   *The soft nation state (pa)*: It draws a line of ethnic antagonism between the majority group and the state. It is constructed around the notion that 'our' state is overprotective of the ethnic minorities, often at our expense. Typically, in this frame, the majority ethnic group is seen as the only constitutive unit of the state:

> *If you are attacked by a Serb [in Kosovo], he would be punished only minimally.*
>
> (FGI01Kosovo 26.06.2015)

3   *Their villain patron state (pa)*: The adversary in this frame is the 'motherland' of the ethnic minority; that state is unjust and constantly attempting to destabilize 'our' ethnic state:

> *[...] rights of the Albanians living in the territory of Serbia are violated every day – they do not even let them educate themselves in their own language.*
>
> (FGI10Kosovo 26.02.2016)

4   *Our traitorous patron state (pa)*: It draws a line of antagonism between an ethno-nationally defined minority and the patron state it sees as its motherland:

> *We fear both Belgrade and Pristina. We [the Serbs] especially fear Belgrade. We don't know what they will decide, and our heads are at stake here, our future.*
>
> (FGI04Kosovo 27.06.2015)

5   *International injustice conflict (pa)*: This variant of the ethno-nationalist conflict frame puts the conflict in the ethnic domain, but it claims that the international actors are to blame for the injustice against 'us'.

> You could see from an airplane, flying 10,000 feet high, they [the
> Albanians] have the support of the most powerful part of the
> international community.
>
> (FGI03Kosovo 24.06.2015)

6   *Disrespectful them (sg); Manipulative them (sg); Violent them
    (sg):* These three variants of the *Ethnic conflict frame* are vectored
    against 'the other' ethnic group because (1) they are disrespectful of
    our ethnicity or nation, (2) they are manipulative when they claim
    that they have been wronged and (3) they are violent and as such are
    a threat to 'our' state:

> They [the Albanians] just ought to have more respect for our
> state, that's all.
>
> (FGI04Macedonia 15.06.2015)

> They [The Macedonians] haven't changed anything in the past
> hundred years. They live with one thought – hating us, even
> though we have no hatred towards them.
>
> (FGI06Macedonia 29.10.2015)

7   *We are our worst enemies (sg):* claims that "we" as an ethno-
    national group are working against ourselves:

> I don't know if this is in our genes? But the present is the same as
> it was in our Enlightenment (meaning late XIX century struggle
> for a nation-state) [...]. We have always won the wars, but in the
> end, we have found ways to ruin all that we have won.
>
> (FGI07Kosovo 18.03.2016)

Civic-ideological Conflict Framing Interaction

These conflict framing interactions define the conflict as antagonism
between irreconcilable ideological (rather than ethno-cultural) positions. This framing may have both individualistic and communitarian
variants, but it always defines the 'us' as ideologically anti-authoritarian
in the sense that it puts the focus of action against the sponsors of hegemony. In this frame, citizens, groups or political actors, on one hand,
may be antagonized by other groups or political actors on the account
that 'they' are upholding structures such as the authoritarian state,
'they' are violating individual rights, 'they' are supressing the struggle
of the poor, and so on (see Table 9.1). This conflict framing is counter-
hegemonic in Kosovo and Macedonia. In contexts where the state and
the media suppress any type of manifestation of ethnicity in the name
of non-debatable individualist consensus, this framing may also be
considered hegemonic. We isolated the following manifestations of the

civic-ideological conflict-framing interactions with respect to political actors (pa) and social groups (sg) as adversaries:

1   *Down the authoritarian state (pa)* is putting the focus of antagonism on the authoritarian state and its sponsors:

> *They [political actors in power] have a political aim to dominate and to control citizens. Not solving any [of their problems] they want to fulfil their own ambitions.*
>
> (FGI10Macedonia 14.04.2016)

2   *Against the un-emancipated (pa and sg)* puts the focus of the conflict on the point of friction between the emancipated and the unemancipated. It frames the conflict in civilizational terms:

> *If you come to look at it in simple terms – citizens ('граѓани' in Macedonian) are those who are conscious and think about issues in this country, people ('народ' in Macedonian), on the other hand, are those who blindly go [to the polls] and simply cast their vote.*
>
> (FGI07Macedonia 19.11.2015)

3   *Liberal/illiberal divide (pa and sg)* places the line of antagonism between upholders and enemies of the open society:

> *The most vocal [counter-protesters] never missed an opportunity to say: "You're gathered here like you are in front a firing squad – you unclean fagots, you lesbos [...]".*
>
> (FGI01Macedonia 18.05.2015)

4   *Class antagonism (pa)* defines the conflict as ultimately one about class. The enemy is the rich and the powerful:

> *The middle class in Kosovo does not exist. Only those who are in the 'tower' have the right to rule and to become rich. The rest of us are the patient ones who barely have enough to live. And tomorrow this is going to create a tension in Kosovo.*
>
> (FGI07Kosovo 18.03.2016)

Institutional/Constitutional Conflict Framing Interaction

These conflict-framing interactions define the conflict as antagonism induced by the reprobate political processes within state institutions or states' constitutional arrangements and legality. This frame stresses that the antagonist's actions are not in accordance with the constitution, they are illegal or not in accordance with international legal provisions. It differs from the previous type of framing interaction in the sense that it (1) sounds practical in that it is not marked by a manifestation of strong ideological wording, and (2) it tends to be contextually transfigured within hegemonic or counter-hegemonic milieus. For instance, an institutional/constitutional conflict frame may be interpreted as hegemonic when it is by implication justified by ethno-nationalist reasoning (see the map below). We isolated the following manifestations:

1 *Constitutional conflict frame (pa)* claims that conflicts in the country are a matter of mismatch between what is written in the Constitution and what the claims of a particular group are:

> *[...] concerning the negotiations about the Community of Serbian municipalities, I believe that they are wrong because they completely derailed from the principles upon which our state is constituted – the Ahtisari plan.*
>
> (FGI08Kosovo 20.03.2016)

2 *Rogue/failed/corrupt state (pa)* constructs friction against the state, which has been framed as a corrupt lawless structure:

> *Freedom has to have limits, if a journalist works on deliberately sparking political or interethnic tensions, then it would be better to address higher courts outside this state, because our courts won't do the trick.*
>
> (FGI03Macedonia 23.05.2015)

3 *War criminals (pa)* problematizes the legality of the leading politicians (former rebels) on the account that they are war criminals:

> *All these people are now politicians [...] but they were slaughtering children for crying out loud and now none of them can sleep calmly – because they know that some of them will have to show up in front of the special court and be imprisoned.*
>
> (FGI05Kosovo 12.09.2015)

4 *Unjustified affirmative action (pa)* claims that state policies aimed at improving the position of minority groups are problematic:

> *They bring in people [in the public administration] in accordance with the Ohrid Framework Agreement – using an ethnic key. This 'girl' just out of University is being employed there, but she doesn't even speak the language, we cannot understand each other [...] she is not fit to work there.*
>
> (FGI10Macedonia 14.04.2016)

Manipulation/Malicious Interest Conflict Framing Interaction

This conflict framing interaction defines the conflict as antagonism between the citizens or social groups on one hand and the state or other political actors on the other. The political actors in this case are framed as manipulative or corrupt structures, and hence, the conflict is an outcome of some kind of manipulation or malicious interest. This conflict frame is tactical and not ideological in its rhetorical appearance, and therefore in some cases can manifest itself as implicitly hegemonic, when, for example, interlocutors claim explicitly that the conflict is a result of manipulation by rogue politicians, but when at the same time (given the context of the conversation), it is implied that only the other ethnic group is being manipulated into conflict. This frame may manifest as counter-hegemonic, when, for example, interlocutors claim that the conflict is a result of a manipulation of ethnicity, and that the real reasons lie elsewhere (see Table 9.1). The FGIs revealed these variants of the Manipulation/malicious interest conflict frame:

1   *Ethnicity manipulation (pa)* claims that political actors are misusing ethnic identity frictions as a smokescreen that covers their background criminality and corruption. This is not an ethnic frame per se because the 'Us' here is not constructed in an ethno-nationalist sense. Rather, the 'us' is conscious of the manipulation of all ethnic members of all ethnic groups – all ethnic groups are the 'Others' in this sense:

> *It is obvious, even today [...] that the political parties are playing with the citizens, especially playing with their national feelings, and they are doing that for their own political gain.*
>
> (FGI08Macedonia 15.11.2015)

2   *Geopolitical interest (pa)* claims that the conflict is a result of global or regional geopolitical positioning:

> *That made me understand that the political games of the international community in Kosovo, and through Kosovo also in Serbia, [...] are still driven by divergent interests of whomever, at the expense of stabilization.*
>
> (FGI08Kosovo 18.03.2016)

3   *Clientelistic manipulation (pa), Predatory political actors (pa)* all claim that, in the middle of the conflict, there is a malicious interest of political actors who exert power, either based on clientelistic relationships or by virtue of blackmail, which causes friction and antagonism:

> *The thing is, when we talk about the news web sites – if I am paid by the red I am going to write in their favour, and if I am paid by the blue, I am going to write in their favour [...] They are writing about the same thing, but it looks different – one against the other.*
>
> (FGI04Macedonia 15.06.2015)

4   *Peace process manipulation (pa)* claims that the peace process is rigged at the expense of the common man.

> *I have had enough of this Brussels agreement thing – where Brussels says one thing, and Pristina says another.*
>
> (FGI09Kosovo 25.12.2015)

5   *Homophobic manipulation (pa)* creates antagonism between liberal groups on one hand, and the illiberal state or its supporters because they are vilifying the lesbian, gay, bisexual and transgender (LGBT) community to create a smokescreen for other issues:

> *Some report was published that suggested that Macedonia is among the poorest in the world, or something like that. And at the same time, the labour minister goes public saying that the state will not legalise same sex marriages! (Laughs) See, no one had an initiative for legalization.*
>
> (FGI04Macedonia 18.05.2015)

6   *Securitization manipulation (pa)* puts the focus of the antagonism between the liberal groups and populist or authoritarian political actors, because the latter are hindering individual rights by making all important socio-political activities a security issue:

> *You cannot get a feel where it [the conflict] is going to explode in this country, except in the VMRO [controlled] TV stations, where the main VMRO-journalists work.*
>
> (FGI01Macedonia 18.05.2015)

Discussion

The maps of the conflict frames and the framing interactions of media-active publics in Kosovo and Macedonia show a wide range of competing frames constructed within four types of conflict-framing interactions. It is, first of all, evident that the Ethno-nationalist conflict frames have prominent status in the interactions of the focus group participants from both societies. Even though in Kosovo they have a far greater frequency, the repertoire of these frames bears a resemblance to those identified in Macedonia, with the exception of the variants that include the patron state of the national minority. The FG interviews in Macedonia did not detect 'Their villain patron state' and 'Our traitorous patron state' variants despite the fact that, in this country, members of the minority ethnic group may tend to claim the existence of such a state. In the political context of Kosovo, the prominent manifestations of these variants of conflict frames are understandable as they are induced by the process of negotiations in which Serbia has an

Table 9.1 Representation of the functioning of the four types of conflict framing interactions

Faming interaction	Type of antagonism	Antagonism 'rationale'	Solidarities it creates	Solidarities it hinders
Ethno-nationalist framing interaction	Against the state → Against the patron state → Against the ethnic other → Against the 'international community' → Against our own kin →	- The state is an extension of their ethnic interests. - Our kin/patron state is selling out the interests of its kin. - Their ethnic group is evil and a threat; disrespectful of the Constitution. - The 'internationals' are protecting them (ethnic). - We have traitors in our midst.	This frame supports ethnic solidarity regardless of political context. Everything is secondary to the interests of our own ethnic kin. Even the questions of class, economy, or ideology are viewed through an ethnic lens.	This frame hinders civic solidarities that make pressure for the rule of law, justice, and equality regardless of ethnicity. **HEGEMONIC**
Civic-ideological conflict framing interaction	Against the state → Against the ideological other → Against the class other → Against 'international community' →	- The state has hegemonic authoritarian tendencies; the crony political elites are the unjust rulers of citizens. - The populist-conservatives have an authoritarian mindset. - Capitalists are predators. - Internationals are imperialists (an extreme left frame not found in FGs, but present in public in a weak form).	It would support solidarities of an ideological or class nature. In the analysed cases these are counter-hegemonic; however, in other context these might be considered hegemonic frames.	It would be skeptical or would openly oppose politicised ethnic solidarities. **COUNTER-HEGEMONIC**

Institutional / constitutional CFI				
Against the state →	- The state is lawless, rogue, captured. The institutions are not complete.	In an ideal typical sense this framing would support solidarities of the ordered society that are based on meritocracy and rule of law. A group would be united under the idea that an ordered society is based on the principles of the law.	It hinders solidarities that are based on informal interpersonal relations (unless it is contextualized in an ethnic – interaction).	**HEGEMONIC & COUNTER - HEGEMONIC**
Against lawless (political) elites →	- The laws are fine, political elites disrespect them so they are not implemented.			
Against the lawless citizens →	- The laws are fine; citizens disrespect them so they are not implemented. Informalities are bad.			

Manipulation/ Malicious Interest CFI				
Against the state →	- State institutions manipulate groups into conflict.	Supports "pragmatic" solidarities of the disenchanted – these may however imply a more durable solidarity, when for example media active publics share identity or convictions.	It aims against solidarities that would be perceived as conflict manipulations.	**HEGEMONIC & COUNTER - HEGEMONIC**
Against rogue politicians →	- Politicians manipulate groups into conflict as a cover up.			
Against ethnicity as such →	- Members of ethnic groups are manipulated into conflict. Ethnicity is a smokescreen			
Against members of class/ideological groups →	- Ideology is manipulation.			
Against 'international community' →	- Geopolitical interests of the internationals manipulate nations into conflict.			

open and formalized interest. One possible explanation for the absence of these frames in Macedonia may be that the media-active publics in the country place the loci of ethno-political action within, rather than outside, that society. This aside, the ethno-nationalist frames resonate strongly with media-active publics in both cases. In times of ethnic tensions, this tends to create a "singularity" for the wider population in which every aspect of political and social life is subordinated to the type of friction that 'essentializes' ethnic identities and creates antagonism along ethnic lines, adding to the conflict's intractability. These frames thus close the political space, discouraging alternative conflict conceptualizations.

In correspondence with our theoretical discussion, the prominent presence and the diverse repertoire of ethnic conflict frames and framing interactions of media-active publics in Macedonia and Kosovo work in favour of a well-established hegemony that has been used by political actors and state institutions to securitize political issues and hinder pressures from citizenry that would demand such aims as greater equality, greater liberty, rule of law and the like. From the focus group interactions that function in this framing dimension, it follows that ethnic conflict defines all societal types of antagonisms. This is why, for example, interactions that create a discourse of antagonism with the 'failed state institutions' would subsume that argumentation into an antagonism, which ultimately suggests confrontation with the ethnic other.

Subsequently, it is important to note that the code co-occurrence maps reveal that the institutional/constitutional and manipulation/malicious interest conflict frames in Kosovo tend to be more frequently dragged into the context of ethnic rather than civic interactions. Media-active publics in Kosovo tend to be more inclined to pull the references to institutional arrangements or to politician's manipulative behaviours, into the ethno-nationalist conflict realm. When interlocutors talk about the conflict as a matter of "disrespect for the constitution", they tend to develop the conversation in ethno-nationalist contexts, when, for example, they would claim that a decision by some political entity is unconstitutional, but only to imply that this is so because it jeopardizes the dominant position of the majority ethnic group in the country. This, in consequence, is also a symptom of a closure of the political space for nuanced argumentations about constitutionality and citizenship because it puts the totality of the political and social processes into an ethno-nationalist singularity. In Macedonia, these frames were dragged both toward ethnic and civic conflict definitions (as can be seen in Figure 9.1 in Appendix).

The comparative data (Figures 9.1 and 9.2 in Appendix) concerning the civic-ideological conflict framing interactions also suggest an important difference between participants in the two cases. There is a wider repertoire and a higher frequency of identified civic-ideological conflict frames detected in the discourse of media-active publics in Macedonia. Speech that places the point of antagonism between the citizens and the 'authoritarian state', or the groups with a liberal outlook against illiberal groups, is clearly more prominent in the focus groups in Macedonia. These frames may be considered counter-hegemonic because they challenge the Ethno-nationalist, hetero-normative and patriarchal hegemony in this country[10]. The media-active publics who are inclined to sponsor the Civic-ideological conflict frames tend to initiate new types of social conflicts, which pose some resistance to the authoritarian, ethno-nationalist and populist grand narratives. This, the results suggest, opens new routes for conflict transformation that vector the conflict away from the thno-nationalist hegemony, and towards a civic-ideological struggle. The repertoire of these types of frames in Kosovo is far scarcer. As these frames have less prominence, in this case it can be hypothesized that it would be harder to bring counter-hegemonic discourses to prominence in Kosovo. This in part may be put on the expense of the political processes in Kosovo in which the Albanian and Serbian communities live in 'territorial isolation' from one another, as in the example of South and North Mitrovica. This 'territorialization' of the ethnic divide closes political spaces and disengages communities from attempting at challenging ethnic hegemony. This may also be a result of Kosovo's contested statehood, which would enhance the feeling of uncertainty in media-active publics.

The focus group interactions that more prominently demonstrated civic-ideological framing when they were referring to the underlying conflict have been more inclined to define the individual manifestations of conflict escalation in the same framing repertoire. For example, if groups claim that the ethno-nationalist framing of the underlying conflict may be considered a manipulation by powerful sponsors and that the real conflict lies in the antagonism between the rogue political institutions, on the one hand, and citizens or civil rights groups on the other, then, they would tend to look at individual escalation instances in the same frame. As a result, they would view the Kumanovo clash in Macedonia or the Jarinje and Brnjak incidents in Kosovo, not as an ethno-nationalist escalation, but rather as a governmental smokescreen to cover strict antidemocratic policies.

Of course, the 'resistance' conflict frames found in Macedonia's media-active publics are evident only *in marginal political spaces*. They are rather more prominent in very isolated media-active public bubbles on social networks than on traditional media, which are still the most popular discourse disseminators in these media systems. Our findings, therefore, do not suggest that Macedonia is a more open society than Kosovo. It only claims that since these frames by media-active publics are nevertheless readily available in Macedonia, they may be more successfully utilized in conflict transfiguration processes to counteract frames that have established hegemony when it comes to conflict definition. These processes may utilize and even further develop frames that open spaces for new types of social conflicts, and by implication create new types of solidarities infusing agonistic pluralism into the public realm.

Conclusion

Agonistic approaches to conflict transformation base their arguments on the idea that conflict is all-pervasive in society and that it is constitutive of democracy (Maddison, 2017). They consequently claim that a real pluralist democracy should acknowledge and develop the possibilities this principle opens for media strategies in conflict transformation by acknowledging "the real nature of [democracy's] frontiers and the forms of exclusion that they entail [...]" (Mouffe, 2000, p. 105) instead of pushing irreconcilable positions into consensus at any cost. However, rarely have there been efforts to transform these abstract principles into detailed, operationalizable concepts and to reveal the kinds of challenges they pose to hegemony, the new possibilities for friction and antagonism they open, and, finally, the residual solidarities they may produce in the process. This chapter suggests that the study of the competing conflict frames within framing interactions of media-active publics is a step in that direction – it is as such a multi-disciplinary attempt at envisioning possible approaches to conflict transformation in the direction of democratization in an age of social media.

In this social media age, the media-active publics may be significant actors in contributing to the conflict dynamic. This study isolated the prominent types of conflict frames within framing interactions that these informal social groups produce and reproduce. The isolation of four types of these conflict framing interactions – Ethno-nationalist, Civic-ideological, Institutional/constitutional and Manipulative/ malicious interest – reveal the varieties in content and symbolic potency these types have for 'constructing' conflict. Furthermore, the study elaborated the functioning of each type of frame and framing interaction by deconstructing their content and revealing what kind of antagonism they encapsulate. Based on the types of antagonism these frames promote, in the context of the two elaborated cases, they are put into an unambiguous mutual disagreement, which in turn has the potential to reshuffle the vectors of antagonism and solidarity in society and move them away from hegemonic terrain. In essence, this suggests that the hegemonic framing of a certain conflict may be deflated by a variety of competing frames, the potential of which needs to be harvested. Finally, the study proposed a possible way to use the nexus of competing conflict frames in conflict transformation processes. In the context of the two cases of moderately violent post-conflict episodes analysed here, it practically proposes that rather than insisting on public circulation of ideas of interethnic understanding and harmony in order to counteract future ethnic conflict escalations – a strategy that often ends in futility – conflict transformation processes should encourage *some* conflict frames that challenge the ethnic hegemony and vector the antagonism and the possibility for mobilization elsewhere – in a less violent symbolic terrain. This process, we claim, would open new spaces for antagonism, but also new types of solidarities.

The notion that conflict transformation strategies should explore the potential of counter-hegemonic conflict frames that possibly open new agonistic spaces seems counterintuitive – it seems like it suggests infusing more risk into an already volatile situation. However, post-conflict arrangements such as the ones elaborated in this chapter tend to be jammed in hegemonic discursive knots holding societies struggling to democratize in an everlasting political limbo. In this limbo, the pressure from the public on the political structures for democratization is perpetually hindered by notions of securitization, ethnic conflict manipulation and so on. In these kinds of situations, exploring and utilizing counter-hegemonic conflict frames that would push friction into a non-violent but agonistic pluralist domain may infuse democratic nuances into the system and destabilize hegemony.

Although the transferability of the presented results does not allow for generalizations applicable to large, heterogeneous populations, mapping the nexus of competing conflict frames offers an idea of an agonistic mechanism at play on a discursive level in conflict transformation concerning the sociologically and politically important media-active publics. Future research in these areas should establish whether and to what extent these conflict frames are applicable to wider populations.

Appendix

Mapping the nexus of competing conflict frames (CFs)

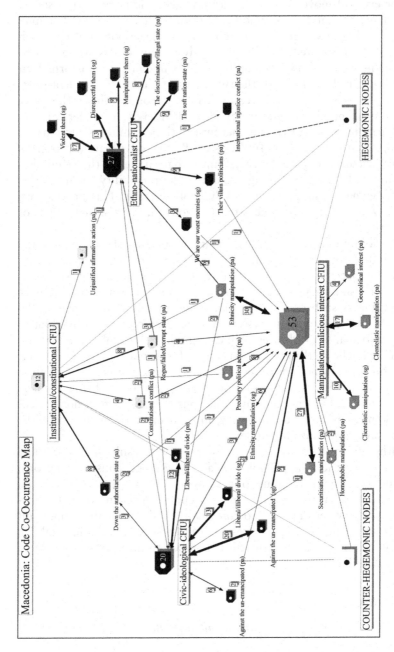

Figure 9.1 A map of competing conflict frames and framing interactions of media active publics in Macedonia.

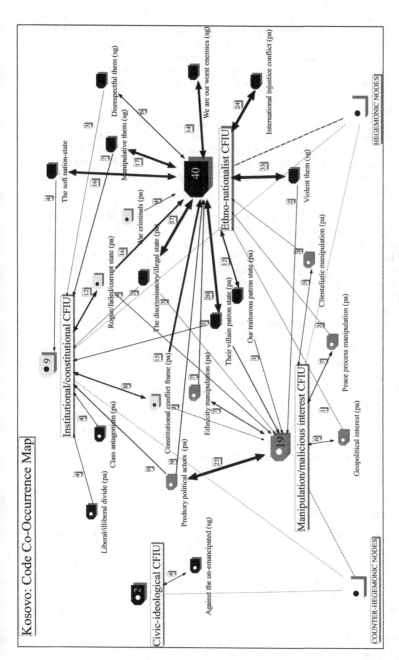

Figure 9.2 A map of competing conflict frames and framing interactions of media active publics in Kosovo.

Notes

1 We elaborate the concept of frame and framing later in this chapter. For now suffice it to say that our definition rests on the sociological tradition. Erving Goffman, for example, viewed frames as cues from which interactionists determine how to understand a situation. Useful definition is also offered by Entman (1993) who theorizes that frames promote a particular problem definition, causal interpretation, moral evaluation and/or treatment recommendation. Conflict frames in our sense define a conflict in a particular fashion, that is, ethnic, ideological, class, manipulative, constitutional, etc.

2 Transformation in this sense means changing violent attitudes/behaviour by applying creativity to contradictions (Galtung, 2000, pp. 31–34).

3 This chapter is a result of a study conducted within INFOCORE – a research project funded by the European Commission's FP7 Programme that aimed to study the role of different actors in shaping conflict by influencing media content.

4 These assessments are based on the methodology of Uppsala Conflict Data Program UDCP, which includes a number of casualties: http://ucdp.uu.se/

5 The choice of the designation 'Postmarxism' instead of the more common 'Post-Marxism' or 'post-Marxism' in our study is best explained by Richard Howson: "This suggests that there is no longer a prefix that seeks to alter the meaning of the second term, but rather it is a term synergized and holding meaning in itself" (Howson, 2017, p. 4).

6 Democratization here is understood as a constitutive element of conflict transformation.

7 We use the term 'frictional domain' as the location of the underlying antagonism. It is discussed later in this chapter.

8 Public sphere here is used in a general sense – as a social realm in which public issues may be discussed between individuals. This realm includes the social media.

9 "Lay" in the sense that they do not belong to governing state or party bodies, peace-building NGOs or media organizations.

10 This assessment is of course a subject of historical change – at a later stage in history or in a different political context this framing may be considered hegemonic – when, for example, the political arrangement supresses all manifestations of ethnicity defending the actions with the individualistic political outlook.

References

Baden, C. (2014). *Constructions of violent conflict in public discourse. Conceptual framework for the content & discourse analytic perspective (within WP5, WP6, WP7, & WP8), INFOCORE, Working Paper 2014/10.* Available online at www.infocore.eu/wp-content/uploads/2016/02/Conceptual-Paper-MWG-CA_final.pdf

Baden, C., & David, Y. (2018). On resonance: A study of culture-dependent reinterpretations of extremist violence in Israeli media discourse. *Media, Culture & Society, 40,* 514 -534.

Bartholomé, G., Lecheler, S., & de Vrees, C. (2018). Towards a typology of conflict frames: Substantiveness and interventionism in political conflict news. *Journalism Studies, 19,* 1689 -1711.

Bieber, F. (2004). *Institutionalizing ethnicity in the Western Balkans. Managing change in deeply divided societies.* European Centre for Minority Issues Working Paper 19. Available online at www.ssoar.info/ssoar/bitstream/handle/document/6315/ssoar-2004-bieber-institutionalizing_ethnicity_in_the_western.pdf?sequence=1

Castells, M. (2015). *Networks of outrage and hope: Social movements in the internet age.* Cambridge, UK: Polity Press.

D'Angelo, P. (2002). News framing as a multiparadigmatic research program: A response to Entman. *Journal of Communication, 52,* 870–888.

Dayan, D. (2005). Mothers, midwives and abortionists: Genealogy, obstetrics, audiences and publics. In S. M. Livingstone (Ed.), *Audiences and publics: When cultural engagement matters for the public sphere* (pp. 43–76). Bristol, UK: Intellect Books.

Dewulf, A., Gray, B., Putnam, L., Lewicki, R., Aarts, N., Bouwen, R., & Van Woerkum, C. (2009). Disentangling approaches to framing in conflict and negotiation research: A meta-paradigmatic perspective. *Human Relations, 62,* 155–193.

Drake, L. E., & Donohue, W. A. (1996). Communicative framing theory in conflict resolution. *Communication Research, 23,* 297–322.

Eidelson, R. J., & Eidelson, J. I. (2003). Dangerous ideas: Five beliefs that propel groups toward conflict. *American Psychologist, 58,* 182.

Entman, R. M. (1993). Framing: Toward clarification of a fractured paradigm. *Journal of Communication, 43,* 51–58.

Fraser, N. (1990). Rethinking the public sphere: A contribution to the critique of actually existing democracy. *Social Text, 25/26,* 56–80.

Frère, M.S., & Wilen, N. (2015). *INFOCORE definitions: "Violent conflict".* Brussels, Belgium: ULB. Available online at www.infocore.eu/results/definitions/

Fuchs, C. (2007). *Internet and society: Social theory in the information age.* New York, NY: Routledge.

Galtung, J. (2000). *Conflict transformation by peaceful means: The Transcend method.* Geneva, Switzerland: UN. Available online at www.transcend.org/pctrcluj2004/TRANSCEND_manual.pdf

Gamson, W. A. (1992). *Talking politics.* New York, NY: Cambridge University Press.

Gamson, W., & Modigliani, A. (1987). The Changing Culture of Affirmative Action. In R. Braungart (Ed.), *Research in Political Sociology* (pp. 137–177). Greenwich, CT: Jai Press.

Goffman, E. (1974). *Frame analysis: An essay on the organization of experience.* New York, NY: Harper & Raw.

Gramsci, A. (1995). *Further selections from the prison notebooks.* London, UK: Lawrence & Wishart.

Harrison, O. (2014). *Revolutionary subjectivity in post-Marxist thought: Laclau, Negri, Badiou.* New York, NY: Routledge.

Hirsch, A. K. (2012). Fugitive reconciliation. In A. K. Hirsch (Ed.), *Theorizing post-conflict reconciliation: Agonism, restitution and repair* (pp. 79–99). London, UK: Routledge.

Howson, R. (2017). *The sociology of Postmarxism.* New York, NY: Routledge.

Howson, R., & Smith, K. (2008). Hegemony and the Operation of Consensus and Coercion. In R. Howson, & K. Smith (Eds.), *Hegemony: Studies in consensus and coercion* (pp. 1–15). New York, NY: Routledge.

Laclau, E., & Mouffe, C. (2001). *Hegemony and socialist strategy: Towards a radical democratic politics*. London, UK: Verso.

Little, A. (2014). *Enduring conflict: Challenging the signature of peace and democracy*. New York, NY: Bloomsbury.

Little, A., & Maddison, S. (2017). Reconciliation, transformation, struggle: An introduction. *International Political Science Review, 38*, 145–154.

Livingstone, S. M. (2005). On the relation between audiences and publics. In S. M. Livingstone (Ed.), *Audiences and publics: When cultural engagement matters for the public sphere* (pp. 17–41). Bristol, UK: Intellect Books.

Maddison, S. (2017). Can we reconcile? Understanding the multi-level challenges of conflict transformation. *International Political Science Review, 38*, 155–168.

Mouffe, C. (2000). *The democratic paradox*. London, UK: Verso.

Ramet, S. P. (2002). *Balkan Babel: The disintegration of Yugoslavia from the death of Tito to the fall of Milosevic*. Boulder, CO: Westview Press.

Rauchfleisch, A., & Kovic, M. (2016). The Internet and generalized functions of the public sphere: Transformative potentials from a comparative perspective. *Social Media & Society, 2*, 1–15.

Reuben, R. C. (2009). The impact of news coverage on conflict: Toward greater understanding. *Marquette Law Review, 93*, 45–83.

Semetko, H. A., & Valkenburg, P. M. (2000). Framing European politics: A content analysis of press and television news. *Journal of Communication, 50*, 93–109.

Schaap, A. (2006). Agonism in divided societies. *Philosophy & Social Criticism, 32*, 255–277.

Sim, S. (2013). *Post-Marxism: An intellectual history*. London, UK: Routledge.

Swanstrom, N. L. P., & Weissmann, M. S. (2005). *Conflict, conflict prevention and conflict management and beyond: A conceptual exploration*. Concept Paper, Central Asia-Caucasus Institute. Available online at www.mikaelweissmann.com/wp-content/uploads/2014/12/051107_concept-paper_final.pdf

Weller, M. (2009). *Contested statehood: Kosovo's struggle for independence*. Oxford, UK: Oxford University Press.

Wolfsfeld, G. (2004). *Media and the path to peace*. New York, NY: Cambridge University Press.

10 Balancing Plausible Lies and False Truths

Perception and Evaluation of the Local and Global News Coverage of Conflicts in the DRC

Marie-Soleil Frère and Anke Fiedler

Introduction

Since the beginning of the 1990s, the region of the African Great Lakes has been oscillating between phases of fragile peace and conflicts (Omeje, 2013; Prunier, 2009; Reyntjens, 2009). In the Eastern region of the Democratic Republic of Congo (DRC), a variety of local and foreign militias and rebel groups (labelled as 'negative forces' by the UN) have been active since 1996. More than three million people have died during the two last decades, either directly or indirectly from the armed conflict. Up to now, dozens of armed groups terrorize the civilian population on a regular basis, engage in skirmishes with the Congolese army and UN troops and plunder national resources, leaving the East provinces of North Kivu and Maniema in permanent insecurity.

It is against this background of sustained conflicts that the local media have to operate, affecting journalists' working conditions to a large degree (Frère, 2011, 2013). The fact that a somewhat professional and pluralist media sector has emerged over the past years in spite of the hostile environment is essentially the merit of numerous individual media professionals who refuse to toe the official line and, for this reason, often work under volatile, precarious and even dangerous conditions including harassments, detentions or assassination, especially in the Eastern part of the country.

In addition to these political factors, there is a plethora of other reasons why press freedom is under threat in the DRC (Fiedler & Frère, 2018): Many media outlets have been facing economic and financial hardships for years, which challenged the emergence of an independent and viable media sector. Bribery, paid-by-the-source journalism and political sponsorship are an integral part of the local media's business models. There is evidence of ethical breaches, professional lapses and misconduct due to corruption and the absence of journalistic standards.

It goes without saying that the media help to build a culture of democracy in African countries like everywhere else in the world.

Yet their role has always been an ambivalent one on the continent. Acting as watchdogs, peace-builders or agenda-setters, they hold governments accountable and provide a basis for good governance, but, in the light of the above, they are also accused of being "irresponsible, self-serving, unaccountable and a threat to the credibility and sustenance of the democratic process" (Tettey, 2006, p. 230).

Against the backdrop of such a complex political reality, we are looking into an important variable in the communication process that has been, particularly in the context of Africa, largely neglected by academic scholarship to date: the *public confidence in media*. It remains unclear what impact an unstable media environment, such as described above, has on domestic audiences: How do people find trustworthy information to help them overcome uncertainty in situations of conflict? Which sources do they trust? These questions gain in importance when we think of the role that the media played in other conflicts in the region, for instance, in mobilizing the audience for murderous purposes during the genocide in Rwanda (e.g. Chrétien, 1995; Kellow & Steeves, 1998; Thompson, 2007).

For the present study, we focus on the city of Goma, capital of the North Kivu province and 2,000 kilometres away from the country's capital Kinshasa. Since 1994, Goma (one million inhabitants) has been deeply affected by the actions of the so-called 'negative forces' operating in the region. According to Büscher and Vlassenroot (2010, p. 257), "[M]ore than 15 years of state decline, violent conflict and massive displacement have transformed this city from a dormant town located at the DRC's border with Rwanda into a notable *siège de rébellion*, attracting rebel leaders, business executives, peacekeepers, refugees and internally displaced persons (IDPs), as well as a rising number of humanitarians."

The population has long lived under unsecure conditions (Oldenburg, 2010) and experienced traumatizing moments, such as the seizure and occupation of Goma by the M23 rebellion in November 2012 (Koko, 2014).

Regarding the media landscape, 19 radio and 7 television stations operate in Goma. *Radio Okapi*, the radio associated with the UN peacekeeping mission MONUSCO, as well as the national broadcaster *Radio Télévision nationale congolaise (RTNC)*, with headquarters in Kinshasa, both have a local office in town. The international French public broadcaster *RFI* is also available on FM for both its French and Kiswahili programmes. The rest of the radio stations are local commercial, denominational or community based. There are a handful of periodical newspapers; none of them is able to publish regularly.

Radio remains the most popular media in Goma, as shown in a 2016 survey implemented by the company IMMAR:[1] 95% of the 503 people interviewed owned a radio, compared to only 71% having access to a television and 39% using the Internet.[2] Radio is the foremost media for both genders, all ages and regardless of education level and occupation. Seventy-four per cent of the people interviewed say that they listen to the radio every day, mostly to *Radio Okapi* (34%), *RFI* (28%) and the local private station *Kivu One* (26%). Therefore, radio plays a central part in access to information in that politically troubled and unsecure context. Despite the centrality of that issue, in a region where radio is viewed as a war weapon or a tool for reconciliation, audiences' motivations to tune in to a specific station and the publics' perceptions of media narratives about the conflict have hardly been researched (Frère, 2017). In this chapter, we try to bridge the gap, at least to some extent, by focusing on the concept of trust. Our study is based on the broad principles of grounded theory, as we basically follow an inductive reasoning approach. The results presented here are heuristic in nature and should provide some food for further reflections on the topic.

Theoretical Foundation and Research Design

Media evaluations include various dimensions, such as objectivity or truth (Kohring & Matthes, 2007, p. 239). There is no consensus about what constitutes media quality, but undoubtedly attitudes toward media have proven "to be important because they affect a host of social and political behaviors" (Tsfati & Cohen, 2013, p. 2). In this chapter, we will focus on the concept of 'trust', for the sake of reducing complexity, but also because we consider trust as an essential element in the processing of media information. Trust, especially when it comes to conflict-related news coverage, is of paramount importance, because only trustworthy information from a trustworthy source can meet an audience's cognitive needs, that is, facilitating orientation and guidance in a situation of conflict or imminent danger (Dotan & Cohen, 1976; Lev-On, 2011). Trust is an attribution; it is not a property inherent to the media. According to Tsfati and Cohen (2013) "the notion of audience trust in media applies the concept of trust, originating from interpersonal interactions"; both "the trustor and the trustee interact in an uncertain situation" in which the trustor risks to gain or lose (p. 2). Mistrust is not necessarily something bad. Following Cappella (2002) "being insufficiently skeptical about the press can get you duped", but having a "healthy, even a strong dose of skepticism about government can enhance democracy and help preserve individual freedoms" (p. 232).

Trust is a subjective notion, derived from the analysis of interpersonal relationships (Blöbaum 2014). It implies that one can 'trust' others when one believes that the other is in good faith. It therefore has a dimension of 'belief' and allows an individual to comprehend future events, in providing confidence about what is currently happening and, therefore, what could happen tomorrow. In the field of media studies, trust is anchored in the credibility of information.

In our study, we asked focus group participants to identify the parameters that contribute to the trust they put in certain media. In total, we conducted eight focus group discussions with more than 50 individuals in Goma between July and November 2015 to discuss about their media use and trust in conflict-related news. Most of the focus groups were carried out by a local researcher who facilitated the discussions in the local language Swahili. All discussions were transcribed and translated into French. Participants were assured of confidentiality (non-disclosure of identifiable information) in order to create an open atmosphere and to build trust with the research team. The selection of interviewees followed the principle of theoretical saturation: The independent variables of focus group participants were varied as often as possible and on several levels (gender, age, ethnic belonging, and educational and professional background) until the discussions did not yield any additional information. Using pictures that were widely circulated by the media during the 2012/2013 M23 armed episode, we tried to frame the debate around the main issue of access to reliable information during conflict.

Results

When asked about why they turn to specific media outlets, especially in a situation of conflict, participants of the focus group discussions put forward that they need to be able to 'trust' the information in order to act. Therefore, we have tried to understand how the participants define the qualities of the media they trust. In the following section, we distinguish between dimensions of trust in media, media distrust in situations of conflict and uncertainty reduction in situations of conflict. These dimensions are derived from the interviewees' own assessment of the media and, as mentioned earlier, they are a product of 'inductive reasoning' and could serve as a heuristic for further research.

Dimensions of Trust in Media

The Importance of Facts for Truth

Trust is based, above all, on the public's feeling that a journalist speaking on the radio or TV says 'the truth', that is, recounting the facts as they happened. For this, a journalist must respect the rules of his profession guaranteeing the veracity of what he reports. "We consider a specific information because we know that a journalist has an 'authorized mouth' to do so. Before spreading the information we believe that s/he has put the feet on the ground and verified the information. The one who lies is not a journalist" said a 56-year-old joint *chef d'avenue* (chief of avenue).[3] Lying is not just simply misinforming, it is considered a potential threat. According to another adjoint chief of avenue, "some radios hide the truth from us. These radios destabilize the country because this sort of misinformation is intended to help one side or the other and that creates unease – the root cause of many conflicts". *Radio Okapi* and *RFI* are regularly pointed as stations providing "real" or "good" information, while the national broadcaster *RTNC* is viewed as constantly lying. Nevertheless, international media are sometimes regarded with a certain suspicion, as they are far away from the field. "They can have correspondents, but they are not in all of the villages", told a 52-year-old housewife. They are also perceived as providing a picture of Eastern Congo that does not correspond with the daily reality of the Gomatracians (inhabitants of Goma): "International media only focus on negative things. When good things happen, they are not here to talk about it", complains a 38-year-old female NGO worker. Because of that systematic negative coverage, she continues, "Outside of the country, people think that we are living in hell. It is true that things happen here, but still, people do live here." Several participants mentioned that they were shocked when the DRC was labelled "the world capital of rape"[4], as it did not match with their daily reality.

Internal Pluralism

Another aspect that was repeatedly discussed was the openness and ability of certain media outlets to reflect a pluralism of views and opinions. Presenting conflicting positions lends greater credibility. *Radio Okapi*, the UN radio station, for instance, is much appreciated because "it gives the floor to both the rulers and the opponents", told a 30-year-old cambist. The radio's evening program, *Dialogue entre Congolais* (Dialogue between Congolese), which brings together various personalities to debate around a specific topic, is regularly cited as exemplary in terms of pluralism. In the eyes of another cambist, 38 years old, the same goes for the French broadcaster *RFI*: "When I listen to this radio station, I feel that I understand the information in its entirety. All sides can voice their opinion. This helps us to understand differences." On the contrary, the national broadcaster will never allow an opponent's voice on its airwaves.

Independence From the Government

Many focus group discussants said that – what they called – "lies" of the public broadcaster *RTNC* had dramatic consequences for their personal life. In November 2012, when M23 rebels approached the city, the national radio, until the last moment, denied the rebel's presence. Interviewees were traumatized by the silence of the national broadcaster during the eruption of the Nyiragongo volcano in 2002, when 70 people perished after lava reached Goma. Although vulcanologists issued urgent warnings, the national radio insisted that there was no need to worry. Focus group discussants were suspicious of all information that is clearly linked to the government. The 56-year-old joint chief of avenue cited above put it on a simple formula: "The official radios hide the truth." Conversely, they trust significantly more local private media such as *Kivu One, Mishapi* or *Pole FM*. Interestingly, the radio stations that were suspended by the state get more attractive for listeners, as a 30-year-old development agent told during the discussions: "By suspending *RFI*,[5] the Congolese government increased the desire to follow this radio." Several participants also stressed that their trust in the private media is linked to the fact that they do not depend on administrative and political authorities.

Actors of Change

Through the dissemination of factual, pluralist and independent information, many participants are convinced that the media can have an impact on the politicians' behaviour and bring changes. About *Radio Okapi* and *RFI*, a 28-year urban development promoter claims that "the journalists who work in these media are more protected, better informed, and willing to inform the Congolese population with no fear. (…) I am convinced that they can bring a change in this country". These media are perceived as able to put pressure on local political leaders. Many participants expressed confidence about the capacity that media and journalists have to foster change in the Congolese society.

Social Responsibility

Finally, and ambiguously, some participants granted credit to the media for not publishing everything. In a situation of conflict, "the journalist must not say everything s/he knows to avoid pouring oil on the fire", said a 42-year-old CEO. The journalist has a particular responsibility since s/he works in a context of insecurity. According to a 23-year-old student, "radios tend to distort information to make them sound less dramatic. We know exactly what happened, but if we tell what happened, people start panicking". This cautious action of the media, coming close to self-censorship, is appreciated by those interviewees who believe it is the media's responsibility to avoid inciting violence. But others heavily criticized the media for being manipulative. This raises fundamental questions here: Can 'truth' be an obstacle to peace and stability? Does reporting facts in a comprehensive and detailed way create risks in a situation of conflict? Interestingly, these questions, which are at the centre of the so-called 'peace journalism' paradigm, have been debated at length in several focus groups.

Media Distrust in Situations of Conflict

The participants explained very clearly why they trust certain radios in particular, at the same time they also told why they distrust others. Generally speaking, local journalists have quite a bad reputation among the participants, as the statement of a 53-year-old NGO worker from Goma shows: "Journalists are amateurs, poorly trained or not trained at all. They write what they want." Several explanations can be put forward:

Insufficient Technical Support and Training

On-the-ground reporting is highly unlikely for small media ventures, in particular in a context of conflict. Most media outlets in Goma operate with extremely limited technical resources and equipment. It goes without saying that they are not able to compete with international stations. "*Radio Okapi* is a UN radio, with effective means for news production. Even the troublemakers in the government cannot get their hands on it. *Okapi* journalists are under the protection of MONUSCO. That's why their information is true", said a 52-year-old peasant. Credibility and technical or material conditions are therefore strongly interrelated, just as safety of journalists.

Safety of Journalists

All participants recognized the risks journalists face in the city of Goma, in particular those who do not support the position of the political authorities. "If a journalist tells the truth, s/he will be killed the next day", told one of the peasants from Mugunga, a locality close to Goma. Indeed, several journalists were assassinated in the past years, and the cases have never been properly investigated. This leads to self-censorship within the profession, as confirmed by a 23-year-old female student:

> *Journalists have relevant information, but they are threatened. They are called on the phone and told not to publish any compromising material. They know that the person calling is capable of everything. Especially here in North Kivu, where you can be shot in broad daylight. And there will be no investigation. You can die as a hero, but who will remember you? Nobody.*

The region of North Kivu has been unstable for years, and the situation of journalists has become particularly difficult: "The police, the military, the security services are always in a stage of alert, especially when it comes to information about the conflict", said a 44-year-old vendor of petrol. For this reason, "a journalist is obliged to protect his life by distorting information", confirmed an unemployed housewife. As the already mentioned peasant from Mugunga concluded: "There is a kind of fear that settles in the back of a journalist's mind who thinks that with the truth, we can go everywhere, even to death."

The Influence of Donors or Media Owners

The results of the focus group discussions show that participants are well aware of the influence on the editorial line exerted by media owners and donors. Although *Radio Okapi* is the most popular radio, it was critisized by some interviewees: "My trust for *Radio Okapi* is at 80%, because sometimes, the station is too pro-MONUSCO. It looks like its editorial line is dictated by the UN mission", said a 45-year-old representative of the civil society. The radio station is accused of turning a blind eye to the deficiencies of the UN peacekeeping mission. Several participants confirmed that they continued to listen to the radio station, arguing that there were no alternatives, but they remained convinced that such a situation is not normal: "We should not have to wait for the foreign media to inform us. It's a shame for our media", says a peasant. Some participants see this situation as "neocolonial" and blame the Congolese authorities for not providing an enabling environment for local media.

The reason why people in Goma lose confidence in *Radio Okapi* is mainly due to the news coverage of conflicts in the region. The United Nations are object of virulent criticisms (Autesserre, 2010). MONUSCO is accused of not defending the Congolese population, although it is obliged to do so, according to its mandate. What is more, the mission is made responsible for fuelling the conflict: Foreign armies borrowing troops to the UN make an enormous benefit from the instability in the region. Another reason for the radio's loss of credibility is the pressure exerted on *Radio Okapi* by the Congolese government. The radio's signal was jammed in January 2012, after the UN station broadcast an interview of Jean-Marie Runiga, political leader of the M23; it was subsequently subject to 'administrative harassment', with the aim to put its legal presence on Congolese territory into question.

But the sharpest critiques from the participants were addressed to the national broadcaster *RTNC*, which is seen as a propaganda instrument of the government: "We have people governing us through lies. Truth is not welcome here", told a 30-year-old representative of the civil society. According to a 38-year-old petrol vendor, mistrust is totally ingrained in the population: "Policy makers prevent the population from being well informed. They want the media to report in favor of their political line."

Corruption

Due to the precariousness of the profession, media users are aware that journalists sacrifice the truth not only for safety reasons, but also to make ends meet. "Journalists are like beggars. They are supported by political actors. It is a hindrance for the fulfilling of the journalists' mission", said a 25-year-old student. And another participant – 26 years old and a student – added: "A journalist has two options: either to tell the truth, but to stay the whole life in misery, or to take the money. A journalist won't think twice, but choose the good life and publish anything." Participants talked about "black sheep", referring to journalists who follow a purely lucrative agenda. They also referred to the practice of "coupage"[6], which means that a journalist is paid by a source of information. "Once you finished the interview, the journalist will ask you to pay five dollars. S/he reminds you: If you want this information to pass, you have give me enough money", told a 45-year-old civil society worker. Even though the participants complained about this practice, they also showed understanding. Journalists in the DRC very often do not earn more than 50 US dollars per month, as a 29-year-old NGO worker emphasized: "Due to the bad pay, they depend on extra money. Journalists have to take every penny they get, even if this means that they have to hide information."

Word-of-Mouth Communication

In case of contradictory information and imminent dangers, it seems that people basically rely on interpersonal communication to verify specific news. Mobile phones play an important role in this 'early-warning system'. "My only source is what I hear here and there. There's no smoke without fire. But it happens that we are told fake stories", said a 52-year-old housewife. Rumours played an important role during the occupation of the M23 rebellion, as most of the media outlets were in the hands of the rebels, as a 54-year-old unemployed housewife remembered: "When Goma was in hands of the rebels, some media outlets didn't go public with their news. Word-of-mouth became the most important source of information by that time. Many rumors were considered true." In a situation of uncertainty, the traditional media do not seem to provide the information needed and rumours gain in relevance. "For me, any rumor is like information because one cannot distinguish between rumors and information", said a female vendor of tomatoes.

Most of the study participants mentioned the rumour of Rwandan President Paul Kagame's death circulating in Goma in January 2014. The announcement on social networks had sparked scenes of jubilation in the streets of the city. Consequently, many interviewees became aware of the unreliable nature of social media channels, as the example of a 52-year-old peasant shows: "They can misguide an entire population and can cause severe damage by mobilizing the population."

Uncertainty Reduction in Situations of Conflict

Aware of the weaknesses of the media, and even of the reasons that lead to an information that does not satisfy their needs and expectations, the participants keep tuning in to these radio stations. That is the core question of this analysis: Why, in situation of insecurity and conflict, does the audience remain attached to (and even dependent of) an information provider to which they grant little trust? Why do they keep listening to radio stations that they perceive as lying?

Very clearly, participants express a need for orientation in the context of uncertainty related to the conflict. A widowed housewife explains:

> *I like information because it allows me to take a particular attitude regarding what is going on in the country, such as killings and massacres that happen every day. Information can warn me about imminent danger and help me to make decisions. Even though I am not very sure of our media, still I follow them, despite of myself.*

The simple fact of accessing to information would be comforting in itself, independently from the fact that the information is reliable or not, because that information can provide a sense of control, and maybe the illusion that the future can be overcome.

> *I want to be reassured about what happened in the country, and about everything that will happen, says a 36-year old taxi-moto driver. The radio helps me to unveil some obscure aspects that come along with rumors that one may hear here or there. I find myself in security when I listen to the radio.*

Participants are seeking information that is a relief for them and that relates to the notions of reliability and credibility. "We would like from now on, in a near future, to enjoy the certainty of an access to good, reliable, credible and reassuring information", declares a rural development promoter aged 30. In that way, "true information" is viewed as able to bring a positive issue to the conflict. Says a female oil retailer, "If the good information reaches us, we will be able to eliminate some evils." Reassuring information is the one that will succeed in reducing uncertainty, giving a sense of control on the present, and even on the future.

Revealingly, one of the shortcomings that the participants identify about the conflict coverage relates to the lack of clear information about the causes of the war. "Sometimes, I don't understand the causes of the war, and that is why I have the feeling that I am not properly informed", complains a chief of avenue. "We get information about the consequences rather than about the causes, concludes another rural development promoter. The reasons of the conflict remain a mysterious issue. But one says that in order to fight easily, one has to know its ennemy (...) That's why these wars never stop, they only change forms."

Conclusion

At the beginning of this chapter, we raised a question about the way audiences in Goma use the media in a context of continuing insecurity and their degree of awareness about the quality of the information they get access to, mostly through the media. The study has demonstrated that the audiences in Goma, whatever social background and level of education, show a wide degree of critical media literacy: Participants to the focus groups had a very clear idea of political or institutional affiliations of media outlets, public and private media financing, corruption or restrictions to press freedom and to information. Obviously, the audience members use a range of criteria in order to assess the credibility of the source of information they get access to: the coincidence between media narratives and the information they get from other channels (word of mouth, social media, interpersonal communication); the degree of internal pluralism of the radio stations and their independence from the public authorities; the working conditions and constraints under which journalists practice their job (poor salaries, "coupage", no protection regarding personal safety, submission to media owners' political line). "Journalists are not well paid. They don't have the logistical equipment and they work under totally unsecure conditions. They don't have access to the whole territory and politicians don't provide them with information either", summarized a 53-year-old peasant from Mugunga.

Nevertheless, despite all these weaknesses, audience members continue to listen to the radio stations available in Goma, even if they do not trust them totally, or do not trust them at all. As a 59-year-old taxi-moto driver explained: "I trust the Congolese media, because the journalists are struggling to inform us. They take risks and sacrifice themselves, to give the best they can despite unsecurity in this area." The permanent uncertainty in which the Goma population has been trapped for the last 20 years has increased the need of the Gomatracians to expose themselves to information, even if that information might be biased or untrue. As Hogg (2007, p. 73) puts it, uncertainty is "highly anxiety provoking and stressful – it makes us feel impotent and unable to predict or control our world and what will happen to us in it". And therefore "we strive to resolve, manage, or avoid feeling uncertain". Media consumption is a part of that strategy to reduce uncertainty (even though not to reach certainty).

In our case, there may be a direct link between uncertainty reduction and survival (as in the case of the M23 seizure of Goma or the Nyagarongo volcano eruption), but, more broadly, uncertainty reduction is in relation to the search for meaning (Hogg, 2007, p. 74). Focus groups participants keep tuning in to international, national and local radio stations not only in order to know if they should flee the city in the following hours, or if they should avoid travelling to surrounding villages, but also to make sense of the wars that they have experienced for more than two decades. In that sense, listening to information from *Radio Okapi*, *RFI* or *Kivu One*, which can be further discussed and crosschecked with friends, neighbours and family members, contributes to build a shared reality, which (be it "true" or not) is already a way to reduce uncertainty and make daily life possible.

Notes

1 The survey was implemented on April 12–16, 2016, on a sample of 503 respondents, chosen according to age, gender, occupation and level of education. The survey was commissioned by *Radio Okapi*. The previous survey had been done in 2013 by the same company and sponsor.
2 Internet access varies widely according to the level of education of the respondents: Only 4% of the people who did not go to school and 15% of the people with a primary school education level have access to the Internet, but 89% of the people with higher education level do.
3 This is a lower level of the administrative organization of the city of Goma that includes a mayor, several "chiefs of neighborhoods", and many "chiefs of avenue" and "nyumba kumi" (about 10 households).
4 The expression was used in 2010 by Margot Wallström, Special Representative of the UN Secretary-General on Sexual Violence in Conflict after she visited DRC.
5 *RFI's* signal has been suspended several times by the Congolese authorities: from July 2009 to October 2010, in January 2012, and from November 2016 to August 2017.
6 "Coupage" literally means "cutting": it refers to many different practices of journalism rewarded by a source of information, or the allocation of material or financial resources to journalists in the exercise of their profession (Elongo Lukulunga, 2012, p. 65).

References

Autesserre, S. (2010). *The trouble with the Congo: Local violence and the failure of international peacebuilding*. New York, NY: Cambridge University Press.

Blöbaum, B. (2014). *Trust and journalism in a digital environment.* Oxford, UK: Reuters Institute for the Study of Journlism, University of Oxford.

Büscher, K., & Vlassenroot, K. (2010). Humanitarian presence and urban development: New opportunities and contrasts in Goma, DRC. *Disasters, 34,* 256–273.

Cappella, J. N. (2002). Cynicism and social trust in the new media environment. *Journal of Communication, 52,* 229–241.

Chrétien, J. P. (1995). *Rwanda. Les médias du génocide.* Paris, France: Karthala.

Dotan, J., & Cohen, A. (1976). Mass media use in the family during war and peace. Israel 1973–1974. *Communication Research, 3,* 393–402.

Elongo Lukulunga, V. (2012). The challenges of journalism ethics in the Democratic Republic of Congo. *Ecquid Novi: African Journalism Studies, 33,* 60–73.

Fiedler, A., & Frère M. S. (2018). Press freedom in the African Great Lakes Region: A comparative study of Rwanda, Burundi and the Democratic Republic of Congo. In H. M. Mabweazara (Ed.), *Newsmaking cultures in Africa: Normative trends in the dynamics of socio-political and economic struggles* (pp. 119–143). Basingstoke, UK: Palgrave Macmillan.

Frère, M. S. (2011). *The media and conflicts in Central Africa.* Boulder, CO: Lynne Rienner Publishers.

Frère, M. S. (2013). Media sustainability in a postconflict enviroment: Radio broadcasting in the DRC, Burundi and Rwanda. In K. Omeje, & T. R. Hepner (Eds.), *Conflict and peacebuilding in the African Great Lakes Region* (pp. 161–178). Bloomington: Indiana University Press.

Frère, M. S. (2017). Audience perceptions of radio stations and journalists in the Great Lakes Region. In W. Willems, & W. Mano (Eds.), *Everyday media culture in Africa: Audiences and users* (pp. 113–139). London, UK: Routledge.

Hogg, M. A. (2007). Uncertainty-identity theory. *Advances in Experimental Social Psychology, 39,* 69–126.

Kellow, C. L., & Steeves, L. H. (1998). The role of radio in the Rwanda genocide. *Journal of Communication, 48,* 107–128.

Kohring, M., & Matthes, J. (2007). Trust in news media: Development and validation of a multidimensional scale. *Communication Research, 34,* 231–252.

Koko, S. (2014). The 'Mouvement du 23 Mars' and the dynamics of a failed insurgency in the Democratic Republic of Congo. *South African Journal of International Affairs, 21,* 261–278.

Lev-On, A. (2011). Communication, community, crisis. Mapping uses and gratifications in the contemporary media environment. *New Media & Society, 14,* 98–116.

Oldenburg, S. (2010). Under familiar fire: making decisions during the "Kivu Crisis" 2008 in Goma, DR Congo. *Africa Spectrum, 45*(2), 61–80.

Omeje, K. (2013). Understanding the diversity and complexity of conflict in the African Great Lakes Region. In K. Omeje, & T. R. Hepner (Eds.), *Conflict and peacebuilding in the African Great Lakes Region* (pp. 25–46). Bloomington: Indiana University Press.

Prunier, G. (2009). *Africa's world war. Congo, the Rwandan genocide and the making of a continental catastrophe.* Oxford, UK: Oxford University Press.

Reyntjens, F. (2009). *The Great African War: Congo and regional geopolitics.* New York, NY: Cambridge University Press.

Tettey, W. (2006). The politics of media accountability in Africa. *The International Communication Gazette, 68*, 229–248.

Thompson, A. (2007). *The media and the Rwanda genocide.* London, UK: Pluto Press.

Tsfati, Y., & Cohen, J. (2013). Perceptions of media and media effects. In A. N. Valdivia, & E. Scharrer (Eds.), *The international encyclopedia of media studies: Media effects / media psychology* (pp. 1–19). Hoboken, NJ: Blackwell.

Part IV

Recapitulation, Consolidation, Implication

11 The Integration of Findings

Consequences of Empirical Results for the Advancement of Theory Building

Romy Fröhlich

The (first) Crimean War in the mid-19th century (1854–1865) is considered one of the very first media wars – or press wars, to be more precise (cf. e.g. Keller, 2001; Lambert & Badsey, 1994). For the first time, a new type of observation and reporting on war events developed that quickly proved itself to be a viable business model: The war reporter as an authentic 'eyewitness' used classic print magazines to report on distant wars; initially, reports were aimed primarily at citizens of the nations involved in the war. That type of reporting had never been seen before, and it was made possible by the development of telegraph technology. This evolution was particularly dynamic in England, which was involved in the Crimean War and at the time was already a society without media censorship,[1] with a fully commercialized media landscape and with the existence of a correspondingly large audience. Further, the government was afraid of war reporting from the very beginning because even in these early years it showed strong effects on public opinion, and the pressure on political decision-makers arising from war reporting was considered to be extremely high from the outset (cf. e.g. Hudson, 1995).

Since then, media war reporting is one of the most prominent objects of social science, especially political science, communication research and media studies. The theoretical and empirical research of very different academic disciplines on the topic can no longer be easily summarized, and the same applies to the (in part) highly heterogeneous findings. In our opinion, the latter is due largely to the extreme dynamics at work in this area (see also, e.g. Allan & Zelizer, 2004). These dynamics can be observed especially in the causes and processes by which wars start, in the way wars were and are conducted in the past and present, in the respective political and social processes and circumstances, in globalization processes, in specific developments in the area of communication technologies, and especially in the dynamics of media and journalism systems that have in turn led to new and accelerated dynamics in the creation of media content and public opinion. These constantly shifting dynamics, which also include ever-changing patterns of media reception and thus also media effects, together with a strong emphasis on single case studies, are the cause of the comparatively short 'half-life' and heterogeneity of scientific findings on war reporting in the media worldwide.

The findings reported in this volume also show: Each war/conflict is different. There are social processes within which the various actors and communicators contribute to the production of war reporting and media content on war and armed conflict. These processes also lead to these actors' continually exchanging roles and functions (from sources and advocates to mediators to users and audiences and vice versa; see Figure 11.1), and they are strongly determined by inherent dynamics that are in turn determined by (systemic, thematic and/or conflict-specific) contextual factors (see Figure 11.2).

Figure 11.1 INFOCORE's actors and roles in the conflict news production process.

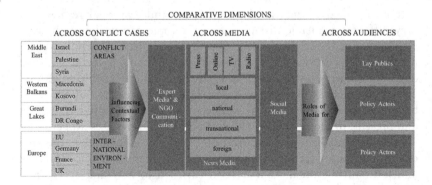

Figure 11.2 INFOCORE's comparative dimensions: contextual factors shaping the roles of media.

Note: I thank Christian Baden who designed the originals of these two figures.

INFOCORE's content-analytical findings confirm our original theoretical assumptions and show, for example, that even specific topics and agendas in journalism and in strategic persuasive communication by political actors and NGOs work as determining contextual factors (see Baden & Tenenboim-Weinblatt, Chapter 2; Fröhlich & Jungblut, Chapter 3). Findings from the INFOCORE interview studies also reveal that the resources to which journalists have access or that are not or are no longer available to them represent key contextual factors for the actual development of specific roles and functions of war correspondents and conflict coverage. The same applies to specific journalistic norms and cultures in very different media organizations and systems that are themselves imbedded in very different political and social systems (see Hanitzsch & Hoxha, Chapter 6). For the theoretical foundation, this means that comparative research in this area cannot only compare the (conflict) cases in and of themselves. It must also compare the social processes of media content production upon which they are based, including the inherent dynamics of media content production as well as systemic and conflict-specific contextual factors of this production.

Based on current developments in the area of media and public opinion on the one hand and our initial empirical INFOCORE results on the other, we will now more precisely describe which key consequences can be drawn for the advancement of theory building in the particular field of research on media and war.

Implications for Theory Building

The global media landscape is being transformed through the interplay of a range of factors: The rise of social media and new communication technologies, new non-Western transnational broadcasting organizations, cutbacks to foreign correspondents and outsourcing production (e.g. Sambrook, 2010) due to decreasing advertising revenue (with NGOs and not-for-profit media trying to fill the gap; cf. Otto & Meyer, 2012), increasing criticism of public (service) broadcasting financed by public funds (e.g. Bardoel & d'Haenens, 2008), dwindling trust in classic mass media by some parts of the media audiences (Quandt, 2012), the crisis of media or journalism or even the public (e.g. Imhof, 2016; Leonard & Schudson, 2009; Levy & Nielsen, 2010; Siles & Boczkowski, 2012) – to name just a few of the developments that have stood out in recent years. At the same time, the nature of violent conflict itself is changing. As explicated in detail in the 'Introduction', the major characteristics of this change are the privatization of wars (e.g. warlords) and military functions as well as security tasks (hiring of military and security companies), decreasing costs for wars (e.g. child soldiers, suicide bombers instead of professional soldiers; acts of war are directed at civilian population instead of at professional armies), a decrease in interstate wars and an increase in military interventions.

Furthermore, the presence of digital media has thoroughly altered the practice of conflict news production. Under the conditions of digital communication and in particular social media, political communication in general is becoming much more pluralized and unclear than in the pre-digital age; today, many more and different communicators and actors are contributing to the production of media content than in the past. New issues are being contested by new actors with new tactics. This enormous growth in the number of communicators and actors has risen in large part from the fact that the strict line between sender and receiver roles that used to exist in public communication has been increasingly blurred in the new media (mobile phones, for instance) and in social media (recipients/users suddenly become senders/communicators and vice versa) or that new roles are also being created such as that of the mediator (see Figure 11.1 above). The monopoly of classic mass media on one-sided push communication is unravelling; pull communication toward the autonomous collection of information and knowledge represents a new mode of public communication that also triggers the creation of new communication roles. When faced with increasingly complex interactions among (very different) communicators and actors on the one hand and organizations and systems (political, social, medial) on the other, theoretical approaches and perspectives that are *solely* based on action theory and/or are mainly actor-centred quickly reach their limits.

In this new scenario,[2] important new opportunities (e.g. mobilization for democratic change, instant eyewitness news, identifying where help is needed) are accompanied by new threats (e.g. quickly spreading hate speech and rumours, propaganda and disinformation,[3] coverage based on unverifiable posts and tweets) that can directly impact the dynamics of conflict and conflict resolution (Kamilindi, 2007; Paterson, Andresen, & Hoxha, 2012). That has consequences for a theoretical reorientation of future research on media and journalism in war and armed conflict (cf. also Baran & Davis, 2012; Bennett, 2015; Vowe & Henn, 2016). In the following, we will describe key consequences that should be drawn given the background of our reported findings and important general developments for a theoretical reorientation of research on media and war. We will start by looking at future research specifically on conflict and war *journalism*.

Key Consequences for the Further Advancement of Theory Building: Research on the Role of Journalism in War and Armed Conflict

The transactionist process model of conflict news production, dissemination and influence outlined in Chapter 1 by Baden and Meyer enables a nuanced, comparative investigation of a wide range of influences that media have on different audiences and it allows us to adequately consider the different media roles. On the basis of the transactionist process model, the various INFOCORE research projects have elaborated on connections between specific representations of conflict and the resulting roles of media, on the one hand, and a wide range of contextual factors (see (a)–(e) in Chapter 1), on the other. Because of the international character of war and violent conflict coverage and the globalized or at least internationalized character of 21st-century news and in particular new/social media applications, the journalists' and the (new) media's role in conflicts cannot be understood adequately from a national perspective. Future theoretical concepts need to be validated via comparative approaches – comparative across different national and international conflict cases, national and international media products, practitioners, conflict contexts, political contexts, etc. INFOCORE rose to this challenge.

Furthermore, because of the speed and interactivity that characterize 21st-century news production processes, media's and journalism's role in conflicts cannot be understood adequately from a snapshot perspective of single conflict moments. Future theoretical approaches must develop research concepts that can observe the production of media content and the creation of public communication on war and violent conflict firstly over longer periods of time, and secondly as an interactive process among numerous participants. Such theoretical concepts must focus more strongly than has been the case thus far on the complex *dynamics* of conflict news production. For these dynamics, valid findings can only be generated using objects of investigation with sufficient scope that also run over longer periods of time. This applies especially to the political system's communication behaviour.

Several contributions in this book show that conflict news is rarely authored by either journalists or sources alone, but emerges from the collaboration and competition of diverse actors. As INFOCORE's results show, for instance, NGOs appear to be highly influential actors in the journalistic production process in contexts with elevated intensity of violence (see Sangar and Meyer, Chapter 7). However, the common assumption that source frames or narratives from strategic persuasive communicators – whether they are political decision makers or NGOs – are highly influential on war and conflict coverage has been put into question by our results (see Baden and Tenenboim-Weinblatt, Chapter 2; see also Fröhlich and Jungblut, Chapter 3).

When looking especially at journalistic performance and roles in times of war and armed conflict, we recommend that future theoretical conceptualizations focus on *journalism as a transformative practice*, which turns information (rendered available by sources, observations, archives, etc.) into news. On the basis of Baden and Tenenboim's findings, we specifically suggest developing theoretical concepts which more clearly differentiate journalistic transformation practices into (a) interventions that follow from general journalistic functions and professional ethics, (b) interventions shaped by the affordances of embedding media systems, technologies used, etc., and (c) interventions that respond to temporary, context-specific constraints and incentives.

Research has depicted many normative transgressions of conflict news, but those recipes detailing how journalists could and should have reported instead (e.g. in the large and growing literature on peace journalism)[4] often have unrealistic assumptions about journalists' autonomy and tend to subordinate the important value of professional journalistic practices to other objectives that collide with journalism's role and credibility as an independent information broker. Critique needs to be based on explicit and plausible normative benchmarks for evaluating journalistic roles in conflict. Such benchmarks need to (a) reflect the important functions performed by journalism for its audiences as political communities (see also Micevski and Trpevska in Chapter 9), (b) take into account those constraints imposed on journalism by the conflict situation and (c) function independently of the normative evaluation of the reported conflict. In place of specific dysfunctions or failures, it may be more fruitful to think in terms of problematic excesses or deficits when applying generally legitimate transformations.

One fruitful perspective for evaluating journalistic performance in conflict is to assess its value added (or subtracted) compared to the information and narratives presented by available sources (cf. Fröhlich and Jungblut, Chapter 3). Another useful point of reference is to contrast its role against the performance of other media channels that lack journalistic moderation (e.g. lays' social media contributions) or whose quasi-journalistic practices are guided by less than professional norms and ethics (e.g. opinion and analysis blogs).[5] Finally, new theoretical concepts should also be broader than was previously the case and, for example, more stringently take into account that journalistic transformation can stand for both without automatically being unprofessional: It may add value in one respect (e.g. include outside voices: political/professional transformation) and simultaneously introduce other, problematic qualities to the news (e.g. naturalize ethnocentric perspectives: cultural transformation). Furthermore, and with a view to the findings from Baden and Tenenboim-Weinblatt (Chapter 2), especially in conflict news and conflict journalism research, there is a need to more systematically distinguish the assessment of the qualities of journalistic coverage from the qualities of covered events.

The study by Hanitzsch and Hoxha (Chapter 6) also suggests this conclusion, as it shows that the characteristics of a conflict, such as its nature and salience, heavily influence the conflict news production process and its outcome. With their theoretical model of news production (see Figure 6.1 in Chapter 6), the authors show that it is worthwhile and fruitful to consider the consequences of conflict-related influences for the way political, economic, institutional, organizational and sociocultural contexts shape the production of conflict news. Particularly, Hanitzsch and Hoxha propose a heuristic model consisting of two parts: a process model accounting for the various stages in news production and a hierarchical model of influences charting the major factors driving those editorial processes. In this line of theorizing, they distinguish among (five) subdomains of influence. One of these areas is sociocultural identity, as journalism usually operates within an existing set of sociocultural value systems. These value systems find expression on three levels – on the level of society/community in the form of normative expectations as to the role of journalism in society, on the level of organization in the shape of newsroom culture, and on the individual level in the form of the journalists' cultural beliefs and identities.

However, theoretical approaches for conflict and war journalism that focus on action theories and/or actors reach their limits when confronted with the increasingly complex interactions between various communicators, actors, organizations, systems (political, social, medial) and communication modes in creating media content and the public. These micro-perspective approaches cannot sufficiently explain, for example, under which conditions or for precisely what reasons interfaces between various communication modes (e.g. between the communication mode 'public relations' and the communication mode 'journalism') are intentionally created in some cases and intentionally prevented in others. That is why alternative theoretical concepts must be developed that more closely compare influences of journalists' individual sociocultural identity with political influence,[6] economic imperatives,[7] institutional arrangements (on the societal level)[8] and reference groups.[9]

Hanitzsch and Hoxha also showed in their work that the taste and desires of audiences are often invoked in journalists' justifications of story selection. At the same time, news media compete with other news organizations and institutions for attention and audience shares, and journalists compete with other journalists for recognition and reputation. As a result, journalism is a highly self-referential enterprise. For research on the performance of war and conflict journalism, it could be beneficial to develop theoretical concepts in the future that take into consideration that excellence in journalism is less dependent on the real preferences of the audience than it is on how a journalist and a news organization is recognized by other actors in the field.

Based on the reported findings, we will now discuss key consequences for a theoretical reorientation of research especially on the role of professional media (coverage) in setting the political agenda on war and violent conflict.

*Key Consequences for the Further Advancement of Theory
Building: Research on the Role of the Media (Coverage) in
Setting the Political Agenda*

Do the media determine the political agenda on war and armed conflict? In political communication and media studies, this has been and
continues to be a key question. While studies focusing on agenda-
building and agenda-setting have shown that crises (of whatever kind)
are "significant catalysts in the agenda-setting process of a political
system" (Schneider & Jordan, 2016, p. 16), findings on the media's determining function for the political agenda have been contradictory.[10]
In part, this may be due to 'politics' being a heterogenous system with
very different types of political actors on very different political levels. Only few studies thus far have dealt with the influence of media
(coverage) on parliamentary debates about violent conflicts. Within the
context of a widespread internationalization of foreign affairs as well
as interpretative frameworks increasingly informed by the 'Responsibility to Protect' (R2P)[11] policy, conflict issues are acquiring greater
importance in parliaments. As the study of Berganza, Herrero-Jiménez
and Carratalá (Chapter 4) confirms, members of parliaments (MPs)
do indeed use communications media as first-hand news sources for
information about violent conflicts. Moreover, adding to a dearth of
first-hand channels of information about conflicts is a lack of institu-
tionalized spaces of communication for politicians from different countries. Because of such needs, traditional professional media appear as
central figures, given that they have become spaces where politicians
themselves carry out political debate, which is often rekindled and further developed within parliaments. The open question for further research, then, is whether such political debates proceed in traditional
media by means of news about events in parliaments, or whether by
means of editorials which explicitly take sides, especially during moments of serious international crises, such as, for example, the Chemical
Weapons Crisis during the Syrian War in 2013.

As for studies on agenda-building during violent conflicts, it is of interest not only to analyse whether the traditional media have the power
to set parliamentary agendas, but also to identify *what kinds of media*
are mentioned *most often* by politicians and MPs as well as *why, in what
context* and *for what purpose*. This appears even more urgent in light
of our findings, which show that in parliamentary debates on war and
armed conflict, public opinion is mentioned more often than traditional
(mass) media.

For politicians beyond parliamentarians, the importance of traditional mass media and their reporting on wars and armed conflicts
seems to vary greatly, as shown by Wolfsfeld and Tsifroni (Chapter 8).

It depends in particular on the question of the importance of the respective conflict on the international news agenda. For domestic and international politicians in the context of, for instance, the Macedonian and the Kosovo conflict, traditional mass media play a twofold role because they widely ignore these conflicts (low rank on the international news agenda) – unless violence breaks out. On the one hand, this means that political actors here do not need to fear (critical) constant observation by the (traditional) media nearly as much. On the other hand, politicians in such 'low relevance' conflicts have a more difficult time than their colleagues in 'high relevance' conflicts (for instance, the Israel–Palestine conflict) when trying to communicate their topics, issues, perspectives and frames through traditional (mass) media. For future research on the role of traditional (mass) media and their conflict coverage in setting political agenda(s) on wars and armed conflicts, according to our findings, theoretical concepts that can explain the variations in the role of these media would be beneficial. These include approaches that more precisely differentiate between conflicts with high and low visibility on the international news agenda (media relevance), for example. The same applies for theoretical concepts on the connection between the determinants of political crisis communication on the one hand and the consequences of this communication on the other.

Robinson (2011) names additional theoretical aspects that would seem to be worth considering in this context. According to him, policy fields which require high economic and political costs are less affected by war and conflict reporting. Conversely, Robinson states that those policy fields for which few economic and political costs are necessary (for instance, decisions on humanitarian aid programmes) are more susceptible to being influenced by war and conflict reporting. Robinson also gives additional suggestions for theoretical differentiation on the question of the influence media reporting on war has on politics and political decision makers: In differing phases of political decision-making processes, media influence seems to be very different ("early agenda-setting stage" vs. "later (...) policy implementation stage" (Robinson, 2011, p. 7)). However, the findings on this are still relatively inconsistent, which suggests that differentiation variables such as the important criteria listed here must be investigated further to provide an expanded theoretical basis for future research.

Based on our findings from the INFOCORE project and considering important general developments, in the following we will now describe key consequences that are important for a theoretical reorientation of research on the role of new (social) media in war and armed conflict. In our view, we need diverse new or at least expanded or adapted theoretical approaches in this area (cf. e.g. Livingston, 2011).

Key Consequences for the Further Advancement of Theory Building: Research on the Role of Social Media and Networks in War and Armed Conflict

Up until now, research has approached social media and networks as a (public) mass media communication phenomenon that is often analysed through the lens of classic theories of mass communication. The fact is, though, that digital media and in particular online social media do not share the institutional characteristics of traditional mass media (e.g. journalism; professionally sanctionable (professional) norms/rules/ethics standards). This fundamental particularity of new (social media) must be more strongly emphasized and mapped out in the future when theoretically conceptualizing relevant studies on the role of online social media and networks in war and violent conflict.

Our findings from INFOCORE suggest that social media and networks provide structural mechanisms and vital platforms for contemporary social movements at three main levels: (a) dissemination, (b) diffusion and (c) organization (see Dimitrakopoulou & Lenis, Chapter 5). In our opinion, these different levels are likely to be decisive for the development of specific roles of social media in war and armed conflict. Therefore, we are convinced that future theoretical approaches to research the role of online social media and networks in war and armed conflict would benefit from stronger differentiation among these three main levels.

The Macedonian case study by Dimitrakopoulou and Lenis showed additional possibilities for differentiation here, as well. It revealed two major categories of communicators: First, an elite group that tweets mostly from a kind of external position on the actual conflict; communicators in this elite group are mostly a part of the group of mainstream media and prominent political actors. Second, communicators in a 'grassroots pool', as the authors call it, which includes participating citizens, bloggers, activists and intellectuals who participate actively in protest actions and regularly tweet while on the ground or in reaction to unfolding events. On the further development of theoretical approaches, it seems worthwhile to consider this differentiation in the future, as well, or at least to keep in mind that these kinds of differentiations among social media communicators exist.

From an INFOCORE study already published elsewhere (Hoxha & Hanitzsch, 2018), we know that war correspondents often use social media as an important source of inspiration. In the case of war reporting, this certainly includes the risk of the breadth of topics related to events, perspectives and interpretations about which war correspondents report being reduced to second-hand research/use by this kind of social media, and the risk of war reporting having even greater consonance than is already the case. This risk is likely to grow as strategic communicators, for example, political actors (especially those in the opposition or who aim to bypass controlled media; see Wolfsfeld and Tsifroni, Chapter 8) or NGOs (see Sangar & Meyer, Chapter 7), are increasingly relying on social media on the topic of war and armed conflict, and Fröhlich and Jungblut also show in their content-analytical study (see Chapter 3) that the scope of narratives on war and armed conflict is already very narrow in NGOs' strategic persuasive communication. This is in contrast to the expectation that social media offers alternative content from communicators in the previously mentioned 'grassroots pool' – alternative to typical standard communication from the usual mainstream communicators, for example, from politics, the military or NGOs. Or as Dimitrakopoulou and Lenis described in their chapter: "At the same time, information appears to be disruptive to the prevailing political and media narratives and brings to the fore under-represented ideas and standpoints." Advanced theoretical concepts about the role of social media in war and armed conflict – whether for content-analytical or interview studies – should focus on these two contradictory expectations and develop a corresponding comparative research design.

In the age of social media, virtually anyone is able to contribute to the construction and dissemination of conflict frames. As a result, the rise of social media has made (lay) publics potentially crucially important contributors to conflict escalation/de-escalation dynamics and potentially important actors in conflict *transformation* processes (see also the section on "The Role of '(Lay) Publics' in War and Armed Conflict" further below). This might add new qualities into conflict dynamics. Against this backdrop, it is necessary to broaden studies on agenda-setting to debates and discourses about war and armed conflicts in digitalized social media. This is particularly important for conflicts such as those originating in the Arab Spring, which have collectively become known as the 'Facebook and Twitter Revolutions'. Another example from our INFOCORE project is the case of Syria: As the violent conflict there intensified over time, the increasing danger to journalists led to an absence of traditional media on the ground. Information and news then often came from local citizens attempting to communicate with each other and record events by means of social networks via the WWW. Therefore, as Micevski and Trpevska argue (see Chapter 9), we need a better understanding of the nexus of fluctuating lines of antagonism and solidarity in media-active (lay) publics' debates on conflict. This is especially relevant during conflict *transformation* processes. Very generally, we call for more research on the debates of media-active (lay) publics on war, conflict and conflict transformation processes than has previously been done. For this, social media offers a previously unknown opportunity, which Dimitrakopoulou and Lenis also point out in their chapter: Media-active (lay) publics (in the sense of Micevski and Trpevska's theoretical approach,) leave distinct digital footprints in social media – a historical visibility online and with this an unprecedented archival functionality that can be traced and followed by researchers. This offers entirely new opportunities for the development of original theoretical approaches and research designs.

In the area of political communication, as well, new (social) media have introduced changes. As Wolfsfeld and Tsifroni (see Chapter 8) demonstrate with their interview study with political leaders, the new (social) media provide these political actors (both in and out of power) with important new tools for their competition over national and international public opinion on war and armed conflict. The political actors interviewed name the following as major opportunities for their use of new (social) media: (1) an increased ability to bypass traditional media, (2) the ability to exploit newer media for generating (their own) news stories (to then be picked up by traditional media for a much bigger audience), (3) the dramatically increased ability for those in government and those in opposition to mobilize support for their causes and (4) the benefits of a much more effective means of communicating with the international community. Interestingly, Wolfsfeld and Tsifroni's results reveal that these opportunities presented by new (social) media are especially important for weaker political actors who aim to overcome the inherent disadvantages they have always faced in their attempts to communicate via the more traditional media. On the other hand, the threats of new (social) media that were discussed by Wolfsfeld and Tsifroni's interviewees were especially likely to create difficulties for political actors in power and in charge of managing wars and armed conflicts: (1) the inability to maintain control over the flow of conflict information and images including the difficulties that political actors in power have in keeping secrets,[12] and (2) the significant shortening of the traditional news cycle. 'Shooting from the hip' in the sense of short-term, general and/or rhetorical responses, however, have the potential to further fuel an already dangerous conflict situation. For future research on the importance of new (social) media for actors in the political/policy field who are dealing with the management of war and armed conflict, what we already said in the previous section about future research on the importance of traditional mass media applies: On this point as well, theoretical concepts that more precisely differentiate among various types of actors from politics – in our case, for instance, between *weaker* political actors on the one hand and *more forceful* ones on the other – are likely to be worthwhile. And the same applies here: We think that future theoretical concepts need to give more thought to those variables that might cause variations in the role and function of new (social) media for MPs and other politicians dealing with (different) wars and conflicts – namely the variable '(high or low) relevance/visibility of wars and conflicts on the international news agenda'.

Finally, as Berganza, Herrero-Jiménez and Carratalá have shown with their study (see Chapter 4), new (social) media have also arrived in parliamentary debates on war and armed conflict. The Civil War in Syria is a clear example of this development: At the beginning of this Civil War, traditional media were mentioned in parliamentary debates about Syria more often than social media. However, the latter acquired greater importance in European parliamentary debates as the Syrian conflict progressed. This might demonstrate that the role of social media (contents) for political agenda-setting through parliamentary debates needs to be addressed in more detail in future studies. Existing theoretical concepts on political agenda-setting should be adapted and further developed especially for the following research questions: (1) Do MPs view and use new (social) media (including platform applications such as YouTube) in parliamentary debates as reliable channels of information? If so, in which contexts and under which conditions do they do so? Do certain strategic persuasive intentions of MPs possibly also play a role in this? (2) Do new (social) media have enough power to set parliamentary agendas and, if so, do they have the potential to facilitate a greater variety of topics, perspectives, agendas for action, etc., in such debates? Up to the present, foundational theoretical concepts and definitions for such important questions are lacking. With a view to the role of social media in parliamentary debates and political agenda-setting in the context of war and armed conflict, alternative concepts of 'reliability' and 'trustworthiness' must be developed, for example, all the more so in the so-called post-factual era of fake news. Or: Is our current understanding of 'pluralism' and 'variety' (for the classic mass communicative offline world) even of any use as a theoretical concept for analysing new (social) media in (parliamentary) debates on war and armed conflict?

In the next section, we will look at key consequences for a theoretical reorientation of research on strategic persuasive communication on war and armed conflict that must be considered with the background of our INFOCORE findings.

Key Consequences for the Further Advancement of Theory Building: Research on the Role of Strategic Communication/ Communicators in War and Armed Conflict

In this area, as well, our findings emphasize the importance of contextual factors: The contextual factors under which strategic persuasive communicators produce and disseminate narratives about war and armed conflict are significantly different depending on the conflict characteristics and/or conflict region/country, depending on the communicator – advocate or source – and depending on the political, media and social system (see Fröhlich & Jungblut, Chapter 3; Sangar and Meyer, Chapter 7). Based on our results, this reveals a highly heterogenous picture of the role, function and impact (meaning success) of strategic persuasive communication in times of wars and armed conflicts. Overarching general patterns can rarely be identified. We were able to find something resembling consistent relevance only for the criterion 'evidence', the findings which we have already published elsewhere (Fröhlich & Jungblut, 2018): The more evidence and transparency characteristics and criteria strategic persuasive communication on war and armed conflict includes, the higher are the chances that corresponding PR material will be chosen for the reporting and enter into the respective media report. What is interesting in this regard: The evidence criterion is at times even more important than the conflict's contextual factors. Overall, Fröhlich and Jungblut's contribution on strategic communication in this book shows that theoretical concepts and research designs meant for international comparisons generate more precise findings because they are more heterogenous.

With a view to the heterogenous findings on the narratives of the strategic persuasive communication analysed, Fröhlich and Jungblut speak of 'narrative flexibility' in their contribution. The authors revealed this narrative flexibility by making a theoretical differentiation between 'narratives' on the one hand and 'measures' (in the sense of 'agendas for action') on the other. The findings show that this was a meaningful differentiation: Their correlation analysis revealed that almost every narrative can appear with all three groups of measures. Future research in this area should pursue this theoretical conception to regard narratives as different semantic constructs that can appear in various combinations. According to this understanding, narratives therefore represent a particular form of persuasive advocacy that can be used to call for a variety of (partly very different!) measures/agendas for action.

Another meaningful differentiation was that between 'frames' and 'narratives'. Unlike Miskimmon et al. (2013, p. 181) and following other authors (e.g. Baden, 2014; Tenenboim-Weinblatt, Hanitzsch, & Nagar, 2016), Fröhlich and Jungblut explicitly assumed a *hierarchical* relationship between both concepts, and provided additional ideas for a way to further distinguish (methodologically) between frames and narratives. They will further elaborate on this theoretical specification in their future work. Against this backdrop, future research will also need to investigate on the (different) relevance of conflict narratives and frames for the agenda-setting process on war and armed conflict and the respective measures/agendas for action.

A final consequence for the further advancement of theory building can be deduced from previous INFOCORE findings published elsewhere by Fröhlich and Jungblut (2018) on NGOs' strategic persuasive communication. There, the authors characterize public discourse "as competitive evidence environments where strategic communicators compete for sovereignty over (problem/issue) definition and resolution" (p. 87). Fröhlich and Jungblut's content-analytical findings revealed that in the competition over the 'power to define', the NGOs who lead the pack are those that rely on convincing and transparent evidence for their claims in their strategic persuasive communication material. Because 'truth' is not the ultimate goal of strategic persuasive communication anyway (cf. Weaver, Motion, & Roper, 2006, p. 19), in our opinion the question whether a claim in strategic communication material is true or false plays a secondary role for future theory building to investigate strategic persuasive communication on war and armed conflict. We believe it to be significantly more innovative to develop theoretical approaches to look into the workings responsible for a particular discourse dominating compared to another. Fröhlich and Jungblut's approach of viewing the 'evidence' and 'transparency' of claims as determining variables for the success of strategic persuasive discourses is a first step in this direction. The approach certainly needs to be expanded, however – for example, by additional determining variables and with the objective of being able to make statements about the weighting of individual variables in comparison to one another.

When it comes to NGOs as strategic actors and communicators, Sangar and Meyer were able to show that NGOs have emerged both as sources of news media and, in some cases, as media like actors producing and shaping news discourses. On the basis of their findings, we identify the following resulting theoretical implications.

More theorizing is needed to conceptualize when and how NGO material is used by journalists as well as what factors determine which NGOs are trusted by journalists and why. Do journalists trust NGOs with a good general reputation, NGOs possessing very specific knowledge about a conflict or NGOs that are successful in 'activating' media attention using their own PR strategies? These questions about trust in NGOs can and must also be raised for political actors – an approach that has hardly been used in respective research thus far. For example, it is entirely conceivable that journalists trust as sources especially those NGOs that are also known to enjoy the trust of political actors.

We also need to theorize more about the implications for journalistic deontology, including the ideal of journalistic impartiality. Just recently, a traditional German prize for journalism was awarded to a story published in Greenpeace magazine. What does this shift towards NGOs as media (like) actors in their own right mean for war/conflict journalism, including efforts to train and assist journalists in conflict countries?

Furthermore: If NGOs' analytical and normative claims about conflict become more influential in news discourse, what does this imply for the intersubjective debate in the general public and the decision-making processes in political institutions? Some authors argue that the dissemination of moralist humanitarianism contributes to the legitimation of military intervention policies, and others fear that conflict diplomacy can suffer from the moral condemnation of conflict actors. More systematic theoretical hypotheses are needed here about the NGOs on which they rely most and what might be theoretical implications for conflict journalism/journalist ethics.

Concerning implications for existing theories on news agenda-making, our results on NGOs as journalists' sources and as media-like actors may suggest that existing theories on the formation of news agendas and the dissemination of specific frames have to be modified: Depending in part on how salient and well-covered a particular country or conflict is, NGOs have become not only increasingly influential news sources for journalists, but also logistical and financial enablers of foreign affairs journalism that gives them extra influence. The most well-resourced and regarded NGOs are able to 'push' their preferred evidential claims and analytical frames in media coverage as a result of their own research and communication efforts, quite independently from newsworthy events or communicative efforts of official actors (cf. also Fröhlich and Jungblut's chapter in this volume). These efforts are typically centred on documenting growing human rights violations and repression, but can also centre on signs of instability, conflict escalation.

Finally, we need theorizing on the question under which conditions NGO media influence translates into influence on actual conflict dynamics – either by influencing decision-making processes in Western capitals, or by drawing media attention to conflict dynamics and HR violations of local actors ('naming and shaming'). While the 'CNN effect' theory has been largely rejected, it might be worth speculating how a potential 'NGO effect' theory might work – and how the greater influence of NGOs on perceptions of conflict might conceptually translate into a positive influence on conflict prevention and peace-building.

On the other hand, we are seeing a significant pushback against liberal/human rights-focused NGOs in many countries, including some Western countries, such that NGOs are seen as the political antagonists/opposition. This combines with pushback in many countries against norms associated with the liberal world order and a crisis of Western foreign policy – a growing disengagement from promoting norms in foreign policy. Pressure against NGOs and pressure against journalism could thus be seen as being part and parcel of the same phenomenon, namely the weakening and/or change of a foreign policy paradigm centred on the promotion of peace and human rights.

In the following, we discuss key consequences arising from our INFO-CORE project for a theoretical reorientation of research on the role of '(lay) publics' and (ordinary) media audiences in war and armed conflict.

Key Consequences for the Further Advancement of Theory Building: Research on the Role of '(Lay) Publics' in War and Armed Conflict

Social media applications make lay publics significant actors in contributing to conflict dynamics. In their study, Micevski and Trpevska developed a promising concept of 'media-active (lay) publics'. Their definition rests on the notion that digitalized social media have enabled the transformation of audiences from receivers of news and information into active producers and reproducers of contents and debates on sociopolitical issues. This is what the authors describe in their contribution as "the transformation of audiences into lay publics". We are convinced that it is key to pursue the path set down by Micevski and Trpevska in future research, thereby linking the theoretical foundation of the concept of 'media-active (lay) publics' with their identification as active communicators in existing protest movements.

Furthermore, the authors have shown with their study that the assumptions of the radical pluralist theories of democracy can become usable aspects of conflict theory. They have proved that theories of radical pluralist democracy and democratic participation can be combined with the framing theory to effectively examine peaceful conflict transformation in political settings with moderate volatility (unstable peace). This is done by exploring the possibility of exploiting rather than arresting the development of wide repertoires of (lay) publics' competing conflict frames. Therefore, we are convinced that exploiting the potential of (lay) publics' repertoires of counter-hegemonic conflict frames is one of the directions that need to be further researched. As our results about the role of (lay) publics's discourse and debate in conflict scenarios demonstrate, it is thereby expedient to identify *(different) types of conflict framing interactions* with the aim to reveal the varieties in content and symbolic potency those types have for constructing conflict in lay publics' discourse and debate. To further assess the *dynamic varieties and complexities* of lay publics' existing competing conflict frames, we suggest extending this particular approach to research on more volatile conflict settings (open conflicts/crises). A more thorough exploration into the fruitfulness of the notions of radical pluralist democracy and the limits of the approach in conflict transformation and reconciliation is necessary, keeping in mind that the literature has deemed radical pluralist approaches to be risky.

In this particular context, from our perspective, an additional consequence arises for the further advancement of theory building in research on the role of (lay) publics: The identification of (lay) publics' repertoires of competing conflict frames (constructed and disseminated through social media) is an important precondition for any conflict transformation effort. Therefore, they need to be further explored in states with *imminent conflict escalation*. Also, more studies need to be focused on the resonance of these repertoires in the *wider population*. Studies need to devise large-N research instruments for operationalizing the identified conflict frames in order to establish the salience of each frame for the general audience.

The widespread assumption that especially in times of crisis media have a strong say in the public's ideas about the crisis is relativized in an interesting way by Frère and Fiedler's findings (Chapter 10), so that once again it must be said: it depends. The authors show that the audience analysed in Goma (DRC) revealed a large range of critical media literacy (regardless of their social background and level of education). Thanks to the study's qualitative design as focus groups, the authors were able to generate very detailed findings on the participants' ideas about political or institutional affiliations of media outlets, public and private media financing, corruption or restrictions to press freedom and to information. With this approach, for the first time researchers were able to collect detailed, concrete criteria that the affected media public can use to evaluate the credibility of media-transported information sources in a specific political conflict context based on long-term (more than two decades) conflict experiences and in a very specific media use context (radio is the key medium in Africa; media content is constantly discussed and cross-checked with friends, neighbours and family): (1) The coincidence between media narratives and the information they get from other channels (word of mouth, social media, interpersonal communication); (2) the degree of internal pluralism of the radio stations available in Goma and the stations' independence from the public authorities and (3) the working conditions and constraints under which journalists practice their job (poor salaries, "coupage", no protection regarding personal safety, submission to media owners' political line). This specific kind of media consumption and assessment in Goma is owed to the media audience there having a certain strategy: To reduce uncertainty and relate the process of reducing uncertainty to the search for meaning in the wars from which they have been suffering for decades. The theoretical approach that enabled these interesting findings assumes that 'trust' in media (coverage) is not a characteristic inherent to the media. Trust in media (coverage) is therefore not subject to a universally definable and shared ascription (least of all one that corresponds only to Western criteria), but instead is an individual attribution by individual members of media audiences. In turn, on this point, it must be taken into consideration that the attribution of trust in media is a culturally sensitive process and that this process is also determined by various, specific contextual factors (see Figures 11.1 and 11.2 at the beginning of this chapter).

The two INFOCORE studies on media (lay) audiences show impressively the benefits of qualitative research designs especially for constellations in which media reception and assessment is done under conditions of ongoing or latent, simmering conflicts. In these situations, media is used and evaluated under completely different conditions. Future research on media use and media effects of coverage of war and armed conflicts in the group of media (lay) audiences should continue to pursue the path of theoretical conceptualization here.

Concluding Remarks

Our research in the INFOCORE project taught us how beneficial it is to anchor relevant contextual factors of communication on war and armed conflict into the theoretical foundation from the beginning (including as variables to be operationalized) and to also systematically vary these factors in empirical investigations. This approach enabled us, for example, to explain differences between individual national findings or different particular conflict cases. However, we cannot (yet) say how exactly the individual contextual factors should be weighted. To make statements about which of the contextual factors have high or low relevance in which scenarios and under exactly which conditions requires more detailed (big) data analysis. This will be one of the future objectives of our continued work on the INFOCORE project.

While established theories and approaches on mediated communication on war and armed conflict provide numerous valuable points of departure, their foundations – typically based on single-case, non-diachronic studies in the West – often point to important limitations that can inform future validation, de-Westernization and the depth and detail of empirical outcomes, if they are properly taken into account. With respect to this, expansions and adaptations of existing theoretical concepts are certainly easy to realize in many areas.

We cannot say often enough: Because of the international character of war and violent conflict coverage and the globalized character of 21st-century (social) news media, their role in conflicts cannot be understood adequately from a national perspective. That is the reason why INFOCORE has been conceived as an internationally collaborative research project. Those, however, represent a particular challenge of their own (cf. Hanitzsch & Esser, 2012) – let alone the intricate management of large collaborative research projects and the funding of such projects. We have intensively shared all these experiences in and with INFOCORE – it was worth the effort.

Apart from the fact that INFOCORE is an internationally collaborative research project, its consortium is also an *interdisciplinary* team of different social scientists. This, too, has been a particular challenge for all participants, as this encompasses a highly complex, culturally sensitive practice of scientific cooperation and collaborative research. This requires researchers who are experienced in international collaboration. In INFOCORE, we needed to apply these culturally sensitive practices of scientific cooperation and collaboration on culturally dependent phenomena, namely on war and conflict journalism and strategic persuasive communication on war and armed conflict (a double-folded culturally dependent scenario). For instance, we had intense discussions about the definition and understanding of key terms (e.g. 'political actor') or about different understandings of 'scientific evidence'. The final results of such discussions were not always reached quickly; however, in the end there were strong and highly robust conceptualizations, which proved to be very viable for the later empirical operationalization across (the partly very) different subprojects of INFOCORE. Key theoretical and methodological concepts of INFOCORE, including many important definitions of terms, can be viewed at www.infocore.eu/results.

Acknowledgment

I would like to thank the following authors for condensed discussions, résumés or keywords on the basis of their respective results: Christian Baden, Rosa Berganza, Dimitra Dimitrakopoulou, Thomas Hanitzsch, Beatriz Herrero-Jiménez, Abit Hoxha, Marc Jungblut, Christoph Meyer, Igor Micevski, Eric Sangar, Keren Tenenboim-Weinblatt and Snezana Trpevska.

Notes

1 However, quickly after the first critical reports came through (about poor morale of under-equipped British troops), the military introduced the first measures restricting the press.
2 Not all of these changes are caused by technical changes of communication conveyed by the public/media. Fundamental social changes have also triggered this development, for example, deliberation, education, internationalization (globalization/transnationalization/Europeanization) or individualization. Or as Dennis McQuail (1999) put it: "Technology only proposes, while society disposes" (p. 24).
3 See, for instance, European Commission (2018).
4 The concept of peace journalism has a comparatively clear idea of what journalists should do. But we think, if journalists did that, they would no longer be journalists but peace activists. There is a reason why journalism exists as a system of its own, so from our point of view, these recommendations are not all that applicable as guidelines in a practical sense.
5 Some online and even some social media contents are journalistic contents in every sense, but we think that there are still distinctions. From our point of view, there is still a difference between producing content for a blog or a social media tool using the same or similar techniques as journalists and formally producing content using professional journalistic techniques and doing this as part of a news profession and organization that is governed by professional rules and protected by particular laws, that is subject to review, and that is sanctionable by the withdrawal of trust. Citing sources and doing research does not make a blogger a journalist, at least not in the sense that audiences can depend on that blogger's professional practices as they can on a professional journalists' practices (whether in print, broadcast or online). And not in the sense that a blogger could benefit from shield laws, which are particularly designed to protect journalists' privilege (for instance, the right which allows journalists to refuse to testify (to keep sources confidential)).
6 Typically exercised by authorities through means of censorship, press bans or, more indirectly, by intimidating journalists and disincentivizing critical reporting. On the organizational level, political influence is typically channelled through editorial policy, which requires journalists to frame their stories within a certain political ideology. This ideology may or may not be in line with the journalists' own political stance.

7 Economic imperatives emanate from the structure of a given media market (e.g. concentration of ownership and availability of advertisement) and, on the organizational level, from the news media organization's business model and allocation of editorial resources to the news desk.

8 A shared sense of desirable occupational practice, usually formalized through professional codes of conduct. On the level of the organization, increased complexity of news work through managerial and editorial regimes (of decision-making, supervision, fact-checking, etc.), which together form an opportunity structure facilitating and restraining journalists' autonomy.

9 Significant groups of social actors who typically serve as a point of reference for journalists' editorial decisions.

10 For a rather sceptical perspective concerning assumed influence of war coverage on policy-makers, see Robinson (2012). The opposite assumption – governments' influence on war coverage – is represented by the so-called 'propaganda model' (cf. Boyd-Barrett, 2004; Herman & Chomsky, 1988).

11 Responsibility to Protect (R2P) is a comparatively novel concept, the application and limits of which are still being debated. It was introduced into the international agenda after the end of the Cold War, although the first time that the United Nations Security Council used it to argue for the use of force was during the military intervention in Libya in 2011. Its aim is to protect populations from genocide and other large-scale atrocities when states affected by these events cannot do so, or when such states themselves are the main culprits. This norm, adopted at the United Nations World Summit in 2005, redefines the concept of sovereignty and challenges the principle of non-interference in the internal affairs of other states (Stavridis, 2016).

12 As discussed by the authors in their contribution: While some amount of secrecy is essential for governments to function, this 'disadvantage' can of course have positive ramifications for other players in the field and might contribute to a broader variety of different information, perspectives, etc., in the debates on war and armed conflict.

References

Allan, S., & Zellizer, B. (Eds). (2004). *Reporting wars. Journalism in wartime.* London, UK: Routledge.

Baden. C. (2014). *Constructions of violent conflict in public discourse. Conceptual framework for the content & discourse analytic perspective (within wp5, wp6, wp7, & wp8).* INFOCORE Working Paper 2014/10. Available online at www.infocore.eu/wp-content/uploads/2016/02/Conceptual-Paper-MWG-CA_final.pdf

Baran, S. J., & Davis, D. K. (2012). *Mass communication theory: Foundations, ferment, and future* (6th edn). Boston, MA: Wadsworth.

Bardoel, J. & d'Haenens, L. (2008). Reinventing public service broadcasting in Europe: Prospects, promises and problems. *Media, Culture & Society, 30,* 337–355.

Bennett W. L. (2015). Changing societies, changing media systems: Challenges for communication theory, research and education. In S. Coleman, G. Moss, & Parry K. (Eds.), *Can the media serve democracy? Essays in honor of Jay G. Blumler* (pp. 151–163). London, UK: Palgrave Macmillan.

Boyd-Barrett, O. (2004). Judith Miller, The New York Times, and the propaganda model. *Journalism Studies, 5,* 435–449.

Herman, E., & Chomsky, N. (1988). *Manufacturing consent: The political economy of the mass media.* New York, NY: Pantheon.

European Commission. (2018). *A multi-dimensional approach to disinformation. Report of the independent High Level Group on fake news and online disinformation.* Luxembourg, UK: Publications Office of the European Union.

Fröhlich, R., & Jungblut, M. (2018). Between factoids and facts: The application of 'evidence' in NGO strategic communication on war and armed conflict. *Media, War & Conflict, 11,* 85–106.

Hanitzsch, T., & Esser, F. (2012). Challenges and perspectives of comparative communication inquiry. In F. Esser, & T. Hanitzsch (Eds.), *The handbook of comparative communication research* (pp. 501–516). New York, NY: Routledge.

Hoxha, A., & Hanitzsch, T. (2018). How conflict news comes into being: Reconstructing "reality" through telling stories. *Media, War & Conflict, 11,* 46–64.

Hudson, R. (1995). *William Russell special correspondent of The Times.* London, UK: Folio.

Imhof, K. (2016). Political, social, and economic crises in public communication. In A. Schwarz, M. W. Seeger, & C. Auer (Eds.), *Handbook of international crisis communication research* (pp. 175–187). Oxford, UK: Wiley Blackwell.

Kamilindi, T. (2007). Journalism in a time of hate media. In A. Thompson (Ed.), *The media and the Rwanda genocide* (pp. 136–144). London, UK: Pluto Press.

Keller, U. (2001). *The ultimate spectacle: A visual history of the Crimean war.* London, UK: Routledge.

Lambert, A., & Badsey, S. (1994). *The war correspondents: The Crimean war.* Phoenix Mill, UK: Sutton.

Leonard, D. Jr., & Schudson. M (2009). The reconstruction of American journalism. *Columbia Journalism Review,* (November–December), 28–51.

Levy, D. A. L., & Nielsen, R. K. (2010). *The changing business of journalism and its implications for democracy.* Oxford, UK: Reuters Institute for the Study of Journalism.

Livingston, S. (2011). The CNN effect reconsidered (again): Problematizing ICT and global governance in the CNN effect research agenda. *Media, War & Conflict, 4,* 20–36.

McQuail, D. (1999). The future of communication theory. In M. Latzer, U. Maier-Rabler, G. Siegert, & T. Steinmaurer (Eds.), *Die Zukunft der Kommunikation. Phänomene und Trends in der Informationsgesellschaft* [The future of communication. Phenomenons, and trends in the information society] (pp. 11–24). Innsbruck, Austria: Studien Verlag.

Miskimmon, A., O'Loughlin, A., & and Roselle, L. (2013). *Strategic narratives: Communication power and the new world order.* New York, NY: Routledge.

Otto, F., & Meyer, C. O. (2012). Missing the story? Changes in foreign new reporting and their implications for conflict prevention. *Media, War & Conflict, 5,* 205–221.

Paterson, C., Andresen, K., & Hoxha, A. (2012). The manufacture of an international news event: The day Kosovo was born. *Journalism, 13,* 103–120.

Quandt, T. (2012). What's left of trust in a network society? An evolutionary model and critical discussion of trust and societal communication. *European Journal of Communication, 27,* 7–21.

Robinson, P. (2011). The CNN effect reconsidered: Mapping a research agenda for the future. *Media, War & Conflict, 4,* 3–11.

Robinson, P. (2012). News media and war. In H. A. Semetko, & M. Scammell (Eds.), *The SAGE handbook of political communication* (pp. 342–355). London, UK: Sage.

Sambrook, R. (2010). *Are foreign correspondents redundant? The changing face of international news.* Oxford, UK: The Reuters Institute for the Study of Journalism, University of Oxford.

Schneider, S. K., & Jordan, M. P. (2016). Political science research on crisis and crisis communications. In A. Schwarz, M. W. Seeger, & C. Auer (Eds.), *Handbook of international crisis communication research* (pp. 13–23). Chichester, UK: Wiley.

Siles, I., & Boczkowski, P. J. (2012). Making sense of the newspaper crisis: A critical assessment of existing research and an agenda for future work. *New Media & Society, 14,* 1375–1394.

Stavridis, S. (2016). The European parliament's contribution to the R2P debate: Lessons from the Libyan and Syrian conflicts. *Global Affairs, 2,* 187–201.

Tenenboim-Weinblatt, K., Hanitzsch, T., & Nagar, R. (2016). Beyond peace journalism. Reclassifying conflict narratives in the Israeli news media. *Journal of Peace Research, 53,* 151–165.

Vowe, G., & Henn, P. (2016). *Political communication in the online world. Theoretical approaches and research designs.* London, UK: Routledge.

Weaver, C. K., Motion, J., & Roper, J. (2006). From propaganda to discourse (and back again): Truth, power, the public interest and public relations. In J. L'Etang, & M. Pieczka (Eds.), *Public Relations. Critical debates and contemporary practice* (pp. 7–21). Mahaw, NJ: Lawrence Erlabaum.

12 Practical Implications and Suggestions for the Applied Fields of Journalism, Media Assistance, NGOs and Politics

Romy Fröhlich

On the basis of INFOCORE's findings, this chapter elaborates on (practical) implications and suggestions concerning three important fields of practice: Journalism, NGOs and politics. In the following, we will discuss the key consequences of selected results for the improvement of:

1 professional journalism in war and conflict coverage and their specific professional role (including the difficulty to be open but not abandon their professional ethos and adherence to quality and critical distance);

2 NGOs' strategic communication and their awareness of the advantages and risks of an increasing blurring of boundaries between media and political actors;

3 options and possibilities for political actors/decision makers and strategic public communication in politics to build policy capabilities for understanding ongoing conflicts and formulating/implementing suitable policies.

Media content is received by media users/audiences to shape their conflict perceptions and agendas, potentially directing and motivating their manifest behaviour (e.g. violent action, policy formulation) toward a conflict. Polarized views can fuel conflict and may heighten susceptibility to rumour and propaganda, while deliberative coverage tends toward reconciliation. Thus, the quality of media content and its sources is very important. It should, however, be considered that news reception is highly selective; it depends on prior attitudes and current concerns (Choi, Watt, & Lynch, 2006; Johnson & Kaye, 2010).

Since conflict news is rarely taken over directly, but undergoes important transformation when it is received, audiences use media information creatively as a resource for their own accounts (see, e.g. Baden, 2010). The empirical studies presented in Part 3 (Chapters 6–10) demonstrated this imposingly. Their scientific results all emphasize how important it is for successful conflict communication to understand different audiences' and target groups' different communication needs and also the obstacles different people might face personally and in their wider sociopolitical context when (actively or passively) participating in public discourse on war and armed conflict. Finally, the extent to which people *feel* informed about a conflict and its resolution is a very important determinant for effective communication and media coverage – more relevant than the actually informative character of a respective communication strategy or media content. Against this backdrop, we hope that our evidence-based suggestions provide a notion about how media, NGOs and policy actors can cooperate to build policy capabilities for understanding ongoing conflict, for formulating/implementing suitable policies and for communicating toward/via media in a manner suitable for assisting mediation and dialogue, reaching out to conflict parties and combating escalatory content.

Practical Implications for Professional Journalism in War and Conflict Coverage

Especially in hyper-partisan and conflict-ridden contexts, journalists and media organizations are well advised to consider multiple perspectives, place special emphasis on journalistic quality and draw clear distinctions between opinions and interpretation, factual claims and verified facts. Emotionalized, polarizing and excessively ethnocentric coverage may offer quick revenue but threatens to erode the selling point of journalism as an entire industry, to the point where audiences may find it indistinguishable from online opinion and rumour, which is free. Practitioners of journalism are challenged to develop ways of rendering conflict news relevant to their respective audiences without compromising their professional ethos, which is what distinguishes journalism from other forms of communication. The main challenge toward a more constructive role of media in violent conflict is not to reinvent or circumvent journalistic news production, but to render it more resilient to the known pressures associated with escalation and violence, and to maintain and reinforce its distinctive contribution amid the cacophony of political propaganda, interest-guided communication, published public opinions and rumour.

In their contribution about the interview study with 215 conflict journalists (Chapter 6), Hanitzsch and Hoxha set out to understand the contextual forces shaping the production of news in times of conflict. According to their findings, it is especially local journalists reporting from the actual conflict zones, who have to deal with safety threats and intimidation. Within the conflict zones, ethnic or religious identity can decide over the life and death of a journalist if caught by the wrong group in the wrong place. The question of war and conflict reporters' safety there-fore remains a key issue. The response of many media organizations to increasing security threats during wars and armed conflicts is to stop sending regularly employed journalists into crisis areas. The risk is too great, and the premiums for the required life insurance policies are now prohibitively expensive. Because of this, it is increasingly freelance war reporters who travel to these areas on behalf of various media. Freelanc-ers bear all risk at their own cost. The collaboration of international journalists with local media is therefore crucial. Hanitzsch and Hoxha's findings also show that local journalists and media organizations often survive on financial support coming from foreign institutions, notably Western governments, the EU, NGOs and various 'humanitarian aid' programmes. Many of these supporting institutions pursue a political agenda related to the conflict, thus creating a gateway to foreign influ-ence and strategic goals. Due to the difficult financial situation of news organizations in many regions, news coverage of ongoing conflict is crit-ical to their survival. That might explain why there is so little reporting globally on pre-escalative phases of violent conflicts and post-war devel-opments. For these and other reasons, NGOs have become a major and often primary source of news where it is difficult for journalists to access information, for instance, in Syria.

These factors are far from perfect conditions or developments for in-dependent war and conflict journalism. We believe that in the Western world, there is still too little awareness of these issues. As a consequence, media organizations and the affected journalists are more or less alone with a growing problem. Ironically, this happens in an arena that has gained a great deal of significance in recent decades due to the interna-tional geopolitical situation. We suggest that political decision makers, NGOs and think tanks that contribute resources toward covering the precarious situation of journalists or that operate in the area of secu-rity training need to connect with the actors at the international level and experts at the local level and look for solutions collaboratively. In this context, a key question needs to be vigorously explored: How can journalists remain independent when their work is supported by exter-nal institutions? Of course, journalists must ask themselves this same question.

Just as Baden and Tenenboim-Weinblatt (Chapter 2), Hanitzsch and Hoxha also emphasize the achievements of war and conflict journalism – especially with the background of constantly deteriorating organiza-tional, structural, and personal resources and working conditions. In that regard, they find the call for more so-called 'peace journalism' from the practice is unhelpful. Since it requires enormous journalistic autonomy, something that is deteriorating as Hanitzsch and Hoxha found in their study, journalists tend to be sceptical about the potential of peace journalism.[1] The chances for peace journalism, as noble and well-intended an idea as it may be, will therefore likely decrease even further in the future.

Furthermore, it is also not clear that 'peace journalism' is necessarily helpful, depending on how one interprets it. After all, journalism performs a function of alerting people to events that may affect their lives. Hence, if journalism were to deliberately de-emphasize its traditional role and instead cover content that does not meet established news values, it is not self-evident that such practice would be accepted by audiences.

Hanitzsch and Hoxha's conclusion is: Peace journalism training programs may help raise awareness among journalists and, as such, are helpful. But those training programs do not change the conditions of reporting. We recommend to all people who work with journalists in war and armed conflicts – whether because they provide information or because the journalists report on them – that when dealing with these journalists, they remember what Hanitzsch and Hoxha stated well at the end of their contribution: "Many decisions conflict journalists are making in the course of news production are dictated less by their free will than they are by external constraints imposed on the reporter." This means that it is less the journalists who are responsible for the state of war and conflict reporting, and ever more frequently the (precarious) circumstances in which they have to work. The fatal aspect of this is that even the best journalistic education can hardly change anything about this bleak situation.

Nevertheless, journalists should make efforts to allow more voices from the 'other side' to be heard by local populations and other audiences (including political decision makers). This also applies to (the often neglected) gender issues and the absence of female voices and women's perspectives in public discourse on war and armed conflict (cf. Fröhlich, 2010, 2016). In addition, journalists need to learn why and how to use a broader network of expert sources. Fröhlich and Jungblut (Chapter 3) showed in their contribution what it can mean to always pick the 'usual suspects' among (powerful, big and traditionally established) sources. And Baden and Tenenboim-Weinblatt (Chapter 2) describe one of their results as follows: "Most journalists not only relied preferentially on sources identified with or culturally close to the ingroup, they also treated out-group sources with considerable suspicion and distance." Social media might be helpful with the aim to broaden journalists' networks of expert sources. In this context, Micevski and Trpevska's contribution (Chapter 9) showed how important it is that the publics are always informed about the existence of other groups' views and attitudes and that various identities, voices and approaches should be permanently provided with access to the content created by the journalists. Journalists should embrace this assumption. However, to contribute to the conflict transformation, journalists should not merely identify and reflect various conflicting views, but also adopt an approach that does not suppress them in order to arrive at a complete consensus. Against this backdrop, journalists should take an approach of cautious openness to social media content produced by media-active publics in order to come to a judgement about a particular way of covering conflict events. In all this, they should keep in mind their specific professional role – hence, to be open but not abandon their professional ethos and adherence to quality and critical distance.

We also advise media to develop their own internal editorial guidelines related to responsible conflict reporting and good governance (e.g. voluntary codes of conduct/ethics related to conflict reporting, to denounce hate speech, to enhance reporting across ethnic and religious lines, etc.).[2] Journalism networks, associations and unions are pioneers here with interesting initiatives which provide a first orientation and good examples.[3] Furthermore, media should firmly apply the 'Monitor Inside and Verify from Outside' principle. One of INFOCORE's policy briefs describes this principle as the establishment of "internal and external quality assurance structures involving managers, journalists, editors, ombudspersons and trade union representatives in order to review the quality of conflict-related reporting, encourage best practices and improve newsroom performance" (Fierens et al., 2016, p. 4).

Practical Implications for Strategic Persuasive Communication of NGOs and Political Actors

General Basics and Challenges

Before we give specific recommendations on improving the strategic persuasive communication of NGOs and political actors based on our empirical findings, we first want to describe the most important basic conditions and challenges that strategic persuasive communication needs to face in the area of conflict prevention, management and resolution. These conditions and challenges apply to the strategic persuasive communication of NGOs and political actors equally. Following that, we will then develop specific recommendations for NGOs on the one hand and political actors on the other based on selected empirical INFOCORE findings.

The greatest challenge for any kind of strategic persuasive communication is, first of all, that it has a basic credibility problem. The field of public relations is now considered a threat to independent journalism or even for democracy as a whole. Since the digitalized social media enables strategic persuasive communications of all kinds to circumvent classic mass media and journalism – that is, the professional gatekeepers – when disseminating their messages and instead speak directly to the intended audience, scepticism about strategic persuasive forms of public communication has continued to grow. The innovations in communication technology have thus simplified practical strategic persuasive communication on the one hand (bypassing classic mass media/journalism). At the same time, in the post-factual/post-truth age in which information needs to be particularly credible and reliable, this technology leads to new challenges to the credibility and acceptance of strategic persuasive communication.

It is therefore hardly surprising that especially in recent years, efforts in PR practice have been increasing to more clearly differentiate between so-called unethical forms of strategic persuasive communication like propaganda on the one hand (in totalitarian systems, for instance), and supposedly ethical persuasion like public relations on the other hand (in democratic systems with free media, for instance). PR theory itself has not yet been able to develop any clearly differentiating models or definitions for 'propaganda' and 'public relations'; the commonalities are too great between these two forms of persuasion (cf. e.g. L'Etang, 2006). Weaver, Motion and Roper (2006) describe selected aspects of these overlaps. They describe public relations as a "strategic attempt to control the agenda of public discussion and the terms in which discussion takes place" and PR practitioners "as working to (strategically) privilege particular discourses over others, in an attempt to instruct what they hope will be accepted as in the public interest and legitimated as policy" (pp. 17–18). Both of these descriptions also apply to all kinds of strategic persuasive communication and therefore also to propaganda.

It is therefore even more important for (ethical) applied strategic persuasion to be recognizable as fair, ethical and responsible strategic communication through the way in which it actually communicates with its stakeholders. This includes, for example, the professional effort of strategic communicators "to communicate 'with', as opposed to, 'to' stakeholders" (L'Etang, 2006, p. 27). According to this understanding, it is recommended that strategic communication is not generally constructed as a one-way monologue but instead as a dialogue[4] (with the intended target groups). This applies in particular to highly controversial social and political *crisis* discourses as in the case of war and armed conflict. Especially in cases of crisis, successful strategic communication is characterized by its discursive (instead of intuitive) nature. Weaver et al. (2006) concisely state what this means: "This perspective [strategic communication/PR as discourse] shifts the role of public relations from information management and control to the production, contestation, and transformation of ideas and meanings that circulate in society" (p. 18). Simple concepts of persuasion (e.g. under-complex 'truths' that are continually repeated; one-sided black-and-white or good-and-evil arguments; intuitive claims; etc.) are very short-lived with the target groups in the Web 2.0 age anyway. Besides that, they do not convince journalists, and they are an easy target for counter-communication.

Against this backdrop, L'Etang (2006) points out the relativist context in which every kind of persuasion takes place: "In a relativist context, beliefs of all persuasions have legitimacy: it is a truism that one person's terrorist is another's freedom fighter. In this context, maybe it is not so much *truthfulness* which counts but *rightness* in terms of moral position and behaviour. This would account for the very necessary ethical turn in terms of the analysis of organisational communication focusing on legitimacy, communication process and intention but also requires attention to the morality of an organisation's overall purpose" (p. 29; italics in original).

Accordingly, the recommendations we give in the following two sections for effective, professional strategic persuasive communication by NGOs and political actors/decision-makers active in conflict prevention, management and resolution also assume that the organizations, institutions and people who are to be advised follow L'Etang's (2006, p. 29) *"rightness* in terms of moral position and behavior". However, we are aware that organizations, institutions and people who do not adhere to this sense of rightness and morality can also make use of these suggestions.

In a policy brief for the respective political institutions of the EU and for NGOs active in conflict prevention, management and resolution, Fröhlich and Jungblut (2016) made further suggestions and recommend: "Security governance and related actions in the political field and the engagement of NGOs must include (1) responsible, coherent and reliable public communication through (2) a sustainable strategic concept and sustainable strategic measures" (p. 6). With a view to "a sustainable strategic concept and sustainable strategic measures", in this policy brief the authors recommend a concept of communication governance. They understand this to be a sustainable, organizationally embedded regulatory framework (i.e. "governance") for the strategic management of all communication activities. Ideally, this governance concept then regulates the entire strategic persuasive communication of the affected organization or institution, explicitly including internal[5] communication, as well. This is the only way to ensure homogeneity between strategic persuasive communicative behaviour directed on the one hand at internal target groups and on the other hand at external ones. In addition, the regulatory framework of a communication governance concept makes it easier to establish a specific organizational culture that is highly relevant especially in crisis scenarios for the external and internal perceptions of an organization's or institution's credibility.

This kind of governance concept offers another advantage: As the outbreak of crises such as war and armed conflict is often almost inevitable, it makes sense to develop specific protocols for actions related to the media and other important stakeholders that can be initiated during such periods. These 'specific protocols' are nothing other than what Coombs (2014, pp. 90–98) understands under the term "crisis management plan". Following Coombs, we recommend developing a specific management plan for *crisis communication* and making it a key element of the communication governance concept. We are convinced that such 'specific protocols' also need to be at hand in phases when the situation on the ground improves (e.g. chances for a ceasefire or a peace process become more probable). This often gets overlooked, since the focus on *crisis* communication is clouding the view. NGOs and policy-makers should have systematic plans in place for exploiting the various types of target groups (including journalists/media) to support and strengthen early emerging signs of de-escalative developments from the very beginning. That is even more important, as it is well known that media focus on negative events and conflicts – even in relatively conflict-free phases of war or during peace negotiations. Even in these phases, media tends to 'swoop' down on the still existing violence. Under some circumstances, this could even mean that they hinder peace processes. Communicators must be aware of this and be prepared for 'headwind' from the media during peace processes (cf. e.g. Wolfsfeld, 2004).

The approach suggesting a media relations governance originally proposed by Fröhlich and Jungblut (2016, pp. 7–13) especially for (strategic) communication with journalists can easily be expanded to a 'public relations governance' framework for the strategic management of communication activities for and with the *general and the specific public* (including particularly intended target groups like donors (in the case of NGOs), lay publics, other (oppositional) political decision makers, war-making parties, public diplomacy actors, etc.). The majority of the detailed recommendations for 'media relations governance' given in the policy brief mentioned above can easily be transferred to many other relevant target groups beyond media and journalists.

And we must mention another recommendation by Fröhlich and Jungblut (2016, p. 13); it also has a rather general character: "Today, a high share of social media content stems from so-called 'bots' – automated accounts (computer programs) that produce automated Twitter or other social media content. Experts estimate that 30 million Twitter accounts do not represent real people/institutions but are automated accounts; Facebook assumes that its platform has 15 million automated fake accounts. (…) It might be a sign of best practice (…) if strategic communicators in conflict prevention, management and resolution proactively assert that they completely abstain from bots (and abide by this assurance). This can contribute to their general reliability and credibility" (p. 13).

Bots may not be ethically questionable as such. For example, they make it easier to run simply structured bureaucratic processes with automated answer or behaviour patterns (e.g. customer service). Using bots with the objective of persuading and influencing the (perceived) public opinion is not a practice that inspires confidence, however.[6] Fröhlich and Jungblut therefore recommend dispensing entirely with the use of bots and proactively and explicitly incorporating this renouncement into an organization's or institution's framework of shared norms and values (communication governance concept). At the same time, all efforts should be made to quickly, effectively and regularly identify 'persuasive' bots on an organization's own social media pages and either offer a well-founded refutation of the bots' messages or delete their messages.

Another important note equally relevant to NGOs and political actors/decision makers was given in Fröhlich and Jungblut's policy brief (2016). It relates to the recommendation of developing a special sensitivity to a conflict, culture and particular (geopolitical) context when designing a communication strategy. As the authors write, this applies in particular when NGOs or political actors are providing analytical judgement/recommendations for problem solving beyond factual reporting. Especially when doing this, counter-productive (escalative) effects can arise. Fröhlich and Jungblut explain this using the example of human rights abuses: "(...) to call prematurely for referral to the International Criminal Court of political or military leaders can make those actors more desperate and less willing to compromise or to negotiate, since they see no way out. Particularly from a short-term perspective, such a recommendation can be counter-productive in preventing an escalation of conflict, although an ICC referral may well be appropriate or just. In this case, being sensitive to a conflict and culture means carefully considering particular conflict dynamics when planning communicative messages. From a communicator's perspective, the strategy might be to achieve justice for the victims and media resonance for himself or herself. It might be well intentioned, but with respect to the conflict development (de-escalation), it might be a better strategy to show restraint, owing to the particularly sensitive context of a conflict and its dynamics. It's the stability vs. justice dilemma" (pp. 9–10).

In the following, we will now describe specific practical implications for successful de-escalative strategic persuasive communication of the two key actors, NGOs and politicians/political institutions that go beyond basic, general recommendations for strategic communication. These implications are based on selected, specific INFOCORE findings that were reported in the contributions to this volume (mainly in Fröhlich and Jungblut, Chapter 3; Sangar and Meyer, Chapter 7; Micevski and Trpevska, Chapter 9). Beyond this, where we believe it prudent, we also integrate recommendations that go back to INFOCORE findings that have already been published, such as in the case of the communication governance concept mentioned above. We start with practical implications for NGOs.

Practical Implications for NGOs Active in the Field of Conflict Prevention, Management and Resolution

Recommendations for Strategic Communication

It is important for NGOs to understand how they are being perceived by journalists, including any perception of bias. Some of the NGOs could do better to promote internal diversity and an open culture of discussion, which would feed into more nuanced approaches to conflict. A more diversified funding structure would help in this process, as would empowering country experts to resist simplifying or misleading messaging that might be motivated by fundraising objectives. Most of the studied NGOs are well aware of the damage factually inaccurate press releases and reports could do to their reputation and put 'accuracy first', but many of the interviewees of our study (see Chapter 7) do acknowledge pressure from the media and fundraising side on the communicated content. Moreover, some of the NGOs do not fully realize the extent to which they are seen as biased by journalists in different settings, which can be partly addressed by doing more research into the most relevant audiences and tailoring information and communication activities better.

Some of the larger and better-funded NGOs could at times refrain more from using their leverage with journalists to advance solutions that lie outside their areas of expertise in human rights. Providing actionable and convincing advice to policymakers on how to act requires dedicated research efforts and few NGOs do this well enough, or they are worried that getting too close to power would undermine their independence and weaken their ability to challenge the prevailing consensus. However, providing poor recommendations can taint the underlying analysis or information gathered by its own personnel, so it would sometimes be better if NGOs were more cautious or refrained from some of the policy advocacy.

Conflicts are by nature highly complex and fraught with many dilemmas, creating problems with some of the moral and value-based framing. Finally, NGOs face trade-offs in terms of using their leverage to influence journalists' reporting and, over the longer term, inadvertently undermining public trust in independent, high-quality journalism. Some forms of sponsorship for journalistic inquiry are problematic, should be reviewed, and if necessary, stopped.

The message from journalists is that most NGOs do have a genuine interest in researching and communicating accurate information on armed conflict and have the necessary resources to do so. However, many journalists and political actors that we interviewed for INFOCORE were sceptical about the 'neutrality' of NGO claims, and some preferred to rely on think tanks as well as academic experts to enhance their understanding. But due to their local presence, NGOs typically have easier access to local populations and are more familiar with short-term dynamics of violence. Many NGOs have employed journalists and academically trained researchers and are using fact-checking procedures very similar to those used by traditional media. If properly triangulated, NGO information can therefore add precious situational awareness especially in conflicts where there is little local presence of international journalists and/or intelligence services. This should be taken into account especially in attempts to improve accuracy of early warning procedures for conflict analysis and response (Meyer & Michaels, 2016; Meyer & Otto, 2016).

At the same time, we caution against an over-reliance on NGOs as exclusive sources of coverage from the ground. The conflict in Syria represents a context in which early on, a lack of local presence of conflict journalists increased demand for factual information from NGOs. But as our results have shown, this has been associated with a lack of critical discussion of the moral frames NGOs such as *Human Rights Watch* (HRW) suggested for interpreting the violent escalation. Journalists should realize that NGOs will not necessarily provide holistic analyses of conflict dynamics, and therefore should triangulate sources and use critical judgment when analysing conflict evolution – even when relying on factual information from NGOs. Furthermore, we would advise to diversify the number of NGOs considered as 'legitimate' sources of information, and also to seek direct contact with NGO representatives to understand how their claims and demands are constructed, rather than solely republishing quotes from press releases and reports.

A similar recommendation goes for the implication of NGOs in early warning and crisis management decision-making in political institutions. In some Western countries, such as France, foreign policy actors traditionally keep NGOs at bay and rely on knowledge and analysis produced by domestic intelligence services, news media and academic intellectuals (Lauer, 2005; Ryfman, 2013). Yet this system displays its limits, as the French decision-making process during the Arab Spring illustrates: "Despite the longevity, breadth and depth of ties with the North African and Middle Eastern region, France failed to anticipate the Arab upheavals that began in 2010" (Utley, 2013, p. 70). Worse even, such relatively closed decision-making cycles can produce echo chambers, where privileged foreign news journalists with exclusive access to foreign ministries anticipate political demands and suggest analytical frames that justify rather than challenge views suggested by political actors (Brauman, 2015; Declich, 2012). We recommend that rather than distrusting NGOs completely, policymakers should make themselves familiar with the most important NGOs present in conflict zones, their individual objectives and their activity profiles. "Analysing sources and inherent biases in such a way is immensely helpful for determining whether and how they can be used" (Meyer & Michaels, 2016, p. 5). By regularly comparing and discussing factual and analytical claims produced by diverse NGOs such as *HRW*, *International Crisis Group*, or the *Secours Islamique*, policymakers will be able to build an additional knowledge base that can complement those provided by academic experts and intelligence services.

Last but not least, so far policymakers have paid insufficient attention to the fact that local NGOs, because of their communication power, are often perceived as opposition forces by authoritarian local governments without good justification. The current wave of repressive legislation and police harassment against civil society organizations that can be observed in countries as diverse as Israel, Macedonia or Burundi can in our view at least partially be explained by the increasing media presence and resulting political influence of local NGOs. Such attempts appear to be even more dangerous as they seem to coincide with either increasingly polarized (as in the case of Israel) or state-controlled media environments (as in the cases of Burundi and Macedonia). Rather than qualifying this pressure as an exclusively domestic issue, Western governments should multiply their efforts to prevent local NGOs from being marginalized. Increasing direct financial or organizational support may be counterproductive, as this facilitates the denunciation of local NGOs as 'foreign agents', but we would recommend adopting minimum standards of NGO autonomy in aid or cooperation agreements with concerned governments alongside devoting greater attention to ensuring freedom of the media and expression.

In Chapter 11, we described previous INFOCORE findings from Fröhlich and Jungblut (2018), according to which the NGO's media-related strategic persuasive material on war and armed conflict was always particularly successful (i.e. selected for use in media coverage by journalists) when the material had a high degree of evidence, evidential facts and transparency. Based on this finding, drawn from content analysis, our clear recommendation to strategic persuasive communicators in NGOs is therefore to improve the evidential and factual character of their strategic conflict communication and to ensure the highest possible level of transparency (transparency of sources used, the actual communicator's intentions, any (still) existing uncertainties about the claims made, etc.). This is how strategic-persuasive communicators can enhance what Snow and Taylor (2006) understand as the credibility of truth.[7] Concerning the communication of uncertainty: Our previously published empirical results on the success of NGOs' strategic-persuasive communication on war and armed conflicts showed that it is considered a persuasive strength to communicate an evidential yet uncertain claim while proactively admitting to uncertainty concerning this claim. This contributes to NGOs' general credibility (Fröhlich & Jungblut, 2016, p. 4; 2018, p. 90).

We believe, however, that this finding on how to deal with uncertainty cannot be directly transferred to other strategic persuasive communicators (e.g. politicians). This is because NGOs – in contrast to politicians, for example – are attributed with a comparatively high moral position and behaviour (in the meaning as described by L'Etang, 2006, p. 26; see above). They therefore enjoy a higher level of trust. This ensures that the uncertainties they communicate are included by their stakeholders and target groups (including journalists) in different credibility contexts than is the case with politicians, for example. For this assumption, we do not (yet) have empirical proof, though, and it is therefore a topic for future research.

Micevski and Trpevska have shown in their contribution (Chapter 9) that and why the (standardized) implementation of democracy during conflict transformation and peace processes with relatively mild conflict episodes is a risky strategy. For the respective society, models of democracy most often are unknown. Against this backdrop, they argue, those strategies cannot be successful since they ignore that conflict is all-pervasive in society and that it is constitutive of democracy. On the basis of their results from focus groups with media-active (lay) publics, the authors suggest the idea that rather than pushing opposing conflict frames into alignment and consensus by all possible means, and instead of pushing irreconcilable positions into consensus at any cost, conflict transformation strategies, including media strategies and communication strategies of institutions in charge, need to examine the possibility of embracing and supporting certain types of counter-hegemonic conflict frames to transfigure violent conflict into non-violent (or at least less violent) conflict outcomes. In their contribution, they show why and how the seemingly counterintuitive strategy to apply the agonistic notion of 'radical pluralist democracy' to conflict transformation makes sense.[8] Consequently, NGOs that work in various conflict settings should focus on developing peace-building strategies that do not solely promote consensus among social groups but also strive to achieve fundamental changes in political, social, economic and cultural conditions that would in turn allow for the variety of competing ideas about society to exist in a dynamic public realm. Their communication's long-term goals and efforts should be based on the recognition of the pluralistic democratic reality and widening the space for new voices, views and approaches to conflict transformation. They should promote a form of peace-building strategies that rely more on recognizing and encouraging contestation and disagreement as a necessary part of any conflict resolution process than on formal discussions on how to achieve absolute consensus that neglects the existence of antagonistic views and attitudes. The application of notions of the radical pluralist democracy approach for NGOs' strategic communication with their diverse stakeholders during conflict transformation and peace processes represents a promising (persuasive) strategy, as it tends to open up the spaces for adversarial manifestations.

Practical Implications for Political Actors in the Field of Conflict Prevention, Management and Resolution

Recommendations for Strategic Communication

The world of strategic persuasive communication practice has changed tremendously in recent years. Digitalization of public communication and the related challenges and other obstacles for strategic persuasive communication have already been mentioned. But there are other substantial changes that are incredibly important especially for strategic communication in politics and that are not yet realized in full in this policy field. These include serious social changes as a consequence of digitalization of communication and (new) social media. L'Etang (2006) very aptly describes them in reference to the survey data from her own study of PR practitioners: "(...) power in society is moving away from its traditional centres in government and business and spreading over a wide social base; national boundaries are reconfigured as regional and global at the same time; legitimacy is defined away from the narrow understanding of what is legal and increasingly in terms of what is moral; citizenship is expressed through consumership, and all this is fuelled by the technological changes in communication and the resulting changes of the mass media. (...) Business compliance with legislation is replaced by the prerogative of earning social trust and approval. Crises are avoided by successful anticipation of issues due to 'creative use of communication technology' (...)." (pp. 282, 286)

Politics has difficulties with the changes described here. This is understandable because politicians themselves are very active participants – for example, as members of a government or a lawmaking institution – in establishing, regulating and exercising 'power in society', in creating 'legitimacy' and 'legislation', in setting up 'national boundaries' or in developing an understanding of what is meant by 'citizenship' in democracies. All of these are part of their inherent tasks and responsibilities. That is why it seems almost illegitimate and utopian that, in democratic systems, the changes described by L'Etang are made essentially *en passant* – without the possibility for democratically legitimated political institutions to intervene. And still – strategic persuasive communicators in politics must anticipate these changes, even those that put into question their own political roles and functions. There are great risks for the effectiveness of political actors' strategic persuasive communication if they ignore these general changes (according to the motto that 'which must not, cannot be') when designing their own strategic persuasive communication.

Besides these general challenges and those that we described as general basics and challenges at the beginning, the individual INFOCORE studies offer specific findings. In the following, we will derive specific recommendations from these results for the advancement of strategic persuasive communication of political actors active in the field of conflict prevention, management and resolution.

Especially considering the contemporary disenchantment with professional journalism, it is important for practitioners from all fields to realize that, despite all its flaws, journalism has also made important contributions that cannot be made by any other institution or actor. The findings by Baden and Tenenboim-Weinblatt (Chapter 2) offer proof of the important contributions of war and conflict journalists. Based on these results, we make the following recommendations: (1) Political actors are ill-advised to bank on social media content over news content for gathering open source intelligence, especially in terms of gaining interpretation; social media content may be more plentiful, but journalistic coverage is still much less susceptible to bias and forgery. (2) Political initiatives to improve public information – both inside and outside conflict areas – may achieve most by focusing on the support and protection of media organizations and journalistic institutions committed to high professional standards (including press councils). Further efforts might need to target the ability of news organizations to remain resilient legally, economically and otherwise against not only political pressure, but also the sentiments of incited audiences. (3) What is also instrumental are media literacy and a public awareness of important differences between journalistic and other news contents (produced by political agents, interest groups or laypeople)[9], including an understanding of the self-correction and quality assurance mechanisms structuring the journalistic field.

The results of Fröhlich and Jungblut's content analysis on strategic communication material (Chapter 3) revealed that the particular political decision makers of their study generally place a higher focus on escalative narratives (especially when conflicts escalate). This especially puts to the test the de-escalative attitude of European politics/political institutions – often postulated from a normative point of view. According to the content-analytical results, however, this escalative attitude has its limits: When it comes to particular appeals for actual conflict *measures* (agendas for action), there is a more intensive focus on de-escalative measures (again: especially during escalative phases). According to the authors, this indicates that the respective political actors assume their particular de-escalative role and responsibility in times of armed conflicts better than when using and communicating via (broader and less binding) narratives. In general, though, this particular finding reveals a kind of inconsistency in the communicative strategy, so that especially European politics/political institutions are in danger of being accused of inconsistent political attitudes. This might be avoided by a more consistent, continuously de-escalative chain of argument.

One aspect must be observed when doing so, however: Decisions about exchanging or modifying narratives that have already been communicated and established involve a very risky and highly complex process that must be well prepared. After all, narratives are not fictitious, unrealistic perspectives on an event. They can only have strategic effects because their meaning is anchored in the real world or in the collective memory of a society (see Fröhlich and Jungblut, Chapter 3). As such, they are not simply idiosyncratic 'views of the world' that can be exchanged at will or as Miskimmon et al. (2013) say: "Leaders cannot create a narrative out of nothing, off the cuff." (p. 8). The modification of narratives in strategic communication must therefore always be coupled with the actual conflict events, the discourse that is actually being held about the conflict, and profound knowledge about the collective memory and trauma of a society. In this, political decision makers and communicators have a particular responsibility, and if they mishandle the situation, they stand to lose a great deal with very long-lasting effects. If decisions are to be made about which strategic narratives should be used, these must therefore be extremely well prepared: (1) With a well-founded analysis of the (actual) conflict events, (2) with sound monitoring of the current conflict discourse in the relevant public spheres (public opinion, media coverage, expert discourses, etc.) at home and abroad in the conflict regions and (3) with a building of profound knowledge about societal collective memories and traumata. With this kind of monitoring and evaluation, political decision makers' quantity of resonance and the quality of how their narratives are processed in diverse publics can also be analysed. It would be best practice to set up this monitoring as a continuous analysis through which the respective strategic communicators could also then receive continual data that can act as an early warning system. Today, once they have been prepared, these kinds of monitoring analyses can be run almost completely automatically by computers as big data content analyses if the required text materials are available. INFOCORE itself is an example of how such computer-assisted, content-analytical big data analyses can be set up and carried out with the help of particular software. However, INFOCORE has also shown that the process of obtaining any meaningful indication of what is going on from that content is still a less than trivial process. Just tracking indicators does not do the job; someone who knows the context and has experience in social scientific analysis is still needed to make sense of that data.

We can derive additional recommendations for improving political actors and decision makers' strategic persuasive communication from Berganza, Herrero-Jiménez and Carratalá's contribution on the dynamics of parliamentary debates on war and armed conflict (Chapter 4). European members of parliament (MPs) need to become more actively aware that, with the arrival of the 21st century, the range of their duties has been expanded beyond its traditional focus: the domestic politics of the nations they represent. The so-called "parliamentarisation of international affairs" (Stavridis & Pace, 2011) is a global phenomenon that underscores the duties parliamentary diplomacy has assumed in recent years, mainly in the prevention and resolution of conflicts. Changes to parliamentary duties can already be seen in the British parliament, for example, where the Syrian War set a precedent according to which the chamber representing national sovereignty must previously approve any deployment of armed forces abroad.

Moreover, parliamentarians must now accept that their duties include monitoring elections in countries undergoing pacification and reconstruction in addition to explaining parliamentary dynamics to their peers in other nations undergoing the democratization process. Travel undertaken by MPs as part of diplomatic delegations to countries in conflict or in periods of post-conflict should be made as often as possible and should be used to forge connections with NGOs, think tanks, journalists/media and members of local civil society organizations, which might serve as sources of information on the ground.

The issue of which sources MPs draw upon for their information is, without a doubt, a priority issue that needs to be tackled. European MPs appear to get their information about conflicts mainly from both communications media inside their own countries and from other international communications media sources. Additionally, these MPs are sometimes privy to reports from their country's intelligence services or from those of other ally nations. On some occasions, they themselves speak of a certain distrust in such reports, owing mainly to the ghost of the Iraq War and the never-found weapons of mass destruction. Similarly, it is crucial that parliamentarians dedicate time and energy to expanding their search for information, so they can stay informed about current conflicts. Among other news sources, MPs need to take into greater consideration reports and other information provided by NGOs – the absence of any mention of such organizations in the French National Assembly is especially notable (see Chapter 4) – and place greater emphasis on opinions and facts gathered by local NGOs; according to Berganza et al.'s results, most allusions to such organizations in parliaments refer to international NGOs. Connecting with these (local) NGOs on the ground should become one of the routine duties that parliaments and traveling parliamentary delegations perform. Moreover, this sort of contact needs to be emphasized during periods of escalating conflict, which apparently has not been the case so far. Thus, for example, during the Syrian War's chemical weapons crisis, MPs referenced information from NGOs much less frequently than they referenced information from communications media and social networks.

Also on the topic of which information sources are used by MPs, we recommend that MPs read/listen to/watch communications media distantly removed from their own political spheres. As Berganza et al.'s content analysis about parliamentary debates revealed, mentions were made about US media, and, during the Syrian chemical weapons crisis, there was no mention of any Russian media source, a country that was a highly important actor during this escalating phase of the conflict. This suggests not only that perspectives on the news tend to be Western, but also that MPs are losing their opportunity to react to potential future policies that important political decision makers beyond the Western sphere may adopt; those decisions can be more easily predicted by the communications media in the respective (non-Western) countries and the conflict countries.[10] Moreover, local media from foreign countries can reflect the pulse of public opinion abroad, which can be useful information to predict the political positions adopted by non-allied states. Hence, MPs need to assess information and opinions provided by media and journalists on the ground, as well as by media from countries involved in the development, pacification or escalation of conflicts, although these may not coincide with perspectives adopted in their countries of origin.

Lastly, given the paucity of information MPs appear to possess during parliamentary debates, it is recommended that Open Source Intelligence be included among other sources of information, since the data it provides, when handled and processed with care, might help to triangulate other news sources, thereby maintaining a level of documental and informational diversity in parliamentary spaces that is currently not as robust as it should be.

As for social media, MPs should be especially cautious. In recent years, there have been several cases in which videos, uploaded to social networks by citizens in countries experiencing armed conflict, have sparked highly emotional debates in the parliaments of Western countries (Geis & Schlag, 2017). It is in such cases that parliamentarians must understand that videos (or texts and pictures) on social networks are not in themselves reliable sources of information and therefore must be compared with and verified through alternative sources.

Finally, the gender issue needs to be reformulated in parliamentary debates. Sexual violence is an important subject in debates about armed conflicts, yet it is often the case that parliamentary debates focus solely on women as victims, overlooking the key roles they play in conflict resolution as both negotiators and peacemakers. If women are treated mainly as victims, they appear as passive subjects who are only acted upon. If, on the other hand, their roles as peacemakers and negotiators are mentioned in speeches, they are instead rightly figured as active agents, a change in perspective that would undoubtedly help foster greater gender equality as the collective imagery of armed conflicts is constructed. In general, MPs and any other political actors active in the field of conflict prevention, management and resolution have a particular responsibility to serve as role models and thus should more often consider the proactive provision of female voices and women's perspectives in their communication material to be a contribution to fair and balanced content production – a key prerequisite for de-escalative effects of communication.

From the perspective of their study on (lay) publics, Micevski and Trpevska (Chapter 9) make an interesting suggestion for political actors: Conflict transformation efforts made by national and especially international political actors in cases of relatively mild conflict episodes have been focused on developing common ground ideologies (in situations where conflict has escalated or is about to escalate) in order for the antagonists to come to a consensus about issues. These efforts have proven shallow and superficial in many instances – they have had obvious effects while international political actors have shown presence by financing peace efforts or by making other gestures of political support for conflict transformation. And yet, soon after peace guarantors decide to decrease attention on consensus-making, peace is destabilized, proving the strategy inefficient in the long run because the roots of the diverse antagonistic views and beliefs have not been adequately handled. Exploring the media-active lay publics' plurality of ideas about the conflict may open up possibilities that would transform the consensus-making strategies of conflict transformation into pluralist strategies in which consensus would be possible but not enforced. With this background, what we already said above about NGOs' strategic behaviour and strategic persuasive communication applies: Political actors and decision makers engaged in conflict management, prevention and resolution should develop peace-building strategies that do not solely promote consensus among social groups but also strive to achieve fundamental changes in political, social, economic and cultural conditions that would in turn allow for the variety of competing ideas about society to exist in a dynamic public realm. Political actors' long-term communication goals and efforts should be based on the recognition of the *pluralistic* democratic reality. They should promote forms of peace-building policies that rely more on recognizing and encouraging contestation and disagreement as a necessary part of any conflict resolution process than on formal discussions about how to achieve absolute consensus, which neglects the existence of antagonistic views and attitudes. The application of notions of the radical pluralist democracy approach for NGOs' strategic communication with their diverse stakeholders during conflict transformation and peace processes represents a promising (persuasive) strategy, as it tends to open up the spaces for adversarial manifestations.

Concluding Remarks

Our project developed several key recommendations and context-sensitive strategies for direct implementation by policymakers, NGOs, media organizations and professional journalists. The aim of this final chapter was to provide knowledge (on the basis of our research findings), which enables media practitioners, NGOs and political decision makers to develop potentials for (political) capacity building and strategic cooperation in conflict prevention and resolution. It should be remembered, however, that strong influences of media coverage and strategic persuasive communication upon public perceptions of war and conflict events are only likely if consistent views prevail in the diverse messages used by specific publics (e.g. Druckman, 2004). Furthermore, the presence of conciliatory messages in the news and in strategic communication can only contribute to mitigating crises if the messages reach both sides of an ongoing conflict (e.g. Ruigrok, Atteveldt, & Takens, 2009).

Moreover, our intention was to contribute to a more reflected, careful reception of conflict coverage and the particular challenges of de-escalative strategic communication. Our findings on how media content and strategic communication shape lay audiences' perceptions of war and armed conflict illustrate how complex and difficult it is to get through to people and audiences inside and outside conflict areas. With respect to this, in summary we would like to highlight the following: Individual efforts toward quality assurance at the actor level (micro-level 'journalist') and at the organizational level (meso-level 'media operations') necessarily reach their limits when faced with *systemic* problems (macro-level). For a start, it appears to us that the general business model of quality journalism has entered into an existential crisis (something to which post-factual and post-truth trends certainly contribute in part). At the same time, we witness a rise in authoritarian regimes worldwide in populist, anti-democratic shifts in power (also in West and Eastern Europe), in hybrid regimes and pseudo-democracies (cf. Diamond, 2002) and a decline or failure of Western efforts to protect, strengthen and promote democratization (cf. e.g. Carothers, 2002, 2004; Huber, 2013, Ritter, 2015) or at least decreasing Western democratic leverage (Levitsky & Way, 2010).

These *systemic* developments at the macro-level lead to deteriorating conditions for both (Western) foreign affairs journalism (e.g. Otto & Meyer, 2012; Sambrook, 2010) and domestic journalism within conflict countries. This problem can be solved neither on the individual (micro) level of journalists nor on the organizational (meso) level of (private commercial) media companies (alone). Here, creative alternative solutions for quality journalism are much in demand – from alternative, properly independent funding sources or the consolidation and stabilization of public service broadcasting[11] to the call for media assistance to become better integrated into development and foreign policy. Concerning the effectiveness of media assistance, we think there is also a need for more long-term emphases on this aspect.

Against this backdrop, professional public communicators and political decision makers who are in charge should make a major effort to raise public awareness[12] of the individual (micro-level), organizational (meso-level) and systemic (macro-level) challenges and biases in conflict news reporting and of journalists' and media organizations' constant attempts to improve existing media practice.

Combating inflammatory media content, promoting dialogue and informing and motivating international conflict resolution by applying 'public communication' remains a major challenge – especially when the people responsible anticipate the knowledge we provided about the diverse *contextual factors* shaping the role and potential of media and strategic communication in conflict prevention and crisis management. We hope that we were able to illustrate on the basis of our research: In this field, a simple recipe would be a recipe for disaster.

Acknowledgment

I would like to thank the following authors for condensed discussions, résumés or keywords on the basis of their respective results: Christian Baden, Rosa Berganza, Dimitra Dimitrakopoulou, Thomas Hanitzsch, Beatriz Herrero-Jiménez, Marc Jungblut, Christoph Meyer, Igor Micevski, Eric Sangar, Keren Tenenboim-Weinblatt, and Snezana Trpevska.

Notes

1 Other approaches have criticized the simplistic epistemological assumptions of peace journalism, its dichotomous nature, advocacy orientation and its insufficient attention to various factors and structural constraints that shape news production (e.g. Hanitzsch, 2004, 2007; Loyn, 2007; Ruigrok, 2010; Wolfsfeld, 2004).
2 See BBC, for example, www.bbc.co.uk/editorialguidelines/
3 See, for example, https://ethicaljournalismnetwork.org
4 On the definition and understanding of 'dialogue' in PR theory and research, cf. Kent and Taylor (2002).
5 The INFOCORE approach focused only on *external* strategic-persuasive communication. Aspects of internal communication were intentionally excluded.
6 See, for instance, accusations aimed at the Russian government on the use of bots www.nytimes.com/2018/02/19/technology/russian-bots-school-shooting.html
7 Snow and Taylor (2006) describe the 21st-century information environment as a space in which "truisms compete with alternative truths" and that for a truth to prevail, it must be perceived as more 'credible' than its alternative (p. 406).

8 This reminds one of Sorensen's (1998) particular understanding of democratization. He argues that any process of democratization must comprise not only measures leading to increasing political equality (inclusiveness), but also those leading to increasing competitiveness (political liberalization and/ or pluralization).

9 With respect to this, see also the contributions of Micevski and Trpevska (Chapter 9) and Frère and Fiedler (Chapter 10) in this volume.

10 Of course, in this context, there is a language problem. To be able to recite Russian media, you need to know Russian. But especially in the case of Russia, there is now English-language media that is easily available online. And we would not necessarily expect media, for example, from francophone Africa to be received and cited in British parliaments, but we would expect it in the French National Assembly.

11 Currently, we witness rather the contrary in Europe; to name but a few, for instance, the *No Billag* initiative claiming the abolition of licence fees for Swiss public-service TV and radio; the law on Public Service Media governance in EU-member state Poland from 2016 according to which guarantees for the independence of public-service TV and Radio were removed (in breach of Council of Europe norms); the plans of the Danish government from early 2018 to abolish the licence fee that funds Denmark's public-service broadcaster and to replace it with a tax (which makes the funding dependent on the government's decisions).

12 Through media literacy programs, for instance. For respective initiatives of the European Commission, for example, see https://ec.europa.eu/culture/policy/audiovisual-policies/literacy_en

References

Baden, C. (2010). *Communication, contextualization & cognition. Patterns & processes of frames' influence on people's interpretations of the EU constitution*. Delft, Netherlands: Eburon.

Brauman, R. (2015). La légende Libyenne de BHL [The Libyan legend of BHL]. *Alternatives Internationales, September, no. 68*, 66. Available online at www.cairn.info/magazine-alternatives-internationales-2015-9-page-66.htm

Carothers, T. (2002). The end of the transition paradigm. *Journal of Democracy, 13*(1), 5–21.

Carothers, T. (2004). Democracy's sobering state. *Current History, 103*, 412–416.

Choi, J. H., Watt, J. H., & Lynch, M. (2006). Perceptions of news credibility about the war in Iraq. Why war opponents perceived the Internet as the most credible medium. *Journal of Computer Mediated Communication, 12*, 209–229.

Coombs, T. (2014). *Ongoing crisis communication. Planning, managing, and responding* (4th edn). Los Angeles, CA: Sage.

Declich, L. (2012). La Libye comme BHL ne pouvait s'y attendre [Libya, how BHL did not expect it]. *Outre-Terre, 33–34*, 471–477. Available online at www.cairn.info/revue-outre-terre1-2012-3-page-471.htm

Diamond, L. (2002). Hybrid regimes. *Journal of Democracy, 13*(2), 21–35.

Druckman, J. N. (2004). Political preference formation: Competition, deliberation, and the (ir)relevance of framing effects. *American Political Science Review, 98*, 671–686.

Fierens, M., Jacquard, E., Khatchadourian, A., Pesic, M., Terzis, G., & Boxel, M. van (2016). European policy brief: Policy recommendations for media and academia. Available online at www.infocore.eu/wp-content/uploads/2017/02/D9.4._Policy_Brief_Media_and_Academia.pdf

Fröhlich, R. (2010). The coverage of war, security, and defense policy: Do women matter? A longitudinal content analysis of broadsheets in German. *European Journal of Communication, 25,* 59–68.

Fröhlich, R. (2016). Gender, media and security. In P. Robinson, P. Seib, & R. Fröhlich (Eds.), *Routledge handbook of media, conflict and security* (pp. 22–35). Oxford, UK: Routledge.

Fröhlich, R., & Jungblut, M. (2016). *Effective and coherent media-related communication during war and armed conflicts. Policy brief for political actors and NGOs. INFOCORE Work Package 'Strategic Communication'.* Available online at www.infocore.eu/wp-content/uploads/2017/02/D6.3_Policy-Brief_Strategic_Communication.pdf

Fröhlich, R., & Jungblut, M. (2018). Between factoids and facts: The application of "evidence" in NGO strategic communication on war and armed conflict. *Media, War & Conflict, 11,* 85–106.

Geis, A., & Schlag, G. (2017). 'The facts cannot be denied': Legitimacy, war and the use of chemical weapons in Syria. *Global Discourse, 7,* 285–303.

Hanitzsch, T. (2004). Journalists as peacekeeping force? Peace journalism and mass communication theory. *Journalism Studies, 5,* 483–495.

Hanitzsch, T. (2007). Situating peace journalism in journalism studies: A critical appraisal. *Conflict & Communication Online, 6*(2).

Huber, D. (2013). US and EU human rights and democracy promotion since the Arab spring. Rethinking its content, targets and instruments. *The International Spectator, 48*(3), 98–112.

Johnson, T. J., & Kaye, B. K. (2010). Believing the blogs of war? How blog users compare on credibility and characteristics in 2003 and 2007. *Media, War & Conflict, 3,* 315–333.

Kent, M. L., & Taylor, M. (2002). Towards a dialogic theory of public relations. *Public Relations Review, 28,* 21–37.

L'Etang, J. (2006). Public Relations and Propaganda: Conceptual issues, methodological problems, and public relations discourse. In J. L'Etang, & M. Pieczka (Eds.), *Public Rleations. Critical debates an contemporary practice* (pp. 23–40). Mahwah, NJ: Lawrence Erlbaum.

Lauer, F. (2005). La France et ses ONG: Les paradoxes de "l'Etat stratège" [France and its NGOs: The paradoxes of the 'strategist state']. *Humanitaire, 19,* 65–72.

Levitsky, S., & Way, L. A. (2010). Why democracy needs a level playing field. *Journal of Democracy, 21*(1), 57–68.

Loyn, D. (2007). Good journalism or peace journalism? *Conflict & Communication Online, 6*(2).

Meyer, C. O., & Michaels, E. (2016). *Utilising open sources for conflict prevention, management and resolution: potential, limitations and recommendations. A policy brief.* Available online at www.infocore.eu/wp-content/uploads/2017/01/D4.3_Policy-Brief-OSINT.pdf

Meyer, C. O., & Otto, F. (2016). How to warn: 'Outside-in warnings' of Western governments about violent conflict and mass atrocities. *Media, War & Conflict, 9,* 198–216.

Miskimmon, A., O'Loughlin, A., & Roselle, L. (2013). *Strategic narratives: Communication power and the new world order.* New York, NY: Routledge.

Otto, F., & Meyer, C. O. (2012). Missing the story? Changes in foreign news reporting and their implications for conflict prevention. *Media, War & Conflict, 5,* 205–221.

Ritter, D. P. (2015). *The iron cage of liberalism: International politics and unarmed revolutions in the Middle East and North Africa.* Oxford, UK: Oxford University Press.

Ruigrok, N. (2010). From journalism of activism towards journalism of accountability. *International Communication Gazette, 72*(1), 85–90.

Ruigrok, N., van Atteveldt, W., & Takens, J. (2009). Shifting frames in a deadlocked conflict? Paper presented at ISA annual convention on "Exploring the Past, Anticipating the Future". New York, USA. Available online at http:// vanatteveldt.com/wp-content/uploads/ruigrok_etal_shiftingframes.pdf

Ryfman, P. (2013). Les ONG Françaises de développement et humanitaires: Une autre "exception Française" en Europe? [French development and humanitarian NGOs: another 'French exception' in Europe?]. *Mondes en Développement, 41*(1), no. 161, 63–78. Available online at www.cairn.info/ revue-mondes-en-developpement-2013-1-page-63.htm

Sambrook, R. (2010.) *Are foreign correspondents redundant? The changing face of international news.* Oxford, UK: Reuters Institute for the Study of Journalism.

Snow, N., & Taylor, P. M. (2006). The revival of the propaganda state: US propaganda at home and abroad since 9/11'. *International Communication Gazette, 68,* 389–407.

Sorensen, G. (1998). *Democracy & democratization.* Boulder, CO: Westview.

Stavridis, S., & Pace, R. (2011). Assessing the impact of the EMPA's parliamentary diplomacy in international conflicts: Contribution or obstacle? In G. Garzón Clariana (Ed.), *La asamblea Euromediterránea – The Euro-Mediterranean assembly – L'assemblée Euro-Mediterranéenne* (pp. 59–105). Madrid, Spain: Marcial Pons.

Utley, R. (2013). France and the Arab upheavals. *The RUSI Journal, 158*(2), 68–79.

Weaver, C. K., Motion, J., & Roper, J. (2006). From propaganda to discourse (and back again): Truth, power, the public interest and public relations. In J. L'Etang, & M. Pieczka (Eds.), *Public Relations. Critical Debates and Contemporary Practice* (pp. 7–21). Mahaw, NJ: Lawrence Erlabaum.

Wolfsfeld, G. (2004). *Media and the path to peace.* Cambridge, UK: Cambridge University Press.

Afterword

Philip Seib

From its outset, INFOCORE has been ambitious. The research project itself and this book were designed to probe and explain ways in which various media venues provide information about preventing and resolving conflict and sustaining post-conflict stabilization. The study covered the construction of news and reached as far as news-informed public discourse. Such topics are not new; other researchers – including many of those who have worked with INFOCORE – have studied and written about these matters in the past. But rare is the project that has addressed so many facets of the issues that have been examined in the preceding chapters.

This is not meant to be self-congratulatory, although we are proud of our work. We hope that the nature of INFOCORE's data collection and the substance of the analyses included in this book will be of use to academic colleagues and those in the policymaking community. Of particular value may be the connections illustrated in the book between news production and broader discourse. More specifically, readers of this work may discern patterns in conflict-related newsgathering practices, news content and news consumers' responses to information. Because of the breadth of the INFOCORE studies – which are based on surveys, interviews and computer-assisted big-data analysis – we trust that INFOCORE provides a foundation for further work in this field.

As is apparent in the preceding chapters, this project was designed to consider the various elements of the conflict information flow as a continuum: from source to content to effects. This is crucial; although information reaching the public may come from disparate origins, ranging from reports by conventional news organizations to casual conversation on social media (along with many other sources), the effects of information on the polity are cumulative. The array of information providers examined in our research includes traditional news outlets, NGOs, the military, public relations practitioners, official and unofficial political commentary and more. These have varied impact in different cases, but it is important to recognize and survey the entire spectrum of information sources if we are to understand all this as a *process* that shapes public discourse and, directly or indirectly, affects policy.

Each of three regions examined by INFOCORE presents its own challenges to researchers. Not surprisingly, the always boiling Middle East supplied diverse content from indigenous and remote sources, and showed that interpretation of events often depends on the eye of the beholder. The Israeli–Palestinian conflict provides examples of competitive news flows that target varied audiences, many of which are highly partisan in the ways they perceive and act upon the information they receive. This case illustrates that the road along which information travels is far from being straight and smooth; it rises, falls and hits bumps and dips, all of which vary in their effects according to the politics of the moment and the predisposition of the information recipients. As the media universe becomes more crowded because of ever-changing technologies, news consumption habits will further evolve, as will the final stage of the INFOCORE continuum: how news affects the public. For some, opinions about the Israeli–Palestinian conflict have been formed over many years based on numerous factors (including religious beliefs and territorial claims), and this affects the amount of influence that news might have.

Still, within the Middle East, much information about the Syrian War is processed differently than news about Israel and Palestine, because for most of its global audience it falls into a more conventional news-to-recipient pattern. Among many, audience partisanship about this conflict has different roots – shallower and less far-reaching – than those related to the Israeli–Palestinian struggle. Here again, technological changes have had significant effect as first-hand reporting from Syrian battlegrounds – which is so difficult and dangerous – has often come from "citizen journalists" who rely on cell phones to reach venues such as YouTube to showcase their reporting. In such cases, news consumers must decide how credible these reports are and how to respond to their information.

As for the western Balkans, our analysis of news about the Kosovo conflict is more retrospective in terms of the fighting itself and more current in the way that it examines how media affect the ability to sustain peace. The cessation of active combat does not mean a conflict has truly ended; "post-conflict" can be a misleading term, as simmering disputes may undermine chances for lasting peace. Media content – particularly from indigenous providers – during such times influences localized perceptions of regional political affairs. It can contribute to a commitment to peacekeeping or it can rekindle animosities.

The Great Lakes region of Africa provided our researchers with an example of conflicts that for various reasons (including some grounded in race) have remained outside the vision of much of the world. In this kind of case, analysis must consider two different audience blocs: the local/regional populations, which mostly depend on indigenous information providers, and the more distant news consumers who receive only limited information about this region from the relatively few globally attuned news organizations. Going forward, an issue to be considered concerns the degree to which global satellite television channels and social media may serve as information bridges between these distinct audiences.

These are the conflicts on which the INFOCORE researchers focused. They may appear to have little in common other than their viciousness, but they provided a wealth of opportunities for media-related analysis. By looking at social interactions related to news production and news-stimulated public discourse, and by including a broad range of "news" providers (such as public relations and strategic communication sources), we hope that this book will have stimulated other researchers' interest in similarly diverse factors.

The findings described in the preceding chapters underscore the importance of relying on a holistic approach to media analysis. Simply studying news content, public opinion shifts, or other such factors in isolation will produce only a partial picture of the media-and-conflict landscape. Such pictures have their uses, but conflict-related information flows and their effects are becoming more complex as newer forms of media increase in their significance. These changes in the media environment profoundly affect the social interactions that are so important in this study. At the heart of the broader phenomena that INFOCORE has addressed are these interactions among individuals. Understanding *people* – not just institutions and technologies – is essential to comprehending the broad, conflict-related, media impact.

Looking ahead, we recognize that findings of INFOCORE are somewhat time-sensitive, given changes in geopolitics and media operations, and so it is important that research on these matters continues. Particularly important will be:

- considering the impact of information warfare (including dissemination of "fake news") on public discourse;
- understanding shifts in credibility within the context of evolving media literacy as the public increasingly relies on social media and other non-traditional venues as news sources;
- evaluating the impact of governments' strategic communication, while the sophistication of such efforts increases;
- assessing the growing impact of non-state actors as purveyors of conflict-related information.

These are just a few of many avenues along which researchers might proceed. INFOCORE was fortunate to have received generous support from the European Union, and we hope that other funders will likewise provide resources for continuing studies in this field.

A final thought: The scourge of war will never be controlled unless those seeking peace have a better understanding of the communication processes on which the public depends, while it forms its opinion about any given conflict. New media tools may foster more comprehensive and timely reports about conflict from a wider range of providers, but more information being delivered faster does not necessarily mean that preventing or ending conflict will become easier. A society that wants to reduce conflict must embrace enhanced knowledge about how news is constructed and how it shapes political and social discourse. We hope this book will help.

Philip Seib
University of Southern California
Annenberg School for Communication and Journalism
April, 2018

List of Contributors

Scott Althaus is Merriam Professor of Political Science, Professor of Communication and Director of the Cline Center for Advanced Social Research at the University of Illinois, USA. His research focuses on communication processes that support political accountability in democratic societies and empower political discontent in non-democratic societies. He is the author of *Collective Preferences in Democratic Politics: Opinion Surveys and the Will of the People* (Cambridge University Press, 2003), which was awarded with numerous prizes such as the Goldsmith Book Prize and the David Easton Book Prize in 2004.

Christian Baden is a Senior Lecturer at the Department of Communication and Journalism at the Hebrew University of Jerusalem, Israel. His research focuses on the collaborative construction of meaning in dynamic, political public debates. Specifically, he draws attention on the processes of cultural and discursive resonance that render specific ideas intuitively plausible and account for their enduring presence in public discourse and thought. His publications have contributed to theory and methodology in research on framing, discourse dynamics and the social and psychological process of sense making in a political public sphere.

María Rosa Berganza is Professor and Chair of Journalism at the Faculty of Communication Science at King Juan Carlos University (URJC), Madrid, Spain. Her research interests include: media content analysis, media effects on public opinion perceptions, comparative journalism research, journalist's practices and perceptions, Big Data and journalism, methodology of research in journalism and political communication. Her research has been funded by several science foundation grants as well as grants from the EU research programs. She is currently vice president of the Journalism Studies Section of European Communication Research and Education Association (ECREA) and member of the editorial board of several international scientific journals, including *Journalism Studies*.

340 List of Contributors

Adolfo Carratalá is Assistant Professor of Journalism in the Department of Language Theory and Communication Sciences at the University of Valencia, Spain. Previously, he has been a post-doctoral researcher at the University Rey Juan Carlos Madrid and Associate Professor of Communication at the International University of La Rioja (UNIR). His primary research interests are communication and conflicts, media and social movements as well as journalistic discourse and framing. His PhD thesis was awarded by the Spanish Society of Journalism.

Dimitra Dimitrakopoulou is Assistant Professor at the School of Journalism and Mass Communication at Aristotle University of Thessaloniki, Greece. From 2014–2016 she supervised an interdisciplinary team studying the role of social media in conflict-ridden societies in the research project INFOCORE, funded under the 7th European Framework Program. Her research interests include online and participatory journalism, social media and networks, new media literacy. She has worked as a researcher for EU projects and is involved in international networks and projects as lead researcher and coordinator for Greece. She has served for four years in the Journalism Studies Section of the ECREA (Chair: 2014–2016; Vice-Chair: 2012–2014).

Anke Fiedler is Researcher at the Department of Communications Studies and Media Research at the LMU Munich, Germany, and Visiting Professor at the Institute for Media and Communication Studies at Freie Universität Berlin, Germany. Following her studies of communication science, sociology and psychology, she worked for UNESCO in Paris and Bujumbura, Burundi, as well as for UNESCO's Iraq Office in Amman, Jordan. Her research revolves around media structures and communication processes in (post-)socialist and transitional states as well as the role of media development in democratic transitions.

Marie-Soleil Frère is Senior Researcher at the Belgian National Fund for Scientific Research and Professor and Chair of the Research Centre in Information and Communication (ReSIC) at the Université Libre of Brussels, Belgium. Her research focuses on the role played by the media in democratic processes, conflicts, elections and social changes in Francophone sub-Saharan Africa. Her publications include *The Media and Conflicts in Central Africa* (2007, Lynne Rienner Publishers) and *Presse et démocratie en Afrique francophone* (2000, Karthala).

Romy Fröhlich is Professor at the Department of Communication Studies and Media Research at LMU Munich, Germany. She was Coordinator of the EU FP7 project INFOCORE (media in violent conflicts) and Principal Investigator of the INFOCORE work package "Strategic

Communication". Her main research interests focus on the influence of strategic-persuasive communication/PR, conflict/crisis communication and news, and the representation of women in media and PR. She has served as (vice-)president of the German Communication Association (1998–2006) and is co-editor of *The Routledge Handbook of Media, Conflict and Security* (2017) and of *Women Journalists in the Western World* (2008, Hampton).

Thomas Hanitzsch is Professor at the Department of Communications Studies and Media Research at LMU Munich, Germany. A former journalist, his teaching and research focuses on global journalism cultures, war coverage, celebrity news and comparative methodology. He was Editor-in-Chief for *Communication Theory* (2011–2015) and has co-edited *The Handbook of Journalism Studies* (2009, Routledge) and *The Handbook of Comparative Communication Research* (2012, Routledge).

Beatriz Herrero-Jiménez is a post-doctoral researcher at King Juan Carlos University, Madrid, Spain. She is a member of the REMINDER research project ("Role of European Mobility and its Impacts in Narratives, Debates and EU Reforms"), funded by the H2020 Programme of the European Commission. Prior to this, she was Visiting Professor of Journalism and Film Studies at the Universitat Rovira i Virgili, Tarragona, Spain. She holds a PhD in Information Sciences from Universidad Complutense, Madrid. Her primary research interests are media discourses, communication and conflict, and gender studies.

Abit Hoxha is a PhD researcher at the Department of Communications Studies and Media Research at LMU Munich, Germany. His research focuses on comparative news production in conflict, conflict and post-conflict journalism as well as journalism and dealing with the past. He is the co-author of *How conflict news comes into being: Reconstructing 'reality' through telling stories* (Media, War & Conflict, 2017) and *The Manufacture of an International News Event: The Day Kosovo was born* (2012, Sage).

Marc Jungblut is a researcher, lecturer and PhD candidate at the Department of Communications Studies and Media Research at LMU Munich, Germany. He focuses his research on political communication, journalism, war and violent conflicts, public diplomacy and news production processes. Since September 2017, he has been part of the project "Responsible Terrorism Coverage (ResTeCo): A Global Comparative Analysis of News Coverage about Terrorism from 1945 to the Present" at the Cline Centre for Advanced Social Research at the University of Illinois, Urbana-Champaign.

Sergios Lenis has worked as a research assistant at the Hellenic Foundation of European & Foreign Policy (ELIAMEP), Athens, Greece, during INFOCORE. He focuses his research on cloud computing, artificial intelligence and network analysis. He studied Mathematics at the University of Patras and holds an MSc in Information Systems at the Hellenic Open University. He is currently a researcher at the School of Natural Science at the University of Patras and has previously worked as a research associate at the School of Social Sciences, Faculty of Humanities at the University of Manchester.

Christoph O. Meyer is Professor of European and International Politics and currently Vice Dean for Research of the Faculty of Social Sciences and Public Policy at King's College London, UK. His research interests are situated at the intersection of EU studies, international relations and political communication. He has specialized in EU foreign, security and defence policy, early warning and conflict prevention and the role of NGOs in the coverage of conflict. He is leading a project funded by the UK Research Council on learning in foreign policy, looking at intelligence production and use in Germany, the UK and the EU (with Mike Goodman). He has published in leading academic journals in International Relations (ISQ, EJIR) and European Union Studies (JCMS, JEPP) and is currently completing a book on persuasion in foreign policy (with Chiara de Franco).

Igor Micevski is a researcher at RESIS – Research Institute on Social Development in Skopje, Macedonia. He holds a master's degree in Comparative Politics/Nationalism and Ethnicity from the London School of Economics and Political Science (LSE) and he is a PhD candidate in Political Sociology at the Cyril and Methodius University, Skopje. He focuses his research on counter-publics, conflict framing and political mobilization. Micevski is a former journalist for the World Service of the British Broadcasting Corporation (BBC). He was also a lecturer in journalism at the School of Journalism and Public Relations at the Institute of Communication Studies in Skopje.

Eric Sangar is an FNRS research fellow at the University of Namur, Belgium, and an associated researcher at the Centre Emile Durkheim of Sciences Po Bordeaux, France. As a member of INFOCORE, he has worked with Christoph Meyer and Eva Michaels on the influence of NGOs on media discourses of armed conflict. He is interested in collective memory, uses of history and the mobilization of emotions in IR. Besides articles in journals such as *Political Psychology*, the *Journal of Strategic Studies* and *Contemporary Security Policy*, he has published the monograph *Historical Experience: Burden or Bonus in Today's Wars? The British Army and the German Bundeswehr in Afghanistan* (2014, Rombach), and co-edited *Researching Emotions* *in International Relations: Methodological Perspectives on the Emotional Turn* (2018, Palgrave Macmillan).

Philip Seib is Professor of Journalism & Public Diplomacy and Professor of International Relations at the Annenberg School for Communication and Journalism, University of Southern California, USA. His expertise lies in the fields of Journalism Ethics, International and Political Journalism and the Middle East. His research interests focus on the effects of news coverage on foreign policy, particularly conflict and terrorism issues. He is author and editor of numerous books, the latest being *As Terrorism Evolves* (2017, Cambridge University Press). He was also founding co-editor of the journal *Media, War & Conflict.*

Keren Tenenboim-Weinblatt is Associate Professor at the Department of Communication and Journalism at the Hebrew University of Jerusalem, Israel. Her research addresses the cultural embedding, societal roles and political implications of journalism, with a particular focus on media and conflict, as well as the various intersections of news and time. Her work was published in the leading communication journals and received several prestigious international awards. She is Chair of the Journalism Studies Division at the International Communication Association.

Snezana Trpevska is currently affiliated with the RESIS – Research Institute on Social Development in Skopje, Macedonia. She has completed her PhD in Sociological Sciences at the Cyril and Methodius University in Skopje. Her research interests extend over several fields: the sociology of news production, audience studies, media policy and regulation and social research methodology. Until July 2009, she was employed as Head of Research and Strategic Development at the Macedonian Broadcasting Council, and since August 2009 she has been engaged as a researcher and assistant professor at the School of Journalism and Public Relations in Skopje.

Linor Tsifroni is Assistant Researcher at the Sammy Offer School of Communication, Interdisciplinary Center (IDC), Herzliya, Israel. She holds a master's degree in political communication studies from the IDC, Herzliya, and a BA in political science from Tel-Aviv University. Her main interests are political communication and political advertising and the age of new media.

Gadi Wolfsfeld is Professor of Communication at the Sammy Offer School of Communication, IDC, Herzliya, Israel, and is Emeritus Professor at the Hebrew University, where he taught for 30 years in the Departments of Political Science and Communication. In 2017, he was awarded the Murray Edelman Lifetime Distinguished Career

Award by the Political Communication Section of the American Political Science Association. His research expertise focuses on the role of the media in political conflicts and peace processes. His most recent book is titled: *Making Sense of Media and Politics: Five Principles in Political Communication* (2011, Routledge).

Index

Abboud, S. 89
absolute frequencies 199–200
Action by Christians for the Abolition of Torture 196
action-dynamic platform 158
activists 228
Afghanistan 107n4, 118
African conflicts 74n4, 100
"Africa Report 169" 204
Agence France-Presse (AFP) 205, 208
agenda-setting process 294–5
agendas for action 25, 27, 35–6, 40; analysis structure for 87, 93–7; strategic narratives and 82, 84, 87, 97–100
al-Assad, Bashar 112, 114
Albanian(s) 91, 93, 176, 177, 220, 221, 242, 258; ethnic-nationalisms 225; minority 224; National Liberation Army 224
al-Gaddafi, Muammar 113, 114
Al Hayat Al Jadidah 59
Al Jazeera 67, 117
alternative models 210
Althaus, S. 9, 18
Amnesty International (AI) 193, 201, 208, 210
amplification of conflict news 36–8
Anglo-Saxon media 66
anti-government protests 146, 147, 200
anti-NATO banners 146
Arab–Israeli conflict 222
Arab Spring 112, 113, 115, 116, 129, 136, 137, 297, 320
armed conflict 210–13
Armed Conflict Location & Event Data (ACLED) Project 87, 203
Assad (Syrian President) 38, 40
Associated Press (AP) 208

Association de Réflexion et d'Information sur le Burundi 204
"Attention Deficit Hyperactivity Disorder" 235
audiences 25–7, 30, 36–9, 42, 68; domestic 37, 42; in Goma 16–17, 304
axial coding, MaxQDA software 252
Ayrault, Jean-Marc 126, 127

Baade, R. C. 175
Baden, C. 9–11, 82, 291, 312, 313, 324
Balkan conflicts 74n4
Bantz, C. R. 175
BBC *see* British Broadcasting Corporation (BBC)
"behind-the-scenes" influence 213
"Belgrade–Pristina Dialogue" 225
Ben Ali regime 112
Benkler, Y. 157
Bennett, W. L. 138, 140, 143, 157
Berganza, R. 12, 294, 298, 325
Bild 58
bloggers 306n5
Boltanski, L. 211
Boolean Search 119
bots 317–18
Bouazizi, Mohamed 112
Boyd, D. M. 162n1
Bribery 271
British Broadcasting Corporation (BBC) 119, 124, 342
British government 85, 85
British media coverage 38
British Parliament 114, 115, 118, 123, 124, 129, 130, 326
Brüderle, Rainer 127
Brüggemann, M. 178
Bruno Le Roux, M. 127

Burundi 179–81, 182, 183, 212; in crisis 202–5; Democratic Republic of Congo 182–7; ethnic violence in 171; journalist, experience of 180–2; statement, journalist 179
Burundian journalists 90
Burundi conflict 53, 65, 70, 72–3, 85, 87, 88, 89, 90, 94, 95, 101
Büscher, K. 272

Cameron, David 114, 115, 128
Cappella, J. N. 273
Carratalá, A. 12, 294, 298, 325
Chadwick, A. 220
Chemical Weapons (CW) 38, 94, 112–18, 120, 294
"Citizens' Movement for Defence of Macedonia" 143, 144
civic-ideological conflict frames 255–6, 262–3
civil resistance 143
'classical' literature 195
classic media formats 5
'CNN effect' 302
Cofelice, A. 113
Cohen, J. 273
Cold War 104n7, 191, 301n11
Collective Action Frames 240, 243
Colourful Revolution movement 13, 136, 138, 141–4, 146, 155–7, 160
communication governance concept 316–17
communications media 125, 126, 128, 129, 130, 294, 326, 327
competing conflict frames 247–8, 265–7
conceptual analysis grid 10
conflict(s): casualties 87, 100–2, 101; classification of 174; communication 311; conceptualisation of 7, 24; framing interaction 303; global 170; salience of 174
conflict casualties 87, 100–2, 101
conflict framing interaction: civic-ideological 255–6; ethno-nationalist 253–5; institutional/constitutional 256–7; manipulation/malicious interest 257–9; in post-conflict societies 243; types of 260–1
conflict journalists 169–72, 174, 179, 181, 198, 311; economic resources, lack of 182–4; information, sources and locations access 180–2;

interview responses of 170, 178–80; mapping influences on news production 171–6; news production freedoms of 178–9; reconstructing conflict news 176–8; safety threats and intimidation 184–6
conflict measures 82, 84, 93–7, 94
conflict news 24–5; amplification of 36–8; contents of 16, 33–6, 42, 170; creation of 28–31; influences of 38–42, 39; normative transgressions of 292; transformation of 31–3
conflict transformation: antagonism vectoring 253–9; coding and validation 252; and communication 244–6; competing conflict frames 247–8; and conflict definition 246–7; efforts 328; frame content 253–9; framing interactions 253–9; and framing interactions 247–8; hegemony, counter-hegemony and conflict frames 248–50; media-active publics, subjectivity of 250–1; postmarxism in 244–6; recruitment and interviewing strategy 251; sociopolitical aspects of 243; validity 252
conflictual collective allotments 137–41
conflict zones 311
Congolese journalists 17
contextual factors 288, 289, 299, 305, 330
Coombs, T. 317
Coser, L. 7
Cottle, S. 27
counter-hegemonic conflict frames 249, 265
country's relationship 154
Crimean War 287
Criminal Tribunal for the former Yugoslavia (ICTY) 97
crisis communication 317
"Crisis Management Cell of the French Foreign Ministry" 197
crisis management plan 317
cross-case patterns 208
cross-cultural difference 237
cultural transformation 58–60
cumulative media effects 23
CW *see* Chemical Weapons (CW)

Dandashly, A. 114
D'Angelo, P. 248

Davis, A. 125
Dayan, Daniel 250
Daymon, C. 78
deactivation model 5
decision makers 37–8; foreign 43; political 3, 41, 312, 325
decision-making process 295, 320
de-escalative conflict measures 93–7, 94, 98, 106, 324
de-escalative narratives 81, 82, 86, 88, 93
Demetrious, K. 78
democratic participation 303
Democratic Republic of Congo (DRC) 171, 180–5, 187; media, dimensions of trust 274–7; media distrust in situations of conflict 277–80; theoretical foundation and research design 273–4; uncertainty reduction in situations of conflict 280–1
Democratic Republic of the Congo (DRC) conflict 53, 65, 70, 72–3, 85, 87, 88, 89, 90, 94, 101
democratization process 331n8
Deutsche Welle (Ozimec) 146
Die Welt (newspaper) 204
digital age 218, 226, 235
digitalization of public communication 323
digitalized social media 303, 314
digitally networked action (DNA) 138
digital media 30, 46n2, 69, 118, 140, 157, 290, 296
Dimitrakopoulou, D. 13, 296, 297
Dimitriev, Emil 143
discriminatory/illegal state 254
DNA *see* digitally networked action (DNA)
Doctors without Borders/Médecins Sans Frontières (DWB/MSF) 199, 206
domestic audiences 37, 42
domestic coverage of conflict 17, 19n6
Domingo, D 175
DRC *see* Democratic Republic of Congo (DRC)

economic imperatives 307n7
'Economic Necessity' narrative 88, 97, 98, 99, 105
Egypt 136, 139, 140, 208
Eidelson, J. I. 248, 252
Eidelson, R. J. 248, 252
Ellison, N. B. 162n1

emotional argumentation 80
emotive transformation 58–60
England 287
Entman, R. M. 268n1
escalation-oriented conflict reporting 3, 53, 60–4
escalative conflict measures 93–7, 94, 98, 106
escalative narratives 80, 82, 86, 87, 89, 100
ethnocentric coverage 311
'Ethnocentrism/Patriotism/Religious Superiority' narrative 86, 97, 98, 99, 104
ethno-cultural groups 253–5
ethno-nationalist conflict frames 259
European colonial rule 185
European decision-making centres 177
European members of parliament (MPs) 326
European Parliament 114, 124; communications media 129; debates 119; foreign policy 113; Libyan crisis 113; Russian media from 129; Syria conflict 118, 122, 299; T3 post hoc test 121, 123
European politics 325
European Union (EU) 85, 85, 107n9, 113, 142, 143, 147, 177, 225, 312, 316, 337
Evans, Gareth 193
evidence-based report 211
evidence criterion 300
evidential beliefs 38, 40–1
evidential claims 24, 27, 34, 36, 38–41
evolutionary factor analysis 54, 66
executive elites 28–9, 44
external police force 113
extremist groups 43

Facebook 116, 120, 130, 155, 157, 181, 196, 197, 219, 227, 231, 297, 317
fake news 34
Fatah 186, 223
Federal Republic of Yugoslavia 225
Felesteen 57, 59
Ferguson, D. P. 81
FGIs *see* focus group interviews (FGIs)
Fiedler, Anke 16–17, 141, 188n2, 304
Financial Times (FT) 208
First Intifada 222
focus group interviews (FGIs) 251

foreign coverage of conflict 17, 19n6
foreign policy 103, 113, 115, 117,
   302, 320, 330
foreign policy actors 320
FP7 Programme 268n3
frames: interactions 253–9;
   interpretive (*see* interpretive
   frames); and narratives 79, 300
France 107n8, 115, 177, 320; foreign
   policy 115
Franco, C. de 198
Freedman, L. 78
Freedom House 223–5
French decision-making process 320
French government 85, 85
French-language media 209
French Parliament 121, 123, 129, 130
Frère, M. -S. 16–17, 304
frictional domain 248, 268n7
Fröhlich, R. 11, 74, 78, 79, 160, 163,
   292, 297, 300-2, 313, 316–18, 321,
   324

Gamson, W. A. 40, 247
Gaza 180, 182, 206
Geis, A. 117
German government 85, 85
German legal system 114
German Parliament 114, 121, 124
Germany 177, 188n2
Ghouta 90, 94, 116–18, 120, 122, 130
global conflict 170
global media landscape 289
Goffman, E. 268n1
Golubovska, Jasmina 155
Goma 16, 17, 90, 94, 185, 272,
   274–82, 304; audience members in
   16–17, 304
'grassroots pool' 297
Greece, refugee crisis 155
Green Revolution 143
Gruevski, Nikola 142, 155
Guardian 204, 207, 210

Haaretz 59, 208, 210
Hamas 56, 58, 59, 186, 207, 223, 224
Hanitzsch, T. 13–14, 160, 292–3,
   311–13
Hargie, O. 103
Hatufim 58
hegemonic 249
Herrero-Jiménez, B. 12, 294, 298, 325
heuristic model 293
'high relevance' conflicts 295

Hogg, M. A. 282
Hoskins, A. 5
Howarth, Gerald 126
Hoxha, A. 14, 160, 292–3, 311–13
Human Rights Watch (HRW) 85, 196,
   199, 205, 208, 210, 320, 321
Hutu 181, 185
hybrid media system 220

ICG *see* International Crisis Group
   (ICG)
identity-based conflicts 43
IDPs *see* internally displaced persons
   (IDPs)
INFOCORE 6–7, 20n12, 85, 296,
   297, 305, 324, 325, 330n5; actors
   and roles in 288; comparative and
   holistic approach 8–9; comparative
   dimensions 288; content-analytical
   findings 289; findings 318–19, 321;
   interview studies 289; policy
   briefs 314
INFOCORE project 192, 195,
   214, 295
INFOCORE team 119, 131n1
information monopolies 4
INGOs *see* International NGOs
   (INGOs)
in-group collective memories 58, 61
instantaneous news cycle 235–6
institutional/constitutional conflict
   framing interaction 256–7
internally displaced persons
   (IDPs) 272
international affairs,
   parliamentarisation of 12, 113,
   130, 326
international community 117, 140,
   183, 209, 219, 221, 236, 245, 298
International Criminal Court
   (ICC) 7, 318
International Crisis Group (ICG) 193,
   204, 207, 210, 321
International Federation of
   Journalists 184
international injustice conflict 254
International NGOs (INGOs) 192
International Organizations (IOs) 194
International Press Freedom
   Award 194
international press reports 116
international treaty 115
Internet 15
internet-based news portals 197

internet technology 141
interpretive frames 25, 27, 35, 39
interstate conflict 43, 176
interview-based research 192
IOs *see* International
    Organizations (IOs)
iProtest movement: country's
    relationship 154; dictionary-
    based approach 144; different
    relations 150; justice, freedom and
    democracy 142–5; research design
    and methodology 144–5; results
    and findings 145–56
Iran 136
Iraq campaign 170
Iraq War 326
ISIS *see* Islamic State of Iraq and
    Syria (ISIS)
Islamic Resistance Movement 223
Islamic State of Iraq and Syria (ISIS)
    114–16, 118, 131n2, 194
Israel 212
Israel Hayom 223
Israeli airstrikes 207
Israeli audiences 38–9
Israeli Defence Forces 206
Israeli journalists 180, 182, 186
Israeli media 58, 61, 66, 67
Israeli–Palestinian conflict 15, 55,
    58, 63, 64, 65, 70, 72–3, 74n4, 85,
    87, 88, 89, 90, 94, 95, 100, 101,
    170, 171, 176, 180, 186, 187, 219,
    222–4
Ivanov, Gjorge 142, 143, 147, 155

JAmCAT *see* Jerusalem Server f the
    Amsterdam Content Analysis
    Toolkit
Jarinje and Brnjak clashes 251
Jerusalem Server of the *Amsterdam
    Content Analysis Toolkit* (JAmCAT)
    9, 85, 119, 199
journalistic deontology 301
journalistic ideology, hallmark of 179
journalistic impartiality 301
journalistic performance 292
journalistic selection 56
journalistic transformations 56, 57–60,
    291–2; persistent patterns in 64–8
journalists' authorship 54
journalists' contribution to covering
    conflict 11, 51–3, 68–9; data and
    approach 53–4; situation-dependent
    60–4

Jungblut, M. 11, 79, 160, 297, 300,
    301, 313, 316–18, 321, 324

Kagame, Paul 280
Kim Jong Un 40
Kosovar Albanians 93
Kosovar journalists 180–2
Kosovo conflict 15, 16, 62, 63, 64, 65,
    70, 72–3, 85, 88, 89, 91, 93, 94, 94,
    95, 225–6, 295
Kumanovo clash 251

Lammy, David 128
'Last Resort' narrative 88, 97, 98,
    99, 106
Latent Dirichlet Allocation 145
laypeople/lay publics 16, 29, 37, 41,
    297, 302–4
Lee, S. T. 173
Lenis, S. 13, 296, 297
L'Etang, J. 316, 323
Libya 113, 114, 118, 201, 307n11
Limor, Y. 5
Livingstone, S. M. 250
local audiences 141, 197
'low relevance' conflicts 295
Lynch, Jessica 80

McCorkle, S. 175
Macedonia: Albanian minority, rights
    of 224; colourful revolution in
    138, 141, 142, 155; conflicts in
    202, 224–5, 246; dictionary-based
    approach 144; government of
    143; internet penetration in 141;
    Ivanov, Gjorge 155; media-active
    publics in 251; media landscape
    of 141; networks, power of 143;
    oppositional leaders in 160, 226;
    police, and relations of 155; pro-
    government rally 143, 146, 147;
    Pržino Agreement 142; in social
    networking performance 141–2;
    social protest 136
Macedonian conflict 13, 15, 16, 63,
    64, 65, 70, 72–3, 85, 88, 89, 91, 93,
    94, 224–5, 295, 296
manipulation, conflict frame:
    clientelistic manipulation
    258; ethnicity manipulation
    258; geopolitical interest 258;
    homophobic manipulation 259;
    peace process manipulation 259;
    securitization manipulation 259

Markham, T. 170
Maslog, C. C. 173
MaxQDA analysis, conflict frame: civic-ideological 255–6; ethno-nationalist 253–5; institutional/constitutional 256–7; manipulation/malicious interest 257–9
media-active (lay) publics 16, 244, 247, 250–1, 297, 303, 322, 328
media actors 4, 7, 13, 30, 32–3
media censorship 287
media competition 30
media content 10, 310; producers 26, 32; social 13, 306n5, 317, 324
media distrust in situations of conflict: corruption 279; donors, influence of 278–9; insufficient technical support and training 277; journalists, safety of 277–8; media owners 278–9; "true information" 280; word-of-mouth communication 279–80
media formats 33
media influence 38–42, *39*
media organizations 32
media outlets 17, 33, 37; conflict coverage 72–3; Palestinian outlets 67; Western outlets 11, 51, 66
'media relations governance' 317
media scholarship 169
members of parliament (MPs) 294, 326–8
Meyer, C. 9–10, 14, 301
Meyer, Willy 124
Micevski, I. 16, 297, 302, 303, 313, 322, 328
micro-perspective approach 293
militant Islamists 184
military intervention 112–15, 118, 130, 301
Miskimmon, A. 77
'Monitor Inside and Verify from Outside' principle 314
Montenegro 181, 225
MONUSCO 272, 277, 278
'Moral Values' narrative 88, **98, 105**
Motion, J. 315
Mouffe, Chantal 245

Nakba 61
narrative(s): de-escalative 81, 82, 86, 88; density 82; escalative 80, 82, 86, 87, 89; flexibility 102–3, 300; and frames 79 *see also* strategic narratives

National Assembly of France 123, 126
national broadsheet newspapers 177
National Liberation Army (NLA) 224
NATO 114, 143, 146, 234, 225
Ndadaye, Melchior 184
Neiger, M. 169
Netanyahu, Benyamin (Israeli PM) 57
NETPRESS 204
newer media, political leaders: cause, mobilizing support for 228–30; generating news stories 227–8; information, flow of 232–4; instantaneous news cycle 235–6; international community, messages to 230–2; opportunities 226–7; role of 219; threats 232; in violent conflicts 219–20
Newmark, Brooks 127
new (social) media 295, 296, 298–9
"new political spaces" 245
news creation: conflict news 28–31; laypeople in 29–30
news dissemination 24, 26
news production 5, 10, 23, 25; conflict-related influences 173; essential stages in 175–6; influences on 172; interactive processes of 26, 27; journalists' freedoms in 178–80; mapping influences on 171–6; organizational factors 171; reconstructing process of 179; theoretical model of 292–3
news selection patterns 66
newsworthy information 26, 55, 56
New York Times 57, 117, 207
NGO *see* Non-Governmental Organisation (NGO)
'NGO effect' 302
9/11 environment 198
Nkurunziza, Pierre 185
NLA *see* Albanian National Liberation Army (NLA)
No Billag initiative 331n11
"No Justice No Peace" 146
non-governmental organization (NGO) (NGOs) 5, 14–15, 18, 32, 69, **85**, 102, 103, 185, 291, 300–2, 311, 312, 316, 318; activity profiles 193–4; advantages of 196–7; analytical and normative claims 301; communication activity of 88, 210–11; as communicators 192–5; conflict cases 197, 200–8; on conflict discourse 195;

decision-making process 320; diachronic evolution of 199; epistemic claims 200; evidence of 209; fact-checking standards 211; funding structure 193; headquartered and geographical reach 194; human rights-base 211; information, supply of 195–7; international 29; liberal perspective of 214; local 321, 326; media debates on armed conflict 210–13; media demand for 197–9; media impact of 191; MPs information sources 326–7; organizational culture 194; peace-building strategies 322; perception of bias 319; policy-makers 317; policymakers and 321; professional information brokers 81; qualitative analysis 208–10; quantitative and qualitative tools 199–200; relative frequencies of 200; selection criteria 85; strategic persuasive communication 314–19, 321–3, 328; trade-offs 319; traditional news media 195
non-state conflicts 3
non-violent escalative conflict measures 93, **94, 98,** 99, 106
non-violent friction 246
non-Western states 199
Northern Ireland 234
North Kivu 272
Nossek, H. 5
Nyiragongo volcano 276

Obama, Barack 115
occupational self-consciousness 170
official fact-finding missions 200
Ohrid Agreement 224
Olmert, Ehud 223
O'Loughlin, B. 5, 77
open coding, MaxQDA software 252
Open Society Foundations 154
Open Source Intelligence 327
Operation Pillar of Defence 207, 223
Operation Protective Edge 89, 92 *see also Operation Pillar of Defence*
opportunities, for modern leaders 226–7
Orange Revolution 143
organizational factors 171
Ottaway, Richard 125
Otto, F. 198

out-group memories 61
Ozimec, Kristina 146

PageRank 150, **153**
paid-by-the-source journalism 271
Palestine conflict *see* Israeli-Palestinian conflict
Palestinian civilians 208
Palestinian community 182
Palestinian journalists 179, 180, 182, 186, 224
Palestinian media 58, 59, 61, 67, 180
Palmer, J. 170
Papacharissi, Z. 138, 161
parachute journalism 198
parliamentarisation of international affairs 326
Parliamentary Assembly of the Union for the Mediterranean (UfM PA) 113
parliamentary debates 12–13, 294, 299, 326, 327; political agenda setting 111–12; quantitative content analysis 111–12; traditional and social media, impact of 117–18; violent conflicts 111
peace and conflict studies 245
peace-building activities 191, 268n9
peace-building policies 322, 328
peace journalism 52, 187–8, 227, 277, 292, 306n4, 312–13, 330n1
persuasion 77, 103, 315–16
persuasive strategic communication 76–7, 80–1
Poell, T. 220
policymakers 321
political actors 17, 55, 69, 102, 297, 298, 301, 311, 314–19, 324, 328
political agendas 210, 294–5, 299
political communication 76, 81, 88, 290, 294, 298
political decision makers 41, 312, 324–5
political influence 23, 173, 180, 181, 183, 220, 293
political instability 141, 185
political leaders, violent conflict: communicate opportunities 221; interviews topics 222; Israel–Palestine conflict 222–4; Kosovo, conflict in 225–6; Macedonian, conflict in 224–5; methodology 221–2; and newer media 226–36; scientific background 218–20;

theoretical claims 220–1; threats 221; undemocratic approach 232
political sponsorship 271
political transformation 58–60
Politics–Media–Politics principle 230
post-factual 299, 315, 329
Postmarxism 244–6, 268n5
Postmarxist tradition 244–5
post-truth 77, 315, 329
post-violent-conflict process 245
Powers, M. 210
pro-Fatah media outlets 223
professional gatekeepers 314
professional ideology 170
professional transformation 57–8
pro-governmental supporters 154
Pržino Agreement 142
'public communication' 330
public confidence in media 272
Public Diplomacy (PD) 18, 77, 78, 81, 103, 317
public hostility 44
publicly available symbolic resources 248
public opinion presence 13, 120, **121**
public relations (PR) theory 314–15
Python script 119

qualitative content analysis 112
qualitative discourse analysis 199–208
quality journalism 15, 215, 329
quality news media, business model of 197
quantitative and qualitative tool 199–200

radical pluralist democracy 244–5, 303, 322
Radio France Internationale (RFI) 204, 272, 273, 275, 282n5
Radio Okapi 272, 273, 275, 276
Radio Publique Africaine (RPA) 185
Radio Télévision Nationale Congolaise (RTNC) 272, 275, 278
Radio Television of Kosovo (RTK) 225–6
Ramallah 180, 182
rationalist paradigms 41
Red Cross 212
Reese, S. D. 171
Reich, Z. 178
relative frequencies 200
relativist context 316
Reporters sans Frontières 85

Reporters Without Borders 116, 174
Responsibility to Protect (R2P) 84, 88, 90, 97, **98, 105**, 113, 294, 307n11
retrospective reconstructive interviews 14
RFI see Radio France Internationale(RFI)
Robinson, P. 295
Roper, J. 315
Roselle, L. 77
R2P *see* Responsibility to Protect' principle (R2P)
RPA see Radio Publique Africaine (RPA)
RTK see Radio Television of Kosovo (RTK)
RTNC see Radio Télévision Nationale Congolaise (RTNC)
Russian media 331n10
Russian press 129
Rwanda 272
Rwandan media 43

Sangar, E. 14, 301
Saveski, Zdravko 146
Schlag, G. 117
scientific literature, in conflict 218–19
SDSM *see* Social Democratic Union of Macedonia (SDSM)
Search for Common Ground 85
Second Intifada 223
Secours Islamique (SI) 197, 321
security hazards 198
Segerberg, A. 138, 140, 143
Seib, P. 18
selective coding, MaxQDA software 252
'(Self-) Defence' narrative 90, 93, 97, **98**, 99, 103, **105**
semantic concepts 81, 84
Serbian ethnic-nationalisms 225
sexual violence 327
Shoemaker, P. J. 171
SI *see* Secours Islamique (SI)
Simmonds, Mark 126
Six-Day War 222
Skopje 142–8, 155, 224
Skopje government 224
Smith, M. F. 81
Snow, N. 321, 330n7
social-cultural value systems 172
Social Democratic Union of Macedonia (SDSM) 142, 146, 147, 154, 155

social interactions 8, 10, 45, 337
social media 13, 15, 25, 46n2, 68–9,
111, 115–17, 119–20, **121**, 122,
122, *122*, 129, 290, 297, 313
social media and networks 296–9
social movements 296
social networking sites (SNS) 162n1
social networks: colourful revolution
156–9; in conflictual collective
allotments 137–8; diffusion
mechanism 139–40; dissemination
mechanism 138–9; in macedonia
141–2; media/public voices 141;
organization mechanism 140–1
social processes 288; of media content
production 289
sociocultural identity 293
soft nation state 254
Somerville, I. 103
Sorensen, G. 331n8
Soros Foundation 193
Soros, George 154
'specific protocols' 316–17
Stalpouskaya, K. 20n12, 82
state-based armed conflicts 3
story ideation 175
story narration 175–6
story presentation 176
strategic actors 12, 36, 42, 68, 301
strategic communicators 9, 26, 54,
81, 90, 100
strategic narratives 11–12, 77, 78,
78–82, 104n3, 319; agendas for
action 10, 25, 27, 35–6, 40, 42–3,
78, 82–7, 93, 97–100, 103, 111–12,
118, 124, 126, 128, 130, 195,
209, 299, 300, 324; analysis of
narratives 87–9; analysis structure
for 86; *vs.* conflict measures 81,
83; de-escalative 81, 82, 85, 86;
diverse (external) political actors
and NGOs 99; escalative 80, 82, 85,
86; in favour of war 79; narrative
density 82; narrative flexibility
102–3, 300; occurrence and
co-occurrence of 82–4; particular,
occurrence of 83; patterns of 81;
persuasive communication, political
role of 77, 79, 81; references,
communicators/actors 88; semantic
concepts 84; as semantic constructs
in public discourse 78–9; on wars
and armed conflicts 79, 81
strategic persuasive communication
80-1, 298–300, 314–19, 323–4; of

non-governmental organizations
321–3; unethical forms of 315
supply-and-demand model 14, 192,
195–9
"Support the SJO" 146
symbolic resources 246
Syria 297; chemical weapons 113;
civil war in 171, 176, 187; conflict
in 112–21, 184; historical and
political background 112–15;
Israeli–Palestinian conflict 171, 176,
187; measure 119–20; sample and
procedure 118–19; social media,
opportunity for 115–17; traditional
media 115–15
Syrian chemical weapons crisis 326–7
Syrian Civil War 111, 114, 121, 122,
138, 299
Syrian conflict *63, 65,* **70, 72–3, 85,**
88, 89, **89,** 90, *91,* 94, **94,** 100, 101,
101, 320
Syrian crisis 12, 13, 113, 114
Syrian journalists 181, 183, 184
*Syrian Observatory of Human
Rights* 194
Syrian Revolution 2011 116
Syrian Revolution Martyr
Database 74n4

Talking Politics (Gamson) 247
Taylor, P. M. 103, 321, 330n7
Tenenboim-Weinblatt, K. 4, 11, 291,
312, 313, 324
theoretical claims 220–1
theoretical-qualitative research 80, 88
threats, for political leaders 232
thruth/thruths 244, 273-279, 301,
315, 321
Toledano, M. 103
traditional and social media: analysis
120–1; diachronic evolution of
129; distributive power of 117;
findings 121–8; international
response 112–20; measure
119–20; on parliamentary debates
111, 117–18; presence 119–20;
qualitative analysis 124; refugees
up-to-date 116; role of 111–12;
sample and procedure 118–19;
Syrian conflict 115–17; violent
conflicts 117–18
traditional media: generating news
stories 227–8; mass media 294–5;
news media 195, 213; role of 218–19
training programs 313

traitorous patron state 254
transactionist process model 10, 26–8, 29, 44, 290–1
transformation of conflict news 31–3
Treaty of Nice 85
Trpevska, S. 16, 141, 297, 302, 303, 313, 322, 328
Trump, Donald 226, 235
truth, authoritative claim 34
truth, exclusive 35
trust in media, dimensions of: change, actors of 276; government, independence from 275–6; internal pluralism 275; social responsibility 276–7; trust, in media (coverage) 304; truth, importance of 274–5
Tsfati, Y. 273
Tsifroni, L. 15, 294, 298
Tumber, H. 170
Tunisia 112, 136, 140
Turkish exile 183
Tutsi 181, 185
21st-century (social) news media 291, 305, 330n7
Twitter 116, 120, 130, 143–5, 149, 150, 155, 157–60, 196, 197, 219, 226, 297, 317

UCDP *see* Uppsala Conflict Data Program (UCDP)
UfM PA *see* Parliamentary Assembly of the Union for the Mediterranean (UfM PA)
United Nations (UN) 80, 114, 225, 231, 234, 278
United Nations Interim Administration in Kosovo (UNMIK) 225
United Nations Security Council (UNSC) 113, 307n11
United Nations World Summit (2005) 307
UNMIK *see* United Nations Interim Administration in Kosovo (UNMIK)

UNSC *see* United Nations Security Council (UNSC)
untruth 34
Uppsala Conflict Data Program (UCDP) 3, 74n4, 87, 268n4

Van Dijck, J. 220
villain patron state 254
Violation's Documentation Center, Syria 87
violence, conceptualisation of 20n11
violence-intensive conflicts 208
violent conflicts 7, 23, 26, 38, 117–18, 243, 294
Vlassenroot, K. 272
VMRO-DPMNE party 143
VMRO party 146, 147

Wallensteen, P. 7
Wallström, Margot 282n4
war journalists *see* conflict news content
war reporting 11, 76, 287, 288; changing conditions of 4–6; risk of 296
"War on Terror" (WoT) 19n3
Weaver, C. K. 315
West Bank 182, 186, 207, 208, 222, 224
Western Balkans 13, 14, 84, 100, 171, 176, 187, 336
Western governments 312, 321
Western media, in global news 4–5
Western news outlets 11, 51, 66
Wolfsfeld, G. 15, 27, 28, 56, 160, 170, 294, 298

Xhaferi protests 251
Xinhua 73, 204, 208

Yedioth Ahronot 59
Yellow Revolution 143
YouTube 117, 118, 120, 127, 130, 336; on ISIS videos 118

Zaev, Zoran 154
Zandberg, E. 169
Zeitzoff, T. 219

Printed in the United States
by Baker & Taylor Publisher Services